EDWARD S. CURTIS AND THE NORTH AMERICAN INDIAN, INCORPORATED

For almost four decades from the 1890s onwards, Edward S. Curtis took thousands of photographs of Native Americans all over the West and his assistants collected masses of other data – myths, recordings of music and ceremonies, folk tales, language vocabularies, and histories. This material was published in *The North American Indian* (1907–30) in twenty volumes of illustrated text and twenty portfolios of photogravures; the project was supported by Theodore Roosevelt and funded in part by J. Pierpont Morgan, and spawned exhibitions, postcards, magazine articles, lecture series, a "musicale," and the very first narrative documentary film. While not unique, the project was bigger, better funded, and more famous than any of its time, and its images still retain their influence today.

Neither a eulogy to Curtis's achievement nor a debunking of it, this book is the first scholarly study of the project as a collective whole: what it was, who was involved, and what it meant. Mick Gidley examines the historical documentation such as letters and field memoirs of Curtis, principal ethnologist W. E. Myers, and other participants – including Native American assistants and informants – and synthesizes the ideological, governmental, aesthetic, economic, and anthropological forces in the project. In doing so, he provides a rich assessment of the significance of the endeavor not only in terms of its representation of Native Americans, but also as a quintessential "American" enterprise.

Mick Gidley is Professor of American Literature at the University of Leeds, England. He has written extensively on American literary and cultural history. His books include a Curtis anthology, *The Vanishing Race* (1976; 1987), and *Kopet* (1981), on Chief Joseph. Among the essay collections he has edited or co-edited are *Views of American Landscapes* (Cambridge 1989), *Representing Others: White Views of Indigenous Peoples* (1992), *Modern American Culture: An Introduction* (1993), and *American Photographs in Europe* (1994).

EDWARD S. CURTIS AND THE NORTH AMERICAN INDIAN, INCORPORATED

MICK GIDLEY

CAMBRIDGE UNIVERSITY PRESS

PUBLISHED BY THE PRESS SYNDICATE OF THE UNIVERSITY OF CAMBRIDGE
The Pitt Building, Trumpington Street, Cambridge CB2 1RP, United Kingdom

CAMBRIDGE UNIVERSITY PRESS
The Edinburgh Building, Cambridge CB2 2RU, UK http://www.cup.cam.ac.uk
40 West 20th Street, New York, NY 10011-4211, USA http://www.cup.org
10 Stamford Road, Oakleigh, Melbourne 3166, Australia

First published 1998

Printed in the United States of America

Typeset in New Baskerville.

Library of Congress Cataloging-in-Publication Data

Gidley, M. (Mick)
Edward S. Curtis and the North American Indian, Incorporated / Mick Gidley
p. cm. – (Cambridge studies in American literature and culture)
Includes bibliographical references and index.
ISBN 0-521-56335-6 (hc)
1. Curtis, Edward S., 1868–1952. 2. Indians of North America – Pictorial works. I. Title. II. Series.
E77.5.G53 1998
770'.92 – dc21 97-44371
[B] CIP

A catalog record for this book is available from the British Library

ISBN 0-521-56335-6 hardback

Frontispiece. Before the White Man Came – Palm Canyon, 1924, by E. S. Curtis. A Cahuilla woman near the site of present-day Palm Springs, California.

There is no document of civilization
which is not at the same time
a document of barbarism.

Walter Benjamin (1940)

CAMBRIDGE STUDIES IN AMERICAN LITERATURE AND CULTURE

Books in the series

118. Wilson Moses, *Afrocentrism, Antimodernism, and Utopia*
117. Lindon Barrett, *Blackness and Value: Seeing Double*
116. Lawrence Howe, *Mark Twain and the Novel: The Double-Cross of Authority*
115. Janet Casey, *Dos Passos and the Ideology of the Feminine*
114. Caroline Levander, *Voices of the Nation: Women and Public Speech in 19th Century American Literature and Culture*
113. Harryette Mullen, *Freeing the Soul: Race, Subjectivity, and Difference in Slave Narratives*
112. Dennis A. Foster, *Sublime Enjoyment: On the Perverse Motive in American Literature*
111. Eileen Gregory, *H. D. and Hellenism: Classic Lines*
110. Beverly Haviland, *Henry James's Last Romance: Making Sense of the Past and the American Scene*
109. Alfred Arteaga, *Chicano Poetics: Heterotexts and Hybridites*

CONTENTS

LIST OF ILLUSTRATIONS

Unless otherwise indicated, all photographs from photogravures by Edward S. Curtis are reproduced from *The North American Indian* courtesy of the University of Exeter Library, with titles as they appear in *The North American Indian*; dates, here and throughout the book, are either those of the year in which it is known images were made or, failing that, the year in which they were copyrighted.

PREFACE AND ACKNOWLEDGMENTS

I have been working on this study of the project that produced the set of illustrated volumes known as *The North American Indian* (1907–30) for a long time. Not for quite as long as it took Edward S. Curtis and his associates to produce their monumental publication, but it has been long enough; and despite the fact that – again like them – sometimes other things had to take precedence, I have accumulated many debts in the course of it.

I was awarded year-long fellowships by the American Council of Learned Societies and the Netherlands Institute for Advanced Study, the former allowing me to start on this book, the latter to complete it. When I began, the ACLS award enabled me to spend a very enjoyable and productive year at the Burke Museum on the campus of the University of Washington in Seattle, and when I finished it was in the supportive and stimulating environment provided by NIAS in Wassenaar, The Netherlands. In between, the American Philosophical Society, Philadelphia; the British Academy, London; the Center for Creative Photography, Tucson; and the U.S. Embassy in London awarded me grants and fellowships to make further research visits to reservations, libraries, and archives in the United States. My own institution during most of this period, the University of Exeter, kindly granted me both study leave and financial assistance. Throughout, certain colleagues at Exeter, at San Diego State University where I spent a pleasant semester, and at my present university, Leeds, were – and have remained – collegial, stimulating and, even, inspirational. Since they are also my friends, they know who they are.

During my visits to the United States a number of people with direct personal knowledge of *The North American Indian* and the personnel associated with the production of its words and images graciously granted me interviews, answered my telephone queries, responded to my letters, or in other ways shared their experiences with me. I am particularly grateful to the then-surviving family of Edward S. Curtis: Harold Phillips Curtis, Billy Curtis Ingram, Manford Magnuson, and, especially, Florence Curtis Graybill; to Betty McCullough, Asahel Curtis's daughter; and to Victor Boesen, Fritz Dalby, Grace Meany Hodge, and Wellington S. Phillips. Curtis collectors and dealers Lois Flury and

Karl Kernberger were very helpful to me. The Notes to this study record some of the nature of these and other similar debts too numerous to list here. Other scholars have also been generous with their findings; I have endeavored to acknowledge these too in the Notes, but must mention here George Quimby, formerly Director of the Burke Museum, Beth B. DeWall, James Enyeart, John C. Ewers, Bill Holm, Robert Bruce Inverarity, the late Robert D. Monroe, Jay Ruby, Clifford Trafzer, and Richard J. Weber.

Unpublished and uncollected primary materials – letters, memoirs, photographs and the like – are at the heart of this book. Some of them come from private collections, but most are reproduced or cited through the good offices of public archives and libraries. I hope all are fully cited in the text itself, in the Notes, or at another appropriate point, but I would at least like to name here the helpful colleagues encountered in various sections of the University of Washington Libraries (though not all of them still work there), especially Dennis Andersen, Andrew Johnson, Gary Lundell, and Glenda Pearson, and those in the University of Exeter Library who supported my work over the years, including Nick Eastwood, Heather Eva, Sue Conniff, and Sue McManus. Other key archival figures for this book were the late Michael Harrison, William B. (Pete) Lee, and Ruth M. Christensen, formerly at the Southwest Museum, Los Angeles.

Parts of the present book have appeared, in very different form, in a number of publications – *History of Photography, Pacific Northwest Quarterly, Prospects, Studies in Visual Communication, The Yearbook of English Studies,* and the book *Between Indian and White Worlds* edited by Margaret Connell Szasz (University of Oklahoma Press). I am grateful to their editors for publishing my work and for granting permission for it to be reprinted here.

Several people gave practical help in the production of this book. I am thinking of Susan Harshberger, Janet Ibbetson, Angela Day, Vi Palfrey, Sandra Skinner, Patricia Dowse, and Sarah Moore. The anonymous readers at Cambridge University Press provided excellent structural advice, as did my editors there, Susan Chang and Anne Sanow. My friend David Nye read portions of it with a sense of involvement that was itself encouraging. The moral and spiritual sustenance has come primarily from my family; Ruth and Ben have contributed more than they know towards the book's completion, and any lift it has – or, indeed, my life has – comes courtesy of Nancy.

Mick Gidley
University of Leeds, 1997

PART ONE

INTRODUCTORY

All the peoples of mankind are human.

Bartolomé de Las Casas (1550)

Figure 1. Navaho Still Life, 1907, by E. S. Curtis. The staple items of Navajo material culture arranged to meet the conventions of western art.

INTRODUCTION

Since the 1970s, when there were a number of exhibitions and books featuring Edward S. Curtis's Indian photographs, there has been a revival of interest in the total output of Curtis and his project. This project comprised *The North American Indian* (1907–30), twenty volumes of illustrated text and twenty portfolios of large-size photogravures; magazine articles for the general reader in *Century, Scribner's,* and the like from 1898 onwards; numerous lectures and even a "musicale" on Native American cultures, which filled Carnegie Hall in 1911; *In the Land of the Head-Hunters,* originally released in 1914, the very first narrative documentary film; popularizing books, such as *Indian Days of the Long Ago* (1914); and, of course, many exhibitions and much incidental publication of the countless photographs created by the enterprise. In fact, the project, which was devoted to over eighty different Native American peoples living west of the Mississippi and Missouri rivers who (in Curtis's prefatory words to *The North American Indian*) "still retained to a considerable degree their primitive customs and traditions," almost certainly constitutes the largest anthropological enterprise ever undertaken.

The collection of ethnological data for *The North American Indian* – including thousands of musical recordings as well as the images and the verbal data, such as myths and folklore – was achieved by a (changing) field team of ethnologists, Native American assistants and informants, photographic technicians, and others. The production and distribution of *The North American Indian,* which became the responsibility of a specially-created business company run by Curtis, involved prodigious organization, massive funding, the cooperation of specialist publishing and photoengraving companies, and considerable attention to publicity. *The North American Indian* was sold on a subscription basis – mostly to very prosperous individuals and major libraries – in a severely limited edition of luxurious, leather-bound books.[1]

When, too long ago, I started work on the present book I intended to produce a biographical and critical study of Curtis. Despite the scholarly – and popular – attention paid to Curtis in recent years, there is still room for such a work. But this book, which deals with the project as a more collective endeavor, involving financial, editorial, and other figures, is not it. For three decades from the 1890s onwards, Curtis did take thousands of photographs of Native Americans all over the West, which were very widely circulated throughout that period, and he was credited with the creation of the monumental *The North American Indian.* He was undoubtedly the project's prime mover and he put it on the map, so to speak. While I trust that my book does illuminate aspects of the man – his dynamism, range, egomania, and charisma, especially – it is neither a eulogy to his achievements nor a debunking of them in the manner to which much of the previous writing on him has accustomed us. Rather, this book is a study of the project as a whole, what it was, and, to some degree, what it meant.

In 1911, after a performance of his elaborate musicale or "picture-opera" at the Brooklyn Institute, Curtis reported to a friend that Franklin Hooper, an eminent scientist of the time, had told him that he "was the first to give them . . . the real Indian." What that audience actually experienced was, obviously, not "the real Indian," or even what Curtis himself had witnessed in the field, but a *representation.* More recently, the British poet Alan Ross wrote of Curtis that "In ceremony and cloud signs, beyond corruptions/ . . . he searched out/ . . . a pure lineage" and "in the set of their profiles/ Not mere paraphrase of history,/ But something of themselves."[2] Despite countless confusions to the contrary, such as these, it has been understood since the time of Aristotle that forms of cultural expression, both "artistic" and otherwise – whether poetry or parliamentary records, songs or statistics, drawings or dramatic productions – do not reproduce reality itself; rather, in their various ways, these and other forms far too numerous to mention each offer something which *stands for* an aspect of reality.

The concept of representation, as a number of commentators have shown, is fundamental but also highly complex, especially in its relationship to ideas of "realism," the sense that some forms, or individual examples within forms, offer closer approximations to reality than others. (Photography and film are frequently cited in this regard.) Hence Hooper, confronted by a show using a range of media in a more highly wrought manner than he had previously encountered, could be led to believe, mistakenly, that he was getting the real thing. What such representations in fact offer are varying *illusions* of reality. Here I do not mean to imply "mere illusions," to downgrade the significance of representations. For a start, they may – like Curtis's images – be replete with skill or art, and, often for this reason, they may impress themselves with haunting and awesome force on those encountering them. The fact that representations are capable of exerting such power – and we know that those treated here have done so – is part of what makes them worth investigating. Also, by referring to them as "illusions," in no sense do I mean to suggest that they function only as symbols of something much more important, and lying behind them, as it were, in real life; rather, these representations have in turn acted to *constitute* "reality" for the cultures that produced and consumed them.[3]

Despite its apparent problems, the use in this study of the term "representation" does have certain advantages. One of them is that it may be enriched, if further complicated, by its association with the idea of political representation. That is, there is a relationship between what W. J. T. Mitchell calls "things that stand for other things" and "persons who act for other persons." "Even purely aesthetic representation of fictional persons and events," says Mitchell, "can never be completely divorced from political and ideological questions," and he points out that just as, for example, literature is often said to be a "representation of life," it is to be expected that "life" will affect the nature of the representation. This study of the North American Indian project instances exclusively representations produced by members of the politically powerful – indeed, dominant – group. In "life," as the next chapter here insists, the subjects of these representations, Native Americans, were also the political subjects of the producers' society, and Curtis often purported to represent them in both senses.[4]

It is a truism that to visitors in a new land – certainly to settlers – the original inhabitants were profoundly *Other*: The settlers may have had to struggle physically with the indigenous people for possession of the land, and in the process the original inhabitants became that which the settlers defined themselves against. It was virtually inevitable that the representations examined here would incorporate, reflect, or respond to, perhaps justify, the assumptions of the dominant (whites). And, as we will see repeatedly, they do. The representations produced by the project tend to conform, in other words, to the lineaments of "the white man's Indian" of their period, as identified by Robert Berkhofer, Brian W. Dippie, and others.[5]

This view of the situation is a long way from simpler questions about the "accuracy" or otherwise of a work's representation of the culture at issue. Indeed, in much recent writing on the representation of other cultures – often indebted to Edward Said's *Orientalism* (1978), a groundbreaking study of European scholarship, political pronouncements, and literature, including travelers' tales, devoted to the Middle East – a kind of consensus has emerged that members of the dominant group, no matter how "intimate" (to use a favorite Curtis term) their sense of their involvement with the people concerned, will represent nothing but the assumptions of their own kind. Rather than seeking out or simply recognizing the features held in common with the subject group, there will be a tendency, as James Clifford has put it, "to dichotomize . . . into we–they contrasts and to *essentialize* the resultant other – to speak of the oriental mind, [etc.]." On one occasion, in relating "How the Indian Composes Songs," Curtis said that his "long acquaintance with the Indian" had shown him that "he [the Indian] does . . . many things exactly as the white man does" – but this pronouncement is an exception that proves the rule. Thus we get the emergence of "*the* Arab," "*the* African," "*the* Indian," and so on, and on. Instead of previously prevalent questions as to whether particular representations produced by white culture(s) depicted indigenous cultures with verisimilitude, in the manner of the repeated claims that tribal people depicted in Curtis's images were "wrongly" dressed, it would seem that the appropriate question to ask today of one of the dominant (white) culture's products would be, What aspect of *itself* has it represented?[6]

And in this "crisis of representation," as it has been called, what may be said about anthropology, the discipline whose central business it has been to describe and understand culture in general and "other" cultures in particular, and the one to which the North American Indian project (if to any) belonged? The Mexican painter David Alfaro Siqueiros gave the suitably enigmatic title "Ethnography" to his 1939 portrait, now in New York's Museum of Modern Art, of someone clothed in a Mexican peasant's smock, surrounded by darkness, and, crucially, wearing a decorative mask under a straw sombrero. The picture is itself literally – or, rather, graphically – only a mask, a mystery hiding rather than revealing the nature of the life of the person and culture it represents. For a start, anthropologists themselves have bemoaned the degree to which, if sometimes unwittingly, the enterprise of their discipline was not immune to the influence of the kinds of inequalities we have noted, but was inextricably linked to the exercise of power by the dominant culture.[7] This larger intellectual and institutional context must be borne in mind as we examine the project.

In fact, it probably cannot be emphasized enough that the representation of any part of the social life of human beings – in any form of cultural expression – is a complicated business. Howard S. Becker, in his notably lucid and wide-ranging essay "Telling about Society," has reiterated some of the difficulties of these issues and pointed out that all representations involve what he summarizes as processes of "selection," "translation," "arrangement," and "interpretation."[8] Curtis himself claimed in one of the documents reproduced at length here that Native American myth material provided a kind of unmediated access: "The thought is often expressed: 'If we could only see from the Indian's point of view, if we could see what he sees, what wonderful stories we could tell,'" and he asserted that "in [the Indian's] . . . legends, and in his myths, we must see from his viewpoint. . . . [W]e must get the Indian's logic" (see Doc. 4A). But the issue is more complicated than this because, even in myth material, precisely what "we" are receiving is already selected, translated, arranged, and interpreted – indeed, incorporated.

We might well wonder whether it is ever possible for a member of one culture, perhaps especially a member of a dominant culture, to represent another culture – or, even, just to hear the voices and truly see the sights of another culture. "If the ways of seeing in different communities are in conflict because their interpretive practices reflect incommensurable presuppositions about the human situation, can such communities understand each other?" asks Paul B. Armstrong. In Curtis's photographs, for example, where European conventions of genre prevailed – producing, say, "Navaho Still Life" (fig. 1: 1907) or "Maricopa Still Life" (1907) – how much truly *Navajo* or *Maricopa* content is communicated? "Can one culture," asks Armstrong, "use its own terms to say something about another culture without engaging in a hostile act of appropriation or without simply reflecting itself and not engaging the otherness of the Other? . . . can we ever escape our provincial islands and navigate between worlds?" Such issues – at least in the abstract – are largely beyond the scope of this book, but I would submit that the first step must be to become aware – and ever more aware – of the problematics of the representational act itself; and the second, at least for members of habitually colonialist groups, must be to attend to the voices of those "others" as they express what the Nigerian novelist Chinua Achebe has termed "The Song of Ourselves."[9]

That being said, this book, in emphasizing representation, does not purport adequately to describe the realities of Native American experience and culture themselves. Moreover, it does not deal with the project *as experienced by* Native Americans, whether during what must have been a common occurrence, the sittings for portraits, or during the project's more targeted forays to secure "esoteric" information. On the other hand, this experience *is* treated throughout at one remove, so to speak, in that much can be inferred from what is covered. Obviously, although Curtis's pictures involved even more Native people than did the gathering of the text, it was inevitably a fairly fleeting encounter, at most seasonal, not the sort of intimate involvement evoked in Jaune Quick-To-See Smith's recollections of her family album in *Partial Recall*, a collection of essays on photographs by Native American artists, or, even more, Leslie Marmon Silko's book *Storyteller* (1981), set in her own Pueblo homeland, where photographs "taken since the 1890s around Laguna" are interspersed through the stories of the book "because they are part of many of the stories and because many of the stories can be traced in the photographs."[10] Nevertheless, in another sense, the Curtis photographs are an important part of the larger, encompassing story of Native Americans this century, and that is why they feature again here.

In the course of my research I came across such a richness of unpublished or previously unregarded materials that I have been impelled to publish some of them in articles and will produce a book-length collection of them. Also, as many as possible are incorporated into the present study, both as extended quotations within the text of each chapter and as documents appended to chapters. It has seemed especially important that reports by North American Indian project workers of their encounters with Native Americans in the early twentieth century be added to the ethnohistorical record so that others may use them and assess their significance; hence the length of documents in such published pieces as "Into Apache Lands," which presents and contextualizes memoirs by Curtis and two other figures who worked on the White Mountain Reservation during a so-called "Messiah Craze" early in the life of the project, and in such chapters as "Adventure in the Field" here.[11] I hope that the documents and extended quotations also serve to amplify the voices of those other than Curtis – whether the principal ethnologist, William E. Myers, other assistants, Native American informants, members of the Curtis family, political figures, or patrons – who were associated with the project.

There are facets of the project that have already been more or less adequately treated in earlier scholarly publications: the production of the first feature documentary movie, for example, or the effects of Curtis's participation in the Harriman Alaska Expedition, or the affinities between Curtis's photographs and the Photo-Secession. In these cases it seemed advisable to grant less space to them here and, within that space, to concentrate on the provision of new material. In general, the same sort of strategy has been adopted wherever there was a potential overlap between previous accounts and my own, whether the issue is a large one or a matter of detail, though in certain cases it has been necessary overtly to correct wrong impressions that had threatened to become accepted facts. On the other hand, there are features of the enterprise – some of the technicalities of its photography and book production, for instance, or the project's fall into virtual oblivion from 1930 until the 1970s – that remain unconsidered here.

This book has three strands, which for the most part are pursued together: The first strand consists of an account of the North American Indian project's manifold activities; the second is an attempt to describe as adequately as possible the key forces – ideological, aesthetic, economic, and anthropological – that were fused in the project; and the third is an assessment, sometimes presented implicitly rather than overtly, of its significance, both as an American enterprise and as a complex representation of its declared subject matter, the culture(s) of Native Americans. It is to the last of these strands that the double meaning of the book's title points: "Incorporated" signifies both business company or enterprise and, metaphorically, the *idea* of incorporation. The latter usage is fully elaborated (if with relatively limited reference to Native Americans) – not only in its "literal sense," as referring to "a specific form of business . . . organization," namely the corporation, but also in its "figurative sense" as applied to "a more comprehensive pattern" – throughout Alan Trachtenberg's important book *The Incorporation of America* (1982).[12] The project was largely organized under the auspices of a New York-based business enterprise established with J. Pierpont Morgan funds, The

North American Indian, Inc., and other corporations were founded to deal with the motion picture work it brought into being. Just as, in Trachtenberg's usage, American culture was "incorporated," so too were Native American cultures incorporated by the project.

Edward S. Curtis and The North American Indian, Incorporated is structured in three parts. After this Introduction, the first chapter, "A National Undertaking" – which takes as its launch-pad numerous remarks by such public figures as Theodore Roosevelt (see fig. 2) that the project was an important American enterprise – completes Part One by making some claims for seeing the project as affecting and affected by national attitudes – and, more concretely, Bureau of Indian Affairs policies – towards Indians. Ronald Takaki has stressed the role of the railroad as an "iron horse in the West," "a *corporate* interest aggressively involved in the white settlement of the West and the destruction of Indians," and the railroad was only the most obvious of a series of corporations to exhibit these two, seemingly inextricably linked, features.[13] Insofar as *The North American Indian* was intended as a monument to a "vanishing race" – even if, unlike Mark Antony, it came neither to praise nor bury – you could be excused for discerning a double edge to my use of that word "undertaking."

Part Two, "Co-ordinates for a Project," attempts to diagram some of the principal co-ordinates which determined the project's particular trajectory: "Cracker Jack Pictures" outlines Curtis's aesthetic aspirations and drive for images; "Trading with the Indians" treats the recurrence of, and linkages between, various forms of appropriation; "Hustling the Eminent" explains the (lopsided) approach necessitated by the project's singular forms of patronage; and "Diffident Ethnology" principally investigates the role of the half-forgotten figure of William E. Myers and, more generally, aspects of ethnological inquiry as it was understood during the project's own time. Each of these co-ordinates is also shown in action, so to speak, throughout the remainder of the book.

The third and final part of the book, "Indians Incorporated," pays detailed attention to the project's extensive output. Its first chapter (6), "Adventure in the Field," analyses and offers sample accounts of the project's actual field experience. "We long ago saw the impossibility of pretending to give a complete survey of all the western tribes in 20 volumes," wrote Myers to Frederick Webb Hodge, his editor, in 1926, when the project was nearing completion, "and have been trying to do the best we could in various cultural areas."[14] I have followed a similar, if more radically curtailed, strategy, and have focused this chapter on just a small selection of peoples. In the reproduction of documents here and elsewhere, divergences from and correspondences with the published volumes of *The North American Indian* are established and, where appropriate, commented upon. The extraordinary musicale is treated in "'The Vanishing Race' in Sight and Sound." The movie work is also granted a chapter of its own: "Bronze in Action." The words and images of the generality of texts produced by the project, especially *The North American Indian* itself, together with some of the project's overt conflicts and covert ambivalences over representation, are discussed in the final chapter. That chapter, "Representing the Indian," also relies, if often only implicitly, on the various accounts and documents that precede it.

The project as conceived and conducted by Curtis and his associates was large in its scope and scale and may have presumed to create a monument, but it was not monolithic; it involved numerous personnel, lasted a long time, changed, and was subjected to changes in the culture which encompassed it. Despite the fact that this very durability and multifacetedness would render redundant any study of the project exclusively from a fixed temporal point, the book – especially the final part – does speculate upon the project's significance. But *not* in its own chosen terms, that is, as a more or less straightforward "record" of Indian life; rather, as I have stressed here, the project is viewed as a complex representation of Indian culture(s) that could not help but represent the assumptions of the dominant culture.

Indeed, in contradiction of previous accounts of Curtis and his endeavor, I hope to show that the enterprise was not an unprecedented breakthrough in its approach to Native American studies. Commentators such as T. C. McLuhan, Florence Curtis Graybill, and other members of Curtis's own family who wrote about him, exhibition organizers and a host of anonymous and semi-anonymous dealers in photographs who promoted the Curtis "revival" of the 1970s, all tended to present his work, particularly the images *per se*, as marking a new and especially sympathetic portrayal of Indian lifeways. The use of Curtis's images as contrapuntal illustrations to McLuhan's widely circulated anthology of Native American texts, *Touch the Earth: A Self-Portrait of Indian Existence* (1971), sanctioned the popular conceptions of Curtis as "*the* shadow catcher" and of his photographs – now reproduced everywhere, from calendars to shoe company labels – as authentic incarnations of essential Indian nobility and spirituality. On the other hand, Christopher M. Lyman's *The Vanishing Race and Other Illusions* (1982), as its title indicates, emphasized the powerful element of staging in the photographs and inaugurated a number of dismissive references to the work, almost as if it had been produced by a charlatan. Subsequent commentary may be seen as subscribing to one of these two positions, usually without reference to other evidence.[15]

By contrast, basing the case almost wholly on primary materials, I want to show that, in many respects, the enterprise was entirely *typical* of its time. Clark Wissler, Curtis's contemporary and a leading anthropologist of Plains peoples based at the American Museum of Natural History, devoted a whole chapter of his memoirs, *Indian Cavalcade or Life on the Old-Time Indian Reservations* (1938), to (unnamed) makers of what he termed "Those Ever Vanishing Types," as if they were as frequently to be encountered as the Indian Agents and other representative figures who populate his text. "Up and down the Indian country roamed . . . artists," he said, "in reality conservationists, since they sincerely believed that when the few old Indians died, the type would vanish forever, and feeling that here was something of incalculable value, they were out to copy, model and photograph for posterity." "I met some of these photographers," he added, and described one with Curtis-like facilities: "a kind of camp studio, an enormous tent and a huge portrait camera." Certainly, photographers other than Curtis were also specifically credited with rescuing "the vanishing race" from oblivion. For example, in an article in *The Craftsman* – which, as we will see in Chapter 2, also favored *The North America Indian* – Louis Akin celebrated the Norwegian-born Frederick Monsen for "the art of portraying . . . the individuality of a picturesque and fast vanishing race." Except for claiming that Monsen's images were produced through good personal relations alone, whereas those of others were allegedly made by figures who "speed through the country with the camera in one hand and the ever-ready dollar in the other," all the qualities Akin noted about Monsen were those so frequently ascribed to Curtis. And there were so many stylistic similarities to Curtis in some of the images produced by another contemporary, Joseph Kossuth Dixon, that Curtis himself believed that Dixon had deliberately copied him. At the popular level, whatever Curtis hoped, Dixon's work was seen as parallel to his own; for example, the *Photographic Times* of April 1912 had an article on Curtis titled "Writing History with the Camera," and two issues later it published one devoted to Dixon, "More History with the Camera," in which it claimed, after mentioning Curtis, that Dixon was "another sympathetic and talented artist."[16]

The North American Indian project both was and was not unique. Along with certain contemporary observers, I believe its images were ultimately more memorable than – and aesthetically superior to – those of the other figures mentioned; Sadakichi Hartmann, as we shall see, dubbed Curtis "*the* photographer of Indians." More importantly, the North American Indian project was a bigger, better funded, and more famous enterprise than theirs. But they were parallel endeavors, and perhaps the Curtis project is best thought of as paradigmatic. Its representation of Native Americans was conditioned by the dominant culture and permeated it. I see Curtis himself as not so much an *author* of words and images – although he was that too, of course – but as subject to what Wai-chee Dimock, in an appropriation from Umberto Eco, has called "a controlling logic of *culture*."[17] That is why his images were so influential for so long, if not in an unbroken, unchanging, and unchallenged line, and why they retain their influence still. That is why the representations produced by the project as a whole have called for our understanding. But this is already to assume what the chapters that follow are intended to reveal.

Figure 2. Theodore Roosevelt, 1904, by E. S. Curtis. President Roosevelt championed Curtis's Indian work.

1

A NATIONAL UNDERTAKING

Beginnings

On February 6, 1906, the President of the United States, Theodore Roosevelt (fig. 2), wrote to compliment Curtis on his success in securing funds from J. Pierpont Morgan for his work with North American Indians: "I congratulate you with all my heart. That is a mighty fine deed of Mr. Morgan's."[1] The establishment of these financial arrangements certainly marked the high point of Curtis's achievement to date, and it had not been easy to secure, either in the short run or in terms of his previous career. Curtis, who was born on February 16, 1868, was approaching forty and deeply conscious of the distance he had travelled and that his true life's work was still ahead of him.

Curtis came from an evangelical Christian family, probably Methodist, which was poor, hard-working, and future-oriented. His adulthood had properly begun when, in the late autumn of 1887, he and his father, Johnson Asahel Curtis, left Edward's elder brother Rafael (known as Ray) to look after the rest of the family in Cordova, Minnesota, and ventured westwards. Johnson and Edward arrived in Sidney (now Port Orchard) on the shores of Puget Sound, on December 17, 1887. Edward was nineteen and his father, a Civil War veteran, was not a well man when they settled on their hillside farm. On May 2 of the following year, only three days after his wife Ellen, daughter Eva, and son Asahel joined then, Johnson died of pneumonia, leaving Edward as the mainstay of the family.[2] William Washington Phillips, who became acquainted with Curtis very soon after this, wrote about Curtis's motivations in a probing unpublished memoir he produced as early as 1911. As Ray was to stay in Minnesota until

1905 before putting down roots in Portland, Oregon, quite separately from the rest of the family, the labor of pioneer farming fell to Edward. "Clearing and grubbing in a veritable jungle became the order of the day," wrote Phillips. Slowly, through the planting of fruit trees and various vegetables, the family began to make a living in its new home.[3]

Then, in the autumn of 1890, "a serious accident befell Curtis," recorded Phillips. "He fell on a log, severely injuring himself. For a year . . . he lay on an invalid's bed, limp, thin and bleached, the constant care of a tireless mother and a girl (Clara Phillips) destined later to become his wife." On his recovery, Curtis had a new conception of what he should do for a living: "he recognized the necessity of starting into business somewhere." Curtis's first business venture was a brickyard, but this never became a success, and – having learned the rudiments of photography earlier, either in St. Paul or Minneapolis, Minnesota – he used the proceeds of the brickyard sale to buy into a photographic gallery in Seattle.[4]

Phillips, Curtis's nephew by marriage, lived with Edward and his family from the age of sixteen, and knew him well. He realized that going into business was a decisive point for Curtis, as it was for so many aspiring new westerners, and framed his observations carefully:

> The city was an overgrown, struggling village then, and the establishment conducted by Rothi and Curtis only a half-grown struggling enterprise. But the enterprise of the junior member of the firm ere long chafed for a freer scope. He had married soon after entering business, and felt the impetus a wife gives to a man's ambition. In little more than a year he withdrew from Rothi & Curtis and formed a new concern in a better business location, that of Curtis & Guptill, Photographers and Photo-engravers. Guptill did clever work at drawing with his pen, and what neither knew of the engraving processes they learned as the business grew. An uncertain growth it was, too, in those panicy [sic] years of the early nineties, but solid foundation stones were being laid.

They certainly were. Thus it was that the son of a sickly pioneer farmer, a man of little formal education and whose first proper job back in Minnesota, as he later liked to stress, had been that of young boss of an unruly railroad gang, was on his way to becoming one of Seattle's most prominent citizens.

Through a hammered fusion of talent, influential friends and patrons, prodigious labor, and unrelenting ambition, Curtis began to achieve national recognition with his camera, especially after his service as Official Photographer to the Harriman Alaska Expedition of 1899. The expedition, which gathered some of the most prominent natural historians of the time under the scientific leadership of Dr. C. Hart Merriam to explore much of the Alaskan coastline, was a private enterprise launched, financed, and captained by the railroad tycoon E. H. Harriman.[5] It was also Curtis's specialization in the photography of Indians, alongside all the regular work of his studio, that drew public attention: He was awarded national prizes for it, exhibited the results widely and, as we shall see, was credited with a particular vision of Indian life.

Nevertheless, when he conceived of turning his Indian work into a major project – even after he had expended much of the proceeds of the Seattle studio on photographic field trips to many parts of the Indian West gathering material for it – his search for sustained patronage proved both arduous and fruitless. In the summer of 1903 he journeyed to Washington, D.C., specifically to secure help from various U.S. Government agencies. Frederick Webb Hodge of the Bureau of American Ethnology encouraged him and, as a result, received a projection of Curtis's plans: "I will be . . . at work in the field by the middle of January [1904], and hope to give practically all of the time from then until the coming Autumn to the Indian work, and on my next trip to Washington, I hope to have another selection of good things." Curtis concluded this account of his aspirations with the hope that Hodge would write to him "if anything" occurred to him.[6]

Whether Hodge helped him at that time or not, by the following October Curtis was able to report on the work of the summer of 1904 with considerable pride. To Gifford Pinchot, chief of the U.S. Forest Service and a fellow Harriman Expedition member, his account was laced with ironic, schoolboy bravado:

> Well, my trip to the South-west has been a very successful one. One of the hardest trips that I have ever made, met with more trouble from rains, accidents and that sort of thing than I have in my work heretofore, but, withal, succeeded in getting a very large amount of splendid new material. Saw the Snake Dance of the Mokis [Hopis]; also the Buffalo Dance and Antelope ceremony of the Acomas, the annual ceremonies of the Jiciralla

> [sic] Apaches and a nine day ceremony of the Navahos. Eight hard, happy weeks! But you know how it is – results is what a fellow wants, and if you get them, what matters a few camp hardships, and the occasional loss of more or less of one's outfit in cloud bursts, freshets, etc.
>
> Until the first of the year I shall be in Seattle doing portrait work and working up the field work of the summer, and after that, a trip to Washington and New York, at which time I hope . . . to show you what the whole collection is like. No one [h]as ever seen it yet, and I am now going to try and get a complete set of prints from all my negatives to show just what I have.[7]

To Hodge, after telling him about the 1904 fieldwork, Curtis was more emphatic: "The longer I work at this collection of pictures the more certain I feel of their great value . . . the thing has grown so. . . . The only question now in my mind is, will I be able to keep at [it] long enough . . . , as doing it in a thorough way is enormously expensive and I am finding it rather difficult to give as much time to the work as I would like." In the same letter Curtis indicated that his interests extended beyond photography *per se* in that he wanted, he said, to return to the White Mountain Apaches "more for information than pictures." And just a year prior to Curtis's success with Morgan, Hodge's superior, William Henry Holmes, the chief of the bureau, declined his agency's support in a letter obviously intended to help Curtis raise money elsewhere: "I sincerely hope that you will succeed in this most commendable undertaking. The series . . . would be a monument to yourself, and especially to the institution or person making the publication possible."[8]

Precisely how it came about that J. Pierpont Morgan, the powerful banker and magnate, was persuaded to make such a publication possible is not certain. Roosevelt gave his general blessing to the venture in a very fulsome tribute after Curtis asked him for "a letter of introduction to Mr. Carnegie or anyone else" who might be interested, but in his reply Roosevelt issued a specific ruling: "there is no man of great wealth with whom I am on sufficiently close terms to warrant my giving a special letter to him."[9] Since the president was engaged in major political and economic tussles with several men of "great wealth" at the time, including Andrew Carnegie and Morgan, doubtless he was *not* in the best position or disposition to seek favors. The financial settlement occurred through the conjunction of a number of factors – the newspaper response to Curtis's exhibitions, for instance, the particular nature of the proposal, and other endorsements of Curtis's work – but the single most effective element was most probably the influence of Robert Clark Morris.

Morris, the scion of a prominent New England family from the town of Morris, Connecticut, was both a teacher of international law at Yale and very active in legal practice in New York City. In 1903 Roosevelt appointed him U.S. counsel to the U.S.–Venezuelan Claims Commission and he was on personally amicable terms with the president's family. He was heavily involved in Republican Party politics and, as he revealed in his unpublished autobiography, the position of president of the Republican County Committee of the County of New York in the early 1900s vested him with notable powers of patronage. Morris may have met Curtis on one of his trips to the West, during which he had found himself fascinated by Indian life, so much so that as early as 1896 he had been privileged to enter the Hopi Snake Dance kiva. Most significantly, Morris was retained as a counsel by the Morgan Bank. Later, in 1911, Morgan interests were to appoint him vice-president and one of three directors of The North American Indian, Inc., the company established in 1910 to run the financial affairs of the project – but by then he and Curtis were less close. In 1906, however, the Morrises – both Robert and his first wife, Alice Parmalee – were very friendly to the westerner. He would visit with them during his early trips to the East, and the couple even offered a home during his vacations to Curtis's son Harold, who attended a boarding school in Pennsylvania. Childless themselves, the Morrises – especially Alice – were lavish with affection towards the boy.[10]

Curtis outlined his project on paper for Morgan's benefit and then, on January 24, 1906, had the favor of a meeting – almost an audience – with the financier. During this meeting – or perhaps in the course of a second one a couple of days later – Curtis had the opportunity to show Morgan some of his pictures; according to Curtis family stories, Morgan, who was of course a major art collector and president of New York's Metropolitan Museum, was so moved by what he saw – including the portrait of "Mosa" (1903), a young Mojave woman, the lines of whose face painting and beaded necklaces seem subtly to accentuate the wistfulness of her gaze – that he was prepared to become the patron Curtis had been seeking. In essence, Morgan agreed to finance the fieldwork for the project at the rate of fifteen thousand dollars *per annum* for five years, while Curtis undertook to look after the actual publication himself.[11] By early February

1906, Curtis was able to tell Roosevelt of his success and, as we have seen, receive the president's jubilant response.

The injection of funds from one of the world's richest and most influential people – which, over the years, would be renewed and augmented in a number of ways – allowed organizational improvements, set a stamp of approval on the project's more ambitious aspects, and gave the Indian work an immediate boost. Arrangements already instituted for the management of the Curtis studio in Seattle were formalized: Its running would be left to Adolf F. Muhr, manager since 1904, and he would have freedom to take on staff extra to the various members of the Curtis and Phillips families who were employed there over the years. An office was established at 437 Fifth Avenue in New York City – usually with its own manager, but with Curtis himself much in evidence – to handle subscription sales and promotion of the monumental publication of *The North American Indian* that Morgan and Curtis had decided upon: twenty volumes of illustrated text and twenty portfolios of large-sized photogravures.

Although the pictorial content was to remain a principal feature of the project, such a plan was much more complicated than the extensive compendium of pictures which had seemed to be Curtis's ambition when, as recently as October 1904, he had relayed the trials and joys of fieldwork to Pinchot; the "information" element, of which he had spoken to Hodge – "the word picture," as he was to call it – was increased almost immeasurably in significance and scope. Because of this, Curtis tried to interest such figures as Charles Doolittle Walcott, Secretary of the Smithsonian, to join with "four or five of the Presidents of the leading educational institutions in America" as "contributors," essentially an authoritative editorial board able to give endorsement and credibility to the massive wordage now decreed by the Morgan agreement.[12]

Walcott declined, but Hodge, Curtis's old contact at the Bureau of American Ethnology, agreed to serve as editor of the proposed text at a fixed fee per word. Hodge was already editor of both the journal the *American Anthropologist* and what was to become the standard reference work *Handbook of American Indians North of Mexico* (2 volumes, 1910). He was one of the most respected figures in American anthropology from the turn of the century onwards. He had conducted important excavations at Enchanted Mesa, New Mexico, had written numerous papers and, most significant of all, was trusted by other leading practitioners of the discipline. He was later to direct the Museum of the American Indian in New York before moving to the same key position at the Southwest Museum in Los Angeles. Equally crucial, if from a different perspective, the Morgan largesse made it feasible to employ Native American informants and interpreters on a regular basis and, in effect, put a team in the field. Much of the organization of all this fell to William W. Phillips (whose memoir we have quoted) and to Curtis himself, but they were also able to take on staff for extended periods. The single most important recruit was William E. Myers, a former Seattle newspaperman who was to become the project's principal ethnologist and, in time, writer.[13]

Later, in August 1906, emboldened by the grant, by much successful fieldwork, and by a euphoric optimism that was to fuel the project through all kinds of vicissitudes until its completion in 1930, Curtis wrote from Hopi country to ask Roosevelt a further favor: "Could you consider in addition to [my] introduction, an introduction by yourself?" "It is only the largeness and historical value of the work which gives me the courage to suggest this," he added. "It is a work of great national worth, during your most active years. Pardon my crude way of saying it, but you as the greatest man in America owe it to your people to do this." The ebullient president agreed, wrote a laudatory foreword, and later even signed individual copies of the book's first volume.[14]

Ethnology vs. Indian Welfare

On July 27, 1924, Curtis delivered a lecture in Santa Fe, New Mexico. By then both Roosevelt and Morgan were dead, fourteen of the twenty volumes of *The North American Indian* had been published, and the end was in sight – or, at least, seemed to be. In his introductory remarks, before going on to other matters, Curtis gave an accurate summary of the coverage and concerns of *The North American Indian*:: "the old time Indian, his dress, his ceremonies, his life and manners."[15] Photogravure Number 1, "The Vanishing Race," the key image chosen to head off the pictorial aspect of *The North American Indian* (fig. 3; 1904), is typical. It depicts a line of mounted Navajos riding away from the camera towards the deep and engulfing shadows of canyon walls, with the penultimate figure in the line, as if in regret, turning in the saddle to look back; according to its caption, "the thought which [it is] meant to convey [is] that the Indians as a race, already shorn of their . . . strength and stripped of their primitive dress, [are] passing into the darkness of an unknown future." In Curtis's images, Indians would often perform the graphic equivalent of riding into the darkness of an unknown future.

The North American Indian project, as subsequent chapters here elaborate, was indeed primarily an enterprise of salvage ethnology, concerned to record traditional ways before – as it was assumed they would – they passed away. For example, one of Curtis's popular books was titled, tellingly, *Indian Days of the Long Ago* (1914). "In other words," Curtis continued the 1924 speech, "in [the North American Indian project] I suppose I am to be classed along with that group . . . occasionally referred to as 'long-hairs,' those who are interested only in the old Indian, [with] no interest whatsoever in the economic welfare of the Indian, his education and future."

This "long-hair" position was one Curtis was generally keen to deny, and on this occasion he went on to outline in particular some of the current activities of the Indian Welfare League, of which he held the Chair. In fact, for the project such a sharp distinction between "the old Indian" and the present was, of course, never tenable. Virtually all the fieldwork was conducted, with official permission, on reservation lands controlled by the policies of the government of the United States – or, in certain instances, of Canada. An extensive network of contacts at every echelon, from Secretaries of the Interior – even presidents – down through Commissioners of Indian Affairs to agents on individual reservations, was established. At the most humdrum level, the project was frequently in touch with the Bureau of Indian Affairs – for letters of introduction to agents, for copies of *Annual Reports*, and the like – and, as Chapter 4 stresses, the nature of the patronage under which the publication was produced frequently led Curtis, as its principal organizer, to flatter figures in positions of power.

The dominant assumption of the Bureau of Indian Affairs – often called the Indian Office or Department – just before and after the turn of the century was that Indians should be assimilated into mainstream (that is, white) society as rapidly as possible.[16] It was recognized that different tribes and individuals would proceed towards this goal at varying paces, and that some, because of material circumstances, historical inheritance, or whatever, would have great difficulty adjusting to the new order. Assimilation meant necessarily that Indians should be de-tribalized, encouraged to see themselves not as members of a preexisting group with traditional practices but as individual participants in a larger society governed by American laws. The principal instrument intended to achieve this result was the General Allotment or Dawes Act of 1887, which provided for the elimination of collective ownership of Indian lands, reservation by reservation, and the establishment of holdings by specific allottees. These indi-

Figure 3. The Vanishing Race – Navaho, 1904, by E. S. Curtis. The project's keynote image.

vidual property holders, if they so wished, could even sell the land allotted to them – and, in any case, the unallotted and supposedly "surplus" reservation land was thrown open for white settlement. Indian owners of individual allotments were encouraged to take up United States citizenship – though this did not usually mean they were granted a vote; as citizens they were subject to the franchise laws of the particular state in which they resided, most of which discriminated against Indians in this as in other civil rights.

However wrongheaded this set of objectives may now seem, and though it was definitely advocated by some interests as a cynical means of acquiring Indian lands, it was supported with reforming zeal by so-called "Friends of the Indian," such as the Indian Rights Association. It held hegemonic status until the 1920s – until, in fact, just about that moment when, as Curtis put it in his 1924 lecture, there seemed to be "an unusual, or abnormal interest in the Indian subject." In line with these assumptions, the bureau was dedicated to: (i) basic guardianship of those Indians deemed to need health care, provision of rations under treaty obligations, bureau policing, etc.;

(ii) allotment of reservation lands, a lengthy legal process involving surveying and conveyancing of millions of acres; and (iii) the progressive acquisition by Indians of U.S. citizenship.

While Curtis's interests in "the old time" and "the future" were definitely not divided "fifty-fifty," as he claimed they were in 1924, from the moment he began to photograph Indians beyond the immediate environs of the Seattle waterfront – perhaps as early as 1896 when he visited the nearby Tulalip Reservation – his work with Indians put him in situations that led him, almost inexorably, to represent them – and/or what he saw as their interests – politically and thus to intersect with the bureau in each of its areas of activity as just sketched. In June 1904, for example, before the North American Indian book project as such was under way, Curtis wrote to Commissioner William A. Jones to tell him of the hard work among the Navajos of a Mrs. H. M. Cole, who was based at Chinle, Arizona, near the mouth of the Canyon de Chelly, and his implicit suggestion was that she needed more help from the bureau.[17] The totality of the project's representation of Indians, whether in images, music, or words can only be adequately understood within the context of official attitudes and policies.

Curtis himself, in the 1924 speech, asserted that he was "strengthened" in his "welfare work" for present day Indians by his "ethnological knowledge," and this may well have been the case; what I hope to show here is that the project's ethnological activities were certainly informed by Indian Office beliefs and practices which, in turn, were consistent with the cultural assumptions of the dominant forces in American society. All told, there was more interplay – sometimes amounting to concordance – between such assumptions and the North American Indian project than might at first be apparent. Let us sample relevant encounters at four different phases in the life of the project: first, during its early, formative years; second, during the period when Curtis reached the acme of his fame and public exposure, beginning in 1911, while William Howard Taft was in power; third, somewhat later, in Woodrow Wilson's presidency; and, finally, in the period during which Curtis delivered his Santa Fe lecture in 1924.

National Dimensions: One

During the first phase, in 1905, on returning from what he called his "Southern trip" to the Southwest, Curtis told Commissioner Francis E. Leupp of conditions among the Havasupai:

> While in the Grand Cañon country I heard considerable of the destitute condition of the Hava supai, owing to the washouts in Cataract Cañon. I gave a little time to learning what I could of their condition, and I am convinced that it is one of these rare cases where help from some source is absolutely necessary. Whether it is possible for the Department to help, is something of which I have no knowledge, but I thought in the interest of humanity, I would send word to let you know how it looked to me.

Curtis had visited the Havasupai in 1903 in what the second volume of *The North American Indian*, published in 1908, rightly described as "the strangest dwelling place of any tribe in America": the floor of the chasm of the Grand Canyon. There, three thousand feet below the surface of the Canyon, the "Blue Water People" subsisted on the produce of carefully tended fruit trees and on small game, though their hunting rights had been drastically curtailed by Interior Department conservation measures. Curtis went on to tell Leupp that, though he had not visited the Canyon in person during the summer of 1905, he had heard the same story from several reliable sources, and it really did seem that not more than six of the Canyon's families had enough food to last the winter. "They need help," he wrote, "and that quite soon."[18]

Leupp had been a renowned journalist and an active member of the Indian Rights Association before becoming Roosevelt's very vigorous commissioner from 1905 until the end of his mentor's presidency in 1909. Curtis knew him personally and, while no record of Leupp's reply exists, it is likely that – though he was known to resent the interventions of the Indian Rights Association and other external pressures once he was in office – he did respond to the critical situation facing the Havasupai. If to little avail: By the time the Havasupai section of *The North American Indian* appeared, it was necessary for it to state the facts starkly: "in 1903 the Havasupai numbered about 250, but in three years disease has diminished their population to 166."[19]

It is interesting that, whether or not Leupp was able to do anything about the Havasupai, he took seriously – despite his aversion to pressure from lobbyists – a set of suggestions submitted by Curtis about the Pine Ridge Sioux Reservation in South Dakota. When he received Curtis's letter, in August 1905, he added a note: "Here's something for the wiseheads of the Office to chew on. Please report on it to me with reasons pro and con."[20] Whatever the identity of the bureau "wisehead" who read it, most of that person's reasons, as we shall see, were "con."

Curtis began his letter by stressing his sense of personal involvement with Red Cloud's people: "The Sioux of the Pine Ridge Agency and their life have rather got into my brain and I cannot shake it [sic] off." "I can't help but believe they are material worth an effort," he said, and implied that this, together with his personal regard for Leupp, had emboldened him to take the liberty of sending Leupp his plan. In 1905 Pine Ridge was due to be allotted to individual Indians under the provisions of the Dawes Act. When Curtis launched into the outline proper, he stated first the facts of this particular allotment process as he was aware of them:

> I understand the [allotment] plan is, to give a certain parcel of land, a team, harness and wagon, one or two cows, perhaps some farm implements, and a small amount of money, I believe fifty dollars. I am under the impression that there is a Sioux Fund. If there is no such fund, this outlined plan is out of the question. If there is such a fund, and this plan could be worked, it would slowly turn over to the Indians who are deserving of it, their portion of the fund, and in a way that they could get some benefit of this money and not be able to squander it.

Curtis's proposal consisted of a series of contractual obligations. Allotment would go ahead as already envisaged, but in addition, "If the Indian has ten or more cows, you will issue him ten more this year, charging them to his Sioux Fund account; but, if you issue these cattle to him, he must give you a contract that he will take good care of the cattle he already has." A similar obligation would apply to crops, with the government "helping" the Indian by breaking the land without charge, fencing it as a charge "to his account," and furnishing his seed, "which he must return from the crop." "I would plan to harvest the wheat with a harvesting crew, taking a portion of the Indian's crop," he continued, so "that the Indian would feel that he was paying for it. I would thresh the grain in the same way, taking a small portion of the crop to pay for this threshing."

The Indian Affairs staff worker who responded to Curtis's plan for Leupp had mixed feelings about these proposals. On the one hand, he seemed to think the actual procedures would work – with the exception that "the Indian should depend upon his own exertions" and, therefore, fence and break his own land. On the other hand, he wrote: "I don't believe a 'contract' with the Indian would be of much avail; . . . the agent should enforce the penalty in the agreement." A similar dismissiveness crept into the next response. Curtis suggested the cultivation of wheat and potatoes to an extent that the Indian family would have "nearly enough food for the year," but the bureau would need to provide a flour mill. The respondent thought the plan "might work," but countered "crops in that part of the country are very uncertain, even when lands are irrigated." "The flour mill would be all right," he said, but then pointed out that the mill at the Santee Sioux Agency had had to be closed down because "the Indians had stopped raising wheat in sufficient quantities to justify [its] running."

In his next paragraph Curtis proposed what he called "a new thought" – essentially *the* new thought of the document: the extension of the contract idea even to those Indians without ten cattle to guarantee their compliance. "I would make this same offer," he said, "to any Indian who could get a responsible Indian to guarantee that he would take care of the cattle issued to him." "I am inclined to believe," he continued, "that where one Indian guaranteed the performance of any act on the part of another Indian, that he would see that the Indian did it." This faith was derided by Leupp's staff worker: "Indians are very cautious and they would not be very prompt in coming forward with a guarantee such as is suggested. Even if he did make the guarantee, the chances are he would try to squirm out of it by saying, 'I no sabe'." Having taken this position, it was logical for the respondent to be almost equally reductionist over Curtis's next suggestion, which was that when an Indian showed he could raise ten cattle, ten more should be allocated to him on the same terms. While approving of the notion of "rewards," the respondent claimed that "just one head of stock might be sufficient." The only part of the plan with which the respondent fully concurred concerned the qualities of hard work, enthusiasm, and dedication required of an effective agency team: "This is the vital point of the whole thing."

Leupp was a supporter of the notion that Indians should be made individually independent, both of the tribe and the government, and this was the emphasis of his first *Annual Report*, in 1905. In 1906, his report stressed how Indians would be forced to earn their living by paid labor, even if it meant compelling them to leave the reservation in search of work. Indeed, in speaking particularly of Pine Ridge, he gave an account of local efforts there to remove Indians from the rations roll and to get them into an employment bureau. It is clear that the details of Curtis's proposal, the idea of a kind of contract with individual Indians, was not put into practice at Pine Ridge or anywhere else, but the generalities of his views must have struck a chord with Leupp. The two men still had much in common in 1913 when Leupp published an article on "The Red Man's Burden," complete, as credited, "With Photographs By Edward S. Curtis." Interestingly, the introduction to Volume 3 of *The North American Indian*, which was published in 1908 and devoted to the Sioux, also contained no such notion, and even fatalistically ascribed the problems of the Sioux to "the fact that they are Indians, and lack by many ages that which is necessary to enable them to meet the competition of the Caucasian race." Perhaps, ironically, this was because in 1907 Curtis had witnessed Pine Ridge Sioux people literally starving as a result of the non-arrival of food rations supposedly guaranteed in treaty obligations by their white "competitors."[21]

National Dimensions: Two

By 1911, the beginning of the second phase, Curtis was at the height of his personal fame and the project as a whole was proceeding apace. Some of this success resulted from all the publicity that year for the elaborate Indian entertainment, the "musicale" – treated in detail in Chapter 7 – that Curtis mounted in New York City and other venues during the autumn. At the same time, while the musicale was given the familiar title "The Vanishing Race," there was some speculation in the press, partly arising from the recent results of the 1910 U.S. Census, as to whether Native American peoples were in fact disappearing; since the project and its chief – as, for instance, in the case of the Havasupai – had frequently associated *The North American Indian* with Indian population decline, this press comment inevitably affected them. A few examples must suffice.

On May 27, 1911, U.S. Chief Forester Gifford Pinchot, who was later governor of Pennsylvania and throughout his career an influential patrician force in American public life, wrote to Curtis with the express purpose of bringing to his attention a newspaper clipping about "probably the only tribe of really wild Indians left in the United States." Curtis had been fortunate to secure the acquaintance – indeed, the patronage – of Pinchot many years earlier, even before that of Roosevelt. Their correspondence reveals that Curtis was usually ready to agree with his powerful friend, and a little earlier he had even supported Pinchot against John Muir, another early mentor and Harriman Expedition member, in the bitter environmental controversy over the Hetch Hetchy Reservoir in the California Sierras. But on this occasion, over supposedly "wild" Indians in California, Curtis was sceptical: "I cannot help but suspect that here is a case where people have let their enthusiasm run away with them." "I have been looking into this matter a little since the first newspaper note of it," he continued, "and I take it that the Indians in question are simply one of the roving bands of Shoshonean stock, which at times are out in the hills, and at other times are, like all the rest of the Indians of that country, hanging about the towns." "All of the Indians of that region are given to going back into the hills for the purpose of hunting, and gathering acorns and berries," he explained. "Of course this little group may be guilty of some special depredation, and for the time being are trying to keep under cover, but I should be surprised if you could not find in the crowd men who could speak English."[22]

Later in the year, in September 1911, Curtis wrote to Clarence Bagley, a prominent amateur local historian he knew well in Seattle, asking him to do "a little serious thinking" to produce an estimate of "the number of Indians in western Washington forty years ago," as such information would be useful to him in the writing of an article in response to comments in the *New York Times* "claiming that we have as many Indians now as ever existed in the United States." Curtis wanted, he said, "to show how absolutely ridiculous such [a] statement is." Later he thanked Bagley for providing statistics – now lost, unfortunately – and promised to send him a copy of whatever he wrote, admitting that comments like those of the *Times* meant that he was "constantly confronted with the statement 'We have just learned that the Indians are not decreasing.'" It may well be that Bagley took some of his evidence from the locally renowned work of the Northwest Coast missionary ethnologist Myron Eells. Among other studies, in 1903 Eells produced "The Decrease of the Indians," in which he had been adamant that there had been a marked decline in sheer numbers of Puget Sound Indians through "the vices of civilization," especially alcohol, and "half civilization." By the latter he meant the replacement of inadequate but reasonably healthy traditional lifeways by poorly learned hygiene methods and inactivity, leading to high infant mortality, tuberculosis, rheumatism, and poisoning, compounded by epidemics of whooping cough, measles, and other diseases against which Indians were not prepared by previous experience.[23]

Present-day analysts of Indian population, most notably Russell

Thornton, have shown that it reached its nadir during the 1890s and, as was revealed by the 1910 Census, started to increase somewhat thereafter, but they have also shown that, even when twentieth-century growth is taken into account, the extraordinary destruction of Native American peoples since Columbus reached the New World can only be described as – in Thornton's borrowing – a "holocaust." Indian population remains, as it did in 1911, substantially below what it was when first contact with Europe occurred. In any case, in the autumn of 1911, Curtis amassed his evidence and tested it on his editor, Hodge, telling him that he had prepared it in response to assertions in the *New York Times.* Writing from the Hotel Belmont in New York City in October, he admitted:

> You may feel that I have rather overdrawn the statement as to the stone house region [the Pueblos of the Rio Grande], but frankly, after giving that subject considerable thought while I was in that country, going over some of it mile by mile and estimating the number of houses in each township, and then attempting to estimate the number of people that it would take to build them, I found the figures more than staggering. There are many localities which we scarcely think of as having been thickly populated by prehistoric people, – for instance, the White Mountain Apache country. Day after day you can ride along the streams there and scarcely ever be out of sight of pottery fragments or mounds indicative of old houses. . . . If this material, as blocked out, is used, it will be in the form of an interview, and I take it, in the New York Herald. It will be good publicity for me. . . . [24]

Fortunately, versions of what Curtis wrote and sent to Hodge survive, and the "interview" with Edward Marshall, one of Roosevelt's acquaintances, was published the following spring, with many attractively laid-out Curtis photographs as illustrations, in *The Hampton Magazine.* Marshall opened it resoundingly:

> The Indians of North America are vanishing. Within the span of a few generations they have crumbled from their pride and power into pitifully small numbers, painful poverty and sorry weakness. A few generations more will see quite bared of them the land they held in an exclusive sovereignty when we white men first discovered it. A vanishing race! There is a majestic

> pathos in the words: a tragedy so great that is must be regarded as an epoch-marking matter. . . .[25]

And he continued in the same vein, asserting that Curtis had been driven by the realization that "even he" would have to "work with great rapidity if he would catch the comprehensive picture of the passing pageant of this disappearing people before it . . . became invisible forever. . . . "

The piece concluded with a return to the question of population numbers and a restatement, by Curtis, of Eells's views:

> In peace we changed the nature of our weapons, that was all; we stopped killing Indians in more or less fair fight, debauching them, instead, thus slaughtering them by methods which gave them not the slightest chance of retaliation. . . .
>
> The most conservative estimate of the number of Indians here at the time of America's discovery places the total at 1,000,000. Some experts claim that there were probably a million and a half. Whatever the number was, they all were fullbloods. We have, to-day, 335,000 gross Indian population, including all people known to have in their veins a trace of Indian blood, even those who are but one-sixty-fourth Indian, and it counts thousands of whites who have joined Indian tribes, because of indolence or greed. There are not, in fact, to-day, upon the Continent of North America, 100,000 fullblood Indians, hence it is not difficult for one to draw a conclusion.

Clearly, there is much more to this issue of Indian vanishment than this, and we will return to it, but it is worth pointing out straight away that these exchanges each had an ambiguous coda. The *Photographic Times* of April 1912 contained an article on Curtis titled "Writing History with the Camera." This included several rather purple quotations from Curtis on the theme of Indian demise, and then pointed out that in the future artists looking for Indian models would be forced to portray "a white man painted in bronze" wearing costumes "borrowed from a museum to which the last trail of the vanishing race will undoubtedly lead." The writer then added: "A museum is a strange dwelling place for human souls and memories." This was a comment more perceptive than its writer knew. While, in the absence of the particular news story, we cannot determine the likely specific California Indian people at issue between Pinchot and Curtis in 1911, we can be sure that Curtis would have been utterly confounded in his scepticism by the appearance a few months later, in Oroville, California, of Ishi, hailed repeatedly as "the last wild man in America." Ishi, the final surviving member of the Yahi tribe, wandered into the (appropriate) environs of a slaughterhouse on August 29, 1911, and ended his days living in the anthropological museum at Berkeley, where he demonstrated aspects of Yahi traditional life.[26]

In the case of the population figure speculation, the leading Seattle newspaper, the *Post-Intelligencer*, one that frequently ran stories on the North American Indian project, printed a brief editorial on October 18, 1916, under the heading "Indians Increasing." It did not mention Curtis – though it later came to rest as a clipping in the E. S. Curtis Biography file of the Northwest Collection at the University of Washington – and claimed that the U.S. Census Bureau was keen to point out that Native Americans were not "dying out," but "increasing," and that "much sentiment has been wasted over the 'vanishing race'. . . ."[27]

It may seem that those authorities who thought that the Native American population was on the increase and Curtis (who, of course, was not alone in his conviction) were firmly on opposite sides – and they were. But there is also a sense in which *neither* position had much to do with the prospects for actual living people. Those who believed in an increasing Indian population were convinced that the figures showed that no special protection or provision for their subject was required; indeed, as the phrasing of the *Post-Intelligencer* piece intimates, specific concern was considered an indulgence, and sentimental. The proponents of Indian vanishment, on the other hand, whatever their views of current Indian welfare, were so overridingly propelled by the desire to create a "record" of their subject before it disappeared that all other considerations paled into insignificance by comparison.

In saying the latter I do not mean to suggest that the North American Indian project was actually unconcerned about Indian welfare, or that Curtis in particular was insincere when he worried Leupp over the famine facing the Havasupai or, in another case, the threat posed by white settlers to the Chemehuevi of the lower Colorado River. Nor do I think that either the project or Curtis held consistent, and consistently fixed, opinions. In fact, during the very period in which Curtis commended the work of Mrs. Cole among the Navajo, he also claimed, as we shall see, that his own ethnological work there had done much to break down Navajo traditional beliefs (see Chapter 3). Again, while the Introduction to Volume 3 of *The North American Indian* ascribed the fate of the Sioux to their implied inferiority – to what they "lacked" *as* "Indians" – the Introduction to Volume 13, published, ironically, during 1924, the same year as Curtis's speech largely supportive of the Bureau of Indian Affairs, was highly critical of U.S. government treatment of the Indians of California, insisting that "the conditions" imposed upon them were "still so acute" that it was "difficult even to mention the subject with calmness." Further contradictions could – and, in time, will – be elaborated.[28]

What probably constitutes Curtis's own definitive statement during this period of his greatest fame, and itself not free of ambivalence, was published by the American Museum of Natural History. "I desire to add my plea to that of others for prompt work by all of those who would gather first-hand knowledge from the North American Indian," he said. "Many take issue with the thought that the Indian is a 'vanishing race'. As far as the ethnologist is concerned, this race is not only vanishing but has almost vanished. We are now working late in the afternoon of the last day," he continued. "Each month some old patriarch dies and with him goes a store of knowledge and there is nothing to take its place. . . . What is to be done in the field as far as original research is concerned must be done in the next few years."[29] Curtis then proceeded to offer personal testimony, using the selfsame words as his introduction to the Sioux volume, composed some years earlier (see Doc. 1C): "In gathering the lore of the Indian one hears only of yesterday. . . . His thoughts are no longer of the present for today is but a living death and the hopelessness of to-morrow permeates his very being." And he contextualized the task by seeing it in national terms. While readily acknowledging that "the greatest blot upon the history of the United States is our treatment of the Indian," Curtis went on to add, "Yet our strong sympathy for the Indian must not blind us to the fact that the change that has come has been necessitated by the expansion of the white population and for once at least Nature's laws have been the cause of a grievous wrong."

Moreover, while stating "that the inevitable transformation of the Indian's life has been made infinitely harder by the white man's cupidity," Curtis reserved his deepest condemnation for the country's *research* policy: "as a nation rightly and proudly giving considerable study to man, we have . . . neglected a very great opportunity." He summarized the situation as follows:

> The American Indians possess many noble traits which were no doubt not common to the average primitive man of the same state of development. By some strange chance the precursors of this branch of the human race were held for ages in the grip of darkness . . . [and] possibly time will throw light upon the cause. This however is certain: the American Indian has afforded advanced science in an age of civilization an excellent opportunity to study primitive man at a most interesting period. . . .

He concluded by asserting that "here in the United States we have a living 'Veda'," worthy of comparison with the great religious documents of the orient, "a great people possessing primitive beliefs and practices." "As a nation," he thought, "we have not given even a small fraction of the attention to this subject which it deserves. Financial support has been lacking. Also men with the ability to do justice to the task have turned their attention in other directions." "It is not however altogether too late," he reiterated. "Let us trust that there will come an awakening and that the utmost will be made of the last of this opportunity."

National Dimensions: Three

Our third phase provides one of the most striking instances of convergence of view between the North American Indian project and government policy. It is most apparent in an exchange of letters, which began in 1915, between Curtis and Woodrow Wilson's Secretary of the Interior, Franklin K. Lane. Lane, a California newspaperman and lawyer, was an extremely diligent worker who believed passionately in the need for public officials to take full responsibility for the business of their departments. He thus exhibited a much greater interest in Indian Affairs than most secretaries of the Interior and imprinted his views on Cato Sells, his commissioner. He wanted to make maximum use of the national land resources consistent with current conservation policies, and one aspect of this emphasis was a concern to pass over to individual Indians as much responsibility as possible. Curtis joined one of the secretary's first-hand investigation parties during this same year and, in general, knew him quite well when he volunteered a response to one of Lane's schemes:

> Since talking with you, I have given a good deal of thought to your plan of establishing organizations with different groups of

> Indians and I grow more and more convinced that it [is practicable] and should prove of tremendous value. The principal problem, as I see it, will be to get satisfactory local men to assist in establishing the plan. In order to get the subject fixed in my own mind, I . . . figuratively placed myself as the one in charge of the Crows and asked the question, "What would I do to bring out the best in these people?" and the answer was, "Lane's plan of a modified fraternal organization with a definite plan of reward of merit for accomplishment."

Curtis did have particularly close ties to the Crow Reservation, as we shall see, and he often visited it. In 1909 the bureau had sought his advice on improving medical services there and, in general, he probably did envisage himself well-qualified to represent the Crows as "the one in charge."[30]

The proposal at issue – "Lane's plan" to awaken greater Indian interest in the responsibilities of quasi-citizenship through participation in fraternal organizations akin to those so popular among whites at the time (the Elks, the Kiwanis, etc.) – was one strand in a network of efforts to speed up the process by which individual Indians could cease to be the responsibility of the bureau and their lands become part of the general agricultural economy of the West and the nation at large. An aspect of fraternal organizations which was actually introduced to the Indian context was the initiation ceremony. Lane himself, who in another exchange of letters with Curtis expressed an interest in traditional Plains initiation rites, such as the Sioux Foster Parent Chant, supervised the first of the "Last-Arrow" ceremonies at the Yankton Sioux Reservation in 1916, in which Indians were encouraged to shoot a symbolic last arrow before donning "citizens'" (white) dress and accepting U.S. citizenship.[31]

In an additional paragraph in his letter to Lane about fraternal organizations and the Crows, Curtis disparaged both the radical senator from Wisconsin, Robert La Follette, a long-serving member of the Senate Indian Affairs Committee who was often seen as a champion of Indian rights, and Helen Pierce Grey, who from 1908 onwards had made a number of allegations about bureau mismanagement of Crow affairs. "If Senator La Follette is still furthering the destructive activities of Helen Pierce Gray [sic], please urge him to drop the matter and give you a chance to handle the situation," he admonished. "What the Crows need the most at this time, is freedom of agitators." Not surprisingly, Lane was very pleased to have Curtis's endorsement, and in his earlier letter of April 13, 1915, had told him, "It is good to have the support of those who have lived close to the Indian and who have some real conception of the problem."[32]

Later the same year, Indian Inspector James McLaughlin told Curtis, "the Secretary . . . is a great admirer of yours," and asked for his views on "the enfranchisement of a certain class of Indians . . . whose competency in transacting their business affairs justifies conferring full citizenship upon them." While there is no record of Curtis's response – the manager of the New York office of The North American Indian, Inc., Lewis Albert, told McLaughlin that Curtis was out in the field at the time – there is reason to believe he would have endorsed this form of selective assimilation. Many other whites were certainly enthusiastic, and on April 17, 1917, with much fanfare, Cato Sells duly declared "the dawn of a new era."[33]

The new policy for Indian affairs – which would be more accurately described as the acceleration of implementation of an existing policy – had as its primary element an effort to change the status of as many individual Indians as possible from that of "half ward and half citizen" to that of citizen. This was to be done by the issue of certificates of "competence" to all educated Indians, and to as many others as could be deemed able to conduct their own business, especially with reference to the disposal of their lands, in the white world. Sales of land were to be made easier, at the discretion of the owner, and many more Indians, especially full-bloods, were to become U.S. citizens. Needless to say, the new policy also witnessed the speedier transfer of a vast acreage of land from Indian to white hands.

National Dimensions: Four

There was always a tension, usually unacknowledged, between various of the bureau's declared roles and objectives. The potential for Indian self-determination implied in the acceleration of the granting of certificates of competence, for example, was at the same time denied by both the bureau's claim to guardianship of the true interests of Indians and its actual absolute authority on each reservation. By the 1920s – the period of the final phase of interaction we will look at – such contradictions were more apparent and, while there was as yet no ready acknowledgment anywhere in the white community that the status granted to Indians was in effect that of colonial subjects, there was increasing awareness of Indian claims to cultural and religious freedom. There were, indeed, many more "agitators" in the field, including the writer Mary Austin, who was particularly concerned about the Indian Office's efforts to suppress traditional Pueblo ceremonies, sometimes on the grounds of their supposed "indecency." The Indian Defense Association, under the energetic leadership of John Collier – later Franklin Delano Roosevelt's long-term commissioner – was beginning to promote policies that, if adopted, could lead to a hedged form of cultural pluralism. It advocated tribal landholding, self-government through tribal councils, religious freedom, the creation of organizations to promote the sale of traditional crafts, and a complete overhaul of the education, health, and water-supply services for Indians.[34]

In that the predominant preoccupation of the North American Indian project was traditional lifeways or, in Curtis's phrase, "the old time Indian," it might be expected that he would have favored such cultural-pluralist approaches. In fact, however, despite the broadening of the spectrum of influential white opinion, Curtis seems to have held more or less to the Indian Office line which, in the face of increased criticism, was becoming, if only temporarily, more entrenched. While Curtis himself may have believed that he was bringing new thinking to bear on "the Indian problem" during the earlier exchanges we have witnessed, and while it may appear that in one of them the bureau "wisehead" was conducting a kind of unacknowledged dialogue with him, as if his position *was* quite separate from the bureau's, in fact the views Curtis articulated were very much within the parameters of conventional assumptions dominant at the time. Certainly, the apparent convergence of view between Curtis and Interior Department officials that we have seen was too close to be explained solely by the project's need to seek favors and patronage.

The extent to which Curtis's position was identifiable with that of the hegemonic consensus in white society was underlined in the twenties when, in 1923, he helped to found the Indian Welfare League. The other leading figures were Marah Ellis Ryan, Dr. John Adams Comstock, and Ida May Adams. Ryan was a popular romantic novelist. Several of her books, including *Squaw Elouise* (1892) and *That Girl Montana* (1905), were devoted to western themes and two, *Indian Love Letters* (1907) and *The Flute of the Gods* (1909), contained illustrations by Curtis, to whom she was very close. Comstock was a successor to Charles Lummis and a predecessor to Hodge as director of the Southwest Museum in Los Angeles; during Comstock's time at the Museum, Ryan – who was also a keen photographer – was for a short time curator of the archaeological department. The League was very much based in Los Angeles, which was home to all of these principal protagonists, including Adams, a prominent local attorney. Others associated with the League were the lawyer William Jennings Bryan, Jr., the cowboy movie star William S. Hart, and Harry C. James, then a young volunteer worker on the Hopi reservation collecting evidence of abuses by a particular agent there.[35]

Unlike the Indian Defense Association, the Indian Welfare League – as its name implied – worked primarily as a charitable organization for Indians: finding work, providing legal services, and raising funds. But, increasingly, as its "Activities of the Indian Welfare League" report of 1924 makes clear, pressure-group activities, especially lobbying on Capitol Hill led by Adams, came to the fore. The single most significant achievement for which it claimed credit (a credit ironically unrecorded in the relevant historical literature), was the successful passage of the Indian Citizenship Act of April 1924, the piece of legislation that extended U.S. citizenship to all Indians. The Citizenship Act, as John Collier and others who opposed it recognized at the time, was a very mixed blessing for Indians: While it endowed many with extended (if sometimes only potential) individual rights, it did nothing to safeguard tribal rights and could be construed as an attack on both tribal rights and the idea of specifically *Indian* individual identity. Moreover, after its passage, despite the ringing words of the League's report ("this bill carried and now for the first time since slavery was introduced . . . we stand as a whole without a subject race, and we can say in truth and without reservation that we are 'A government of the people, by the people, and for the people'"), the legality of the bureau as "guardian" of its Indian "wards," with all its implications of Indian inferiority, remained in force. Perhaps this was why it could be supported by *both* Congressman Edgar Howard of Nebraska, progressive co-sponsor of the Wheeler-Howard Bill of 1934, which was initiated by Collier to repeal the provisions of the Dawes Act, *and* Senator Clarence C. Dill of Washington State, who also believed in the guardianship of Indians as wards and who was to sponsor an amendment to the Wheeler-Howard Bill, which allowed for the continuation of disposal to whites of "surplus" Indian land.[36]

This was the context for this final sample phase, during which Curtis, introduced as both a leading authority on Indians and chairman of the Indian Welfare League, addressed his audience at the new anthropological museum in Santa Fe in July 1924, a lecture that itself constitutes our primary focus. The bulk of the speech concerned various white attitudes and activities that Curtis believed were inimical to Indians, but it began with a disquisition on "the greatest weakness" – not of whites, but of Indians. This "weakness," as Curtis thought, was "self pity":

> The Indian as a whole from North to South, from East to West, in this year of 1924 is the star sob-sister of the Universe. He spends a great part of his time weeping on his own shoulder. Self pity is absolutely fatal to the individual or to the Community. It is worse than dope. We as people are very much given to encouraging them in this self pity. We listen to their tales of woe and we agree with them that they have been robbed of everything – most of them have – and that we are going to help them in all their problems.

Having seemingly doused in his audience all sympathy for Indians, as if such sympathy were indeed incendiary, Curtis went on to discuss "the Indian's greatest burden": "his white friends, the amateur and professional 'mussers.'" He concentrated on the professionals, using expressions commonly adopted by bureau apologists at the time – "call them propagandists, call them whatever you like" – and, whatever their motives, lumped them all together as "assisting Indians for selfish purposes only." Some of them, he said (possibly with D. H. Lawrence, or even Austin, in mind), were "writers going upon reservations . . . in search of original material . . . something sensational." The remainder of the lecture recounted the activities of such persons in a series of anecdotes.

One such figure, unnamed (but probably Helen Pierce Grey), had allegedly incited a northern Plains tribe to physical violence to prevent her own justifiable arrest by Indian Department police. Another, Jonathan Tibbets, had apparently appropriated for himself dues paid into his Cooperative Indian Organization by 20,000 Southern California Indians. Tibbets, Curtis claimed, was supported by a woman, unnamed, prominent in "the women's clubs of California," possibly Florence Haman. A third figure, also unnamed, a "professional fixer" based in Northern California, had allegedly collected dues from 8,000 Indians and was in the process of "binding all the Indians into a six year's contract to pay him" at an annual rate of three to six dollars, with the promise that he would "recover . . . all of the lands they had lost under the old original treaties," which, as Curtis put it, was "absolutely impossible."[37]

Finally, again without naming anyone, but with New Mexico and the defense of ceremonial practices in view – and presumably, with leaders like Austin and Collier in mind – Curtis laid down a distinction "between religious practice and wrongdoing": "as long as a man carries on his religious beliefs and wrongs no one, well and good, – but if he commits a wrong in the name of religion, it does not right that wrong." By placing this anecdote in the same series as the others, which, if proven, were about obviously "criminal" figures, Curtis was deeply disparaging to people who considered themselves, and were considered by others, as reformers. It was a position Curtis developed at greater length in an article of this same period entitled "The Indian and his Religious Freedom," in which he claimed that certain ceremonies were "obscene" and that traditional religious leaders exerted dictatorial powers that infringed the individual rights of certain members of the tribe, thus humiliating them (see Chapter 9). In essence, of course, while seeming to embody empirical commonsense, such a distinction – between religious beliefs and wrongdoing – works very much against notions of cultural pluralism in that it reserves to the speaker, and to the speaker's (white) society, the sole authority to decide that which is "right" and "wrong," as if the referents of these were universal transcendent values.

Curtis's conclusions were shot through with ambiguities, even with downright contradictions. On the one hand, he advocated that problems and abuses on Indian land should be taken to "the Department" – which, within the limitations of its own red tape, would, he claimed, always make a serious effort to find solutions – whereas discussing them with Indians themselves would only foment unnecessary aggravations. From such a perspective, Indians would not be capable of making up their own minds, let alone taking decisions and acting. On the other hand, in arguing against the preservers of traditional ceremonies and customs, he was categorically assertive: "an Indian cannot be a museum specimen. Nor can he be an exhibit in a zoological park." Rather, as he put it, "they must take their place with advancing civilizations, alongside the white race. They must solve their own problems as we have, otherwise, they perish." From *this* perspective, Indians would *have* to think and act for themselves. Finally, despite the previous demand for Indian advance "alongside of the white race," as if in step and at the same pace as whites, Curtis cautioned, "we must not expect too much. . . . The change must come very slowly. . . . "

This tangle of attitudes was by no means unique to Curtis. Because expressed in a speech, in abbreviated form, it may have been somewhat knottier than appearances elsewhere, but several historians have shown that the same strands ran through the dominant society as a whole.[38] Indeed, it was precisely the benumbing confusion in the unrelenting and confident battery of decisions and dicta to which Indians were subjected over a long period that helped to create the sense of dependency and powerlessness that has still to be set aside completely.

National Dimensions Underlined

In 1910, Curtis informed Roosevelt of the further capital subvention from Morgan, made partly at the request of Henry Fairfield Osborn, director of American Museum of Natural History. This subvention enabled the establishment of The North American Indian, Inc. The former president, as he had before, couched his comments in national terms, telling Curtis, "Mr. Morgan is a trump and Osborn is one of the most useful citizens we have. Your work is a real asset in American achievement." The previous year he had used a very similar expression: "You are doing admirable work for America."[39]

Curtis himself repeatedly cast the project in just such a national context and did so again in the special commemorative declaration produced after Morgan's death for both insertion in *The North American Indian* and separate publication, "In Memory of J. Pierpont Morgan" (1913): "The American Indian possesses many unusual qualities and affords Science the opportunity of studying primitive life in one of its most interesting and important phases. Mr. Morgan made possible this study. . . . Those who have joined us in furthering this national undertaking must feel like members of a great family bonded by the desire of creative accomplishment. . . . " (Of course, in using the metaphor of the "family" here, Curtis doubtless also had the Morgan family itself in mind, so it must have been gratifying when Morgan's son, "Jack" Morgan, decided to continue the family's support for the project.) Proponents of "Science," too, used the same language – at least, according to Curtis; for example, he told one of his Seattle patrons, Mrs. M. Prager, that after a performance of the musicale at the Brooklyn Institute, "Prof. Hooper, who has charge of the Institute, . . . stated that it was one of the most important affairs . . . ever given [there] and [delivered] a message . . . of the greatest national importance."[40]

For the time being we may leave aside the irony here, which should be obvious to a present-day reader: that, generally speaking, an "American achievement" so often entailed a Native American *loss*, even destruction. There was in 1910, and indeed through all the episodes we have looked at, a sense in which the project's reflection of political attitudes towards Indians made it so entirely *typical* that it was actually appropriate to describe it as an "American achievement." (Of course, the irony is a double one: When Roosevelt commissioned the sculptor Augustus Saint-Gaudens to design new coins soon after his inauguration in 1904, the figure of Liberty on the ten-dollar gold piece, at his insistence, had her Phrygian cap, an iconographic necessity in French versions of Liberty, replaced by an Indian headdress. After all, claimed Roosevelt, "American Liberty should . . . have something distinctly American about her"!) In *The West as America*, William H. Truettner stressed the existence in western expansion of "a controlling entrepreneurial group," pointing out that "most 'pioneers' were prompted to act by the marketing policies of the nearest metropolis," and that the very "existence of a metropolitan-based expansion system clarifies the relationship between patrons, artists, and [their] images." Truettner has argued that artistic observation of the West occurred essentially in association with (even from the point of view of) "those who stood to gain most from the westward movement – the leaders of the industrial East." If granted, this means that, far from being depictions of the "true West" that they have so often been described as, such images have functioned as ideology; they were such powerful embodiments of prevailing myths of the West that they conferred upon their subject matter what Truettner has called "a quality of absolute legitimacy," as if "what is being described is natural and unquestionable and, therefore, a fully sanctioned enterprise."[41]

While Truettner's comments were addressed mainly to paintings, they also apply to other forms of representation. And the Curtis project, as we shall see in greater detail in subsequent chapters, must be viewed in this context: The richest man in the world was its chief patron; its other primary subscribers encompassed not only government figures like Pinchot and the Canadian governor-general, but also railroad entrepreneurs such as Harriman and Henry E. Huntington, several bankers with western investments, men with western mining and property interests, Andrew Carnegie and a variety of other prominent industrialists, and numerous others who were undoubtedly members of "a controlling entrepreneurial group"; and significant establishment scientists joined Walcott of the Smithsonian in giving support, including George Byron Gordon of the University of Pennsylvania Museum, for instance, and F. W. Putnam of Harvard.

(In this re[tro]spect, the most dubious supporter of the project was, in fact, the figure celebrated by Roosevelt, Henry Fairfield Osborn, in that by the second decade of the century he was an influential scientific racist.[42])

The North American Indian project, as should be increasingly obvious, did not follow a rigid ideological line, but it is precisely the self-contradictory nature of some of its pronouncements that tend, in themselves, to disclose the presence of such an ideology. The fundamental issue of the "vanishing," the "passing" or demise of Indians, reveals this most tellingly. With reference to the Havasupai, for example, *The North American Indian* gave no sense that they had suffered a major catastrophe, the worst effects of which might have been averted, and instead ascribed their decrease in numbers by over a third in just three years to the wholly natural cause of "illness." Similarly, the starvation of the Sioux went unremarked in *The North American Indian.*

The ideological imperatives outlined here were also expressed in visual terms by Curtis, sometimes attended by the same sense of contradiction. In 1924, the same year as the Santa Fe lecture, he made an image of a semi-naked Indian woman standing before an idyllic pool among the foliage of one of the thick palm groves of Palm Canyon, California, to which he gave the title "Before the White Man Came" (frontispiece). Such a photograph, so captioned, is, of course, both an optical and a conceptual illusion. While purporting to render *Indian* life before the advent of white people, its existence and essence were totally determined by white, Euro-American culture. Taken, obviously, with a camera, an instrument of that culture, it even fulfills the white myth of Eden: The as-yet-unashamed Eve awaits her fate. Truly, however beautiful as imagery, such Indian figures were not so much *just* representatives of "the old time Indian" – rooted in the landscape, pushed into the past – as caught in stasis, *removed* from time and its passage altogether. In such a position, Indians could be, at best, makers of their own world; they could never take their place as producers and consumers of the American national economy. Their "national" role was unique.

DOCUMENTS

Document 1A. Outline of the North American Indian Project, by Edward S. Curtis, 1906.

Curtis was allowed to see Morgan on January 24, 1906, and a day ahead sent the following outline to the financier so that, as Curtis put it, Morgan would "have the matter before [him] briefly and concisely." "I feel that the work is worthwhile, and as a monumental thing nothing can exceed it," he claimed.[43]

> The plan in mind is to make a complete publication, showing pictures and including text of every phase of Indian life of all tribes yet in a primitive condition, taking up the type, male and female, child and adult, their home structure, their environment, their handicraft, games, ceremonies, etc.; dividing the whole into twenty volumes containing fifteen hundred full page plates, the text to treat the subject much as the pictures do, going fully into their history, life and manners, ceremony, legends and mythology, treating it in rather a broad way so that it will be scientifically accurate, yet if possible, interesting reading. It is presumed that I and my field assistant will collect and compile the text [which] will later be turned over to men in the scientific field, recognized as authorities, to edit, thus affording unquestionable authenticity.
>
> In addition to the book, the plan includes the publication of seven hundred of the more important pictures in the size now on display 14 × 17 to be placed in portfolios containing 35 pictures each. Illustrations, both large and small, to be of the best photogravure work, and both pictures and text on the best paper. Binding and paper to be such that it will be as lasting as paper can be made.
>
> It has been estimated by publishers that a work of this nature would have to sell at five thousand dollars a set, and that one hundred sets could be disposed of in this country and abroad.
>
> To finish the field work will require five more years at an approximate annual expense of $15,000 for the five years'——$75,000.
>
> One suggested plan for securing the necessary money for the field work is to interest some one of means in the work, getting

him to make an advance subscription to the amount of field expenses, he having that equivalent in sets of the work for distribution to such institutions as he may see fit to so honor, with the understanding that he receive credit for his patronage of the work by its being published as his edition, whatever the title might be. These sets furnished him will represent the greater part of my royalty from the publishers on the publication. To show my good faith in the matter, all negative plates could be kept in a safe deposit vault with such patron having a mortgage over the same.

As the collection now stands, it represents the expenditure of a number of years of time and some $25,000 in money on the work.

To further safeguard the patron of the work, I could insure my life, if necessary, for the amount of his subscription to reimburse him in case I should not live to finish the work.

A Second Suggested Plan of Reimbursing the Patron of the Work.

The complete results of the field research will exceed ten thousand of the large pictures. An agreement could be made between the patron and myself that he should receive one copy of the final publication and a sufficient number of the pictures to cover the amount of his subscription. I have suggested this thinking that the patron might prefer to have this complete collection at one museum rather than the several copies of the publication for distribution to different institutions.

This document was accompanied by a list of "Estimated Annual Expenses" totalling just over $15,000 and covering everything from the salaries of three assistants, through rail transportation, hotels, "food for Indians while at work," livery and pack animal costs, and interpreters, to "money paid indians [sic]," photographic plates and motion picture films (which Curtis justified in a separate note), and such items as copyright fees.

Document 1B. "Foreword" to Volume 1 of *The North American Indian* by Theodore Roosevelt, October 1, 1906.[44]

In Mr. Curtis we have both an artist and a trained observer, whose pictures are pictures, not merely photographs; whose work has far more than mere accuracy, because it is truthful. All serious students are to be congratulated because he is putting his work in permanent form; for our generation offers the last chance for doing what Mr. Curtis has done. The Indian as he has hitherto been is on the point of passing away. His life has been lived under conditions thru which our own race past [sic] so many ages ago that not a vestige of their memory remains. It would be a veritable calamity if a vivid and truthful record of these conditions were not kept. No one man alone could preserve such a record in complete form. Others have worked in the past, and are working in the present, to preserve parts of the record; but Mr. Curtis, because of the singular combination of qualities with which he has been blest, and because of his extraordinary success in making and using his opportunities, has been able to do what no other man ever has done; what, as far as we can see, no other man could do. He is an artist who works out of doors and not in the closet. He is a close observer, whose qualities of mind and body fit him to make his observations out in the field, surrounded by the wild life he commemorates. He has lived on intimate terms with many different tribes of the mountains and the plains. He knows them as they hunt, as they travel, as they go about their various avocations on the march and in the camp. He knows their medicine men and sorcerers, their chiefs and warriors, their young men and maidens. He has not only seen their vigorous outward existence, but has caught glimpses, such as few white men ever catch, into that strange spiritual and mental life of theirs; from whose innermost recesses all white men are forever barred. Mr. Curtis in publishing this book is rendering a real and great service; a service not only to our own people, but to the world of scholarship everywhere.

Document 1C. "Introduction" to Volume 3 of *The North American Indian* by Edward S. Curtis, 1908.[45]

In gathering the lore of the Indian of the plains one hears only of yesterday. His thoughts are of the past; to-day is but a living death, and his very being is permeated with the hopelessness of to-morrow. If the narrator be an ancient nearing the end of his days, he lives and relives the life when his tribe as a tribe flourished, the time when his people were truly monarchs of all they surveyed, when teeming buffalo supplied their every want; and his wish is ever that he might have passed away ere he knew the beggary of to-day. The younger man, if a true Indian, is a living regret that he is not of the time when to be an Indian was to be a man.

Strong sympathy for the Indian cannot blind one to the fact that the change that has come is a necessity created by the expansion of the white population. Nor does the fact that civilization demands the abandonment of aboriginal habits lessen one's sympathy or alter one's realization that for once at least Nature's laws have been the indirect cause of a grievous wrong. That the inevitable transformation of the Indian life has been made many-fold harder by the white man's cupidity, there is no question.

Those who do not comprehend the limitations of primitive people protest, "Why sympathize with the Indians? They now have every opportunity that civilized man has, and more, for the Government grants them lands and renders them aid in many ways." The question might as well be asked, why the man born without eyes does not see. The Indian is an Indian not alone in name and in the pigmentation of his skin or his other physical characteristics. He developed gradually and through ages to meet the conditions of a harsh environment exceedingly well, but these conditions were so vastly different from those we have thrust upon him that to expect him to become adjusted to the new requirements in a generation or two would be much like expecting of a child the proficiency of ripe manhood.

Perhaps among no tribe has the encroachment of civilization wrought greater change than among the Sioux, or Dakota. . . .

The great change that now comes to the Sioux and to other tribes of the plains with the opening of their reservations to settlement and in the consequent increased contact with alien influences will, within the present generation, further demoralize and degenerate. This, however, is one of the stages through which from the beginning the Indians were destined to pass. Those who cannot withstand these trying days of the metamorphosis must succumb, and on the other side of the depressing period will emerge the few sturdy survivors. . . .

PART TWO

COORDINATES FOR A PROJECT

Indian people have been measured . . . against a fantasy over which they have no control. They are compared with beings who never really *were*, yet the stereotype is taken for truth.

Michael Dorris, *Modoc* (1987)

Figure 4. Homeward, 1898, by E. S. Curtis. Taken on Puget Sound, this image won prizes as a picturesque genre study and was featured in vol. 9 of *The North American Indian* (1913).

2

CRACKER JACK PICTURES

"Outside the photo studio, the lake, the sound, the sea, the forests and mountain ranges afforded limitless fields for the camera and a seeing eye," wrote William Washington Phillips, in his memoir of Curtis's early years in Seattle. "These fields he soon invaded, acquiring a series of beautiful scenes." And, according to Phillips, Curtis's "invasion" was a prepared one:

> By night at home, when the actual work of the studio didn't occupy his time . . . he studied pictures; the whys and wherefores; the ifs and the ands: landscapes, portraits, marine views and studies from old masters. He reveled in such, in his musings, in his thoughts and conceptions. I can see him now, sitting on the floor, his knees drawn up and held between clasped hands, his head tilted back against the wall, with clippings and pictures of all sorts scattered about in front of him, a book of poems by his side, lighted only by the flames from a fire place – glanced at and then left apparently unnoticed. When he broke the silence, his usual remark was, "Wait till you see the next picture I make; it's going to be a 'cracker jack.'" And he kept his word unfailingly. Happy compositions in out door pictures, and art studies made under his skylight would later adorn the walls of his studio, and make attractive the photo case at his main street entrance.[1]

Curtis was clearly first and foremost a maker of images. This reminiscence by Phillips constitutes the earliest direct biographical evidence of Curtis's determination to produce what he here calls "cracker jack" pictures, a concern that may well have preempted all others throughout his career. Certainly, at this early stage of Curtis's life all of his work absorbed him totally. "Those sprawly nights at home were rare," Phillips wrote. "Work at the office, in the dark-room, toning-room, printing-room or engraving shop kept him at the grindstone night after night till the last cable car jangled its call as it slid down hill to its terminus." And this became an established pattern; for example, during the height of printing and developing work at the conclusion of the Harriman Alaska Expedition of 1899, Curtis himself told the expedition leader, C. Hart Merriam, of continuous nights of work.[2] Phillips elaborated:

> At an early date Curtis acquired the habit of treating home as a boarding place; all thinking and planning he did at his studio desk. Clubs, lodges, or social gatherings he almost never attended; theaters rarely. Work was his duty, pass-time and recreation; all else was incidental. His children occasioned him no apparent delight as infants, and no great concern. But it is not to be understood that he was cold, or wanting in attributes that make one, as we say, truly human. His sense of humor, keenness at repartee and ready reciprocation to proffered friendship marked him human enough. However, intelligence, mature intelligence, alone strongly appealed to him; neither did he have patience with the dull or uncomprehending. His children have become much to him since acquiring age, but their training to date has caused him only a modicum of thought. . . . Self education has occupied him, always, to the exclusion of assisting in educating others. If any one ever acquired knowledge from him . . . that person did so through his or her own ability to glean, but never through an effort on Curtis'ss part to impart to another knowledge of his professional or technical skill. . . .

Curtis was an extremely ambitious visionary with a tremendous sense of his own capacity to achieve. Such dynamism could have propelled him into one of any number of occupations allied to picture making. One of the first he tried was studio portrait work. The other was literally an ascent: landscape photography, primarily of mountains and mountaineering.

Mountain Landscapes

Curtis climbed Mount Rainier "several times," Phillips claimed, and became "a member of a western mountain climbing organization, the members of which he more than once afterward guided safely to dizzy heights. And always he . . . returned with a collection of pictures remarkable for breadth and boldness. Paradise Park, the valley above which towers Mt. Rainier, the mountain itself, and its glaciers, are to be found at his studio in picturesque compositions." It is worth observing that, perhaps because of his own familiarity with photography and its fashions, Phillips was adopting here the same pictorialist principles that we will later see deployed by such well-known advocates of pictorialism as Charles Kurtz. Both considered that the kind of imagery just described was artistically superior to photographs full of what Phillips called "tedious detail." Another critic of the time wrote that pictorialist photography was a "protest against the niggling detail, the factual accuracy of sharp all-over ordinary photography. Concentration, strength, massing of light and shade, breadth of effect are the highly prized virtues."[3]

Curtis often climbed with the Mazamas, the Portland-based mountaineering club; indeed, issues of the *Mazama* magazine listed him as an honorary member from 1897 on, when almost all of the other honorary members were persons with national reputations, such as the naturalist, writer, and conservationist John Muir. And Curtis was determined to get his "picturesque compositions" to as wide a public as possible. In 1898 his studio published *Scenic Washington*, "a catalogue of Rainier series views available from Edward S. Curtis, 614 Second Avenue, Seattle." This lists, by title in a numbered sequence, 217 photographs and a prefatory note promises that "in October we will publish a complete catalogue, including a later trip to the west side of Mount Rainier." Moreover, some of the goods on offer were 18" × 60" panoramic views at $25 mounted, $15 unmounted. "We have," boasted the Curtis Studio, "the most complete collections of photographs of Puget Sound and surrounding country in existence." Thus it came about that many Pacific Northwest publications could – and did – print evocative Curtis views of Mount Rainier and environs, including *Washington Illustrated* (1900) compiled by O. M. Moore and *Art Work of the State of Washington* (1900) compiled by Edmond S. Meany. Obviously, Curtis was not engaged in landscape photography of this sort merely as "a hobby."[4] In fact, he built his first reputation *on* his mountain pictures.

This is borne out by Curtis's work in 1900 for *The Western Trail*, a short-lived cultural magazine that hired him to write a column on the practice and aesthetics of photography (thus contradicting Phillips's view that he was an inveterate nonteacher); in it he drew upon his own experience and often addressed his comments to the problems of mountaineering photographers. "Do not fail to pack your plates or films in water-tight packages," he admonished. "I have . . . found that it was necessary to use a stronger developer in a cold climate as well as warming it to some extent," he said. Or, again, he added a further "precaution for one who is starting for the mountains": "Take among the supplies a piece of mat celluloid to replace the ground glass in case it should be broken. It makes a much more satisfactory ground glass than a piece of brown paper covered with butter." At the end of 1898, the year after Curtis first set up a studio completely on his own and gave up engraving, when he moved into what was to be *the* Curtis Studio, in the Downs Building at 709 Second Avenue, it was his scenic views that the Seattle magazine *Argus* chose to stress in a brief news note: "It is the intention of Mr. Curtis to make his new studio first class in every respect, that the city may be justly proud of it. He will place on exhibition a large number of scenic photographs, depicting the wild and rugged beauty of the Pacific Northwest, making [the studio] an object of interest which no visitor to the city can afford to overlook."[5]

In his endeavor to build such a reputation, Curtis probably benefited from the Mazamas' tragedy-marred ascent of Mount Rainier in the summer of 1897. Some eighty members started out on July 19 and, a few days later, when the climbing in earnest began, their outing committee appointed Curtis "to guide and command the expedition."[6] Divided into four "companies," each under a "captain," most of the Mazamas – 59 of them – reached the summit in two days, stopping the night at Camp Muir and using lifelines that Curtis rigged up at particularly treacherous places. It was on the way down that disaster struck. In virtual darkness, after most of the climbers had decided to stay the night at Camp Muir, one of a party of four that had gone ahead, Professor Edgar McClure of Eugene, Oregon, slipped to his death down a steep slope. The following day two other climbers fell; both were rescued, one – Walter Rogers – eventually being pulled, frozen but just about alive, forty feet out of a crevasse. These events brought the expedition to a halt on August 3, when it might well have continued for another two weeks.

One dramatic death and a rescue from the very brink of death meant that the climb was big news in the region. Even the national magazine *Harper's Weekly* contained a brief feature that mentioned Curtis. The catalogue of *Scenic Washington* lists photographs directly related to the accidents: "163. Crevasse from which Rogers was rescued" and, rather gruesomely, "205. Rocks where McClure met his death." Later, in 1901, the popular British magazine *Good Words* had an article by another member of the expedition, Arthur Inkersley of San Francisco, which was illustrated by Curtis photographs – as, of course, was the account in the *Mazama* by Edward T. Parsons.[7]

Despite the Mazamas' use of military terminology in their expeditions – captains, companies, and the like – they were relatively undisciplined. Since individuals on outings made their own decisions as to whether they would spend the night here or there, stay with the group, or strike out alone, Curtis as commander could not have been held responsible in any way for McClure's death. And it did not discourage him from further mountaineering exploits. His big chance lay in the aftermath of the first Klondike gold rush, as may be inferred from a letter he wrote to the publishers of *Century*, dated October 14, 1897:

> Gentlemen:-
> I have just returned from a trip over the different trails to the Alaskan gold fields, and have secured the most complete as well as the latest series of photos of the various trails yet taken. These views, one hundred and fifty in number, picture the Argonauts in their mad rush to the gold fields, showing camp scenes, storms in the mountain passes, river crossings, etc. They exhibit the flimsy quarters in which many expect to endure the rigors of an Alaskan winter; the caches of those who have abandoned their supplies and fled to the towns for shelter; and the deserted camps, with dead horses literally in piles, – the number that have perished on the Dyea and Skagway trails being estimated at three thousand. In fact, these views depict every phase of the mad rush to the gold fields, and portray the situation and the difficulties to be encountered more clearly and truthfully than can any mere pen picture.

Curtis offered to supply *Century* with either illustrated articles or "the photos alone." With Whitmanesque bravura he pointed out that they would not be written "from hearsay": "I have myself passed over the trails, climbed the mountains, crossed the rivers, waded through the mud and snow, and endured the cold and hunger." Finally, he claimed that during the following spring he would have "at least four competent photographers in different parts of Alaska and the Northwest Territory," all of whom, he said, would be "able to write comprehensive articles to accompany the photos, if desired."[8]

The letter worked. A few weeks later Curtis dispatched thirteen photographs of the Skagway and Dyea Trails, together with a short article, and on December 6 he telegrammed his acceptance of the editor's offer of $125 for photographs and text. The article appeared in the March 1898 issue of *Century* as "The Rush to the Klondike Over The Mountain Passes" and marked Curtis's first achievement of any national recognition. As a graphic, general account of the "assault on Nature" mounted by the desperate Klondikers of 1897, it still reads well.[9]

Although the by-line at the head of the article said "Pictures from Photographs by the Author," some of them were probably taken by Edward's younger brother, Asahel, then an employee of the Curtis Studio, who certainly went along with his brother on this expedition. It was common until quite recently for photographic entrepreneurs not to give individual credits; often photographers even copyrighted the work of employees and others under their own names. The ambiguity was nicely maintained in a news note printed in the *Argus* in December 1897 which reported on Curtis's entry "into the Alaska view business." "As soon as practicable in the spring, Mr. Curtis will start a party for the fields of gold in charge of Mr. A. Curtis. . . . " The note concluded: "Mr. Curtis has already received a number of offers from publishers and others for first choice from the collection." Sure enough, Edward S. Curtis Alaska mountain pictures appeared in the elaborate Christmas souvenir editions of the *Argus* in 1897, 1898, and 1905, and when Gilbert H. Grosvenor announced Curtis's appointment as official photographer to the 1899 Harriman Alaska Expedition in the *National Geographic Magazine*, he spoke of him as "the photographer of *several* expeditions to Alaska."[10]

Curtis also remained active in Washington mountain photography. In the summer of 1898 the Mazamas' main outing was to the summit of Mount St. Helens and, as the reporter for the *Mazama* recorded, Curtis was again "given command of the expedition." Thirty-one climbers succeeded in reaching the mountain top, left a record of their names in a copper box, and were photographed. Several members of the party were especially interested in the volcanic history of Mount St. Helens, and of "the small group" who searched for evidence of the previous eruption, the only one to make such a discovery was Curtis himself. There was, as the reporter noted, a marked scientific element to this expedition, and three of its members were distinguished scientists. The most prominent was Frederick V. Coville, chief botanist at the U.S. Department of Agriculture, and Curtis made him a captain of one of the companies. Scientific interest was also high in 1901, when Curtis and other Mazamas joined Professor

Harry Reid of Johns Hopkins University to explore the glaciers of Mount Hood.[11]

In later life Curtis told the story of meeting with other scientists and natural historians on the slopes of Mount Rainier:

> For two seasons prior to the [Harriman] Expedition I spent some weeks on Rainier making pictures. In the second season a party of scientificos came to study the mountain. A couple of times they got lost, & I managed to get them to my camp where I thawed them out and bedded [them] down; following that I acted as their guide in giving the mountain the once over. In the . . . volumes of the Harriman Expedition [reports] you have seen pictures and names of all the wise men I met on the mountain. . . . It was the same men who sold Harriman on the thought of spending a lot of money on an Expedition to Alaska [and] suggested that I accompany the Expedition as official photographer. . . .

It is conceivable that the meeting on the mountain incident occurred within the context of a Mazama outing, though probably not during the summer of 1898 when the Mazamas climbed Mount St. Helens. It is not certain precisely who it was that Curtis guided in this way, but one of them was C. Hart Merriam, head of the Biological Survey of the U.S. Department of Agriculture, later to be the main scientific convener of the Harriman Expedition. The others often mentioned include Gifford Pinchot; George Bird Grinnell, authority on Indians and editor of *Forest & Stream*; and Coville, a "scientifico" who was certainly in Curtis's camp in 1898, and who would be, like the others, a member of the Harriman team.[12]

Curtis's own participation in the Harriman project was not on a salaried basis but, as he put it in a letter of agreement to Merriam of April 20, 1899, under an arrangement in which "each . . . of the scientists [would] purchase such negatives as they want and the head of the party anything that they see fit." Though he expressed some financial concern – "owing to having spent a great deal of money in fitting up [his] new studio" and over the fact that equipment for "the photographic trip [was] going to be expensive" – he was surely confident that expedition members would buy his work. Also, some of that work was to be visually innovative: "I shall arrange to take my 18 × 22 camera with me [and] I have been working for some time on a panoramic camera which will make a picture 10 inches high and 36 inches long and including in the view just half the horizon." Curtis told Merriam that he was pleased there was to be a dark room aboard and that there was "no question" but that he was "delighted with the proposition of making this trip, especially where the arrangements are so fine for seeing and exploring," and that he had wired his acceptance "at once." He also offered to find "two or three men who would make good packers," and said he awaited developments with a sense of excitement. "I feel," he said, "that it will be the best chance of photographing Alaska that I shall ever have."[13]

Curtis also asked Merriam, "Do you plan the climbing of many of the peaks?" and such a question might well be expected from a leading member of the Mazamas. He made many Rainier treks and in later life remembered especially the time he "bossed 108 men and women on a climb to the summit. I do not recall how many I started with but the 108 reached the top of the mountain." "Miss Ella McBride," he continued, "was one of the women who reached the summit unaided." Then, in tones redolent of the 1890s he was describing, he added, "She [was] my star helper in herding the women and sorting out those who had made false statements to our M.D. as to their physical condition." It is worth pointing out that just as Curtis benefited enormously later from his meetings with natural scientists in the mountains, so he did in his relationship with Ella McBride: A Portland schoolteacher, born in 1863, she went on to run the Curtis Seattle Studio office in 1911 and later became a significant photographer in her own right.[14] "She lived with our family as one of us," Curtis remembered, as "a second mother" to Beth and Florence, his elder daughters.

The crucial thing about these meetings was not really their coincidental, fortuitous aspect – or, even, that they resulted from a sense of adventure on both sides – but that Curtis fully realized their significance. Again, Phillips was most perceptive:

> On his earliest summer trips out into the mountains in the middle nineties, he made the acquaintance of government foresters, biologists, botanists and other scientists working in the same regions, forming friendships that have grown stronger and more valuable with the passing years. He gravitated to those active thinking men, and they to him, at once, while at home he knew few people, and few knew him. In that ability to draw to himself those most able to help him in his efforts, – a native, unstudied ability – lies a great secret of his success. In such

> respect he is a marvel. His earnestness, industry, simplicity and innocence are positively contagious. . . .

Although Curtis had photographed Indian scenes at least as early as 1896, it was partly under the tutelage of "active thinking" people like Grinnell that he became increasingly interested in Indians as subjects (and, indeed, semi-systematically photographed them for the Harriman Expedition). These natural historians reinforced his emerging conviction that the Indians' future existence was doubtful and, at best, limited – that they needed to be recorded urgently. Also, as previous studies of his life's work have shown, he achieved marked success with his Indian pictures extremely rapidly; in 1900, for example, three of his Puget Sound Indian views won major prizes in the national photographic convention in Indianapolis. The following year, Arnold Genthe, probably the best known pictorialist on the West Coast, a renowned society portraitist who was himself also conducting a visual investigation of San Francisco's Chinatown, proffered extremely high praise:

> E. S. Curtis's Indian studies occupy quite a place by themselves. They are of immense ethnological value as an excellent record of a dying race, and most of them are really picturesque, showing good composition and interesting light effects. "The Moqui [Hopi] Chief" is a stunning portrait of the haughty Indian, and is, perhaps, even of greater artistic merit than "The Mother" and "The Moqui Girl," both pictures of great human charm. "The Three Chiefs" just misses being great. If the head of the foremost horse could have been turned so as to break the straight line formed by the three horses the composition would have been perfect. But, even as it is, the photograph is a very beautiful rendition of the picturesque phase of Indian life.[15]

In contrast, Curtis's mountain landscapes of the same time were *not* reaching the audience he wanted. *Century*, which had taken his Klondike story, rejected an illustrated feature on Mount Rainier in 1899, despite the fact that Rainier had recently made headline news by becoming a National Park. Perhaps ironically, it was Asahel Curtis who was to become the most prominent photographer of Mount Rainier in the first half of the twentieth century. He started his own photographic business, specialized in promotional work – especially commercial and industrial views – and campaigned for better roads in the belief that more people should have access to mountain scenery.[16]

In Edward's case, at least part of his ambition continued to incline upwards to the mountains. For instance, one of his views of Mount Rainier provided the frontispiece for an issue of the *Lewis and Clark Journal*, the magazine produced to commemorate the events of the huge Lewis and Clark Exposition held in Portland in 1904. In 1905, in an extremely enthusiastic endorsement of Curtis's work, Gilbert H. Grosvenor of the National Geographic Society mentioned the landscapes just as prominently as the Indian pictures: "Mr. Curtis has the most unique, remarkable and beautiful colored pictures of Indians and of American Scenery I have ever seen." And in 1915 Curtis planned to visit a number of mountainous areas and National Parks – the Grand Canyon, Yellowstone, Yosemite, and, of course, his beloved Rainier – to make both movies and still pictures of "the beauty spots of America." Nonetheless, despite the inclusion of what were probably just some of the resulting photographs in *The National Parks Portfolio*, a popular collection compiled by Robert Sterling Yard and issued in several editions, he was destined to scale other peaks.[17]

Portraiture

"Public recognition first came to Curtis," wrote Phillips, "through the publication by magazines of some of his photographic art studies: 'The Cuban Patriot'; 'Summer'; 'Spring'; 'Devotion' and numerous others made in his studio in eighteen ninety four and five." These "art studies" were of various sorts, including nudes, and as late as 1930 Curtis produced "Aphrodite," a depiction of a nude lying back in water, as if rising from the deep like the goddess herself. But they were predominantly portraits. Very rapidly the early "art study" portraits, along with more workaday portrait work, established Curtis's studio as *the* place in Seattle for fine family pictures. In 1896 a group of 101 portraits of Seattle citizens was awarded a bronze medal at the National Photographers' Convention in Chatauqua, New York, and the *Argus* reported that Curtis portraits could be found in nearly every home.[18]

One face featured among the 101 was that of Judge Thomas Burke, perhaps the most progressive of Seattle's more patrician civic leaders. Burke had a lively interest in a variety of cultures – the Thomas Burke Washington State Memorial Museum at the University of Washington, devoted to the peoples of the Pacific Rim, including

Native Americans, was appropriately named after him – and did much to advance the humanities and the arts in the city, especially in the leadership of the campaign to establish a fine Public Library. As well as boosting Curtis's work in the early years, Burke seems to have acted as something of a patron to the ambitious photographer, and both he and his wife, Caroline McGilvra, posed for his camera. Other prominent Seattle sitters included Samuel Hill, who built the railroad along the north bank of the Columbia River; poet Ella Higginson, who composed "The Vanishing Race" after seeing Curtis's famous 1904 image of the same title; Trevor Kincaid, a Harriman Expedition member who was a professor of zoology at the University of Washington; and Edward Camano Cheasty, major clothing merchant and president of the city's park commission.[19]

With the passage of time fewer of the portraits executed in the Curtis Studio were actually made by Curtis himself. Phillips took some, after 1904 Adolf Muhr made many, and over the years a variety of other operatives, including Ella McBride, took a hand. Also, it is likely that for large commissions, such as portraits of virtually the entire membership of the prestigious men's business and social organization, the Arctic Club, all who could be were pressed into service. It is therefore difficult to determine precisely who was responsible for such surviving Arctic Club portraits as those of Erastus Brainerd, a politician and vociferous advocate of Washington State's interests in Washington, D.C., who may have helped boost Curtis in the capital, and Cecil B. de Mille, for whom Curtis was later to work in Hollywood. Usually, however, it was the practice for Curtis himself to take the portraits of members of Seattle's elite when he was in town, and often celebrities visiting the city were brought to his studio for likenesses to be made. For instance, Curtis's friend Professor Edmond S. Meany escorted Chief Joseph of the Nez Perce to the studio in 1903 when, on a speaking trip sponsored by Samuel Hill to plead his people's case for the return of land in Oregon, the Chief addressed meetings both in the city and on the University campus. Similarly, Curtis photographed Jacob Riis, the pioneer reformer, when he lectured in Seattle in 1904.[20]

In 1909 Curtis was awarded the honor of both exhibiting his Indian pictures and running a rather grand portrait studio within the grounds of the enormous Alaska-Yukon-Pacific Exposition mounted in the city; a Curtis Studio portrait of the Exposition's director-general, I. A. Nadeau, survives, as does one of William Duncan, the autocratic founder of Metlakahtla, the mission to Northwest Coast Indians dedicated by Duncan to the eradication of all signs of aboriginal cultures (a mission visited by the Harriman Expedition ten years earlier). Portrait photography in his own studio was to remain an aspect of Curtis's career, and notable Curtis Studio images made by him or other operatives include ones of Anna Pavlova, the dancer, and members of her troupe; Rabindranath Tagore, the Bengali Nobel laureate for literature; Hollywood film stars; and Ezra Meeker, pioneer extraordinary.[21]

In one of his 1900 photography pieces for *The Western Trail,* Curtis urged his provincial readers not to be afraid of national competition and to enter a *Ladies' Home Journal* contest. If not then, in 1903 he seems to have followed his own advice when one of his pictures of a Seattle child, Marie Octavie Fischer, was entered for a *Ladies' Home Journal* competition to find "the most beautiful children in America," prizes for which were to be paintings of the winning children from life by Walter F. Russell, then at the height of his career as a society portrait painter. Of eighteen thousand photographs received, Curtis's was given third place.[22] According to Phillips, when Russell visited Seattle on his painting tour, "he quite lost self control" over Curtis's "gallery portraits and Indian pictures," and – having covered Roosevelt's activities in the Spanish-American war as an artist for *Collier's* and *Century* – he happily introduced the photographer to the president's family. The Roosevelts, said Phillips, "found him a capable portrait maker and a winsome friend."

In 1904 (and, possibly, 1905) Curtis spent periods of time with the Roosevelts at Sagamore Hill, their home in Oyster Bay, Long Island, and made a series of portraits, both formal and informal. Eight of these were presented in such a manner as to give maximum exposure to both subjects and photographer in "The President's Family From Photographs by E. S. Curtis Now Published for the First Time," which appeared in the popular *McClure's Magazine* in July 1905. Curtis was euphoric about this work. In August 1904, in completing an order for pictures secured at the president's home, Curtis wrote to Roosevelt's friend and ally Pinchot:

> My picture of the President is great. It is quite different from anything before taken and, I believe, will be considered by all who know him, a splendid likeness. I made no effort to re-touch up the face and make him a smooth-visaged individual without a line or anything to show his character . . . background, clothing and everything is carried in one great mass of shadow, bringing the face, with its great strength of character, the only thing that we see, and I believe it is good.

Pinchot, who heeded its maker's comments, was quick to order a print and was probably gratified to hear further praise of the picture by Jacob Riis, who had both worked with Roosevelt in New York City and made many distinguished photographs himself. Riis, recorded Curtis, had said that the portrait was "more than a picture: it is the man himself." Not surprisingly, Pinchot was soon having his own family portraits made by Curtis. Roosevelt, for his part, used some of Curtis's Sagamore Hill family pictures in his *Autobiography*.[23]

In one letter to Pinchot, Curtis spoke of his portraits of the president's daughter Alice, as "quite a victory." Alice was something of a firebrand and, though Curtis may have pictured her as early as 1902, he clearly worked long and hard to establish a rapport with her. In April 1905, writing from the Waldorf-Astoria Hotel in New York City, he gave her the benefit of his opinions on some of the portraits:

> The one which I like best is the large head; and the second best I will mark – it is one of the three-quarter lengths, with a very dignified pose. Beyond that, they all seem good, and it would be hard for me to express a preference. . . . I have unfortunately been very ill and confined to my room here at this gilted cage of a camping place. The arrival of your pictures seemed the first ray of sunshine for many days. . . . Not having been allowed newspapers . . . I quite lost track of the different members of your family [except] the President, of course we cannot help but know where he is if we only pick up a paper once in a while.
>
> Hoping that the pictures are at least a part of what you expected. . . .

In all probability they were everything Alice had expected, for Curtis was appointed official photographer for her wedding the following year to Nicholas Longworth, the senior senator from Kansas.[24] With commissions such as this, Curtis was clearly going from strength to strength as a society portrait photographer; but, while he never avoided the earnings and opportunities inherent in such work, for him the attraction of the ungilded "cages" of true camping places of the West took precedence.

Pictorialist Aesthetics

Curtis's aspiration to create "cracker jack" pictures – and his conception of what might constitute that level and kind of achievement – did not spring from nowhere. In Seattle at the turn of the century – though a frontier town or, in Phillips's phrase, massive "overgrown village" that it was – Curtis was heir to a surprisingly rich photographic culture. One of the most distinguished professionals was Frank La Roche, an enormously successful maker of striking portraits who also did unconventional views of the Klondike gold rush: a group of prostitutes, or, as he called them, "actresses," for instance, fording a stream on their way to the diggings. Another was Frank H. Nowell, primarily a commercial photographer for local industries and "official photographer" to the Alaska-Pacific-Yukon Exposition who had also spent time – in his case, some years – in the frozen north. A. C. Warner, who had made the very first exposures from the summit of Mount Rainier when he accompanied John Muir and Thomas Keith, the artist, in 1888, was another. Though living a little further afield in Sedro Woolley, Darius Kinsey was a frequent visitor to the city. Kinsey was a professional dedicated almost obsessively to recording the timber industry, who financed his enterprise mainly by selling portrait prints to individual loggers. And in Bellingham there was E. A. Hegg, who went from photographing family portraits and local Indians to make an enduring visual tribute to the hardships of the Alaska gold rush.[25]

Curtis was materially indebted to La Roche in that he purchased what was earlier referred to as *the* Curtis Seattle studio – in the Downs Building – from him, and the facilities that La Roche had installed were in the main to prove suitable for the remainder of Curtis's residence in the city. Once firmly established, Curtis himself was responsible for bringing his manager, Adolf Muhr, from Omaha, Nebraska, where he had worked for F. A. Rinehart for about six years and, among other things, had himself made numerous Indian images at the 1898 Trans-Mississippi Exposition. Among the interesting photographers – besides Asahel Curtis – who got their start at the Curtis Studio were Ella McBride, Imogen Cunningham, later a member of the f64 Group with Ansel Adams and Edward Weston, and Frank Kunishige, the Japanese-American pictorialist. (Also, out "in the field," it is probable that Curtis gave a start to the prolific Crow photographer Richard Throssel.)[26]

For the most part, though far from entirely, professional practitioners like these, however accomplished, were more concerned with the completion of assigned tasks, with commercial, even workaday, aspects of photography than with efforts to create "cracker jack" pictures. At the turn of the century, at the time of the Linked Ring in Britain and leading up to the Photo-Secession in the United States, it was often amateur photographers like the readers of Curtis's photography pieces in *The Western Trail* who were more preoccupied with the aesthetics of the medium. Typical would be A. W. Denny, scion of one of Seattle's first families, who won several commendations in *The Western Trail*'s photographic competitions. Through membership of organizations like the Mazamas and in his efforts to secure patronage for his studio (and, increasingly for his Indian work), Curtis befriended such figures. Duncan George Inverarity, for example, a New Zealand-born and Oxford-educated lawyer, was a personal friend of Curtis, his exact contemporary in age, and also sufficiently proficient in photography to accompany Curtis as his assistant on the Harriman Expedition.[27]

Both professionals and amateurs would have benefited from the publication of *Anderson's Photographic Monthly*, which was put out by the Anderson Supply Company of 111 Cherry Street, Seattle, between July 1901 and June 1902. Although this consisted primarily of "how to" articles of one sort or another, usually reprinted from East Coast specialist magazines, many of the illustrations were by figures already recognized as artists of the medium, such as Alfred Stieglitz and, from Britain, Frank Meadow Sutcliffe. Also, some of the essays included serious discussion of photography from an aesthetic point of view. Thus C. H. Caffin's influential *Photography as a Fine Art* (1901) was very favorably reviewed; an anonymously authored article entitled "Photography Recognized as a Fine Art" was reprinted from the *New York Journal* and this, too, provided illustrations from the work of Stieglitz. Also, even without magazines like *Anderson's*, pictorialist "how to" books like Otto Walter Beck's *Art Principles in Portrait Photography* (1907) were very widely known.[28] Curtis himself, if his column in *The Western Trail* is taken into account, was already familiar, at the turn of the century, with this range of pictorialist imagery and, equally important, ideas.

Curtis's first *Western Trail* piece, "Photography," which carried the subheading "This Department will be of especial value to Amateurs," was composed essentially of two long quotations on the need to work directly from nature and not simply to imitate paintings from, respectively, George B. Sperry's address to the National Photographic Convention and an article by Edward W. Newcomb reprinted from *The Photo American*. Curtis's second piece urged, among other things, the need to specialize: "Remington made his reputation drawing horses. Had he spent his time on a variety of subjects, the chances are that no one would know who Remington is today." It also cited his own example in preparing for a picture, thinking it through, before actually exposing the plate, in a looser version of what Ansel Adams was later to advocate as "previsualisation" – a theme continued in the two final *Western Trail* pieces. "Study the photographs of the recognized workers and the reproductions of the many landscape painters," Curtis admonished. "I have spent four summers on the slopes of Mount Rainier trying to photograph it . . . and a number of the pictures I worked up in my mind the first season are not yet made." "Perhaps," he added, "I shall never go back to . . . make these pictures I have in my mind, but the study of the subject has helped me to compose other pictures." Or again:

> Let every one's work show individuality. Try to make it pronounced enough that a friend could pick up one of your pictures anywhere and know it was yours. Some one will say that landscapes all look alike and the photographer cannot put enough of himself into his work to show his character. I believe that it can be done. After looking at a dozen of Horsley Hinton's photographs any lover of pictures can tell them instantly.[29]

The honors that Curtis received in photographic conventions at the turn of the century attest that just as he was able to recognize the work of the British pictorialist Hinton, so others were able to discern his individual style. While through his travels to the East – and, indeed, to Indian country, especially for the Hopi Snake Dances (see fig. 15), which were virtually rendezvous for photographers – he became personally acquainted with a range of photographic practitioners, and they with him, there was also an element of reciprocity in appreciation of the work. In one of the Curtis Studio leaflets, "The Curtis Portraits," it was reported that its proprietor had devoted time "to the study of the best work of the eastern portraitists," and that "a visit to the Saint Louis Exposition" had "rounded out this tour of study." And we have seen that in 1901 Arnold Genthe praised Curtis in detailed pictorialist terms. Or again, at the Fine Arts Exhibit of the Lewis & Clark Exposition in Portland, Curtis could have seen at first hand photographs by twenty-four figures who – together with himself, the twenty-fifth exhibitor – were then considered at the forefront of art photography; they included Gertrude Käsebier, Frank Eugene, Alvin Langdon Coburn and Clarence White. And at least the selectors of this show – who also exhibited – must have known the Seattle artist's output. The most influential of them was undoubtedly Alfred

Stieglitz (who in 1907 was also to include Curtis in the first Canadian pictorialist exhibition). The others were Edward Steichen, who in 1903 had so brilliantly portrayed Curtis's patron J. Pierpont Morgan (his hand grasping the high-lit arm of a chair that looked for all the world like a dagger), Joseph T. Keiley, a founding member of the Photo-Secessionist group and an Associate Editor of Stieglitz's new journal *Camera Work*, and F. Benedict Herzog, president of the powerful New York Camera Club.[30]

It cannot be emphasized enough that Curtis carried the freight of artistic ideas he picked up from the pictorialist avant-garde – including, as the contemporary critic Charles Caffin noted, the domination of one tone throughout a composition, avoidance of detail in favor of broad masses, and, most tellingly, "looking at objects through a great gauze veil" – into his Indian work. My contention is that the faces of Curtis's Indians were often also "carried in one great mass of shadow," and certainly – especially in the cases of older figures whose facial lines were sometimes accentuated by a slightly downward camera angle – "character" rather than "likeness" (in the sense of "accuracy") was stressed, somewhat similarly to the manner adopted in Frank Eugene's famous 1898 profile of the doyen of American Photo-Secessionists, Stieglitz. Also, such notions were taken into the dark room, the print shop, and, even, to the gravure stage; in the portrait of the Jicarilla chieftain "Vash Gon" (fig. 10; 1904), for example, much effort was expended after the initial image was made to accent the line of the shadow of his proud silhouette and to "lose" the detail of his chest, all of which tended to thrust his profile up in the frame, dramatizing his presence. There is even a structural resemblance between this image and some of Käsebier's portraits, including "Portrait [of a Woman in Profile]."[31]

As early as 1903, the Seattle *Sunday Times* reported that, "according to his own statement," Curtis was "led into his present habit of flattening the Indian up against a negative through the desire to reach out after a *picturesque* subject." Most obvious of all, out in the field Curtis tended to make portraits of Native Americans according to the particular posing practices and stress on lighting then current in studio portraiture – and which he had described in part to Pinchot in the case of his Presidential portrait. Sometimes we may discern in the Indian images allusions to established pictorial conventions: in Chapter 6 here connections to a whole category of visual production – popular orientalist views – are advanced and, at the level of the individual image, it is possible, as William Goetzmann has claimed, that in his portrait of the behatted young Apache in "An Ostoho Cow Boy" (1903) Curtis alluded to the common trope of Hamlet as the melancholy Dane. Always, in every genre, Curtis was after spectacular images. In 1907, for instance, he confided to Hodge that in the coming season "the special effort" of his camera work would be "pictures illustrating the incidents of the myth stories." "This," he said, "will give me a splendid chance to make the most of the nude." And nudes, both male and female, did appear in the pages of *The North American Indian* (see fig. 8). Curtis also produced Indian nudes that did not conform to the conventions of ethnographic work, such as his "Maid of Dreams," which depicts a young Apache woman holding a sheet in front of her to hide her nakedness – while the curves of her back and buttocks were turned to the camera.[32]

The anonymous author of "Writing History with the Camera," the *Photographic Times* article cited in the two preceding chapters, certainly recognized that much of Curtis's success was due to the aesthetic qualities of his work:

> In 1904 an Indian photograph was taken in Arizona, which has done more to awaken interest in the original American, than any other in our day and age. . . . It was simply a group of Indians on the trail going into the shadows of great cañon walls. Without a face being visible, the picture grips one with its pathos, its dignity – and above all – its mystery. It haunts one with its suggestion and silent question. The title, "A [sic] Vanishing Race," caught the fancy and copyrighting has been insufficient protection to Mr. Curtis for this picture. Imitation, that most sincere form of flattery, has been in evidence for seven years, until between prose and verse, picture and sculpture, there has grown up almost a literature based on the mystery of the cañon's shadows, and the title of that one eloquent picture.

The success of the Curtis Studio, the article continued, was due to "Mr. Curtis's experience and artistic taste alone." "Even childhood, when photographed by Mr. Curtis," it said, "contains the real Indian characteristics. One cannot imagine him photographing a child . . . without retaining the indescribable atmosphere of the prairies or the mountain slope." Moreover, the writer of this article also discerned that there was an aesthetic relationship between the work of the field and that of the studio: "Mr. Curtis has been very fortunate in obtaining sittings from interesting people. . . . [His] collection of pictures, therefore, affords the double interest of being a record of photography of the Indian race, and also of representing a great many tribes of Anglo-Saxon people."[33]

Similarly, Dr. Charles M. Kurtz, director of the Buffalo Fine Arts Academy, a person who did much to promote Photo-Secession photography – including, just before his death, the initial planning of the major 1910 international exhibition mainly selected by Stieglitz (and which included works by Curtis) – was very certain about the nature of Curtis's aesthetic achievement. In 1908, when he came to write a piece on Curtis in his museum's *Academy Notes*, he proceeded as if what he had to say was obvious:

> Many of these photographs have the qualities one finds in paintings – qualities obtainable only by the artist educated in composition, in the management of light and shadow masses, and the sub-ordination of undue detail when the spirit of the work demands it – combined with the skill of the competent photographer knowing all one should know [about] . . . exposure . . . development . . . and [the] making [of] prints that are in the highest degree artistic.[34]

But, while certain figures – Roosevelt and Grinnell, as well as Kurtz, among them – recognized the artistic component to Curtis's Indian project, it was certainly not an aspect that was *fully* appreciated. Indeed, it was as if, in following his own aesthetic advice to amateurs to specialize, Curtis removed his Indian work into another dimension altogether. At the Portland Exposition, for instance, while participating in the Fine Arts exhibition, Curtis's main appearance was in a completely separate show of his Indian work in the Forestry Building. The triumphal progress of that Indian work, coupled with the opportunities that Curtis's relationships with natural historians and other influential figures provided, helped to determine the particular trails he would try to ascend. By the time he gave two stereopticon lectures to his old companions among the Mazamas in 1904, his subject was not mountains, or even portraiture or artistry in photography, but his Indian project, and he was declared "the foremost living authority" in the field.[35] Even if that description was an exaggerated one, Curtis as the Indian photographer, "the shadow catcher," had come into being. But, after all, these dimensions were not so far apart.

One of the primary features of pictorialism – as hinted at by Kurtz – was *manipulation*. Some of Curtis's Seattle studio work, such as his portrait-cum-fashion pictures of Caroline McGilvra Burke, in which she is posed in rather theatrical positions – about to open a curtain, say, as if on stage – exemplify this clearly. Not surprisingly, Curtis also took manipulative techniques like this into the field. "Chief of the Desert" (1904), for example, presents a Navajo man with his face turned fully to the camera, but with his shoulders at an angle, as if he had *just* looked back at the viewer and had been caught like that; in other words, a seemingly straightforward full-face portrait is really already subtly dramatized – a process which was continued in the use of an exotic title for the image. Such exoticization is more apparent in "Judith – Mohave" (1903). This image depicts a bare-breasted woman, and the presence of her bunched blouse, unintentionally visible just above her waistline behind her, indicates that she had been asked to disrobe. In this case, the effect is not to remove the woman from the discourse of ethnographic photography, as happened in the "Maid of Dreams" nude mentioned above, but to accentuate the representation of the "primitive." Similarly, the male figure in "The Whaler – Makah" (1915) is equipped, as if in readiness, with a thick harpoon and a heavy seal-skin float – despite the fact that the Makah (this one wearing a wig) had not hunted whales for a generation.

In fact, very many of these views – especially those devoted to Plains peoples, such as the one praised by Genthe, "The Three Chiefs – Piegan" (1900), or "The Old Cheyenne" (fig. 5; 1911), in which the ancient rider displays a human scalp – were in reality reconstructions or, more accurately, *constructions* produced at the behest of a prevailing ideology to which we will repeatedly return. The Plains Wars were long over, all these people were incarcerated on reservations, and none of them roamed the prairies at will as depicted, for instance, in "Ogalala War Party" (fig. 13; 1907), where a group of mounted Sioux descend a steep hillside. (Such images, as is noted in a later chapter here, fed into the iconography of the Western as refined by John Ford and others.) One view of a mounted Crow war-party is actually called "The Spirit of the Past" (1905) and, of course, the title is ironically accurate in that war-parties *were* by then a thing of the past.

The Secessionist avant-garde, especially Stieglitz, increasingly in pursuit of what Caffin called "the qualities of photography that are fundamentally *photographic*," began to abandon the pictorialist aesthetic in favor of the oft-invoked "straight tradition." As has frequently been noted, the contrast between the work by Käsebier featured in the

Figure 5. The Old Cheyenne, 1911, by E. S. Curtis. He displays a human scalp.

opening numbers of *Camera Work* and that of modernist Paul Strand in the final number in 1917 could not have been greater. Interestingly, Curtis – though unsteadily, at a much slower pace, and without overt aesthetic underpinning – moved in the same direction. Nevertheless, because the photographs for each volume of *The North American Indian* were made over an extensive period of time – for example, those for the two Pueblo volumes, which appeared in 1926, were mainly taken between 1903 and 1906 but some also in 1912 and 1924 – their cumulative impression was predominantly pictorialist.[36]

Perhaps the single most significant strain in pictorialism – if its most elusive one – was, as its very name implies, a stress on the picturesque. This is a large and intractable topic; loosely, of course, picturesque means "pretty as a picture," and in the picturesque work of the Secessionists there was almost always an effect of completeness and composure, a tendency towards the preferred view, the prospect suitably framed. In Curtis's output this is apparent in such images as "On the Little Big Horn" (1905). While of ethnological and historical interest because it depicts a Crow encampment located at the site of Custer's defeat by the Sioux and Cheyenne under Crazy Horse in 1876, this is also, we might note, a most delicately framed landscape: The brushwood in the foreground is echoed by the bend of the river and the darker tones of the left river bank "balance" the greater mass of the right bank, with the tipis sheltered between. Sometimes these picturesque scenes feature reflections, or equivalent such devices, which act as testimony to the status of the image as, precisely, a *picture.* Clear cases are "At the Water's Edge – Piegan" (1906) and "A Kutenai Camp" (1909); in the latter a strikingly-prowed canoe, a small group of tipis, and some soaring pines are replicated in the water below. Among numerous other instances are the literally-titled "Still Life – Puget Sound" (1912), "A Smoky Day at the Sugar Bowl" (1922), with its young Hupa fisherman gazing wistfully over the lake before him, and "Before the White Man Came" (frontispiece), discussed earlier.[37]

While it is predominantly Curtis's portraits of Native Americans that are constantly reprinted, it is worth remembering that the earliest of his Indian pictures to achieve national prominence as prize-winning entries in major competitions were categorized as "picturesque genre studies," such as "The Mussel Gatherer" (1896) or "Homeward" (fig. 4; 1898). (It will be recalled that the Seattle *Sunday Times* had even claimed in 1903 that Curtis had been drawn to Native American subject matter precisely *because* of what were considered its "picturesque" aspects.) The Secessionists, with their knowledge of P. H. Emerson's overtly pictorialist treatment of the vanishing folkways of the Norfolk Broads during the 1880s, probably always considered Curtis in this light. There is certainly a kinship of style as well as of subject matter between such views as Emerson's "Rowing Home the Schoof-Stuff" and Curtis's "Homeward," both of which feature boatfolk and their harvests returning to base as evening comes on, or between Emerson's "Gathering Waterlilies" and Curtis's "Kutenai Duck Hunter" (1909). John Berger has observed of picturesque genre studies of ordinary, everyday life that the figures depicted in them often smile, and that this form, *as* a form, favors the way things are: "Such pictures assert two things: that the poor are happy, and that the better-off are a source of hope for the world."[38]

Such a note of reassurance is very evident in certain of Curtis's images: for example, "The Pima Woman" (fig. 6; 1907), who smiles as she holds her basket to the saguaro cactus, as if beseeching it (and the viewer) for sustenance. The person portrayed is content, or at least accepting of his or her condition, and the viewer – inevitably in Curtis's time, a member of the dominant culture – is reassured that everything is in its proper place. And, even when the figures in such views do not smile, which is the majority, they are at one with their surroundings: witness the sheer stillness of the women and the water in Curtis's extremely popular "At the Old Well of Acoma" (1904), or the Kwakiutl man supposedly ready to make fire by rubbing wood together in "The Fire Drill" (fig. 17; 1914), and who seems to have been rooted there at the base of the ancient tree since the origin of fire itself. *Historical* change is kept at bay, despite the fact that, as we have seen, during the period we are considering sheer population figures for Native Americans were at their lowest point ever, the allotment process breaking up communal tribal bonds with the land was in full swing, and ever more Native American individuals were becoming hungry and destitute.

The fullest early appreciation of the North American Indian project, by George Bird Grinnell, both embodied the principles of pictorialism as sketched here and performed the same conceptual dance as his protegé's work. It spoke of the demise of Native American peoples and cultures, of the monumental task faced by the project, even underestimating the time it would take to complete, stressed the scientific value of the enterprise, and repeatedly emphasized Curtis's pictorialist artistry:

> Here was a great country in which still live hundreds of tribes and remnants of tribes, some of which still retain many of their primitive customs and their ancient beliefs. Would it not be a worthy work, from the points of view of art and science and history, to represent them all by photography? . . . The idea . . . overpowered [Curtis, and] he has visited many tribes . . . to picture the Indian as he was in primitive times; the Indian unposed, unartificial, . . . going about his daily affairs. But while he does this, he considers also – and, I fancy, considers chiefly – the art side; and the result is that his pictures are full of art. . . . It is through the manipulation of light and through beauty of line and of composition that Curtis is able to make his personality felt. . . . The results stir one as one is stirred by a great painting. . . . These pictures show not what an ordinary photographer would have obtained – for Curtis is an artist.

Figure 6. The Pima Woman, 1907, by E. S. Curtis.
The saguaro cactus, as the woman's pose seems to indicate,
was a source of food, fibre, and much else
for the Pima people of Arizona-Mexico borderland.

Finally, and tellingly, in his closing cadences, Grinnell evoked Nature. To accomplish the task before him, he said, Curtis had "exchanged ease, comfort, home life, for the hardest kind of work," including "the heart-breaking struggle of winning over to his purpose primitive men, to whom ambition, time, and money mean nothing, but to whom a dream or a cloud in the sky, or a bird flying across the trail from the wrong direction means much."[39]

In essence, the picturesque genre approach to Native American culture, when fused with the ideology of Native Americans as a vanishing race, created images that *naturalized* the predicament faced by indigenous North American peoples at what was, in fact, at the turn of the century, the very nadir of their experience on the Continent. Thus, as in the keynote "The Vanishing Race," or in "Homeward" and other images discussed above, Nature – rather than anything cultural – is invoked as the indicator of the passage of time: A "primitive" horseman is suitably and nobly alone by "An Oasis in the Badlands" (1904); "The Three Chiefs" (1900) face the fading light; and another Emersonian gatherer steadies her frail craft on Klamath Lake in "The Wokas Harvest" (1923). And, repeatedly, as in the latter image, evening shadows engulf a representative figure in a repertoire of visual metaphors of demise.

Moreover, to the viewer of such images, the larger contextual situation evoked will not be an affront, but – however sad – natural and inevitable. This is partly because, despite the fact that Curtis's subject matter was exotic, western, and so forth, the *formal* aspects of his work made it palatable to sophisticated eastern viewers; that is, it was framed in such a manner as to make the possibly provincial, the regional, suitable for *national* consumption.[40] The ideological thrust of the heritage of photographic pictorialism in Curtis's images worked, almost synergistically, to disguise, even deny, what was, in fact and effect, a seemingly almost endless series of damaging political and economic decisions made by human individuals and agencies.

DOCUMENTS

Document 2A. Extract from "Telling History by Photographs," anonymously authored article in *The Craftsman*, 1906.[41]

> In the recent exhibit [at the Waldorf-Astoria] in New York, about two hundred prints of the thousand already made, were on the walls. But something of the purpose in making the collection is quickly felt even in this limited display. Each primitive tribe – as far as captured by Mr. Curtis's camera – is presented in its own group, with every variation of type, young and old, with home structures, environment, handicrafts, games and ceremonies presented intimately and sympathetically. These pictures tell the history, the legends, the myths, the manners of customs of a vanishing tribe as no printed page, however vivid, could set forth.
>
> And the photographs themselves, quite apart from their historic and scientific value, show a fresh, far step in the progress of photography into the realm of fine arts. Mr. Curtis has so far improved on old methods of printing and finishing as to have

practically invented processes in photographic presentation. His tones, his rough surfaced papers, his color combinations are a new art, or a new science, as one classes camera work. And to those who know nothing of methods and improvements these photographs of picturesque people, employed in primitive ways, their homes and their country, are beautiful pictures, as paintings are beautiful, because of the marvelous way in which nature is reproduced. There are most luminous atmospheric effects, a glimmer of sunlight, a deep still night, desolate plains seen through dust clouds and astonishing contrasts of light and shade as sunbeams gleam down gorges through narrow crevices.

There is apparently nothing in the way of difficulties that he cannot overcome, from the shyness of the Indian nature to illusive quality of air and sunlight. . . .

Mr. Curtis is first of all a craftsman, and after that equally a historian, a scientist, an artist and an understanding human being; if he collects facts, they are accurate; if he traces the civilization of Indian tribes, he is consistent; if he makes a picture, it is with the latest improvement in methods; if he wants the confidence of a tribe of people, he visits them and wins their liking and trust – so that each phase of his endeavor can stand alone; his pictures by themselves are perfect, his ethnological researches are of themselves also complete. . . .

Document 2B. Extract from "E. S. Curtis, Photo Historian," by Sidney Allan, 1907.

Sidney Allan was one of the pseudonyms used by the prolific writer on arts subjects, Sadakichi Hartmann. His article, which was clearly partly based on publicity put out by the Curtis project, was a careful mix of praise and pique, but it registered well the impact made by Curtis's images, especially in the comparison with Gertrude Käsebier.[42]

Although it is difficult to tell the whereabouts of E. S. Curtis at this moment, there is no doubt that he is just now the most talked-of person in photographic circles. Curtis is the pictorial historian of the Red Man. . . . And it was the camera that won out for him. A painter is apt to let his imagination run away with him . . . [whereas] accuracy is what makes Curtis's records valuable to posterity. There is no making of pictures for pictures' sake; a Sioux must be a Sioux, an Apache an Apache. In fact every picture must be primarily an ethnographic record. Being photographs from life they show what exists and not what one in the artist's studio presumes might exist. . . . The workmanship of the Curtis print could be improved upon and I do not agree with some of his lay critics, that "he has created the most beautiful and artistic series of photographs that the world has ever known."

Not even as far as photographs of Indians are concerned. Some of the Käsebier . . . Indian pictures are way ahead artistically. But they are merely isolated examples. They do not count when one considers the aim and intrinsic value of Curtis's work. He has done what no other photographer has done. He is *the* photographer of Indians, and will live as such.

Much could be said, I suppose, about his methods as a photographer, and the adventures of his various canvas wagon journeys when he is "gunning with his camera," but as I am not familiar with either it is best to leave it to others. He himself would probably prove the best narrator of his manifold experiences. . . .

Document 2C. Extracts from a Speech by Edward S. Curtis, 1907.

The typescript of the following speech – untitled, unattributed, and undated – was discovered in the uncatalogued part of the papers of Edmond S. Meany in the University of Washington Archives. Professor Meany was a pioneer historian of the Pacific Northwest, an amateur photographer, an inveterate collector of documents, and a good friend to Curtis. Curtis spoke at Meany's institution, the University of Washington, on other occasions, so it is likely that the present address was delivered there, perhaps to a camera club. It is probable that, like the more formal lectures he delivered at various points in his career, the talk was illustrated by stereopticon slides; certainly the pictures he specifically mentioned, such as the portrait of Alchise, did exist, as did others which could have dramatically illustrated his experiences as a field photographer. Since Curtis did not return to Seattle from the 1906 field season until the January of 1907, the talk was probably given soon afterwards, and certainly before his departure for New York City sometime before the end of March 1907. Although the typescript was probably given to Meany for him to publish somewhere, perhaps in the *Washington Historical Quarterly*, which he edited, Curtis had to dispel any such notions when the piece appeared in *The Photographic Times.* "The dope I sent you on the work . . . has been published . . . in a small photographical magazine," he wrote. "You should only use it to bolster up your personal knowledge."[43]

> You ask me to tell you something of my work that would be of interest to photographers. I question anything in connection with it . . . being of much help to my fellow photographers, unless it would be to convince him that his life is one of comparative ease and comfort. To begin with, for every hour given to photography two must be given to the word picture part of this record of the vanishing Indian. True, many of the hours given to the writing are those of the night time, and the light is not a 32-candlepower stand lamp, but most likely . . . a half dozen tallow candles fastened with their own wax to a scrap of plate or grub box. The everlasting struggle to do the work, do it well and fast, is such that leisure and comfort are lost sight of. . . .
>
> The field season of 1906 was nine months long, beginning in the mountains of Apacheland, with snow still in sight, and long before the season ended we were snow bound in the mountainland of the Walapai. The field party for the season was, firstly, Justo, our Mexican cook; two helpers, who could best be called ethnologists, collecting the lore, logic and history of the people, one of whom acted as my stenographer – and myself, I doing the photography. There being three of us at work there had to be three interpreters, which, of course, we secured from each group with which we were working. During the season we have worked with fourteen languages and no end of dialects. Our camp equipment weighing from a thousand pounds to a ton, depending upon distance from a source of supplies; in photographic and other equipment there were several 6½ × 8½ cameras, a motion-picture machine, phonograph for recording songs, a typewriter, a trunk of reference books, correspondence files covering over a year of business affairs, as being always on the move it is necessary to keep up my regular correspondence in connection with the work, its publication and the lectures all from the field. Tents, bedding, our foods, saddles, cooking outfit, four to eight horses – such was the outfit. Someone has to boss the job; usually that falls to me. Everything must be kept on the move that no time is lost. Teams have to be

bought, supplies secured, both commissary and photographic, arrangements made for getting and sending mail. On long stretches the whole outfit has to be shipped . . . and, withal, the one thing that must never be lost sight of, the purpose of the work; a picture and word history of the Indian and his life. But at times the handling of the material side of the work almost causes one to lose sight of art and literature. . . .

All [these adventures and mishaps have] not happened in one season. There have been nine of them, each having its good share, and yet I have not spoken of the people with whom we have to deal. Each tribe or village is like unto no other, but all have their full share of superstition and secretiveness, to say nothing of stubbornness. Each tribe visited is a new situation to be taken up and mastered, and that quickly. Every phase of their life must be noted and, as far as possible, pictured, and the gathering of this lore, logic and myth must go hand-in-hand with the picturemaking, as without the knowledge of their life, ceremony, domestic, political and religious, one cannot do the picture work well.

How do I manage the portraits and the handling of the life? In every way. Conditions cannot be changed. I must fit myself to them. Some of the portraits can be made in my tent, which is a fair sized one made for photographic work. More are made in the open, in the soft light of the morning or in the intense glare of the midday sun. The subject secured, it matters not the time or conditions. The picture must be made. My fine picture of Alchise, the Apache chief, was made in the strong light of the midday sun, the back-ground of a juniper tree. The picture of Red Cloud, the Sioux, was made in the strong sunlight on the open prairie. The particularly fine one of the Jicarilla chief was also made in the strongest glare of the open sun and the background a red blanket. A certain fortunate picture caused the question, "How did you get that beautiful soft effect?" It is easy to answer. The picture was made in a blinding snow storm and the falling snow between the lens and the sitter caused the semi foggy effect. The results were satisfactory but the doing of it exceedingly uncomfortable.

My mood tonight seems to have been to tell of the difficulties and hardships. Do not think that this is the only side of the work. For . . . the most stormy days have had glorious sunsets, and for every negative that is a disappointment there is one which is a joy. . . .

Figure 7. Advertisement for Curtis Studio in *The Western Trail* magazine, photograph probably by E. S. Curtis, 1901. (University of Washington Libraries.)

3

TRADING WITH THE INDIANS

On October 31, 1905, Curtis wrote from Seattle to J. S. Candelario, the Santa Fe trader, about a "shipment" of "three dozen" blankets he had ordered. "Send them to me by express at once. Now, don't," he said, "pick out all the poor ones you have, simply because I am not there to see to the selection. You know that I am larger than you are, and if you don't make a good selection there will be trouble when I am in Santa Fe next year." This was but one purchase in a series that Curtis entered into to maintain a stock of Indian items – blankets, pottery, baskets – for exhibition and sale in his Seattle studio. He wanted his studio to be an attraction for both tourists and Seattle's citizens. An advertisement from as early as 1901 showed a room at the studio strewn with Indian arts and crafts (fig. 7); visitors would experience his Indian pictures in an "Indian" setting. After the inauguration of *The North American Indian* he seems to have wanted the studio to be known not only as the photographic base for the project but as "the home of the North American Indian."[1]

Trading in Indian arts was an inextricable element of the Curtis enterprise from very early on. On July 31, 1899, back in Seattle at the end of the Harriman Expedition, George Bird Grinnell recorded in his diary: "Bought lot of baskets from Curtis," and the day before, the leader of the scientists, C. Hart Merriam, wrote in his: "I spent much of the day in [the] Curtis studio looking over photographs and Indian baskets, some of which I purchased." (Merriam was in fact a major collector of baskets, and in 1906 Curtis succeeded in getting Phillips and himself invited for dinner at Merriam's Washington home in order to see them.) In 1903, in a typical transaction, Curtis found a particularly good Snokomish basket for the editor of *The Ladies' Home*

Journal, Edward Bok, and, at the same time, reminded this patron of the virtues of his photographs.[2]

Once the publication of *The North American Indian* was underway, Curtis would keep in touch with his prosperous subscribers – as well as with some potential ones – and several of them made use of his services as a broker in acquiring Indian arts. He was exceptionally assiduous in his efforts on behalf of Miss Charlotte Bowditch of Santa Barbara. In May of 1908 he agreed to collect baskets for her while in the field; in 1910 he offered to rummage through the studio collection in search of a particular one that would "answer" her "desire" and also pressed upon her a "Yaque [sic] bowl" (price $3) that he had taken north a few years before. In 1913 he was prepared to let her have a Nootka hat from his "personal collection" and sent her a picture of baskets numbered in such a manner that she could make a selection or buy them all at a reduced price. She was evidently much taken by the hat and wanted more; Curtis gave her a full account of it and promised to look out for others, saying "the first time I find a proud lady who can be induced to sell her hat, I will send it on to you." And in 1915 he sent her a picture of a Haida argillite carving he wanted to sell.[3]

Many of the items collected by Curtis and his associates in the field were passed not into private hands, but were sold or, sometimes, donated to museums. In the summer of 1911 Curtis dickered by mail with George Byron Gordon of the University of Pennsylvania Museum over the sale of a basket, for which he wanted $80, admitting in a later letter that it was slightly broken, but cheekily expressing pleasure that it was to go into the museum rather than stay where it was, given "the careless handling" it received at the studio. Several other such instances centered on the editor of *The North American Indian.* Hodge worked for a time for the New York collector George Heye, originator of what was to become the Museum of the American Indian, and several pieces entered those collections. Later, when Hodge moved on to the Southwest Museum in Los Angeles, the array of Eskimo artifacts gathered by Curtis and Stewart Eastwood, his assistant on the final field trip to Alaska in 1927, were acquired for the museum's holdings and remain there as a feature to this day.[4]

Lest it be thought that Curtis exhibited a unique pecuniary spirit in these practices, it is important to realize that they were a common feature of ethnological activity of the time. Occasionally there was disquiet. Curtis himself, in a 1908 letter to Hodge, expressed a degree of ambivalence over the activities of Gilbert Wilson among the Hidatsas:

> As to the Hidatsa shrine and skulls, yes, I knew Heye had them. The Rev. Wilson who did the collecting was a guest in my camp for some days the past season. Incidentally, as you perhaps know, there is a considerable feeling in the Dakotas in regard to said skulls. Understand I am not saying anything as a criticism but only stating how it looks to some of the people out that way. Wilson was ostensibly gathering information and material for the American Museum of Natural History, and now some of the local people say that there was nothing in that but a bluff, and that he was merely collecting and selling to whoever would pay him the best price. Personally I have no objections to their acquisition by Heye.

The shrine and skulls referred to here certainly did mean much to some of "the people out that way": their original owners the Hidatsas. The Hidatsas were Siouan-speaking people closely related to the Crows. They lived adjacent to the Assiniboin, but whereas the Assiniboin were nomadic, the Hidatsa, like the Mandan, lived in villages of huge earth lodges. The last one was at Fort Berthold, North Dakota, which is where the Curtis party found them.

According to *The North American Indian*, the myth of the sacred skulls tells of the parting of two spirit men in the form of eagles, Shiwahuwa, who settled among the Assiniboin, and Big Bird, who settled among the Hidatsa. Each thought he had the better deal, Shiwahuwa preferring the mobile life of the Assiniboin, Big Bird the more sedentary one of the Hidatsa, with all its rich agricultural produce. Apparently Shiwahuwa abused the hospitality of the Hidatsa, a conflict arose between the Assiniboin and the Hidatsa and all the visiting Assiniboin were killed except Shiwahuwa. His end came about through the trickery of Big Bird, who cut off his head and placed it in an ant hill, where he visited it daily until one day a voice from the skull intoned, "I will aid you." Thenceforth the skull was revered and, when he died, Big Bird's skull was placed with it. These two skulls were the most important sacred possession of the Hidatsa; their keeper always travelled at the head of the column when they moved to a new village, and the shrine where they were kept was venerated above all others. "Until the disintegration of the old native customs," said *The North American Indian*, "the lodge in which they reposed was not entered on trivial errands. Fire was never borrowed from the lodge, and those who entered were required to sit down quickly." "In 1907," the note concluded, "the shrine containing the skulls was disposed of by Wolf Chief, its custodian, and it is now in a private collection in New York City."[5]

These days, as the writings of James Clifford and others testify, there is concern, at least among museum curators and anthropologists, over the bitter legacy that the expropriation of cultural items has created, with resultant calls for their repatriation. But such misgivings are of only recent origin. Removals like the one just described, especially of items of less centrality, were commonplace and, for the most part, viewed as unproblematic. The files of Dr. C. F. Newcombe, the indefatigable Northwest coast antiquarian of Victoria, Vancouver Island, for instance, are full of letters about purchasing Indian items. Among his purchases, negotiated by the anthropologist Samuel M. Barrett, was the fine tall Haida totem that now stands in front of the Milwaukee Museum, and a dozen others that grace ethnological collections from Europe to Australia. In the summer of 1899 the Harriman Expedition spent a whole day loading the Expedition's ship with trophies from Gash, a Tlingit village on Cape Fox, Alaska – two large totems, Chilkat blankets, masks and carvings – all selected by the most eminent natural historians of the day, from botanist Coville and U.S. Chief Geologist Grove Karl Gilbert to Grinnell and the leading conservationist of the era, John Muir.[6]

Charlie Day, Trader

One of the most prominent traders Curtis dealt with was Lorenzo Hubbell of Ganado, Arizona, on the Navajo Reservation. The two probably met in 1904, and by 1906 Curtis was relying on Hubbell to bring him extra photographic plates for use during the Hopi Snake Dance ceremonies of that year. Later in the same year, in pursuit of blankets "more or less old" for "a friend," and having already acquired one such himself, Curtis asked Hubbell if he had in his possession "one of the so-called old chief blankets" – a request Hubbell was able to fulfill. When hustling for subscriptions to *The North American Indian*, Curtis was even prepared to take payment from Hubbell – should he have agreed to subscribe (which, as it happens, he did not) – "in blankets." He used a Hubbell blanket in his important "Navaho Still Life" (fig. 1; 1907), an ensemble of Navajo material culture deployed as artfully as those traditionally used by painters of the genre. Also, Curtis chose to decorate his newly opened New York office-cum-showroom with blankets supplied by Hubbell, and secured further ones for use in his grand exhibition room at Seattle's Alaska-

Yukon-Pacific Exposition of 1909. In later years, partly as a gesture of goodwill towards a regular customer, Hubbell tried hard to exert influence as a member of the Arizona State Legislature to get the State to buy a set of *The North American Indian.*[7]

Intriguingly though, when Curtis wanted help in acquiring information rather than material goods from the Navajos, he sought it not through the biggest trader on the reservation but through the one with the closest family ties: Charlie Day, son of Samuel Edward Day, Sr. By the early 1900s Sam Day had homesteaded for twenty years just south of the reservation at St. Michaels. He had learned Navajo well enough to teach it to the Franciscan missionaries there, and Charlie and his brothers Bill and Sam Jr. – who later married a Navajo woman, Kate Roanhorse, daughter of Manuelito – grew up speaking Navajo as readily as they spoke English. At the opening of the twentieth century the Days operated trading posts at Fort Defiance and at Chinle, near the mouth of the Canyon de Chelly. Each of them was interested in the preservation of Anasazi Indian relics and ruins, and in particular in 1903 Charlie was appointed the official guardian of the ancient Canyon de Chelly sites by the Department of the Interior. Both Charlie and Sam Jr. made amateur records of Navajo stories and ceremonies, and Charlie even purchased early gramophone equipment to record Navajo songs. He also acquired a camera to begin a photographic archive, and it was probably this shared interest, as much as the fact that he was single and relatively free of obligations, that brought him within Curtis's orbit. It is likely that, had Day's life not been cut short by an automobile accident on the reservation sometime towards the end of the first decade of the twentieth century, Curtis, who kept in touch with him at least through a terrible fever Day endured in November 1908, would have engaged him again when the project returned to the area to gather more data for the Hopi volume of *The North American Indian*, eventually published in 1922.[8]

Each of the Days interceded at various points on behalf of the Navajos in opposition to Bureau of Indian Affairs policies or personnel, and they may be regarded not just as traders but also as cultural brokers. In 1905, and on through 1906, relations between Charlie Day and the bureau were at their worst. Together with Daniel Holmes Mitchell, who traded with the Hopis, Charlie wrote to President Roosevelt to ask for the removal of bureau officials, including Navajo Agent Reuben Perry, who he believed had grossly infringed Indians' rights. Indians had been accused of various crimes, tried and punished, even jailed on Alcatraz Island, without the benefit, in the traders' view, of the due process of law. It seems that the intercession was ultimately successful, in that the Indians were released, but in the meantime Charlie was awkwardly placed. Perhaps in retaliation for his activities, the bureau prohibited him from attending any Indian ceremonies. So when Curtis, having received Day's help in 1904, sought it again in 1905, Charlie wrote as follows:

> An Inspector came out here and I think I will be all right. But he told me not to have any thing more to do with dances in any way. His name was Mead. So if you want me to help you out . . . with my masks etc., you had better go to the Commissioner of Ind. Affairs and get a written permit for you to get what you want and for me to help you. Otherwise I would be running to [sic] much risk of being put off of the Reservation, and I do not want too [sic] get out of here for awhile, at least I would like to finish my sand paintings. . . . [9]

Curtis complied with Day's request and his long letter to Commissioner Francis E. Leupp revealed much more about Day's position. "It is as natural for him [Day] to [go to the ceremonies] as it is for a duck to swim," he said. "He was but a year old when he went to the reservation; his playmates were always Navahoe children, and when the Navahoe children went into the ceremonies, so did he. To him, Yobochai ceremonies count more than the fourth of July to the average youngster." And Curtis admitted how much of his own work in 1904 had been dependent on the younger man, who was only in his early twenties at the time; in particular, Day's rapport with "the medicine men" had led to "the chance of a life time to secure a large number of sand paintings and their stories." Clearly, Day devoted much energy to this task and it added immeasurably to the store of Navajo lore recounted in the first volume of *The North American Indian.*

While in the preface to that volume Day did not receive the acknowledgment that was probably his due – though he was always remembered by Curtis and his family as a key figure in the Navajo work – the depth of his involvement may be registered by both the content and tone of one of Curtis's 1904 messages:

> The basket reached me several days ago. I am tickled to death, but tell Billy [Day] he should have gone a little bit further and put the tobacco in the cigarettes. However, I will forgive him as

> he says I can have another dance whenever I want it, and you bet I want another dance next summer.
>
> Just a few days more of this Holiday rush and then I am at my Navaho notes and getting ready for my series of exhibitions and talks, and say, Charley, I am terrifically anxious about my sand painting of the Yebichai, as I want to use lantern slides from those sand paintings in my . . . lectures (say, I do hate the word "lecture") – but I do wish you could hear one of my talks; however, you have heard me talk until you were tired, any way.
>
> The people who have seen my motion picture of the Buffalo Dance say that it gives them the creeps; they feel that the whole howling mob of Indians is coming right at them. Now, Charley, strain a point and get me your Yebichai Dance description and the sand paintings, if possible; and . . . I will do a little looking around on the sand painting subject while I am East. I am much in hopes that things go more than well with me on this trip [to the East], and if they do, you and I will have some great old trips. . . .

The Day material helped to make the first volume of *The North American Indian* a solid achievement; its ceremonial descriptions, which are the parts most attributable to Day, certainly stand comparison with longer ones provided by other authorities (however we answer the vexed question of what constitutes a "good" ethnography). The visuals, on the other hand, the numerous plates of sand paintings and, especially, masks, some of them *looking* almost new, might well give pause for thought. It seems that the masks were especially and secretly made for the occasion by Curtis and three Navajos who, in exchange for calico and cash, appeared prepared to defy the tribe, despite what a newspaper reporter called a "powwow" held to argue them out of it. The masks contained small "errors" or deviations in representational conventions. This was because Charlie knew that the seemingly literal taking of the image itself by the camera would not have been acceptable to his Navajo kinsmen. Also, it may have been the case that Day himself posed as a Navajo for Curtis's camera wearing Yebichai masks. Certainly, he was able, as a broker, mostly with Curtis's cognizance, to achieve a visual production satisfactory both to the Navajos and to Curtis.[10]

One of the things which made the arrangement satisfactory to the Navajos was that they were paid. Matilda Coxe Stevenson, a Bureau of American Ethnology worker and a prolific contributor on Indians of the Southwest, was distressed about this issue, though she was a supporter of Curtis in other ways. "I have always maintained," she wrote to Charles D. Walcott of the Smithsonian, "that the native peoples will not sell their religion and the beliefs sacred to them for money." "Mr. E. S. Curtis declared to me," she continued, "that to reach the inner life of the Indian one must have his pocket book overflowing until the money runs out in a stream upon the ground. Had Mr. Curtis been an anthropologist I would have taken issue with him but I never argue for the mere sake of argument. Mr. Curtis's work is beautiful as it is." The American Museum of Natural History anthropologist Clark Wissler similarly pointed out in his reminiscences that an "artist" was received as "a superior person" at Indian agencies and that even "the Indians were infected by this white hero worship and looked upon the artist as a kind of magician, though rarely overlooking the supposed commercial value of the product and driving hard bargains for their services as artists' models." While the back-biting element in these comments may be attributed to professional jealousy, especially in the case of Stevenson, who was well-known for extracting information and materials by pressuring her Indian subjects, it is true that such trading became a consistent feature of Curtis's relationships with Indian peoples.[11]

George Hunt, Paid Informant

In his old age Curtis wrote to Harriet Leitch of the Seattle Library that his very first Indian picture had been of Princess Angeline, Chief Seattle's daughter, a clam digger: "I paid the Princess a dollar for each picture made," he said. "This seemed to please her greatly and with hands and [Chinook] jargon she indicated that she preferred to spend her time having pictures made than in digging clams." But the best documented case of such unequal trading is probably that of the Kwakiutl of the Northwest Coast. There the figure in the middle was George Hunt, the offspring of a Tlingit woman and a Scottish Hudson's Bay Company trader, a native Kwakiutl speaker with considerable standing in the tribe who had also long since made himself indispensable to a number of scholars, especially Franz Boas. Ronald P. Rohner has rightly dubbed him an "anthropologists' anthropologist."[12]

Hunt was born in 1854, met Boas in 1888, and worked closely with him from 1894. Between 1896 and his death in 1933, Hunt supplied Boas with objects of material culture, several series of photographs, and, most importantly, some six thousand pages of tales, vocabularies, ceremonial descriptions and the like, covering not only his own immediate people but the Nootka, the Bella Coola, and other Northwest Coast groups. He was granted joint named credit with Boas, if not equal scholarly recognition, for a range of collections of myth material, especially *Kwakiutl Texts* (1905), and the title page of Boas's groundbreaking *The Social Organization and Secret Societies of the Kwakiutl Indians*, published by the U.S. National Museum in 1897, reads: "Based on personal observations and notes made by Mr. George Hunt." While Hunt's crucial role in salvaging a coherent record of the complexities of Northwest Coast culture has been acknowledged by a number of scholars – including Irving Goldman, who has pointed out that Hunt was sometimes more precise and more telling than his mentor Boas in his literal translations from Kwakiutl dialects – it is unfortunate that his biography remains unwritten.[13]

It is not surprising that when Curtis and his assistants came to work on Vancouver Island they too sought out Hunt. Curtis and his chief ethnologist William E. Myers most likely first met Hunt and his family in 1909, and for several seasons thereafter one or both of them journeyed to Fort Rupert and employed him as an informant, photographic assistant, translator, actor, and, perhaps most important, organizer. Curtis – and hence his family – remembered Hunt as prodigiously effective in achieving whatever was desired for the project as a whole. Hunt himself both sat for portraits or performed ceremonially for the still camera (see figs. 16 and 17), and many of his family acted in or helped out on Curtis's documentary film, *In the Land of the Head-Hunters* (1914). At the same time, improbably enough, Curtis recalled that the Hunt family's miscalculation of the tides had caused a group of them to risk drowning on a rocky island during the filming of a sea lion hunt. In a separate story, Curtis let on that Hunt was profoundly changeable in mood, irascible – subject, he even hinted, to homicidal rages.[14]

That such accounts were most likely dramatic travelers' tales designed to play on the dominant culture's fears of "savage" and libidinous Indians is borne out by the fact that, at the very material level, for the film alone Hunt organized the construction of a whole village of false house fronts; also, massive canoes were repainted, masks were refurbished, cedar bark clothing was manufactured, and, just as he had for Boas, Hunt traded for and collected an array of traditional ceremonial items, many of which survive in museum collections. And Hunt's account book also survived, complete with a record of the payments made. The full extent of such transactions – and, perhaps, some indication of their meaning – may be gauged through an analysis of the following newspaper item:

> In his studio yesterday, Mr. Curtis was found arranging the prizes he brought from the North Coast country, the land of totem poles, of strange and grotesque masks and costumes, and of the strangest of secret dances; a land where in the old days head hunting was a common and popular pastime, and where man even now seems to hark back to the days when the human race was young and where the gloomy forests still retain something reminiscent of the somber ages before the faintest dawn of history.
>
> On the floor was a chest half filled with ghastly human skulls and containing also a mummified leg and foot. Asked of what use were the grewsome relics, Mr. Curtis explained that they were part of the paraphernalia he had to have as a member of one of the many Indian secret orders. Part of this paraphernalia proved to be a necklace with bangles consisting of four human skulls. Were they the domes of wisdom of chiefs or slaves? Of men or of women? The artist-writer seemingly knew not and cared not. They were the requisite skulls. That was all he cared to know.
>
> [Curtis] said that [Volume 10 of *The North American Indian*] will be of deepest interest, for it deals with the vigorous tribes of British Columbia, and will contain a wealth of material, in pictures and text, the great problem being to find room for even the best of the facts and illustrations. . . . In point of original genius in designing, [the] masks are in a class by themselves. Each separate costume has its own religious, family or historical significance, the stories of which Mr. Curtis naturally keeps to himself at this time.[15]

Needless to say, it is unlikely that Curtis would have needed any of these objects "as part of the paraphernalia he had to have as a member of one of the many Indian secret orders." Over the years there were often references in the press, especially in Seattle papers, to Curtis's membership of Indian esoteric organizations, so it was clearly a feature of the publicity for the project. The project was written up as "discovering" unknown things, and *The North American Indian* was featured as being written by someone who knew Indian life from "the inside." (Volume 10 has indeed acquired among scholars the reputation of being a – perhaps the – most subtle and comprehensive version of Kwakiutl culture.) In later life Curtis wrote a very vivid account of stealing skulls from Kwakiutl burial islands – "islands of the dead" – and, even, of securing the help of Hunt's wife in getting hold of a complete mummified body. It may be that Curtis exaggerated somewhat, but as the above contemporary newspaper account testifies, something of the sort must have happened.[16]

The context, however, was not any participation in secret ceremonies preparatory to whaling, as Curtis's memoir has it, but the gathering of props for a film. *In the Land of the Head-Hunters* includes a number of sequences in which skulls appear and it even has a section on whaling, never a feature of Kwakiutl culture and one no longer extant for any Northwest Coast peoples when this newspaper item was composed in 1912. If Curtis needed a mummy to go in the prow of a whaling canoe, as he claimed, it was not to hunt whales but to film the hunting of whales. Either way, graves were robbed and the dead disinterred. On one occasion some grave boxes accidentally fell from trees while Curtis was photographing. "There was a veritable deluge of bones and skulls," he reported. "Like a boy gathering apples, I quickly picked up the skulls, thus adding five more to my collection." He himself called this an "unholy quest."[17]

Harold Phillips Curtis, Edward's son, told of a more extreme case of trading: One of his most vivid memories was of his father buying cattle to feed the Pine Ridge Reservation Sioux who, in 1907, were literally starving because of the non-arrival of the food rations supposedly guaranteed under treaty obligations. Also, Professor Edmond S. Meany, a friend of Curtis, left among his papers a list of payments that he had made in 1907 to individual Sioux on Curtis's behalf for allowing portraits to be made or for providing myth material. Perhaps the starkest instance of this kind of trade was the project's dealings, according to Curtis's own testimony, with various Apache shamans in pursuit of a ceremonial artifact and its meanings:

> When starting my work among the Apaches, I found that there was not a word in print dealing with their religious beliefs and practices. I quickly learned that all information relative to their religious beliefs was jealously guarded. . . . One of my interpreters told me who the foremost medicine men were . . . at the same time telling me that a certain medicine man had a chart which told the whole story. . . . I talked with the owner of the sacred chart. He first disclaimed any knowledge of anything of

> the sort, in fact, had never heard that the Apaches possessed anything like that. I then asked him, "If you had such a painted skin and I offered you one hundred dollars to see it, what would you say?" "I would say no, for if I showed it to you, I would be killed by the other medicine men and all the spirits would be angry and misfortune would come to our people." Then I asked him, "If I would give you five hundred dollars, what would you say?" "I would still say no, for if I was dead the money would do me no good. . . . " To make certain that he would realize the magnitude of my offer, I spilled out on a blanket several hundred dollars in silver. The silver held his eyes but did not change his "no" to "yes". . . .

But later, as Curtis was able to boast, after the shaman's death, his wife *was* induced, by money, to part with the chart.[18] And someone even modeled for a photograph of the chart being prayed over (fig. 8).

Again, it would be mistaken to think Curtis was alone in such practices. In 1888, Boas, despite recording in his diary that it was "unpleasant work to steal bones from a grave . . . [even if] someone has to do it," collected 85 crania and 14 complete skeletons from Northwest Coast sites, and later he got George Hunt to arrange the shipment to the American Museum of Natural History in New York the *whole* of a Nootka island burial site, complete with skeletons and carved insignia. Both photographers and anthropologists habitually paid Indians. Hunt himself received a monthly allowance from Boas to cover his expenses for the extended periods during which he was collecting information and sending it from the field to New York – and after his death Boas offered his widow a stipend, "if necessary."[19] In fact, payments were made as a matter of course by Boas and his students and colleagues, and employees of the Bureau of American Ethnology were given a special allowance for the purpose. On the other hand, it may well have been the case that the North American Indian project, as a strictly private enterprise, was able to distribute sums in excess of those available to other fieldworkers.

There was at least one certain instance of this: In 1915 E. W. Gifford, a colleague of Alfred Kroeber at the University of California's Museum of Anthropology, Berkeley, urged Myers to keep costs down in the following terms:

> In the matter of your work with the Miwok I have one request to make. Please do not pay either informant or interpreter more

Figure 8. Apache Medicine Man, 1907, by E. S. Curtis.
It is not known whether the person who prays over this hide chart of deities is the medicine man who refused to show Curtis such a chart.

> than $1.50 a day. This is the amount which has been paid by the Department throughout the state; and it is the amount which I will be paying the Indians of Tuolumne Co. in October. Our funds are very limited, and if you set the precedent for more than $1.50 a day, you can well see that it would cripple my work in October. I now have one Miwok paper in the hands of the Editorial Committee, and another in preparation. . . . [20]

Keeping costs down in this complex trading of information meant depressing the living standards of the primary subjects, the Indians, in just the same manner as could so easily happen in the trading of baskets, blankets, and beads.

At the same time, money alone, as Matilda Coxe Stevenson had discerned, truly was not always effective in securing the required goods. Phillips, Curtis's first ethnological assistant, included in his memoir a record of one of the earliest thorough attempts of the Curtis party to gather data – in Eastern Washington in 1905 after the reburial ceremonies for Chief Joseph of the Nez Perces:

> The Indians continued their rites and festivities for several days, dancing at night, racing horses and playing games by day. All throughout the period they were assembled, hard endeavor was made to secure "inside" information, to but little avail. A centenarian, Quiquitas the elder, withered till his flesh conformed to the very contour of his bones, was prevailed upon by his son to promise us tales of Indian beliefs, and life in the early days, but visits at his camp three miles distant, on as many recurring days, netted only a few short myths of animal antics, and nothing of primitive life, religion, or history. Yellow Bull, the old warrior, though carefully approached, effectually evaded all attempts to get him to reveal anything relative to ritualism, legends, gods, or worlds hereafter. The very seriousness of the deference to the gods and spirits gone to the Great Beyond proved a barrier to the securing of details of its underlying causes. Persuade, reward as we would, veterans of the tribe refused point blank to divulge information. . . . After the dispersal of the gathering . . . I scanned the pages of my notebook, and wondered if succeeding efforts were to be as barren of results.

Phillips's notebook did in fact survive, and – given his assumptions about the purposes of ethnography – it is, as he said, "barren of results." He and Curtis became, as he phrased it, firm in the conviction that "Indians must be employed to conquer Indians."[21]

Alexander Upshaw, Cultural Broker

And this is how they came to seek out Alexander B. Upshaw, a man Curtis probably first heard about from Adolf Muhr as the Crow interpreter at the Omaha Exposition in 1898. Although the Curtis party had high hopes of Upshaw, the white people at the Crow Agency in eastern Montana had a different view. "No one knew his whereabouts," reported Phillips, "but all knew that he would be of no use to us: lazy, dishonest, meddlesome, here today and there tomorrow; 'a regular coyote', said the livery-stable man where he hired horses, 'and a damned bad one. Don't leave anything layin' around loose.'"[22] Finding, indeed, no trace of him, Curtis and Phillips drove alone to the Crow Fourth of July gathering on a tree-shaded bend of the Little Big Horn. They joined the revelers. "Though not without protest. Oh No!" expostulated Phillips. "But objections were soon overcome by a liberal use of silver, the men in charge pacified, and our own camp made beside a giant cottonwood." "Upshaw, The Terrible?" he continued. "Not there; but the Indians knew where he could be found. Admiration showed in their faces at the mention of his name, and we had no difficulty in securing a messenger to carry word to him at his home some sixty miles away."

After a fruitless week, at least as far as data gathering was concerned, they returned to the agency. In reporting what happened next, Phillips made one of his rare excursions into the realm of opinion:

> It was while we were there that Upshaw, the Renegade, joined us. The reasons for his unpopularity among the white people soon became apparent, the chief being that he was both observing and discerning, and that he had a thought and care for the welfare of his copper-skinned brothers. Such characteristics in an Indian capable of conveying his impressions . . . to sympathetic listeners from the "outside," or to Washington . . . prove fatal usually to his reputation among local reservation authorities. . . . No abler character among Indians . . . have we met than Upshaw; educated in English and in his mother tongue, kindly, honest and shrewd; but to little avail. The odds against the advance of the educated Indian – barriers interposed by the white people who ought to aid them – are too many to be overcome. . . .

Upshaw, son of Crazy Pend D'Oreille, a prominent Crow leader whose name was a byword for fearlessness, was born in 1875 in St. Xavier, Montana, and, after graduation from Carlisle in 1897, eventually became a teacher at the Genoa, Nebraska, Indian School. In 1897, in an article in the Carlisle paper, he expressed both assimilationist views and what can now be seen as a debilitating self-hatred: "Unless we break away from our tribal relations and go out into the world as men and women, we will remain Indians and perish as Indians." As late as 1901 he helped survey the Crow Reservation in preparation for allotment. But by the time he came to work for the North American Indian project, as Phillips saw, he was regarded as someone who had indeed almost "returned to the blanket," as the pejorative saying of the time had it.

Perhaps because he had largely turned his back on white ways, he was able to get the confidence of the older folk; very early on in their relationship Curtis went so far as to tell Hodge: "Upshaw . . . is proving of great assistance to me. Through him I am getting into the heart of the Northern Plains Indian in a way that gives me the greatest satisfaction." Certainly, the Crow volume of *The North American Indian* – as if in fulfillment of Upshaw's ambition (as remembered by Curtis's son) – proved one of the richest collections of data in the series, frequently cited by other anthropologists of Plains peoples, such as Clark Wissler and Robert Lowie. Much of the actual writing of the early volumes of *The North American Indian* was completed by Curtis, Myers, and others in the Crow country, in a Pryor Valley cabin that Upshaw probably owned. He worked for the North American Indian project throughout the West until his death in 1909. The Curtis family remembered Upshaw as a gentle man, but perhaps not too surprisingly – in that he aroused racist ire by his marriage to a white woman and by his determined defense of the tribal land base – he came to a violent end: murdered in a brawl just off the reservation.[23]

At the end of the first season with Upshaw, in 1905, Curtis used a revealing expression when he told a newspaper reporter: "In the Crow country I had an Indian interpreter who in some respects was the most remarkable man I ever saw. He was perfectly educated and absolutely uncivilized." "Through him," Curtis continued, "I was able to get some pictures of the July dances of the Black Lodge clan that were very interesting. And also through him I was able to meet the great Five Bears. . . ." Phillips recalled the way Upshaw worked as he took Curtis and himself through Crow territory in the company of two extremely aged informants:

> We could have found no better interpreter than Upshaw, and as he translated the words of Bull Chief or Shot-in-the-Hand into almost fluent English, by the light of the flickering campfire, stretched close beside it, flat on my stomach, I jotted notes at a rapid rate. Shifting winds, changing the drift of smoke and sparks mattered not, tradition and ethnology had to be booked on the instant. Since the old story-tellers rested through the days, they lasted well through the nights, and not once did midnight find the camp asleep. On the day following each long night of note making, while the narratives were fresh in mind, I rounded out my notes, filling in gaps where a deadened fire had made it possible to scrawl suggestions only of the context of the reminiscences.

In 1907 Upshaw helped arrange a thorough investigation of the Custer battlefield, in the company of elderly Crows who had served as scouts under the ambitious general (see fig. 12). Over the years he collected ethnological data from members of a number of tribes, including the Sioux, the Arikara, and the Blackfoot. Most of this material, if without specific acknowledgment to him, found its way into the published volumes of *The North American Indian.* All round, by March 1909 his prominence was such that – though he also had to suffer the attentions of the press, which lent *him* a deliberate touch of the exotic by dwelling on *their* surprise that such an educated person was "a full-blooded Crow Indian" – he was able to accompany Curtis on a morning visit to President Roosevelt's White House.[24]

While Upshaw's ethnological work was for the most part to his material advantage, and to that of his people, there were prices to pay that Upshaw may have regretted. For instance, Curtis himself recorded an anecdote of the time when, under arrangements Upshaw had painstakingly made over a period of months, the two of them were able to participate in a purification ceremony which enabled them to see the Sacred Turtles – effigies made of thick buffalo hide – of the Mandans. Curtis badgered their keeper, Packs Wolf, and his two "confederates in the unethical affair," into letting him make photographic plates of the Turtles (fig. 9), even getting them to "strip" the Turtles of their decorative adornments and move them into better light, all the while worried that other members of the tribe would discover this transgression of Mandan lore. When in fact more circumspect Mandans appeared, "with their horses snorting clouds of vapor" in the winter air, they "found me," Curtis said, "making notes in a little book." "I blew on my hands," he continued, "and told Upshaw to tell them we were learning about a tribal myth. As we rode away I hoped we had convinced [them] that our own story was not one too."[25]

Some prices Upshaw *must* have regretted. There were periods, for example, when a shortage of funds for the fieldwork meant that he went unpaid or was virtually laid off. Edwin J. Dalby, another of the Curtis field team in the early years of the project, remembered that on one occasion he and Upshaw had to be physically restrained by Henry B. Allen, a Skokomish friend and interpreter, from waylaying Curtis and manhandling him for the money he owed them.[26] Money was also at the root of another divisive encounter, as recorded by Phillips:

a

b

Figure 9. Mandan Sacred Turtles (a) Dressed (b) Undressed, 1911, by E. S. Curtis. The keeper of these venerated objects was paid to unveil them for the camera.

> When we bade good-bye to the two old fellows who had been such boon companions, their per diem, for we paid all Indians for every assistance . . . , was handed to them in paper and silver. The amount was noted by the younger Indians with us – a half-brother of our interpreter, and his brother-in-law who had hired for the trip under a different rate, – so when the time came to settle with them at their homes on the following morning, there was trouble in the air. The surly half-brother couldn't understand why old men were worth more than young men, and demanded equal compensation. He was stout and savage; expostulations addressed to him in English were useless, so he got his demands in full. He had been living a lazy life at Upshaw's expense for a long time, but then and there he received orders to leave the Big Horn Valley and return to his own lands on Prior Creek. . . . His wife and Upshaw's sister were bosom friends and when the rupture occurred between the two men, tears streamed their cheeks. To feel that we were even indirectly responsible for the breaking up of the happy home circle there on Upshaw's ranch filled Mr. Curtis and me with deepest regrets. I have often wondered to what extent the bad blood flowed; Indians, though, are quite the same as mankind in general, forgetful in time, forgiving and accepting forgiveness, but for the day and night that we spent on Upshaw's place, exchanging horses and fitting up for another long drive, the men were grumpy and ugly, and the women tearful.

On another occasion Curtis actually succeeded in purchasing a tract of 120 acres of the Crow Reservation for a relatively paltry sum by virtue of "the non-competence" of "Crow allottee no. 2232." The Dawes Act of 1887 had done its utmost to extinguish tribal ownership of reservation land and vast areas had been individually allotted, but often the allottees, usually untrained in necessary farming methods, had been unable to make a go of their individual plots and were forced to sell out. Upshaw fought hard for tribal members caught in this kind of fix. In 1909 especially – with, ironically, a letter of support from Curtis – he mounted a vigorous campaign of letters and petitions to the bureau to try to prevent Indian land being leased out from under them for cattle grazing.[27] That a figure as well-known as Curtis, Upshaw's own mentor and employer, could buy Indian land – on the railroad line, too – would have been at least an embarrassment to him. As a cultural broker he was betwixt and between: like piggy in the middle, unable to catch the ball. Perhaps fortunately for him, by the time this land transaction took place, in 1911, he was dead.

Trade Imbalances

Something similar happened between Curtis and Charlie Day. In Curtis's letter to the commissioner for Indian Affairs, in which he sketched Charlie's upbringing on the reservation and asked for permission to have him allowed on the land to help with fieldwork again, Curtis, unbeknownst to Charlie, said this:

> As to the harmful effects of my work there, I am of the opinion that in breaking their old superstitions sufficiently to get the pictures which I did, did more to disintegrate the same superstitions than any other one ever has. The fathers at St. Michael say my work of the one season did more to break down the old superstitions [than] all the years of their missionary work. . . .
>
> Hoping that I am not overstepping any bounds in communicating with you in this way, and at the same time putting Mr. Day in perhaps a more favorable light than he would be otherwise. . . .

One interpretation of this is that Curtis was cynically playing on Commissioner Leupp's known prejudices against native ceremonial life to place his own activities in a better light. Another interpretation – especially considering how easily brokerage shades over into trading which, in turn, often allows, even encourages, expropriation by the stronger party – is that Curtis did, indeed, recognize the disintegrative nature of getting people to perform for money rather than for meaningful ceremony. Such episodes constitute sharply dramatic examples of the enforced substitution, in quasi-Marxist terms, of exchange values for use values.

In any kind of trading the buyer does not always get what he or she pays for. Curtis himself admitted that on one of his visits to Hopiland he took a picture – what he called "a character pose" – of a "chief" holding a shield that a Smithsonian ethnologist later told him was "wrong." Curtis "wanted that particular Moki chief," the newspaper reporter put it, "to have a shield, as that was one of their ways of dressing years agone, but as the regular Moki shield was missing Mr Injun rung in one from another tribe." Interestingly, in this instance, *both* Curtis and his Hopi subject participated in the creation of the image. And in the dealings with Charlie Day and the

Navajo people, it is worth recalling as a kind of coda that the expropriation, if such it was, does not appear to have been definitive: present-day Navajos knowledgeable about the Yebichai, when shown the Curtis film footage and still images of the ceremony, have wryly pointed out that their forebears who performed for Curtis did everything *backwards*, presumably in order *not* to contravene tribal restrictions on the recording of such sacred rites. What that "powwow" actually hammered out, presumably without the image maker's awareness, was not the total acquiescence to Curtis's wishes, as the newspaper journalist reported, but an ingenious way of placating him. The episode may thus be considered an example of what Mary Louise Pratt, in emphasizing what she calls "transculturation" in preference to "acculturation," has seen as a two-way process when representatives of one culture encounter representatives of another in "the contact zone."[28]

Nevertheless, insofar as Curtis apprehended at least the potential cultural destruction involved, it is awesomely paradoxical that the primary thrust of the North American Indian project was the memorialization of the Indian cultures as they existed prior to that destruction. In light of this, the cultural brokers in the middle – whether by parentage fully Indian like Upshaw, partly Indian like Hunt, or white like Day – were in a position already essentially undermined. They each responded differently to the pressures of the situation in which they found themselves, and more could be said about the differences between them. But just as I am stressing that Curtis was not unique – or even exceptional – in his position, in that, as he saw, many aspects of the salvage ethnology of the time helped to "break down" Native American cultures, I believe it is more appropriate to emphasize not the special nature of their experience, but its characteristic *ordinariness.* Upshaw, Hunt, and Day wished *both* to contribute to a significant study of the Native American culture with which they identified *and* to honor the laws, customs, and traditions of that culture; they were – in their very typicality – representative figures. They simply had to wrest the best they could from an always unequal relationship. But it is to their own credit as individuals that they did this so well.

Further Implications of Transcultural Trading

The irony just mentioned – the project's stress on memorialization of traditional, "pre-contact" cultures even when its own activities could be seen as agents of destruction for such cultures – constitutes an aspect of a more encompassing issue: Clearly, as has been asserted here from the Introduction onwards, for Curtis and similar figures of his time the "preservation" of Native American cultures took the form of the production of *representations* – well-bound books, fine photographs, vivid films – rather than efforts to ensure the living continuity of tradition or, sometimes, even of the people themselves. A particularly grotesque affirmation of this may be found in an early newspaper celebration of Curtis's accomplishments:

> The American Indian fought, weakened, and vanished. Instead of the painted features . . . we find him in [the] blue jeans . . . of semi-civilization. Enshrined though he may be with the weird habits and mysterious rites of his forefathers, the mystery has vanished and the romance has gone in the actuality of the present day. . . . And so . . . Curtis . . . found him. For the time being Curtis became an "Indian". . . . The best years of his life were spent . . . among the Indians. He dug up tribal customs. He unearthed the fantastic costumes. . . . He took the present lowness . . . and enshrined it in the romance of the past. He builded even better than he knew, for, with a byronic flight of imagination, he changed the degenerated Indian of today into the fancy free king of yesterday. . . . He has picked up a bundle of broken straws and erected a palace of accuracy and fact. . . . He has caught the redskin, as it were, in a flashlight of fancy; has transplanted him from his wildwood haunts into the art galleries of Gotham. . . . Curtis isn't a photographer. He is an artist. . . . [29]

One reason for such sentiments – including the usually less strident formulations of them that we have seen emanating from the North American Indian project itself – is, of course, the pervasiveness of the concomitant conviction (implicit here too) that the demise of such cultures was absolutely inevitable. Given such a view, that nothing could save them *as* cultures, representations were considered the best that could be achieved.

There is in all this, obviously, a profound Eurocentrism. Indeed, there is a sense in which traditional Native American cultures were revered not so much for their intrinsic values as for what, in a worldview subservient to the idea of Progress, they might reveal about the "past" of the dominant culture. In the case of the North American Indian project, this notion lies behind the repeated use of "primitive" in the titling of such images as "Primitive Mohave" (1907), "Primitive Dress – Quinault" (1912), and "The Primitive Artist – Paviotso" (1924), but it was most clearly embodied in the formation of another of the business enterprises in which Curtis was a prime mover: The Modern Historic Records Association.

This short-lived and almost oxymoronically-named organization, which was not a definite corporation and may have had charitable status, offered its members "authentic" records of the past, and on at least one occasion this consisted of a Curtis Indian photogravure. On the verso of one copy of "The Oath – Apsaroke" (1908), published by the association in 1913, Curtis inscribed the following in his own hand:

> The American Indian [offers the] best opportunity to study primitive man as a living human document of supreme importance. His life history in its evolution of thousands of years is a unique story of beginnings early stages and developments in language, customs, manners and institutions. The complete scientific study of this subject seems a natural and important duty of the Modern Historic Records Association. The rapid changes make quick action essential. It cannot be deferred if it is to be done at all. For this work there is no tomorrow.

Native-American author Michael Dorris has correctly characterized the attitude behind such opinions as one in which the Indian is seen not "on a human being to human being basis, but . . . through an ancestor-descendant model"; "Indians," he said, "though obviously contemporary with their observers, were somehow regarded as ancient, as examples of what Stone Age Europeans were like."[30] In the minds of those holding this attitude it was precisely *as* such representations that Indians had their fullest meaning and, possibly, being.

In a further twist to this tangle of ideas, despite the importance of representations in the sense just described, the Curtis project, as we have observed, characteristically placed the emphasis on making a record – indeed, *the* record – of Indian life. That is, Curtis frequently presented his work as offering an apprehension of preexisting reality rather than what it was, the *construction* of a record. In this, to be fair, the North American Indian enterprise shared much with other anthropological activities of that time, and since. The record as we have it, written and/or visual, constitutes, of course, text. The original enactment of, say, a ceremony is not seen as text by its participants but becomes so when the subject of ethnography. In other words, if for the North American Indian project the preservation of traditional cultural phenomena – such as Kwakiutl seafaring ways, the Navajo Yebichai ceremony, or Mandan sacred artifacts and their lore – typically took the form of representation rather than the maintenance or fostering of living practices, the same could be said of most other anthropological endeavors. As an individualistic yet corporate enterprise obliged to appeal for funds in the market place (in ways to be explored in the following chapter), the North American Indian project may have been different in *degree* to the emergent academic anthropology of the period, but not in kind. Clearly, this is a topic to which we must return.

DOCUMENTS

Document 3A. Extract from "Edward S. Curtis: Photo-Historian of the North American," 1903.

The following portion of a newspaper account, replete with racist wisecracks, was based at least partly on interview comments by Curtis himself and appeared in *The Seattle Sunday Times.*[31]

> But before Curtis enters the smoke-begrimmed [sic] domicile of the medicine man he passes through the village, giving a nod here, a handshake there, candy to the babies, silk and calico to the squaws; and after he has chucked a few of the youngsters under the chin and made himself a good fellow generally, he subdues the government agent in charge of the reservation, peels his coat and begins business. . . . [32] One time down in Arizona he engaged a Moki [Hopi] boy, a mighty bright youngster, to act as his interpreter. . . . While they were working among the Apaches this lad was a host in himself. For instance, he would say in reply to a suggestion by Mr. Curtis: "Um, no brudder. Me no hire pony for $1. We git him two bits." And it was "Me no

hire Injun to pose for $2. Me get him 10 cents." And so Curtis got his Apache photos for about a quarter of the price he expected to pay for them.

But what a difference once they entered the Moki's own country. For example, Mr. Curtis would say this to his interpreter: "Now, Charley, you offer this bunch of Indians 50 cents a head if they will pose for me." And Charley would turn to his brothers and cousins and say in his native tongue: "This man says he won't take your pictures unless you charge him $5 apiece, and I think you are big damn fools if you let him off that easy." Charley would then turn to Curtis and say: "Red brudder no savey 50 cents. Want ten dolla'." "Now, see here, Charley," Curtis would say severely, "you're lying to me." "Uh! Me no savey lie. You no like Charley's way doin' business, talk to 'em yousel'. Ugh!" And Mr. Curtis was up against the real thing from Arizona.[33]

But according to the California Camera Club, a bunch of rank amateurs, Mr. Curtis has ruined the field from their standpoint. They sometimes go among the Southern California Indians and want them to pose for pictures. It is then that the ruination business develops nicely in the sun of understanding. Drawing himself up, Mr. Indian says: "Ugh! Brudder Curtis he give Charley t'ree dolla'. Me no savey cheap."

Document 3B. Newspaper Report by Edmond S. Meany, 1907[34]

WOUNDED KNEE, S. D., Saturday, Aug. 10 – The E. S. Curtis Indian expedition has moved from Pine Ridge to this interesting locality, where the great Sioux Nation made its last stand against the swarming white men who had driven away the buffaloes and taken the lands of the Indians. Only a few miles from the camp is the field of the Battle of Wounded Knee. Around the camp are many warriors who took part in that battle and a few survivors of the greater Custer battle, while most of the older men count their inter-tribal contests by the tens and twenties.

Two years ago Mr. Curtis had a few of these Ogalalas on a special trip into the Bad Lands, when among others he obtained the famous picture known as "The Oasis" [sic], showing Chief Red Hawk watering his horse at a small pond in the midst of the desert. At that time Mr. Curtis promised his Indian friends that he would come back and give them a feast in return for which they would reproduce for him an old-time Sioux camp from which should be excluded all the new clothes obtained from the white people.

The chief who stood sponsor for the success of the undertaking was the same Red Hawk who figures in "The Oasis." On arrival here it was found that Chief Slow Bull, cooperating with Red Hawk, had erected a huge scalp tipi for the councils between Mr. Curtis and the Indian chiefs and head men. This tipi is in itself a beautiful exhibit of the old life of the Sioux. It is held aloft by twenty-five long slender lodge poles. One of the poles is about five feet longer than the others, and from its tip floats in the air a large black scalp. It is in reality a horse's tail, but so arranged as to closely resemble the scalp from a woman's head. Around the sides of the tipi are arranged with perfect grace and beauty according to aboriginal standards, about fifty scalps, while all the fastenings are polished rods of cherry wood and clever imitations of snake rattles.

The first evening Mr. Curtis was sent for, and as he entered the tipi he found the council assembled. The place of honor at the back of the tipi, facing the entrance, was saved for him, and soon, through Interpreter John Monroe, he had explained the object of his visit and read from letters how much interest President Roosevelt and Commissioner Francis E. Leupp had manifested in this effort to save a record of the true old Indian life. There was a chorus of "Hows" and then Chief Red Hawk talked in a friendly way about the long time they had waited for Pazhola Washte (Pretty Butte), the Sioux name for Curtis. Their hearts were all glad because he had come at last with the promised feast.

Then Iron Crow waved for the interpreter and relieved his mind of a speech, the main part of which was that there were more than 300 Indians assembled and the two beeves promised would not make much of a feast and if Curtis was a brave man he would give four beeves. An adroit answer about a good feast and all being happy restored good feeling and then Big Road, the young chief of the Wounded Knee district, arose and made a fine speech about the respect for white men who did what they promised.

The writer was then introduced . . . and told the Indians how much interest the white people all over the country were manifesting in this work of Mr. Curtis, and how, after many snows [and] we are all dead the children who grew up would look at the pictures and read the words and learn the truth about the American Indians. "Hows" and applause showed that they entered into the spirit of the work.

Figure 10. Vash Gon – Jicarilla, 1904, by E. S. Curtis.
Note the accentuation of this image at the printing and gravure stages.

4

HUSTLING THE EMINENT

The role of professional photographer in Curtis's time – especially that of the portrait maker – inevitably involved frequent searches for clients and patronage. In Curtis's case, because of his commitment to the Indian project, the quest was intense and unceasing. Thus, supposedly "at the request of several of his friends,"as the invitation phrased it, Curtis "consented to give an exhibit and description of his Indian photography at [Seattle's] Christensen's Hall" on December 2, 1904. The "friends" included Judge Thomas Burke, who introduced him; Joseph Blethen, a son of the owner of *The Seattle Times,* Alden J. Blethen; and a number of Seattle notables. At the beginning of the same year, Curtis's true friend, Edmond S. Meany of the University of Washington, joined with others, including Professor of Mining Engineering Milner Roberts, one of Frederick Webb Hodge's companions on his 1898 ascent of the Acoma Enchanted Mesa, to try to persuade the University – in exchange for the permanent acquisition of the pictures – to pay for the framing of two hundred of Curtis's photographs ready for showing at the St. Louis World's Fair. And the following year Curtis's successful exhibition of photographs at the New York Waldorf-Astoria was put on "under the patronage" of Mr. and Mrs. E. H. Harriman, his employers during the Alaska Expedition; Corinne Roosevelt Robinson, the president 's sister; George Bird Grinnell; H. C. Bumpus of the American Museum of Natural History; Mrs. Richard Watson Gilder, wife of the editor of *Century* magazine; and several other leading figures from New York society.[1]

It might be thought that once Curtis had won over the notoriously obdurate – and flagrantly wealthy – J. Pierpont Morgan and was enjoying his patronage to the extent of fifteen thousand dollars each year, a sum for fieldwork which was the envy of certain professional ethnologists of the period, his need to hustle for patronage would end. But it was not to be. The 1906 agreement with Morgan was not, in fact, as munificent as it seemed in that it exacted, in true Morgan fashion, a heavy obligation from Curtis: He was to publish the expensively produced volumes and be responsible for their sale, on a limited edition subscription basis, *out of his own funds.* That is, the high printing costs of producing a lavishly illustrated series of books on the very best paper was to come out of the sale of subscriptions at the then staggering (and still now large) sums of $3,000 per set (or $150 per volume) if printed on Van Gelder paper and $3,850 per set (or $192 per volume) if printed on Japanese tissue. Moreover, these prices rose, with costs, over the years, until in 1924 the Van Gelder set sold for $4,200 and the Japanese tissue for $4,700. Curtis was put on a kind of treadmill of constantly having to try to raise the cash to pay for the publication – and Morgan's employees, such as C. W. King, the accountant Curtis dealt with in the early years, were ever watchful in his interest.[2]

Subscriptions – and, of course, potential subscribers – were seen as the principal means of deliverance. But the building of a subscription list took time and Curtis had major financial problems almost immediately. The severe depression of 1907 caused printers and engravers to demand their money and his own bankers refused to service the large loans he had taken out to tide him over. For a time it looked as if *The North American Indian* might have to cease publication even before it had established itself.[3]

In the hope that his energetic and popular friend Meany could persuade some Seattle businessmen to lend him $20,000 to meet his publication bills, Curtis wrote him a series of desperate letters through the late summer and autumn of 1907. Out on the plains, he and his field team struggled to collect final data, then to write up Volumes 3 and 4, and matters were further complicated by the severe illness from typhoid of Harold, Curtis's young son, and what Curtis saw as the laziness and incompetence of C. H. Levin, an assistant he had taken on to replace the absent Phillips. Then, in a long and virtually unpunctuated outpouring of August 20, 1907, Curtis reported, "I am tied up here [Cheyenne Agency] for the present but now hope Hal can be moved to gettasburg [sic] in a week if so I can then go on and take up my work – the boys started work yesterday I did not get money to start them on till then," before elaborating at length on the reasons why he was reluctant to let the negatives and manuscripts of *The North American Indian* be stored permanently at the University of Washington. Clearly, Meany wanted a commitment to this effect from Curtis as part of the security for the loans and promissory notes he was arranging.[4]

"I am not yet so far out of the woods with the publication but that it may be necessary," Curtis continued, "to make some big move which might include the final ownership of field material." "You see," he claimed, "I am in the position of an unknown man trying by sheer bull dog determination to carry through a thing so large that no-one else cared to tackle it." After expressing a series of similar worries, Curtis raged against Levin: "I shall let him go back early in October. I cannot stand him this is no baby job he is a spoiled calf I am mighty sorry I had hoped he could make good I have reached the point where I cannot have him in my sight. . . . " The stress was, he knew, destabilizing him: "Yes I will try to cheer up but when I think of some of the Seattle bunch I go mad." And in his next letter, of September 4, despite admitting that he "likely needed the rest" that – enforced by circumstances – he had just had and that he would, in the future, "try not to be childish," he reiterated in the same tones much of the preceding letter, adding "your good words in regard to the work . . . are about the only [ones] that I have had from any one in many weeks." It seems that even Phillips had lost faith; Curtis quoted Phillips's letters as saying: "'you are insanely optimistic,'" "'I don't think you can succeed in getting through,'" and so on for "30 typewritten pages." "If you hear any one say I am not to succeed," he admonished Meany, "tell them they don't know me." "I am not going to fail and the sooner the whole 'Damn Family' know it the better," he asserted. "Remember I am doing the best I can and keeping 17 helpers from having cold feet and at the same time get together something over forty five hundred dollars a month to pay the bills." Then, without a pause, he added: "ask the studio for a new prospectus."[5]

Meany's success in his persuasive efforts must have brought much peace of mind to Curtis, for by the end of October he was simply sending straightforward instructions about the placing of promissory notes. By January 1908 he followed these requests with such tongue-in-cheek comments as, "I suppose I could on a pinch pull through March without this [activation of one of twenty notes], but it is going to leave me in an uncomfortably cramped condition if I do, and I find it rather hard to do good work on the books and puzzle over how I am going to pay my bills at the same time." By June 1908 he was presenting some volumes of *The North American Indian* to the University of Washington Library "in the name of" the figures from whom Meany had raised loans on his behalf.[6]

Hodge always had to ask Curtis for his editorial payments several times, but it is clear from the tone of one of Curtis's responses that towards the end of 1908, despite everything, Curtis was able to undertake further fieldwork in the Southwest and a sense of confidence was returning to the project. "Seeing you are inclined to be funny about money matters I shall presume that you do not need any for six months," he quipped, "as to mortgaging the studio on your account, have no fear of my doing that, for the simple reason that like everything else I have or expect to have [it] now bears more mortgages than is comfortable to contemplate." "If I had an earthly thing that was not mortgaged," he added, "I would immediately start out to find some one to loan me a few dollars on it right here in Santa Fe." Curtis ended the letter with a disarmingly insensitive or mischievous reference to Hodge's newly acquired financial responsibilities: "I will be in Seattle during most of October, and when you need a few hundred dollars to buy the baby's shoes with let me know."[7]

Paradoxically, some of Curtis's ease of mind was secured on the national stage by the very person with whom he had made his own hard bargain, J. Pierpont Morgan, who acted to allay the panic which gripped financial institutions at that time. Curtis could claim to speak, as he put it, for "millions" – and truly did speak for himself – when he thanked his powerful patron for his interventions: "you saved the country when no one else could." Not surprisingly, despite the exacting conditions of his agreement with the financier, Curtis sought to renew it when it was due to lapse in 1910. And, as Curtis was pleased to inform his subscribers, Morgan did agree to advance a further $60,000.[8]

This time, however, the agreement was not with Curtis as such, but with The North American Indian, Incorporated. And The North American Indian, Inc., according to its records retained by the Morgan Company, was essentially a small subsidiary to the Morgan Trust, with most of its shares owned by J. Pierpont Morgan, soon to be succeeded by his son J. (Jack) P. Morgan. Its funds were held by the Morgan Bank; its affairs were run either by former Morgan employees, notably Lewis Albert, or actual Morgan employees, such as Edward S. Pegram; and its meetings were held at the law offices of Robert Clark Morris, the man who probably acted as Curtis's first link to the financier. Moreover, each shortfall experienced by Curtis was as likely as not to lead to a further appeal to Morgan interests, often through

Pegram, who as the first treasurer of the North American Indian, Inc., was able between 1911 and 1915 to get Morgan's agreement to loans of up to $20,000 each (later rising to $30,000 each) to cover expenses in the field. The arrangement also led to The North American Indian office exerting some control over the movements of Curtis and other fieldworkers, including one occasion in 1925 when Myers was specifically forbidden to travel East to discuss with Hodge volumes then in press.[9]

Other financial requests went through Belle de Costa Greene, J. Pierpont's trusted librarian and general book purchaser, who was also directly responsible for the distribution of the twenty-five sets of *The North American Indian* which Morgan always received as part of his return from his investment in the project. In 1914, writing from Port Hardy in British Columbia, and clearly downed by exhaustion, Curtis entered into a very intense correspondence with her over his supposed "extravagance." He claimed that an extraordinary amount had been achieved in relation to the funds available and enclosed an "extract from [the] annual report of January, 1913" in support of the contention. He almost begged for her understanding, declaring: "Practically, the only desire of my life is to carry this work on and complete it in a way which will be of the greatest possible credit to Mr. Morgan's name; but to do this it is necessary that I have the hearty sympathy of those on the inside of our organization. . . ." Unfortunately, when such appeals were successful, as this one proved, if with little grace on Greene's part, Curtis would be made to pass over more of his rights in exchange; for example, between 1923 and 1928, in a succession of legal documents, he relinquished copyright in all the pictures published in *The North American Indian.*[10] But by then he was a chronic debtor.

Selling Subscriptions

The primary means of avoiding shortfalls was to sell subscriptions. But this was no easy task. Curtis spent many arduous winters devoted to it. From time to time he also employed experienced salesmen in the effort; one such, William Dinwiddie, he described as "so constantly on the go" that he was "about one hundred percent harder to catch than a California flea." Only the wealthiest individuals could afford to pay the level of subscription demanded, and it was obviously a long term commitment. Creating opportunities to speak directly to potential subscribers about the project – in effect, to buttonhole them – was one of the most difficult phases of the operation. A variety of stratagems were brought into play, from mounting exhibitions in prestigious venues like the Waldorf-Astoria, through delivering stereopticon lectures under the sponsorship of exclusive clubs like the Cosmos or the Century, to attendance at upper-crust social occasions: musical evenings, balls, and, in particular, men's dinner parties. In 1910, for instance, Curtis virtually invited himself to the National Geographic Society's annual banquet.[11]

The single most effective means of securing the desired meetings was through letters of introduction written by figures who were already pivotal in these well-blessed circles. One such was the independently wealthy Gifford Pinchot, a Curtis supporter from Harriman Alaska days. Another was Mrs. Douglas Robinson, the president's sister Corinne. Pinchot, who sponsored Curtis's exhibition at the Cosmos Club, wrote many letters of introduction: to Oliver La Farge, son of artist John La Farge and a person who would himself become an authority on Indians; to Anson Phelps Stokes, the secretary of Yale; to George W. Vanderbilt, the wealthy "amateur" stock breeder and forester with whom Pinchot himself had worked prior to his appointment as Roosevelt's U.S. Forester; and to numerous others. Indeed, when the publicity for the Sioux volume of *The North American Indian* caused a stir by calling into question General George A. Custer's military and moral judgment, Mrs. Elizabeth Custer complained to Pinchot about Curtis as "the man . . . for whom you have made so many friends."[12]

In one of his letters to the patrician Pinchot, Curtis confessed, "I am hustling like a good fellow, and matters seem to be going very well. Mrs. Douglas Robinson has been doing a great deal to help the cause." She had. For instance, when Nicholas Murray Butler, the president of Columbia University, wrote to Curtis in January 1906, he specifically said, "At the suggestion of Mrs. Douglas Robinson, I telephoned yesterday to the hotel, hoping to have a talk with you about your work." It is not surprising that when Curtis came to inform Mrs. Robinson in December 1909 of Morgan's further sixty thousand dollars "to strengthen the cause," he added, "I wish I had words to express to you just how I feel about this. If it had not been for your splendid help in this 'Indian' work, whatever it may be worthy of to future generations, would have been impossible."[13]

And just as in the same letter Curtis went on to shower his benefactor with good wishes – "My every thought for you is almost a prayer that your year abroad will give you rest and happiness" – he was inclined to fulsome praise of many others who supported him. New subscribers would receive letters of thanks, almost of congratulation, which in expression assumed an ongoing relationship. To E. Francis Riggs, retired banker, Curtis affirmed "that every effort of my life will be to make the work one that will in every way justify the encouragement and assistance of my friends," and to C. B. Boothe, after saying something similar, he added, "One great satisfaction in the work is the personal acquaintance of the majority of the subscribers." These letters of thanks were also used to deepen the individual subscriber's knowledge of both the publication and the person credited with its making; the recipient could well feel thoroughly involved in the project's ups and downs. The following letter, received by the railroad financier Henry E. Huntington in 1911, was typical – or, rather, even more gushing in its entirety than this extract can show:

> The publication of these three volumes [6, 7, and 8] is a source of much personal happiness and satisfaction. Each volume . . . brings me that much closer to the goal set for myself, and the fruition of my life ambition. . . .
>
> As to the three volumes, they contain a great variety and quantity of material. Much of this has been in hand for some years. It is, in fact, fourteen years since I began the collecting of parts of the material contained in this installment of volumes. And in placing them in your hands, I can only hope that you will get a small fraction of the pleasure in their possession that has been mine in their making.
>
> As to the cause as a whole, I am glad to be able to report that steady progress is being made, and that the interest in the work and enthusiasm for it is on the constant increase, and I desire to take this opportunity to once more thank you for your assistance to the undertaking.[14]

Mrs. J. B. Montgomery helped Curtis try to sell subscriptions in Portland; later he wrote to tell her of some successes in Los Angeles, saying "so you see everything goes well with the work – I fear you felt a bit discouraged with our effort in Portland but I cannot see that we should, for [with] the chances we had we certainly did as well as we had a right to expect." It was, as he told her, "a large matter and takes time." A few months later, he confided in her again: "I know that you will be more than pleased that Mr. Pinchot has bought the work for Yale library. Someone else might have bought it for them, but you and I are glad that it was Mr. Pinchot who did it." "He has been very good to me," Curtis added, "and helpful in many ways."[15]

Subscribers were also *urged* to be "helpful" in different ways. In March 1906 Curtis offered Pinchot and others a bronze bas-relief costing $75 sculpted by Alfred Lenz from his own 1904 photograph of Vash Gon, the Jicarilla chief (fig. 10). (Pinchot declined.) In 1911 he was able to suggest the purchase of a wooden case that he had designed specially to house *The North American Indian* volumes in either oak ($100) or mahogany ($125). (Roosevelt, for one, claimed, after some prevarication, that he couldn't find room for such a case.) Later in the same year Curtis requested the honor of having various subscribers act as "patrons" of specific appearances he was to make on a major lecture tour. Roosevelt, for his part, agreed that his name could appear on the Honorary List for Curtis's New York City lecture. In 1912 certain subscribers were approached with the suggestion that they might consider subscribing also to a related venture, the Modern Historic Records Association, which at least once offered its members a Curtis Indian gravure.[16]

Often, as might be expected, subscribers to what was, after all, a part work, were urged to consider the benefits of converting from payments as they received volumes to a kind of paid-up status. Also, some subscribers to the less expensive form of the publication were asked if they would like to change over to the Japanese tissue version. Huntington, on one occasion in 1909, received both suggestions in the same letter.[17]

All subscribers were encouraged to publicize the project and seek out further new subscribers. This might take the form of a signed letter of commendation which Curtis would use in a series of prospectuses about *The North American Indian* which issued from his New York office in the early years. In his request to Pinchot, for example, Curtis said, "you might hesitate to speak in regard to the ethnographic value of the work, but you cannot incriminate yourself by speaking enthusiastically of the pictorial and general value . . . find a few points that you can rave about a little bit, and that will help me beautifully." "I am trying," he concluded, to carry the book-buyer "clear off his feet." Among the subscribers who supplied the required rave notices were Huntington, General A. W. Greely, who was chief signal officer of the army, and Pinchot; their comments were printed among ones from such other figures as Grinnell, Merriam, Gilbert Grosvenor of the National Geographic Society, and Commissioner of Indian Affairs Leupp. Another way of asking subscribers to find others was by issuing them with special nomination forms on which they could provide details of likely contacts. In turn, with the intention of retaining their loyalty and interest, subscribers would receive regular information about the project – commendations of new volumes, announcements of Curtis lectures, occasional gifts of unbound photographs or gravures, especially of the project's camps (see fig. 11), and copies of what Curtis called "supplementary readers," his two short books *Indians of the Long Ago* (1914) and *In the Land of the Head-Hunters* (1915).[18]

Most effective of all, probably, was Curtis's successful presentation of his own image as that of an archetypal westerner. From very early on the photographic portrait usually chosen to accompany articles about the project was what he later called "the standard publicity picture" of himself in "field costume," wearing a very jaunty, wide-brimmed western hat (see fig. 14). Despite the fact that – willingly or not – he spent much of his time in the East, he would often write to subscribers as if he was uncomfortable in "civilized" surroundings and keen to be off into the wilds. To C. Hart Merriam in 1908, for instance, after thanking him for a letter of commendation, he wrote: "I shall get away for the West in a few days now. I am getting more than tired of this grind here in New York, and want to be in camp with the Indians."[19]

This image was given full rein by Curtis's knack of sending all subscribers what would now be called personalized form letters, relaying at some length, often in dramatic terms, his "adventures" in the field. A quintessential example was his 1909 account of a time among Plateau and Plains peoples when his party was in fact joined by one of his patrons, Ambassador Jean Jules Jusserand of France, the scholar-diplomat who later agreed to lend his name to a Curtis lecture in Washington, D.C. Amidst a detailed record of the work of various field parties, especially his own on the Colville Reservation in eastern Washington, he presented this moment in which picture-making, trading, appropriation, and hustling were all implicitly fused:

> While the party was encamped . . . , I made a hurried trip to Montana to bring together a group of the Crows to entertain Ambassador and Mrs. Jusserand [during] their long western tour. . . . News of the Ambassador's coming had already reached them, and they were encamped on Pryor Creek in a splendid circle of about a hundred lodges. Mr. Jusserand arrived a couple of days later, the party making the trip from the railroad, thirty miles away, in automobiles. The Indians came out across the plains to meet us – hundreds of them in old-time war costume consisting mostly of paint and noise, making a picture which no

member of our party will soon forget. Night found us again at the railroad, the Ambassador and his party en route to the East, and I on my way to camp.[20]

It was a moment which was in fact more orchestrated by Curtis than his account allowed. In a letter to the commissioner for Indian Affairs he admitted that to grant Jusserand "at least a slight glimpse of the Western Plains Indian" he had decided "to do what [he] could to please him" by inviting the Crows at Pryor Creek to entertain him. "I, of course, asked [the Agent] for permission to do this," Curtis added, "explaining that I would write you . . . and assume all responsibility in the matter." "I furnished Beef and Provisions for the Indians so that they had a splendid feast and a very good time," he continued, "and think they were better off for having had the pleasure of meeting the Ambassador and showing him what the Plains Indians were like." In his response, Acting Commissioner F. H. Abbott wrote that while there were no grounds to object to such a course of action, the "ambition" of the bureau was to "so transform the Indian that he will in the near future cease to be an object of interest to the curiosity seeker and the ethnological student because of his peculiar racial habits and customs." "But the Crows," he added, "have not attained that desirable status."[21]

Sometimes Curtis was able to propose a straightforward commercial arrangement, as he did when he asked J. J. Hill for a loan of $15,000 dollars for which the Northern Pacific Railroad would have been entitled to receive "considerable advertising in connection with Indian pictures." Hill declined. Certain very special subscribers – notably friendly ones and extremely rich ones with philanthropic inclinations towards the arts – were asked to go much further in support than the generality of their fellows. Pinchot, certainly a good friend to Curtis and to the project, was entreated for a loan of $7,000 to meet field expenses during the summer of 1905. This, of course, preceded the arrangements made with Morgan, but in any case, saying he was "simply not in a position to take the matter up," Pinchot declined. In June 1915, however, he did agree to lend Curtis $1,000, to be repaid at the end of the year. The following February Pinchot had not been reimbursed, and it was only after a series of reminders that he received $800 of the debt in May 1916. He never did see the return of the other $200, despite further requests, and the "friendship" came to an end after G. W. Woodruff, one of Pinchot's advisers, made one last – and unsuccessful – attempt to secure the money in January 1920.[22]

While in his 1911 appeal to Henry E. Huntington for a loan of $10,000 for two years, Curtis said, "I appreciate that it is a mighty shabby thing to do, to appeal to one's friends for a loan," friendship was not actually at stake as it was in the case of Pinchot. What was proposed, in fact, was a relatively straightforward transaction in which Huntington would advance the money against the security of $20,000 worth of Curtis's own common stock in The North American Indian, Inc. As it happened, despite full disclosures by Curtis of the financial soundness of the company, Huntington did not respond. Curtis's requests for such assistance always offered as the rationale the exigencies of "the work"; in the letter to Huntington he actually admitted, "had I not at several times imposed on the good natures of my friends, 'The North American Indian' would have died almost before its birth."[23] Instead, certain relationships died.

Securing Scientific Endorsement

In their efforts to secure subscriptions to *The North American Indian* from institutions – museums, colleges, libraries, etc. – Curtis and his associates adopted and adapted a similar array of tactics to those they employed in the cases of rich individual subscribers. In response to Curtis's request for "a little something from some of [his] western friends," for instance, Dr. Stuart Penrose, the president of Whitman College, Walla Walla, Washington, supplied a letter of commendation aimed at both individuals and libraries, saying, "The effort to secure all possible records now is one for which the Scientist, Anthropologist, the Historian and the Artist must be grateful."[24]

One of the "scientists" pressed into expressing his gratitude was Merriam, leader of the Harriman Expedition and distinguished in government circles. He in turn deepened relationships and helped make contacts elsewhere. In 1908, for example, Curtis told him, "Relative to our last few words in regard to a possible subscription by the Geographical Society, I believe if you take this matter up with Mr. Grosvenor . . . it can be carried through"; and, presumably through Merriam's efforts, the National Geographic Society did become a subscriber, helping to fulfill Curtis's hopes, as he put them to Merriam, that there "certainly should be a few sets in Washington, D.C." Earlier, in April 1906, Curtis wrote to Merriam from the Waldorf-Astoria, telling him that he was shortly off to Seattle, then the Southwest, via San Francisco:

> While in Boston I had several splendid talks with Prof. Putnam. He is most enthusiastic over the work and very encouraging. In fact, I found the men at Harvard more than enthusiastic, and nothing has encouraged me more than their interest in the work. Prof. Putnam has expressed a desire that I meet some of the California men, and I thought it possible if you were going to San Francisco . . . I would try to arrange that we get a number of the men together. Perhaps we could have a glass of beer and a sandwich.

Whether this proposed meeting came off or not, Frederick Ward Putnam, the archaeologist and anthropologist, certainly did commend the work, and in general the campaign to raise subscriptions from institutions relied heavily upon building and boosting the scientific credibility of *The North American Indian.*[25]

For this reason, much energy was expended attempting to achieve the backing of the nation's premier scientific establishment, the Smithsonian Institution. Prior to the Morgan agreement, the Smithsonian, as has been shown, was approached for actual funding, and in the planning stage, as has also been demonstrated, Charles D. Walcott, the secretary of the Smithsonian, was asked to serve on the editorial staff of *The North American Indian.* In the early days of the publication, both Curtis and William Dinwiddie, the New York Office manager and a former employee of the institution's Bureau of American Ethnology, made strenuous efforts to sell a subscription to the institution. When Curtis reported the Morgan arrangement to Matilda Coxe Stevenson of the Bureau of American Ethnology he said, "This, of course, does away with the necessity of getting this matter before the Government with a view of their buying a set of the pictures for the National Museum. However, it is only a question of time when the Museum should have such a set." "In the near future," he added, "I shall be in Washington, and will then talk over the matter with my friends there the thought of a set being purchased for the Museum regardless of Mr. Morgan's part in the work." Curtis and Dinwiddie did talk over the matter with one "friend," Charles Walcott, repeatedly, but – despite Hodge's backing from within the institution – to no avail.[26]

Over the years Curtis would report to Walcott on the progress of the work, sometimes using the same form letters that he sent to actual subscribers (such as the description of fieldwork in 1909, including Ambassador Jusserand's visit to Crow country), and he would also send gifts of photographs. Thus the secretary even received the archly romantic "Signal Fire to the Mountain God" (1909) *twice.* But no progress occurred until, as a result of orchestrated urgings by both Curtis and Walcott, Mrs. E. H. Harriman took out a subscription on behalf of the Smithsonian in April 1911. Sure enough, from then on Walcott and the Smithsonian seem to have given their blessing to the project, with Walcott, for instance, acting as another of Curtis's Washington patrons during his major lecture tour of 1911–12.[27]

A particularly effective means of demonstrating scientific backing for "the cause," as Curtis often put it, was to exhibit the Indian photographs under the auspices – and, often, in the premises – of notable institutions. Thus, to give a few examples only, in September 1906 Curtis offered to put on an "afternoon's informal exhibition" at the University of Pennsylvania Museum the following spring. Later in the year, with some misgivings, he agreed to let the Bureau of Indian Affairs – on which government department, of course, he was dependent for permission to work on reservations – exhibit a selection of his photographs at the Jamestown Exposition of 1907. His worries proved justified in that the bureau failed to reimburse him for the full cost of the framing – though he was given a diploma! – and the experience made him reluctant to participate in the 1911 Turin International Exposition under the bureau 's auspices. On this second occasion, however, involvement certainly proved worthwhile, in that the work received an overseas showing and Curtis himself was awarded a photographic *grand prix.* In 1908, despite having failed to secure its subscription in 1907, Curtis was pleased to have a large two-month exhibition put on in Madison at the prestigious Wisconsin State Historical Society, then under the direction of the *doyen* of Western history promoters, Reuben Gold Thwaites. In 1912 some of his pictures were "placed" with appropriate artifacts in the halls of the largest ethnological collection of all, the American Museum of Natural History in New York City – an honor repeated in 1916. In 1914 Edgar Hewett offered Curtis the possibility of a show in either the Arts and Crafts Building or the Ethnological Building at the massive San Diego Panama Pacific Exposition. And in 1924 – to conclude this round-up of typical exhibitions – *The North American Indian* work was displayed at the New Mexico State Historical Society, an occasion that was used to give formal thanks to Robert Clark Morris for his good offices in obtaining a subscription for the society.[28]

A further potent factor in demonstrating scientific backing for the project was the series of reviews by leading natural historians and writers, especially anthropologists, that Curtis, often in concert with

Hodge (also editor of the *American Anthropologist*), was able to line up. Grinnell, presumably of his own volition, wrote laudatory comments on Curtis's work in a 1905 article, illustrated by Curtis photographs, for *Scribner's*. Perhaps partly prompted by the success of that piece, Curtis wanted Grinnell to review the first volumes of *The North American Indian* for the *American Anthropologist*. "I should like to do it," Grinnell told Hodge on April 24, 1908, "but am so absolutely driven with work, that I felt I must decline." Nevertheless, an enthusiastic unsigned notice of *The North American Indian* did appear a little later in Grinnell's own journal, *Forest & Stream*, perhaps from his own pen, and Curtis moved immediately to find someone else for the *Anthropologist*, suggesting either George Byron Gordon of the University of Pennsylvania or George Grant MacCurdy of Yale. Gordon, having been approached earlier for a general endorsement, responded to this particular request, composing a piece so judiciously fulsome that Curtis was able to send offprints to people he wanted to impress, such as Pinchot, Walcott, and Huntington.[29]

Curtis hoped to repeat the process with succeeding volumes, and in April 1909 he suggested William J. McGee, a former Director of the Bureau of American Ethnology, as an appropriate reviewer for the *Anthropologist* of Volumes 3, 4 and 5. McGee was a supporter of Curtis's work; indeed, in 1906 he had both commended Curtis's pictures to the Carnegie Museum and, while he had reported that "thus far, the way is not open for getting [them]," he had promised to join the movement to secure them also for the Smithsonian. Not surprisingly, though Curtis had to prod both McGee and Hodge about its production, when the review (of Volume 5 alone) appeared in the Autumn 1910 issue of the *Anthropologist*, it was one of unqualified praise and concluded with the hope that the first edition would be succeeded by "a more popular issue."[30]

A similar point, though he chose not to express it in his actual published review, lay at the back of the mind of the next chosen reviewer, Dr. H. F. C. ten Kate, the respected Dutch Americanist who was particularly interested in literary and visual depictions of Indians. Ten Kate, Hodge's friend since at least 1889, was probably approached as a result of Curtis's request to his editor, during the summer of 1909, that he try to find European reviewers. Certainly, by November of that year Curtis was able to forward Hodge a copy of a very laudatory letter ten Kate had sent him from Geneva. "You are doing a magnificent thing," the letter said, "building not only an everlasting monument to a vanishing race, but also to yourself. I am sure that if the Indians could realize the value and purpose of your work, and perhaps a few of them do, they would be grateful to you." "In fact," ten Kate continued, "viewed in a certain light, your work constitutes a redemption of the many wrongs our 'superior' race has done the Indian." And he went on to praise the writing as "masterly" and the photography as, without doubt, "art." The letter was so full of praise, in fact, that though in private ten Kate expressed some reservations to Hodge – "But who, except very rich people and big institutions will be able to buy these volumes? I am afraid you won't find many buyers in Europe" – it was determined by January 1910 that his full-blown review for the *Report of the Royal Netherlands Geological Society* (1910) should be reprinted in one of *The North American Indian* prospectuses and as a small brochure in its own right.[31]

The most elaborate puff of all came from Julian Hawthorne, writer Nathaniel's son and author, among innumerable other works, of *The Evergreen State from Early Dawn to Daylight* (1893), a boosting history of Washington, Curtis's adopted state. Hawthorne's essay was syndicated to papers throughout the nation in June 1911 and then printed as a pamphlet to advertise *The North American Indian.* It was so effusive that Curtis felt obliged to tone it down; as he wrote to Hodge when seeking advice and giving instructions about its production as a brochure, it "was considerably modified after . . . coming from Mr. Hawthorne . . . largely in the removal of superlatives and statements which might offend other workers." At the same time Curtis, of course, was equally capable of expressing gratitude in a manner appropriate to his supporter – that is, with all superlatives retained:

> My friends the Hopis have a fashion of placing prayer plumes at shrines and places where water springs from the bosom of the earth – and to them all sources of living water are, in fact, shrines – and the placing of the plumes, so they say, is as a visible offering to the gods, a constant sign of their faith. Thus as the Hopi makes his visible offering, do I send this picture as a token of my constant appreciation of your friendship and assistance to the cause of our "Record of a Vanishing Race". . . .[32]

Reassuring the Authorities

All round, Curtis was justified in his worries. On the one hand, the subscription arrangement and the huge sums of money which needed to be raised virtually dictated the existence of a continuous effort – or, better, campaign – to do so. Thus the (repeated) solicitation of public endorsements from national leaders, especially Roosevelt; thus the employment of Meany to write a supposedly independent piece on Curtis's adventures in the field ("Hunting Indians with a Camera") for *World's Work*; thus the collaboration between Curtis and Meany to secure financial and political assistance from Senator Levi Ankeny of Washington State; thus the similar cooperation, already mentioned, between Curtis and Lorenzo Hubbell to get the State of Arizona to subscribe; and thus the use of popular writers like Hawthorne.[35] On the other hand, "other workers" in the natural history field *were* sometimes "offended," some by Curtis's own lack of professional training, some out of envy of the financial resources the project could command for fieldwork, and some, understandably, by the campaign itself.

At the Smithsonian, for instance, as has been intimated, there were reservations. In one letter to Matilda Coxe Stevenson of May 1907, Curtis himself, in referring to talks with Walcott and William Henry Holmes, wrote, "I think that what I said placed the matter in such a light that . . . I hardly believe that any feeling of the kind that existed will reoccur [sic]." Whatever the precise nature of that "feeling" at the Smithsonian, similar uncertainties were initially apparent in some quarters at the American Museum of Natural History in New York, where in 1909 Curtis asked Clark Wissler, the esteemed anthropologist of various Plains peoples, to put in a "good word" for the purchase of *The North American Indian.* There though, Curtis had been fortunate to secure some sponsorship early on from H. C. Bumpus, the secretary, who acted as a patron of the Waldorf-Astoria exhibition, and he went on to win over the director, Henry Fairfield Osborn, who not only helped secure further funding from Morgan in 1910, as we saw in an earlier chapter, but undoubtedly influenced his institution's decision to subscribe. Osborn even personally introduced one of Curtis's New York City musicale performances in the fall of 1911. By 1913 Curtis was reporting to him almost on a regular basis, and readily displayed his discouragement:

> Business matters make it necessary that I start for the west at once. I have not been able to accomplish as much in securing new orders as I had hoped, and unless the rather unexpected should materialize there seems to be no possibility of any real field work this season. I will, however, continue my effort for

> funds for a few weeks, and if nothing comes of that I will give up thought of work this season and see what can be done for another year. For the past two years I have drawn so heavily on my slender resources that I have practically nothing left to further the cause. Still if there is no other way out I will try from personal affairs to secure enough for a month or so in the field. I must do this in order to finish Vol. 10 and get it ready for the press.

"I want to thank you most heartily for your interest," he concluded, "and should anything come up you can reach me through this [New York] office."[34]

By contrast, the opposition of George P. Winship, an authority on Coronado's Southwestern expeditions, to the book's acquisition by the John Carter Brown Library at Brown University incensed Curtis. "By the time I get through with the Southwest country," he told Hodge, "I will have so much to say that no library that presumes to be complete on Americana can refuse us," and he urged his editor to bring his influence to bear on the case. Similarly, a little later in 1907 he requested that Hodge use his good offices with three figures associated with the Field Museum in Chicago: Edward Ayer, wealthy collector, and anthropologists George Dorsey and Frederick Starr. In this case Curtis was on a hiding to nowhere: Though Ayer was relatively frank with him (he was, Curtis said, "skeptical as to what the text would be"), he had no intention of changing his mind. Years later, Ayer told Hodge – for whom he had much respect, and with whom his wife had worked on a 1901 English language translation of Alonso de Benavides's 1630 *Memorial* of his visit to the Southwest – "I assumed that Ex-President Roosevelt had asked you to edit this work. I knew that particular part of it would be ably done, but simply editing the Curtis writing, unless you entirely re-wrote it, . . . would not give an authentic history, so I have always turned it down."[35]

Curtis himself undoubtedly always sought the backing of "authorities." A typical instance was his attempt to secure Rockefeller support in 1914. "Feeling the great need of a brief word with you," he wrote to Osborn, "I telephoned to your secretary asking if she thought it possible for me to see you. Her word that you are at the point of starting for California answers my question. She was good enough, however, to suggest you would no doubt have time to read a brief letter." In this letter Curtis explained that, through the good offices of Corinne Robinson and Mrs. Bernard Berenson, the wife of the prominent art dealer and scholar, he had the chance to make a case during an interview with Dr. Abraham Flexner, the educator and Carnegie Foundation trustee, that he be allowed to put in for "an annual grant to further the field research." "Such a plan," he said, would require "the very strong commendation of a few who are in a position to speak with knowledge relative to the work." As well as "Walcott and others of the Smithsonian," this meant, of course, Osborn who, if the bid had been successful, would have been expected also to smooth things over with the premier patron, Morgan. If Curtis's reliance on Osborn was already clear, in this letter that sense of dependency was redoubled, almost tested. In response Osborn did dash off a letter, which Curtis could have used if and when he saw Flexner: "I have fully satisfied myself of the serious scientific spirit being carried out and the genuineness of the results."[36] But it seems that in this instance their efforts came to nothing.

To some extent, the hostility of figures like Ayer may have reflected the factionalism then rampant within the American anthropological world, with apologists for a more professional approach opposed to an "old guard" of data collectors and recorders whose "members," such as Holmes and, even, Frederick Ward Putnam, seem to have been more sympathetic to Curtis. Curtis himself, in memoirs recorded in later life, certainly felt that he was opposed by Franz Boas, professor of anthropology at Columbia and the acknowledged leader of the advocates of a more rigorous, scientific approach to race and other anthropological issues. While there is no documentary support for the existence of any particular dispute between Boas and Curtis over the anthropological authority of *The North American Indian*, on a couple of occasions Curtis certainly expressed suspicions of Boas to Hodge over matters unrelated to *The North American Indian*, and relied on Hodge's ability, revered both by Boas and his opponents, to stand above factional disputes. It is quite possible that different stories of animosity between these figures became conflated in the retelling.[37]

Essentially, in a curious reversal of employer/employee roles, Curtis counted on Hodge to vouch for the scientific credibility of the project. On one occasion, in 1907, Curtis clearly felt obliged to respond to intelligence Hodge had conveyed about the hostile views of certain authorities:

> As to the text being a rehash, every volume will speak for itself. As to whether I have been able to bring the material together in a satisfactory way, they must, at least in a measure, judge for

> themselves. It will not be necessary, of course, to explain to them that the work is not intended wholly for the scientific reader, but rather to make a lasting picture of the Indian, showing as much of the beautiful of his life as we can.

In a further irony – to come full circle – nowhere was the need to improve credibility greater than in the offices of The North American Indian, Inc., itself. Thus, in February 1914, Curtis hustled Hodge for complimentary letters about Volumes 9 and 10: "For some reason Mr. Pegram has apparently got it into his head that I did not keep up to standard [in Volume 9] . . . and I am particularly anxious just at this time to convince Pegram that the work is growing stronger rather than weaker, and if you can help me in this I will appreciate it very much." "My annual meeting [of The North American Indian, Inc.]," he added, "comes up on Tuesday of next week, so I need to have this quite soon. . . . " Hodge, as ever, complied.[38]

The Shaping Power of Patronage

In his 1911 report to subscribers (Doc. 4A), Curtis revealed some of the ways that the patronage under which the project proceeded conditioned its nature. *The North American Indian,* we find, was unashamedly aimed at leading members of the urban, Eastern business community: "You who have followed in the pathway of commerce and do not know the byways and nooks of nature," to whom central facts of normal life would be "Wall Street" and the "Stock Exchange." In keeping with the thesis associated with William Truettner's *The West as America* (as raised here in Chapter 1), it was made to appeal to such elites. Most obviously, while the work was being commended quite directly to "those of us who have crushed out most of his [the Indian's] life and are fast perpetrating extinction," in *The North American Indian* itself maltreatment of Indians by the dominant culture was to be downplayed: If white dealings with Indians had been, "in many cases, worse than a crime," nevertheless "the pages of this work [were] not to be taken up with a continual reiteration of their wrongs"; rather, where mention of the issue was deemed "necessary," it was being treated in an "unbiased" way. Indeed, much of "the apparent wrong" was just a working out of "the inevitable." In a sentence reminiscent of many self-justifying statements by men like Andrew Carnegie (with his notion that competition "cannot be evaded" and, even though it may be "hard" for the unsuccessful, was "best for the race because it insures the survival of the fittest in every department"), Curtis said, "Civilization, with its tremendous force and its insatiable desire to possess all, must necessarily crush the weaker life of primitive man." Such sentiments, if this is not too much of an oversimplification, encapsulated the very thoughts of the business leaders who subscribed to Curtis's publication.[39]

And, as we have observed elsewhere, the processes by which domination was achieved, from the "insatiable desire to possess all" onwards, were deemed *natural.* Indeed, the employment of natural imagery throughout the report is most noticeable. Curtis claimed, in fact, that *The North American Indian* was itself a product of "Nature" *per se*: "Nature tells the story, and in nature's own simple words I can but place it before the reader." Hence the point of stressing that the report now being written came directly out of the wilds: "At this moment, I am sitting by a beautiful stream flowing through the forest of Apache-land," within sight, sound, and almost within reach of instinctual animals and, crucially, equally instinctual indigenous people. The language of these Apache people was a product of culture ("the words of the children and lovers I do not know"), but their stories were "universal" and needed "no interpretation." The invocation of universality for some things (here "childhood and love") and not for others (note the emphasis on the essential "deep-rooted superstition, conservatism and secretiveness" of Indians) is a problematic area to which we will return.

At a more mundane level, the report also indicates that the project had a due regard for the presumed tastes of patrons in the format chosen for the publication to which they were subscribers. It was to be comprehensive: If the subject was much too grand to be treated between the covers of one volume, it was at least being covered in one publication – the implication being that it was a very solid work meant for very busy people. Moreover, much of the information in the text was pictorial – "truthful, yet artistic" – and, despite the fact that there were very many words in the twenty volumes of *The North American Indian,* they were there "to round out and intensify the interest of that told in . . . a strictly graphic manner." Also, while there would be an undoubted intensity to the information conveyed in words, it would not have any unnecessary density; it was "freed from the technical, cumbersome terminology" of specialists. That is, while the authority of *The North American Indian* had to be unquestionable ("as scientifically founded as the rocks on the mountain"), it would be accessible to the "general" reader. Finally, of course, as we have already seen, it was a sumptuous publication, exhibiting very high production values. And, precisely *because* it was so expensive in its beauty, it was a piece of conspicuous consumption entirely suited to the uses of its elite subscribers.

Curtis himself was uneducated and came from humble origins. Yet, as we have seen, the nature of the project – and ultimately of the representations of Native Americans that it produced – was conditioned by the very privileged interests in which it was deeply, and very materially, embedded.

DOCUMENTS

Document 4A. Extracts from draft of a report to subscribers by Edward S. Curtis, 1911.

This draft, a typescript among the Curtis materials deposited in the Morgan Library, was probably meant to form the basis of a document to coincide with the launching of the musicale in the autumn of 1911. In places the wording used is similar to that in other publications, but the piece as a whole was not published.

> Long after time has obscured from popular sight the world over practically all traces of the primal rise of the American People, and supplanted in its stead the vision of certain social and political customs only as distinctive features of the Americans, America will stand out boldly as having been the home of a race as different from any other found on the globe as the Caucasian is from the Ethiopian. Yet the nearest approach to anything like a complete, systematic treatise on these American Indians to be found today in a single book of accessible dimensions, including illustrations even purporting to be thorough, is that of Catlin, but, valuable as that work is, and many others of somewhat similar import, it remains that the student, or he who would know the true status of the primitive, aboriginal American in his various ramifications – more numerous than the world's races – must peruse practically as many authors as there are tribes.
>
> Nor can words alone, freed from the technical, cumbersome terminology of the ethnologist, anthropologist, or other

scientist, give to the reader of general topics, for whom this work is specially designed, anything approaching an adequate conception of all that has to do with the physical discussed herein, whether it be the physique of the red man himself, his infant's cradle, or his house.

Believing that a work, aimed primarily to picture the native American in his primitive haunts in a truthful, yet artistic, manner, could not but commend itself to all – those of us who have crushed out most of his life and are fast perpetrating extinction, and those abroad as well, interested in mankind – I took up this great task, appreciating, too, the necessity of a word text to round out and intensify the interest of that told in such a strictly graphic manner.

It is the purpose of this series of volumes to give a complete record of all the tribes of North American Indians, within the limits of the United States, which are at the date of these studies (1898 to 1911) living in anything like a primitive condition.

The value of this work in a great measure will be in its completeness and breadth, and from the fact that the whole is the result of actual first-hand study by one person, which assures each group of receiving its proportionate share of time and study in the general grouping.

All phases of the Indian life are pictured. The Indians and their environment, the types of the old and young, their primitive home structures, their handicrafts, their ceremonies, games, life and manners, all are being pictured with an object, first to truth, then to art composition.

In these illustrations there is no making of pictures for picture's sake. Each must be as it purports. A Sioux must be a Sioux and an Apache an Apache – in fact, every picture must be an ethnographic record. Being photographs from life and nature, they show what exists, not what one from the artist's studio presumes might exist.

The extent of the work is tremendous beyond comprehension, entailing fifteen years in camp life; and the railroad travel by myself and field assistants would twenty times encircle the globe. But greater than that of time and travel is the problem of securing access to the lives of these people, to an extent making it possible to get the story of their life in pictures and words. The work is a constant daily hourly struggle against deep-rooted superstition, conservatism and secretiveness. Not only does this secretiveness make the work different, but the fact that in many of the tribes the ceremonies are being abandoned makes the task of finding the old men who know the esoteric rites in their purity a difficult one.

The word-story of this primitive life must, like the pictures, be drawn direct from nature. Nature tells the story, and in nature's own simple words I can but place it before the reader. In its entirety it must be written as these lines are – while I am in close touch with the life, by the brookside, in the deep forest, on the broad plains, the scorching desert, or crouched by the campfire or in the candle-lit tent. At this moment, I am sitting by a beautiful stream flowing through the forest of Apache-land. In the forest's depths uncountable birds sing the song of life and love. Within reach of my hand, only last night a beaver, with his home-building instinct, has felled a tree, and even now he dodges out of his concealment into the light a moment, looks about with his blinky eyes, and dodges back. A flock of mourning doves fly down to the water, and in their delicate way, slake their thirst. By the brook-side path now and then wander the chattering children; or perhaps a youth and maiden, free from prying eyes, hand in hand, wend their way along the cool stream's pathway. The words of the children and lovers I do not know, but the story of childhood and love needs no interpretation – it is as universal as a belief in the something beyond this life.

The story must be that of the life and its history; not that history which will burden you with uninteresting statistics, but the broad record of the life as it can be had from the old men of the tribes.

While I am a photographer, I do not see or think photographically, and you must not expect me to tell the story in that minute way. And while I hope that my scientific knowledge of the subject is such that my mistakes will be few, I have endeavored not to make pictures or text so scientifically dry that there is no red life-blood in them. It should be a work pulsing, throbbing with life and nature, and yet as scientifically founded as the rocks of the mountain.

You who have followed in the pathway of commerce and do not know the byways and nooks of nature and primitive life, do not tell me that I picture a life which does not exist. To you it may not exist, but to the primitive man there is no Wall Street and no Stock Exchange.

In the story of the Indian life there is much which we can deplore, even come to abhor. On the other hand, there is much that is beautiful – much in the study of which we can profit immeasurably. In so far as it can be made so, this is a truthful record of the Indians and their lives – bad with the good.

While the treatment of the so-called savage by the civilized and Christian people has been, in many cases, worse than a crime, the pages of this work are not to be taken up with a continual reiteration of their wrongs. Where it has been necessary to mention these matters, it has been done in as unbiased a way as one who loves the Indians can make it. Much of the apparent wrong was the working out of the inevitable. Civilization, with its tremendous force and its insatiable desire to possess all, must necessarily crush the weaker life of primitive man. As an individual and as part of a tribe the aborigine would naturally resent this encroachment. He cannot see why he must give up that which was his and had been his father's, merely because advancing civilization demands it. On the other hand, the person whose parents were killed by some band of Indians who were forced on the war-path by an unscrupulous government employe can see no good in an Indian. . . .

The thought is often expressed: "If we could only see from the Indian's point of view, if we could see what he sees, what wonderful stories we could tell." In his stories, his legends, and in his myths, we must see from his viewpoint. No structure can be greater than its foundation, and certainly the legends and myths of a people are its foundation. From this source we must get the Indian's logic.

While it is possible to include but the smallest portion of the myth stories in this work, enough are included to give a good idea of them. As far as it is possible, the creation legend of each tribe or group is given; also the legend of the miracle performer – the person of miraculous birth, or Indian culture hero corresponding to Longfellow's Hiawatha, the character he so beautifully elaborated from Schoolcraft's studies – together with such other myths as seem necessary to give my readers a clear insight into that phase of Indian beliefs. In all cases these are legends collected by myself and assistants, confirmed by getting the same stories from different members of the tribe, under constant effort to keep them in their purity without adding our own thoughts.

> While there is a marked similarity in these culture stories, some tribes certainly show a distinct advancement over others, such advancement perhaps indicating greater age. We must of course presume that in the beginning man had no conception of a deity. As the human mind evolved, it grasped vaguely the thought of a Supreme Being. As the Indians' pantheism developed, there was, as with the Greeks and Romans, a deity for every occasion and hour. The Pueblos, who at least seem to have the greatest age, have evolved such an elaborate ritual that the half of their lives is devoted to prayer, supplication and giving of thanks. . . .

The report continued for several more pages, with paragraphs of speculation on the evolution and "savagery" of Indians, reiterations of the belief that material already collected could not then be duplicated ("Before the ink is dry in the last volume of this work, the primitive Indian life will be almost of the past, and in twenty years from now the Indian as an Indian will have passed from the face of the earth"), notes on the organization of the work, and expressions of fulsome thanks "to the many friends who have helped and encouraged in the work." This "heartfelt sympathy," which had come "from the humblest dwellers in the cabins on the plains" as well as from "the most wealthy" was deeply appreciated – and would be so by "future generations."[40]

Figure 11. Curtis Camp, Kitsap, 1910, by E. S. Curtis.
This Curtis-signed photogravure of the site where Myers
and Curtis prepared volumes 5–7 for publication
was sent to patrons to involve them in the project's activities.
(Washington State Historical Society.)

5

DIFFIDENT ETHNOLOGY

When recounting his 1907 argument with Edward Ayer, Curtis told Hodge, "he thinks I have attempted too big a task for one man, saying 'It looks to me as tho' you were trying to do fifty men's work,'" and in the draft of his 1911 report to subscribers he claimed that much of the value of *The North American Indian* came "from the fact that the whole is the work of actual first-hand study by one person."[1] Ironically, though much of the publicity for the project relied on building an image of Curtis's own monumental role as "the photo-historian of the North American Indian," it might well have better served his interests to reveal more about the involvement of others, especially William E. Myers. Certainly, however slight the public record of Myers's role, his presence through most of the years of the project was one of the key determinants of its character and, even, significance. As we will see, a greater awareness of Myers's work might have endowed the project with just that sense of scientific purpose and credibility that some of its critics claimed it lacked. (It should also be said, though, that Myers too had his prejudices.)

In a reminiscence composed two decades after the final volumes were published, Curtis said, "For a . . . period of twenty years I had the invaluable services of Mr. W. E. Myers. He was a rapid shorthand writer, a speedy typist who had majored in English literature and had developed an uncanny ear for phonetics. In spelling he was a second Webster." As Curtis himself always had trouble with spelling – more often than not he would commit common errors and sometimes he would even write his editor's name as "Hodg" – his respect for such complementary abilities to his own was doubtless genuine. "To the Indians," he continued, "his skill in phonetics was awesome magic. An old informant would pronounce a seven syllable word and Myers would repeat it without a second's hesitation, which to the old Indian was awe-inspiring – as it was to me." Myers even had the gift, according to Curtis, of being able to sing accurately by ear Indian songs he had recorded, even though he did not understand their literal meaning. Curtis elaborated on Myers's general role in the field:

> At most times while extracting information, Myers sat on my left and the interpreter on my right. I led in asking questions, Myers and the interpreter prompted me if I overlooked any important points. What chance did the poor old Indian have when confronted by such a combination? By writing all information in shorthand we speeded the work to the utmost. Our trio could do more work in a year than a lone investigator, writing in longhand, and lacking phonetic skill, could do in five years. That is why we did so much in the time we had. Also we knew nothing of labor union hours in our party. Myers neatly typed his day's collection before going to bed. In that way field notes were kept up to the minute. Our average working time for a six months' season would exceed sixteen hours a day.

There was also, as we have seen, a Curtis family tradition that it was a trunk full of Myers's meticulous notebooks which had exonerated *The North American Indian* project from a charge of incompetence brought to Roosevelt in 1907 by a leading professional anthropologist of the day.[2]

Closer in time to the project itself Curtis's estimation of Myers was equally fulsome. "In the field research covering many years . . . I have had the valued assistance of Mr. W. E. Myers," he wrote in the preface to the eighteenth volume, "and it is my misfortune that he has been compelled to withdraw from the work owing to other demands, after so long a period of harmonious relations and with the single purpose of making these volumes worthy of the subject and of their patrons." "He joined me in the field in 1906, while research among the Navaho was in progress," Curtis continued, "and thereafter we spent practically every season in camp together until the close of 1925. His service during that time has been able, faithful, and self-sacrificing, often in the face of adverse conditions, hardship, and discouragement. It is with deep regret to both of us that he has found it impossible to continue the collaboration to the end."[3]

Not surprisingly, Myers's work was indeed acknowledged in each of the first eighteen volumes of *The North American Indian* and what his role meant to Curtis receives further corroboration from the latter's report to the January 1913 annual meeting of the North American Indian, Inc. In it he recorded how at the close of the first season of fieldwork his "party of three men and a stenographer settled down in obscure rooms to do the final work in getting [the first] two volumes ready for publication"; how a further winter was spent with such a party, again including Myers, in a log cabin in Montana; and how he and Myers only "took two Sundays a month off" from their cabin in Kitsap County (see fig. 11) to visit their families across the Sound in Seattle during the preparation of Volumes 5, 6, and 7. He indicated later in the report that there were seasons during which only Myers was in the field: "Myers, in addition to a fairly successful piece of work in British Columbia did six months of most successful work in the Hopi country; but I, personally, had only a few short weeks in camp."[4] In effect, Myers was the project's chief fieldworker, and by 1914 he was actually listed as an "ethnologist" in the Seattle *City Directory*. It was in such a capacity that he conducted the correspondence with E. W. Gifford of Berkeley's Anthropology Department that we have already noted.

Persons other than Curtis saw Myers's role as even more central than this – as not just that of an ethnologist, but also that of a writer, an ethnographer. Such a position is at least implicit in Curtis's accounts of Myers's incarceration in various cabins with him as successive volumes were completed. Hodge, in an oral history interview conducted in 1956, remembered his own function as editor: "It was a pretty good job altogether, but I must say that Mr. Myers, who accompanied and assisted Curtis in the field, was the one who really wrote the text. I took over the text and checked every word of it, of course, and edited it, in other words, before it went to the printer. . . ."[5] The bulk of this chapter consists of an account of Myers and an assessment of the degree to which he *was* the one who really wrote the text.

Myers

William Edward Myers was born in Springfield, Ohio, on September 20, 1877, the son of Daniel Otto Myers, who died in 1913, and Ellen L. Garver Myers, who lived until 1920. Daniel Myers, a Civil War veteran, had a number of occupations over the years, from gas fitter to sewing machine agent, but by the time William reached maturity he was established as an insurance agent, a profession he left during the last decade of his life to become superintendent of the Springfield

Methodist City Mission. William had two brothers and a sister, but in his later travelling years maintained only intermittent contact with them, though his ashes were returned to Springfield for burial in the family funeral plot.[6]

He attended the local high school and Janesville High School, Wisconsin – where, according to the principal, he was one of the "best students" – before entering Wittenberg Academy (now Wittenberg University), the Lutheran college in Springfield. He was an able student there for two years from 1895, pledged the Beta Zeta Pi fraternity, then transferred to the more prestigious Northwestern University in Evanston, Illinois, from which he received his bachelor's degree in 1899. He was an excellent student, linguistically gifted, who on graduation was honored by Phi Beta Kappa and other societies. Myers majored not in English literature, as Curtis supposed, but in Greek, and on graduation commenced graduate work in German, proposing to write a thesis on "Goethe and Hellenism." He never completed this and quit Northwestern in 1900 to become an instructor at St. Alban's Academy, Illinois.[7] His whereabouts during the next few years are not known, but at some point he must have obeyed the oft-repeated injunction to venture westwards: When the Seattle *City Directory* for 1906 was issued he was listed as a reporter for the *Seattle Star* newspaper (possibly the position in which he built up his much vaunted skills in shorthand). At some point in 1906, as Curtis remembered, Myers joined the North American Indian project to begin a productive, if largely unrecognized, new career.

Myers worked alongside Curtis, W. W. Phillips, A. B. Upshaw, and others in the field, collecting and collating data on tribal organization, myth and folklore, history, vocabulary, and the host of other topics treated in volumes of *The North American Indian.* Permission to camp and research on the various reservations was sought and received from the commissioner for Indian Affairs in Washington, and it is interesting that Myers was the only one of the team for whom Curtis ever requested separate such access. Typically, once a decision had been reached as to which tribes should be covered, Myers would set about establishing where to locate the most appropriate informants. Thus in April 1913 he wrote to Dr. C. F. Newcombe, the renowned repository of Canadian Pacific Northwest knowledge, seeking assistance on the timing and other factors relevant to his work on the Haida: "You no doubt can give some valuable information as to the most favorable places for work and the best interpreters and traditionists." "You of course will understand," he added, "that for my purpose a full population of a village is unnecessary. I need a good, preferably middle-aged interpreter, and a few old men or women – I am told that the women are the repositories of knowledge among the Haida."[8]

Often Myers's work took in as much organizational as ethnological activity. At the height of one of the late field seasons among the Kwakiutl, probably 1914, he wrote to Curtis's main photographic assistant of the time, Edmund A. Schwinke, with a welter of requests, some for himself, but more for George Hunt, the project's mainstay in the field there:

> I am leaving Cape Mudge for Rivers Inlet – address Beaver, B.C. – where doubtless I shall be when you come up, as Hunt says we shall find several tribes there.
>
> I have with me both vols. of the Handbook, Boas, and my Kwakiutl MS, my tent and floor cloth, bedding and cot, and typewriter. Unless we are going to live aboard ship, you had better leave your machine. Hunt has the phonograph here, but we shall need records.
>
> Following are some wants of Hunt: the old white one-pole tent (unless we have our own cruiser to live in): some small clips or wire springs to be used for catching the skin and pulling it away from the flesh, as if a thong had been inserted in the flesh (the cedar rope will be attached to the clip and conceal the metal); a camera to take a picture about 10 × 12, of a grade comparable to the one he has, a 5 × 7 costing $17.50. Or if the chief thinks it would be better for him to use his 5 × 7 and enlarge to 10 × 12, get him the necessary apparatus for the process.
>
> Your Maka notes from page 106 to the end came a few days since, but 1–105 I have not seen. Better have them traced.
>
> Some pretty good material has turned up since my letter to the chief, especially the war stories. These fellows were the champion murderers and pirates of the coast.

If, as we saw in Chapter 3, Hunt was a most active broker, he acted as much for Myers as for Curtis. (The business of the "clip" probably refers to their efforts to recreate for the camera sleight of hand tricks used by *háwinalahl*; these war dancers would give the impression of hanging from thongs attached through slits in the skin of their shoulder blades and thighs, showing that their power made them insensitive to pain.)[9]

In the main, however, Myers seems to have tried to concentrate on the project's more strictly ethnological activities. We find, for example, that just as he had sought help from Newcombe in 1913, in 1915 he contacted E. W. Gifford of Berkeley, saying, "I shall be much indebted to you if you will kindly tell me where I can best work with the Maidu and Miwok. Also if Tule River reservation will yield the best results for Yokuts, and what is to be had in the Tuolumne country." "Lest you . . . have difficulty in placing my name," he added, "we met at the College [Berkeley], in January, 1914, when I was bound for the field in connection with the Curtis *North American Indian*."[10]

When so bound for the field, Myers prepared himself by acquiring and reading previous scholarship, if any, on the people concerned. On January 25, 1910, for instance, he wrote to Hodge requesting that he send on anything recent by Clark Wissler on the Blackfeet, and in 1915, again in a letter to Hodge, he expressed a degree of exasperation over requests to the American Museum of Natural History: "Bulletin XVII, Pt. 3 (Dixon's Northern Maidu) is exhausted. Can you supply me with a copy at Weitchpec, Humboldt Co., Cal.? If there is in the series anything else of value on California tribes, I would be glad to have it. I asked them to send me a list of their publications . . . , but they failed to do so." Florence Graybill, Curtis's daughter, remembered that in the field Myers could dig into "a tailor-made 18-by-24-inch metal trunk filled with books about the tribe they were with."[11]

Myers's dedication to keeping abreast of scholarship naturally led him into correspondence and conversation with other ethnologists. He communicated with Hodge, for example, in March 1910, asking him to get in touch with Alexander Chamberlain "to find out what he thinks of the word Kutenai," saying that he had written to Chamberlain himself with Kutenai words, but had received no response. In 1913 Myers engaged in a probing exchange with Newcombe about the aforementioned so-called "cannibal feast" of the Kwakiutl:

> You no doubt remember telling me what one of the Indians told you about the "cannibal feast" in which George Hunt participated and for which he was put on trial. I neglected at the time to record the information, and I would appreciate it greatly if you will write me the facts as to the composition of the "corpse." Next spring I am going to get at the bottom of this alleged cannibalism. . . .

Then, in his own hand, Myers jotted a postscript about head-shaping, as if maintaining a discussion already underway.[12]

Very early in 1914, as Curtis reported to Hodge, when Myers was in California "spending some time with [Alfred] Kroeber in work at the Library," he seems to have established an enduring relationship. And in the spring of 1919 Myers entered into a lively exchange with Kroeber, the doyen of West Coast anthropologists, that very nearly resulted in separate publication of some of Myers's findings. Writing from Santa Fe, during a period of fieldwork among the Pueblos, Myers said, "Herewith are some odds and ends that have been in my note-book for some time," and enclosed three items: a list of Indian place names, probably for locations in California; a short treatise on the origins of the mother-in-law taboo (see Doc. 5A); and a list of thirty-three words in English, Yurok, and Wiyot, in order to suggest a close kinship between the languages of the two California tribes, the latter based on a "rather casual examination of [his] vocabularies, containing only some 350 words." Myers also added to his letter a table of eight words in English with their Haida, Kato, Wailaki, and Hupa equivalents to advance a case for serious consideration of a link between the languages of the Northwest Coast Haida and some of the Southern Athabascan languages of California.[13]

Only two days later, Myers addressed Kroeber again:

> At the Museum [of New Mexico] Library today I saw the latest number of your [departmental] publications – Ethnogeography and Archaeology of the Wiyot Territory [by L. L. Loud]. You can perhaps picture my chagrin on learning from the author that you and [Roland B.] Dixon affirmed the genetic unity of Yurok and Wiyot in 1813 [sic], and that [Edward] Sapir showed them to be Algonkin, thus antedating my little "discovery" by some five or six years.

In his final paragraph, Myers revealed, in his very self-deprecation, the degree of his scholarly involvement. "The incident," he said, "shows that one can spend so much time in the field as to lose contact with what is being accomplished. I always try to catch up with the periodical publications on returning after a season's work, but evidently I have missed some of them."[14]

In his genial response, Kroeber for his part expressed gratitude for the place names, took issue with the explanation of the mother-in-law taboo, and put Myers's other "discovery," on the connections between

Haida and Athabascan, into perspective. "You may be amused," he said, "that Sapir has anticipated you also on the relationship of Haida and Athabascan. He had a paper in the Anthropologist some two or three years ago on the Na-dene family in which he advocates your proposition." "I do not know how far it has been extended," he admitted, "and know of some people who still fight shy." Kroeber was clearly keen to keep in touch: "I hope you will let us hear from you from time to time . . . and that we may count on seeing you whenever you blow in here." Kroeber's regard for Myers's abilities, moreover, was readily apparent in another letter sent out on the same day in which he urged Myers to collect data on Southwestern kinship systems. "A good Keresan system seems to be the chief desideratum," he wrote. "Zunian, Tanoan, and Hopi are represented fairly well. I suppose Acoma would be the best place to secure a Keresan system." Then, in terms as concerned with "tradition" as any that Curtis might have used, he added, "In any event, it should be secured where Spanish influence is least likely to have modified the aboriginal system." He enclosed a list of the kinship terms he hoped would be collected.[15]

On reflection, Kroeber came to see further value in the linguistic work Myers had sent him:

> I am wondering whether you would have any objection to my putting your Yurok-Wiyot and Haida-Athabascan lists into the Journal of American Linguistics with a prefatory note explaining the belatedness of your discovery. I think the fact that you have independently come to the same conclusion as Sapir will be valuable corroboration. The battle between him and [Truman] Michelson on the one hand and between him and [Pliny Earle] Goddard on the other took on a technical character so far as the combatants were concerned, and the line up of the spectators was more largely on the basis of their prejudices . . . than anything else. The very fact that you have been so completely an outsider gives your finding the value of being totally unprejudiced, and I think will go farther to convincing neutral people like . . . Wissler and [Alfred] Tozzer than a hundred pages of the most detailed additional proof that Sapir might bring. The question of relationships has in the last five years got to be the most prominent one in the field of American linguistics, and I think we should do everything possible that will help to elucidate it. I hope you can get yourself to feel the value of my using your material as I feel it.

Whatever Myers felt, his lists did not appear in the *International Journal of American Linguistics*, and in academic circles he remained, in Kroeber's phrase, "completely an outsider." His findings did appear, however, under Curtis's name, in the pages of *The North American Indian*. In the succeeding months, perhaps years, Kroeber and Myers kept in contact – indeed later in 1919 Myers offered to collect information on "Hopi subjects" – but then drifted apart. As late as 1932 Kroeber made an effort to find Myers, saying "We should like to get in touch with you, or at least to know how you are."[16]

Myers and The North American Indian

Hodge was probably the one professional anthropologist for whom Myers was emphatically not "completely an outsider." While Myers was denied or missed an opportunity to contribute directly, as an author, to a hot issue in linguistics, Hodge was in a position to witness his contributions to *The North American Indian*.

Scarcely a year after Myers joined the project in 1906, Curtis informed Hodge in June 1907 that Myers was among the Sioux at Pine Ridge in advance of the remainder of the Curtis party, which was about the join him. By January 1908 Myers was writing authoritatively to Hodge on matters of substance on Plains ritual and the letter is worth quoting in detail because it encapsulates Myers's empirical knowledge and inquiring spirit:

> All of the Titon bands observe a ritual called Hu ^{n}kálowa^{n} pi [Foster Parent Chant], the purpose of which is to implant certain virtues in the child for whom it is given. Priest and child assume the relation of godfather and godchild. It is found among the Yankton, the Assiniboin, and in slightly different form among the Hidatsa and Mandan. The same songs appear everywhere, but with the three tribes last named Arikara words are set to the music.
>
> I think the Siouan tribes borrowed the ritual from the Arikara version of the Pawnee Hako; either that is true, or else the Caddoan ceremony is an adaption of the Siouan. But the use of Arikara words by Hidatsa and Mandan certainly favors the former supposition.
>
> Do you not think that the question would be answered conclusively by the presence or absence of the ceremony among those Santee who have not come in contact with the Caddoan?

> One other piece of information I should like to have: Do the Santee bands relate a legend of the Gray Buffalo Woman, mentioned in Clark's Sign Language under head of *Buffalo, White*?

Similarly, Myers wrote to Hodge a few months later with a series of questions, the answers to which would relate events in a winter count to episodes in Sioux-white contact recorded in the journals of white travelers. Understandably, by the winter of 1908 it was Myers who went East to see volumes through the press, a task he appears to have shouldered from then on, sometimes early on with assistance from Phillips or Curtis, and always in cooperation with Hodge. In November 1908, for instance, he was wondering how to render "in type the surd syllables occurring so frequently in, for instance, Atsina . . . ," or how best to express the difference between Yanktonai and Yankton, and a host of other matters.[17]

Not surprisingly, Curtis began quietly to defer to Myers on such issues and Hodge came to refer to him as an authority. In September 1908 Curtis was already writing to Hodge in such a vein. "As to the vocabularies," he said, "you no doubt spoke to Myers in regard to that, and arranged it with him. If not, it would probably be best to write him. . . ." Hodge, for his part, entrusted to Myers an article submitted to the *American Anthropologist* on which he needed a reader's report. It was a paper on the shrine of skulls that, as was reported in Chapter 3, had been taken away from the Hidatsa and deposited in the Heye collection. Myers was firm in his response:

> Under separate cover you will find . . . the Hidatsa shrine article. In my opinion the authors, in striving for scientific accuracy, have dwelt at too great length on unimportant minutiae. This is more apparent in the quotations of the natives. To be sure, they did not set out to produce a masterpiece of literature, but I never could see why such things should not be readable as well as scientifically accurate. I have appended a note or two on points which our [field] notes seemed to elucidate a bit. . . .[18]

It is tempting to see such comments as a partial expression of Myers's own hope that *The North American Indian*, too, would be "readable as well as scientifically accurate." At about the same time, he reported his progress on the section of *The North American Indian* that he was working on. "I am endeavoring to make the Atsina text read more like a finished product and less like pages from a field notebook," he said. "The work among that tribe was not at all satisfactory. A 'green hand' was set at it in the fall of 07, but did not get far beneath the surface, partly because nearly all the people were in the mountains and he had no camp equipment to enable him to go to them. Last summer I was sent to round out his notes," he continued, "but accomplished little for the same reason. Then in September Mr. Curtis and a *very* 'green hand' went back, mainly for pictures. They secured the battle tales and the pseudo history." Work like this by Myers lay somewhere between editing and writing as such, but it certainly included the latter. In fact, in the surviving field and manuscript material for *The North American Indian*, Myers's hand is very evident. Among the notes on the Atsina, for instance, there are a disproportionate number of pages by Curtis and the marginal clarifications and amendments are almost all attributable to Myers. In several other parts of this manuscript material – on the Yakima, on the Nez Perce and other Plateau peoples, for example, or on the Nootka and Haida of the Northwest Coast, or on the Sioux and Piegan of the Plains – his is either the only hand, or at least the most prominent one, in evidence.[19]

Myers's responsibility for the texts grew over the years. By 1913, when Volume 10, on the Kwakiutl, was being produced, his letters to editor Hodge were indisputably those of an author. At the end of the year, for example, he said, "I am sending back by express MS of Vol. X, so that you can go through it during the winter." "There will probably be some changes regarding alleged cannibalism," he added, "but they will be of such a nature that I can make a duplicate copy of them for your inspection. You therefore will not have to cover the same ground twice." (In the same letter, incidentally, there is further data on the kind of trading frequently entered into by Curtis and other anthropologists. "Will you kindly write a note to Curtis informing him of the name of the little shells such as you sent to your Zuni friends at the time I was there?" Myers asked. "Some of the Hopi have requisitioned him for a quantity of the shells, and it is rather important that he respond.")[20]

It will be remembered that Myers had already promised Newcombe that he was going to "get at the bottom" of the "alleged cannibalism" of the Kwakiutl. When Myers's Kwakiutl fieldwork and writing were put together as Volume 10, the nonpictorial aspect of the resulting book was substantially his, including at least some of that element in the text which characterized the Kwakiutl as, in

Myers's abbreviated judgment already quoted, "murderers . . . and pirates." Curtis's words in the book's preface should, in fact, be taken at their face value: "Myers has done his best work here. . . ."[21] This instance underlines again, of course, that in considering the representation of Indians constituted by *The North American Indian* and associated works, its nature as a collective production cannot be ignored.

Despite some delays in publication – certain of them considerable, such as that between the appearances of Volume 11 in 1916 and Volume 12, on the Hopi, in 1922 – Myers worked steadily, unobtrusively, and authoritatively to produce the texts of succeeding volumes. On July 4, 1914, for instance, he was not celebrating but at his desk to address Hodge on plans for the Hopi volume: "I will go to Walpi about August first, and the MS should be ready for your reading by September first." In August of the following year he dispatched Hodge an urgent request from his field camp among the Hupa of California. Although he was immersed in fieldwork for a volume on California peoples – as his request for relevant publications showed – it concerned the minutiae of one devoted to the Northwest Coast: "The New York office is inquiring what will be the approximate number of pages in Vol. XI. I think my estimate is found on a sheet attached to the MS. Will you please inform the office what the estimate is; or, if you find none there, will you make one for them? I have no means of doing so here. About 25 pages should be allowed for music [transcriptions]." On August 5, 1919, he reported on his summer's work, signposted the autumn work to follow, and then gave a flavor of the intervening period he was to spend with Curtis:

> . . . I have been here at Gallup since the 31st, waiting for Curtis, who by riding on work trains and carrying his luggage across arroyos contrived to come from Winslow in three days.
>
> We are leaving for Polacca tomorrow. The delay caused by washouts, and the unexpectedly long time it will require to drive out (we had counted on going with a car), make it quite improbable that we shall return before you have closed your camp. I had looked forward with the greatest pleasure to the opportunity of seeing you again and hearing about your [archaeological] work at Hawikuh [part of Zuni], and shall be much disappointed at this turn of affairs. If you should chance to remain there longer . . . drop me a line at Polacca. . . .
>
> It is possible that I shall spend a part of September at Zuni.

> If so, had I better count on camping, or is there a sufferable lodging house?[22]

On June 28, 1923, he wrote, "I am sending you today 31 pages of KLAMATH material. If you make no radical changes, please send it along to the printer," to which he tacked on comments to the effect that his Appendix was ready, barring a few points "to be verified." In September of the same year he reinstated a procedure whereby he, rather than Hodge, would have the final word on proofs, "for the reason that not infrequently, as in the case of aboriginal spellings, you suggest corrections that are open to question and can be verified only by reference to original MS or field notes." The following March he sought Hodge's bibliographical help in preparing for fieldwork in western Nevada and New Mexico, adding "All [the] New Mexico pueblos must be discussed in two volumes." On September 7, 1924, he commented adversely on Matilda Coxe Stevenson's observations in comparison with his own findings on the Tewa and on the Pueblo snake cult and explained some of the motivations for one of his last journeys:

> We are off to Gallup Tuesday, partly to see the show, but principally to look for an exiled Jemez man. Apparently nobody has ever obtained any information of importance at Jemez, Santo Domingo, or Taos. There is a fair chance that we will make the proper connections for the first two, but Taos remains, and probably will remain, (for us), pretty nearly a blank. However, I hope to get some good Tigua [Tiwa] dope at Isleta (already have part of it), and am going to try for a Picuries man. Picuries is so near extinction that I see no logical reason why the survivors should be reticent. . . . [23]

A little later, on September 21, Myers reported what he called "good progress" in these endeavors; in this letter, his vocabulary was marked by a strong subjectivity, in that he said he was especially happy over "perpetrating a very satisfactory *coup* on Santo Domingo, one of the very worst nests of the lot." At the end of the year he wrote as follows: "I am hard at work on the Pueblo material, and if I don't get lost in the mazes two more volumes will be ready for you by the Spring."[24]

As is the case with so much writing, the Pueblo volumes, 16 and 17, took longer than expected; they were not completed until August of 1925, and Myers wrote to Hodge about them from his camp on the Piegan northern plains reservation while gathering material for Volume 18. "You will see," he said, "that the Appendix is not complete, and that in a few places the text is not in its final shape." "If you will be good enough to read it as it is," he continued, "leaving the pages of field notes where they are, I will make necessary additions later. Vol. 16 is already over size, and I don't know just what to do about it." Then, after outlining the project's plans for ethnological and photographic fieldwork among the Sarsi and Cree, he returned to the Pueblo volumes: "'Sex stuff' became such a frank and common subject of conversation with many of my informants that I grew quite hardened, and it may be that this is too clearly reflected in the wording of passages dealing with this phase." "If it appears so to you," he requested, "try to eliminate the rawness of phraseology without concealing the points involved." The ensuing letters log a protracted discussion on the organization of the volumes, including Myers's acceptance of Hodge's suggestion that a separate paper of the so-called "phallic dope" be prepared.[25]

In 1925, when it was decided to tackle peoples of the Canadian plains that year, Myers sought a letter of introduction to the Canadian reservation authorities and hoped to have full planning discussions with editor Hodge. As it happened, he received the necessary letter but was unable to see Hodge, who was still working at the Museum of the American Indian in New York City. The field party had to travel very long distances for the summer's work and while enjoying a brief stop among the Piegans in Montana during August, Myers wrote Hodge that he appreciated the copies of the almost miniature *Indian Notes* Hodge had sent him from the Museum of the American Indian. "Thanks for the little handbooks," he said. "They are convenient camp companions, and I am going to settle down with one of them this evening." "After a few more days here," he reported, "we are going north to the Calgary country, with the idea of giving the greater part of the proposed volume to Sarsi and Cree, rather than repeat on Piegan-Blackfoot." Then, noticing a typing error in what he had just written, Myers added a marginal note: "My typewriter is still dizzy from the trip."[26]

At the end of the summer, back in San Francisco, he included in one of his letters to Hodge the following brief report on the work in the Calgary country: "We had a satisfactory season in Alberta. The outlook was discouraging at first, but as we went further north it became more promising. We were lucky to find a very good source of information for Cree and Chipewyan, and pumped it dry." Eventually, by early 1926, Myers was able to get down to writing up Volume 18 on the peoples of Alberta, including these tribes and the Sarsi.[27]

In February 1926 Myers was starting to plan the final volumes, to be devoted to Oklahoma peoples, but there was a very slight element of testiness with Curtis which may well have augured the break that was to come:

> Curtis writes me that he wants to start field work by May 1, on which date there is to be an intertribal gathering somewhere in Oklahoma. He expects to get a large number of his pictures there.
>
> If we visit such a gathering without definite plans, the result will be a miscellaneous collection of photographs around which a text is to be written.
>
> To avoid this, I want to know in advance just what tribes we are going to do in the next volume. I should like to limit the number to two, if possible; always remembering that it is sometimes possible to collect abundant text material in tribes that yield insufficient pictures for our requirements.
>
> Will you be good enough to give me your opinion on what tribes best suit our purpose? A bibliography of such works as are not mentioned in the Handbook, and such series as the American Museum papers, will be appreciated.

In his reply, Hodge concurred, saying that he assumed "Curtis's plan is the same as ever, to include only those tribes that retain many of their primitive traits . . ." and what, in Oklahoma, such a requirement meant.[28] His list of tribes, which was clearly intended for Myers to select *from*, reads something like the table of contents of the *The North American Indian* text that eventually appeared as Volume 19 in 1930. Perhaps this was because, by then, Myers was no longer the principal ethnologist and writer.

During the spring of 1926 Myers, whose health was apparently deteriorating, felt he had to leave the project to take up a real-estate opportunity in San Francisco. Curtis was stunned, both by the loss of Myers and by the scale of reorganization that would be necessary. On the latter, he sought Hodge's help, either in the field himself or in finding a replacement, but neither worked out: Hodge could not get away and both of the anthropologists Hodge suggested, T. T. Waterman and Leslie A. Spier, who were already well-known and much published, must have refused. Myers was distressed at his own inability to continue and, perhaps even more, by the possible harm to the project as a whole. "I suppose it will be next to impossible," he wrote to Hodge in April 1926, "to get either of the men you mention, or anyone else, to do the fieldwork and prepare the text without insisting that it be published over his name." "That of course is the nub of the whole problem," he concluded, "and the thing that made me hesitate so long before deciding to withdraw." The man who did replace Myers, Stewart Eastwood, proved less than adequate, at least at first, and Hodge must have communicated this fact to Myers. In a letter written during May 1927 enclosing galley proofs of Volume 18 that he was seeing through the press, Myers said, "I am distressed by your report of vol. 19 – It really causes me to regret that I yielded to the lure of Mammon." "Curtis writes me that he is leaving for Alaska on the 25th," he added. "I wish I were going."[29]

Quitting the Project

Myers's fortunes at the hands of Mammon – indeed in relation to much of the workaday world, apart from scholarship and the field – were always somewhat mixed. It is not certain how much salary he received from the North American Indian, Inc. but it could not have been much, and for it he was perpetually on the move. Although he was listed as an assistant at the Curtis Studio in the 1907 Seattle *City Directory*, he enjoyed no home address of his own in the city until his marriage to Sophie or Sophia Myers – and then, in 1913 at any rate, only a downtown hotel, the Hotel Perry. Moreover, except for 1914, when he was listed as an "ethnologist" living at 1736 26th Avenue N, Seattle, he had no stable address until he settled in San Francisco during the twenties. He was a tireless workaholic, whether out in the field or tied to his desk. His letters were sent from numberless lodging houses, camps, Indian agencies, cabins, hostels, and hotels, and his capacity for sheer labor was registered in one of his later communications with Hodge, in which he commented on his ailing physical strength: "I am hardly fit to adopt baggage smashing as a profession, but am in better condition than I have been for several years, ever since my sacroiliac went on the bum. I am at my desk regularly until 2 or 2.30 am. A few months ago I was all in at 8 and went to bed at that hour."[30]

The Myers had no children and Sophie, it seems, either did not have a job outside the home or was a school teacher, so she was free to join him in the field in the summer on occasions, and probably helped him out, taking notes and discussing issues. They certainly traveled around New Mexico together. In July 1920, the Myers settled in Belmont, in the Bay Area, and in October 1923, they moved into 274 Russ Building, in San Francisco itself. In 1925 they relocated again, to a new building at 1750 Pacific Avenue. It was this building, purchased in Sophie's name in 1920 and for which Myers was given planning permission to undertake a further $20,000 worth of building work in 1923, that seems to have featured strongly in his real-estate ambitions, as expressed to his North American Indian colleagues in 1926.[31]

At any rate, in 1925 Myers felt flush enough to at least consider spending the winter in Europe. "Curtis gave me to understand that there would be no more printing until all the fieldwork was completed, and with this in mind," he told Hodge, "I had promised Mrs. Myers a winter across the pond. I have not yet accumulated the courage to impart the sad news [that printing plans have changed]; and when I do I shall have to offer a compromise in the form of a winter in any place or places in the USA she may select." "And at that," he quipped, "I'll be lucky to get away with my life." Myers described the particular form in which Mammon beckoned to him when he informed Curtis of his withdrawal in a letter written at the beginning of April 1926:

> It is an unpleasant thing to have to write you that I shall not be able to do any field work this summer. An opportunity has presented itself to make a lot of money in the next two or three years – a real estate transaction. It is one of the kind that rarely occur, and I am getting too old to pass it up in hope that another will be at hand when the Indian work is finished. It will necessitate my being here from June 1 on . . . [As to the remaining fieldwork,] failing any better solution, I imagine I can have an organization perfected so that I could get away for three months next summer. As you probably know, the desire to finish the job is what has kept me at it these last few years on a salary that doesn't amount to much in these times, and only a very remarkable chance could have induced me to drop the plowhandle. . . .[32]

As it happened, the opportunity proved far less "remarkable" than Myers hoped. He became manager of the apartment building at

1750 Pacific Avenue and secretary-treasurer of Braemer Inc., a real-estate company, which in 1928 occupied the fifth floor at 244 Kearny before apparently ceasing to exist. The 1930 edition of the San Francisco *City Directory* listed Myers as, simply, an "author" living at 1750 Pacific Avenue. The following year, as the Depression worsened, he took a job as company secretary at the Prima Vista Company Ltd., a beverage manufacturer, and for the remainder of the decade he occupied the same home and similar positions at the soft-drinks company. At the end of the thirties, after a move together to 204 Hugo, San Francisco, either Sophie died or the couple separated. His final years were spent as the manager of small motels, the last at Petaluma, north of San Francisco. By then he was married to Eveline M. Roberts Myers of Glen Ellen, Sonoma County. He died of heart disease on April 29, 1949. In the brief obituary notices which appeared in the Santa Rosa *Press Democrat* there was no mention of Myers's contribution to *The North American Indian.* He himself, on encountering the tribute to his efforts in the preface to Volume 18, as quoted above, expressed himself characteristically: "Reading the last paragraph gives me a heart-ache and spoils the day completely."[33]

Eastwood

When Myers became unable to conduct fieldwork for *The North American Indian,* he was replaced by Stewart C. Eastwood, a young graduate of the University of Pennsylvania who had successfully completed a number of anthropology courses and came highly recommended by Frank G. Speck, an authority on Eastern Woodland Indians. Hodge made the arrangements, offering Eastwood a fee of $4,000 plus expenses on May 15, 1926. Within a month, Eastwood, who was the son of a doctor from Brandon, Vermont, had discussed the project with Hodge in New York, talked to the business managers of The North American Indian, Inc., at the Morgan Bank, and was with Curtis on the plains in Oklahoma. He wrote most of Volumes 19 and 20, on the Oklahoma tribes and the Alaskan Eskimos, based on two hard seasons of fieldwork in 1926 and 1927. The end of his association with the project in November 1929 roughly coincided, of course, with the onset of the Great Depression, and Eastwood felt his job prospects were poor. He and his wife Gertrude, married during his Curtis years, seem to have eked out a living in Los Angeles until, partly on the strength of a glowing reference from Hodge, Eastwood was granted a commission in the U.S. Navy at the beginning of World War II. He appears never to have returned to ethnology.[34]

In a long letter to Hodge from Quapaw, Oklahoma, of June 17, 1926, Eastwood set out his initial sense of the fieldwork required for Volume 19:

> We stayed in Pawhuska while the conventions lasted, camping in the Osage village. There were Indians here from all over the state and from adjacent states so we were able to make contacts for real ethnological work in the future. However, we did get some good pictures and we have made quite a bit of historical research for the opening chapters. Now we are in Quapaw for four days getting more pictures and any other data that may spring up. Summer life for the Indians seems to consist of a round of visits from one village to another each trying to out do the others in hospitality. Our real ethnological work will begin with the Oto, probably, about the 21st, then the Cheyenne, Comanche and Pawnee. The program is tentative; . . . we are up in the air since so many problems have arisen, but we figure that four studies of four representative groups of linguistic stocks will more than keep us busy.
>
> The five civilized tribes are so much civilized, so white, that they will be impossible while the wealthy Osage are not only becoming civilized but wealth gives a haughtiness difficult to overcome. On the other hand we have been met more than half-way by the Oto and Cheyenne and from them are [anxious?] to get a wealth of material. With the Pawnee we are thinking of a new idea to embody in the volume tho the details of the program are still vague. This surely is an odd situation but we are beginning to see our way clear tho' vaguely. It seems certain that we'll have a great deal of material; then perhaps things will clarify more. . . .

As things did "clarify more" for Eastwood and Curtis, they abandoned some of this plan, mainly in that they ultimately chose to concentrate on the Oto, Cheyenne, Comanche, and Wichita peoples, with only a few pages on the Pawnee. The volume on the Oklahoma peoples that they produced did have "a new idea" in comparison with previous volumes, but it did not concern the Pawnee. Rather, the initial part of the book was devoted to thumbnail sketches of almost all the tribes domiciled in Oklahoma at that point, including the Osage and the five civilized tribes, however "white."

By September, Eastwood was at least sounding more professional and relaxed; he wrote to Hodge with enthusiasm, saying, "I should have kept you more fully informed concerning work in the field but you know how it is – one day is very like another and they slip away fast when we put off doing things." His report is again worth quoting quite fully, for it offers a succinct indication of his stance:

> I told you of our progress with the Oto. We tried to get the generic story of the Osage and the Ponca for comparison with the Oto. The Osage were "summering" in Canada and the mountain resorts of Colorado but we did get some information from the Ponca, enough to justify the effort.
>
> We were with the Cheyenne for several weeks, staying in camp with them . . . while they had their arrow ceremony and sun dance.
>
> We were lucky enough to get the arrow ceremony ritual complete tho' of course we couldn't see the arrows. It might be interesting to know that the vow-givers who put it on were two northern Cheyenne who came down for that purpose. We took the story of the origin of the arrows from three different men which we worked into one detailed story.
>
> The sun dance was a trifle disappointing on account of some modern innovations but our data on it is good.
>
> The Cheyenne also put on the Buffalo Ceremony and Animal Dance, both starting in the [illegible] land and both being given together. Those we have in detail together with pictures. After some difficulty we took the pictures of the sun dance lodge and altar – rather, Mr. Curtis got the pictures while they were arguing whether we should or not.
>
> I liked the Cheyenne. They treated me O.K., especially some of the older chiefs such as Howling Wolf, Old Crow and Man-on-the-Cloud, all gory warriors in their day. So far they have been the most primitive I have seen in Okla. I mean by that that they have held on to their old customs and ways with greater tenacity.
>
> Now we are with the Wichita – and having our troubles. Part of the tribe are strong baptists, hence they will give no information because the old ways are sinful and pagan. Couldn't even take a picture of one of their grass houses. The tribal grass house, a fine specimen, has a high broad fence around it to keep away cattle so as a picture it is no good. Some of the chiefs

have made trouble saying that the government has full knowledge of the Wichita through [James] Mooney and [George] Dorsey; that it is useless to go over the same ground. However, thro much talk, a diligent interpreter *and dollars* we are getting some good stuff. Slow but worthwhile.

We aren't taking folklore stories but the stories and rituals of ceremonies, the deer dance, Rain Bundle ceremony; Around the Fire; Buffalo Bundle etc. are fine. We haven't drawn conclusions as yet on their religious life but these stories are replete with animism, the attaining of a "power" thru animals or spirits; earthly and heavenly gods, magic such as sleight of hand entailing mass hypnotism and cataleptic trances.

Further, one of their ceremonies, the Around the Fire, is nearly identical with the peyote. There are some conclusions that may be drawn from that but we need further evidence . . . but on the surface it seems as if the use of peyote north of here, as spread by Wilson, might have used this ceremony as the basis of its ritual. Wilson was a Caddo. That is merely an unchecked statement, hence valueless.

When we finish here, and there is quite a good bit to be done yet will go to the Comanche. . . . We have stumbled across the peyote ceremony so much that, if a paper or any information whatsoever has been published concerning it, we would like to check up with our findings. . . .

We have been working with the Oto, as one of the Siouxan [sic] stock, with cross references to others of the Southern Sioux. Just about finished with them with a lot of good material. We were lucky to get a number of songs, accompanying the creation story. We have had to be very careful about anything of a religious nature since there is an enormous mixture of Mormonism, Christian theology, peyote ceremony and ghost dance all jumbled up in a seemingly inextricable mass.

Some day I'm going to prepare a paper on the ghost dance, "stomp" dance, and peyote ceremony since there is a possibility that the latter two either became connected with, or developed out of, or borrowed the ghost dance in some of its particularities. It is, of course, in many respects comparatively recent.

The progress Eastwood described here was very much reflected in the contents of Volume 19 of *The North American Indian.* The text describing the Cheyenne arrow ceremony and its mythology, for example, included the information that "the author" had been unable to witness the rites in the sacred lodge, which were led by two votaries from the Northern Cheyenne, and that the account had been blended from three different sources. Interestingly, however, the published text on their sun dance did not reveal the extent of any "modern innovations," though it did indicate that in one respect it had been more intricate in its "undebauched form."[35]

In the case of the descriptions of the Wichitas, too, there was a high degree of correspondence between these field descriptions and the content of the published account. Thus, though the published version did in fact include photographic representation of one of the grass houses, the record of the Surround-the-Fire Ceremony was certain enough by then to include the promised "definite statement" that the widespread peyote rituals had been adapted from this Wichita ceremony. Also, Eastwood's belief that "Wilson" – presumably not Jack Wilson, the founder earlier of the Ghost Dance cult, but John (Moon Head) Wilson, the most prominent peyote messiah figure at the turn of the century – "was a Caddo" was correct; though partly Delaware, Wilson had been raised among the Caddo. It is strange that, despite his prominence, Wilson went unmentioned in this volume, one that contained much else on the peyote cult; indeed, Eastwood did not wait for "some day" to prepare a paper on the "stomp" dance and related matters, but included fullish descriptions of them as a special note in *The North American Indian*.[36]

In his final letter from the 1926 field season, written on September 24, Eastwood expressed his satisfaction with what had been achieved: "I feel that we have a fine lot of material, more than we can use." "We were with the Comanche, but got little from them – as we expected," he reported. "We then returned to the Wichita to complete our collections. This I did while Mr. Curtis went north to the Cheyenne again for more pictures." His note explained what, pictorially, Curtis was after: "There is a paucity of good settings for pictures here – it seems to me that the Cheyenne have kept more to the old ways, with more objects of material culture than any tribe in the state." He also indicated certain other constraints on their achievements:

> I was unable so far, either from some Pawnee friends or Wichita, to find out anything about the Morning Star ceremony, story or sacrifice, or anything in connection with it. I did get a good Wichita story of the morning star.
>
> I couldn't get any satisfaction on the word "quivira."

> I did find, if memory serves me right without consulting notes, that there are four bands making up the Wichita tribe. . . .

Eastwood's impressions and tone in this last letter were borne out in the writing up of Volume 19 of *The North American Indian.* The few pages devoted to the Comanche were literally only "general description," and they served primarily as a kind of preface to a series of Comanche folk tales. The morning star ceremony of the Pawnee people went unexplored. "Quivira," which presumably referred to the name the Spanish gave to the province originally inhabited by the Wichita, went unexplained. And, as his memory did serve him "right," the Wichita were said to be comprised of four distinct bands.[37]

When Hodge received what Eastwood vainly believed constituted the final version of the text, in April 1927, he was not pleased. Eastwood had written, "I had a lot of fun helping make it up and I hope you have as much pleasure at your end," so he must have been greatly discomforted when Hodge virtually accused him of *actually* making it up. "The entire compilation lacks that care and precision which so thoroughly characterize Myer's [sic] work," Hodge wrote. He berated Eastwood's spelling, his style, his orthography, his Cheyenne vocabulary, his over-reliance on myth material at the expense of ethnography, and, in general, his lack of critical distance. Ultimately, after arguments which involved Curtis as well, Eastwood had to rewrite the entire volume.[38]

Diffident Ethnology Underlined

Further evidence of the formative role of what I have dubbed diffident ethnology – both its importance and, as we saw in Eastwood's case, the constraints upon it – may be seen in the relationship between the project and Alfred Cort Haddon, reader in ethnology at the University of Cambridge and a Fellow of Britain's premier scientific body, the Royal Society. Haddon, who had been leader of the 1898 Torres Straits expedition, one of the first thoroughgoing exercises in empirical fieldwork, was a founder of anthropology as a social science, and had achieved respect throughout the world. He had a particularly good grasp of anthropological developments in the United States, and in 1901 he had joined George A. Dorsey of the Field Museum, Chicago, in fieldwork among the Pawnee. He was eminent-ly suited to be invited to give a series of talks on the evolution of culture around the Pacific, and – though his presence also worked to legitimate the public exhibition of tribal peoples (what he called "living bronze") as a Midway attraction – he did so during the 1909 Alaska-Yukon-Pacific Exposition in Seattle.[39]

Haddon came within the project's orbit either through Hodge, who was British by birth and also knew virtually everybody in the profession through his various official positions in American anthropology, or, more likely, through his long association with Henry Fairfield Osborn, Curtis's chief patron at the American Museum of Natural History. In any case, in November 1908, Curtis told Hodge that Haddon was to be involved with their fieldwork during the following summer: "He will probably spend more time at one of the branch camps, which will be on Puget Sound, than he will with my personal party." This branch camp was in the charge of Edwin J. Dalby, who had been a student at the University of Washington when Meany recommended him as an ethnological researcher. Dalby was a practiced speaker of the Chinook jargon, the *lingua franca* for Pacific Northwest Indians. He was somewhat overweight but used to an outdoor life, bright, keen to write, and ambitious. When he started in the field earlier that summer Curtis reported to Meany, as he put it, "Your boy Dalby has had an experience he will not forget in a few days. Every few minutes he cries out wanting to go back to Washington. The mosquitoes proved almost too much for all of us, to say nothing of a juicy boy like Dalby." Despite such hindrances, Dalby settled to the work, became known to some Indians as "Man Without Hat," and was entrusted with a field party of his own – the one to be joined by Haddon – in the summer of 1909. He worked for the project for at most one season thereafter.[40]

Curtis was acquainted with the British newspaper tycoon Lord Northcliff and hoped that this contact would make it possible for Haddon to review *The North American Indian* in a British publication, thereby encouraging the sale of European subscriptions. As an incentive to Haddon, Curtis and Osborn tried to persuade Morgan to grant Haddon his own free subscription. This particular initiative eventually came to nothing, but Curtis was always at pains to please Haddon. In a note about him to Dalby, Curtis urged that they do their best to accommodate the eminent Englishman, adding, "he would be with you but a couple of weeks so it won't seriously interfere with your work." But at the very time this admonition was delivered, in November 1908, Haddon himself was beginning to wonder what he had let himself in for. In a letter to a friend of some standing, ethnologist Clark Wissler, he asked, "By the by – who is Mr. E. S. Curtis? & what is he doing in the N.W.? He has offered to take me on some Expedtn. & I don't know who the devil he is and what the devil he is doing. Do enlighten me." "In reply to your . . . letter . . . asking [about] Mr. Curtis," wrote Wissler, "he is an enthusiastic photographer who has a great deal of interest in the ethnological side of Indian life, but whose chief effort is to photograph as many of the living Indians as possible. He is publishing a magnificent book of some twenty volumes. . . . While he is primarily an artist, I believe you would enjoy spending a day or two with him."[41]

Haddon was very sympathetic to photography and visual anthropology in general. His Torres Straits expedition had been the first ever to take along a movie camera together with still cameras and sound-recording equipment. Nevertheless, he seems to have taken Wissler's reservations to heart, at least for a time, for he wrote a detailed letter to Dalby, advocating that the Curtis parties utilize the systematic means of recording family relationships in any given community that had been devised by the British anthropologist W. H. R. Rivers and pioneered in the Torres Straits. While Haddon may well have thought that his strictures on the need to surpass the mere collection of folklore data, as he sometimes saw it, were not taken to heart by Curtis and his associates, his period with them appears to have been a happy one. For a start, the "day or two" recommended by Wissler stretched to several weeks as plans developed over the following months. Haddon told newsmen in July 1909 that he was to spend about two weeks with Dalby's "Curtis" party among Indians gathered for their annual summer fishing season at the mouth of the Fraser River, British Columbia, and he also spent some time with a Curtis party among the Nez Perce in Idaho and the Kutenai on the U.S.–Canada border. But his biggest experiences took place the following month in Montana, with Curtis himself, among the Blackfeet. According to a newspaper story, by the time that journey began Haddon had become "much attached to Mr. Curtis" and intended to have "a thoroughly delightful trip," making observations and taking physical measurements among the tribe. He wrote up this fieldwork in some detail in an unpublished memoir.[42]

In the years that followed, Curtis and Haddon seem to have remained in touch in only a desultory way, but with the passage of time Haddon's experiences in Montana became an ever-more vivid and cherished memory. His reviews in 1911 of *The Old North Trail,*

Walter McClintock's account of the Blackfeet, resonated with remembered excitement. His short piece on "The Soul of the Red Man" (1914) included a mention of his Pawnee and Piegan fieldtrips and testified eloquently about "intensely religious nature" of Indians. Haddon told the *Christian Science Monitor* that he had no intention of publishing anything on the Blackfeet, and he never did, but he did collect data from several authoritative writers on the Northern plains – including Grinnell and his own friend Wissler – which he incorporated into his memoir. It was probably written during World War I, though Haddon may well have first started it soon after his return from America in response to Curtis's call for a review-cum-endorsement of *The North American Indian*.[43]

One of the most interesting aspects of Haddon's essay is that it is a *memoir*. It does not include the kind of kinship data that he advocated to Dalby, yet it does contain a good deal of what he had castigated as "folklore" material, such as the story of the origin of buffalo stones, and at its heart are records of Haddon's personal sense of such experiences as the all-night sweat lodge. That is, it was the depth of Haddon's *subjective* experience that was memorable. Considering Haddon's stature as an advocate of neutral observation, this is more than paradoxical. It is reasonable to question – and we must do so – whether such a stance should be located within the discourse of ethnology at all.

DOCUMENTS

Document 5A. "The Mother-in-Law Tabu – A Possible Explanation," by William E. Myers, 1919.

> Among the Indians of the Western United States there is very generally a tabu on conversation and association of any kind between a man and his mother-in-law, and less generally between a woman and her father-in-law. The tabu is a rigid one, except where it is obviously due to external influence or is not a true tabu at all, but merely a question of treating an honored person with respect. The writer has made inquiry of a very large number of tribes regarding the origin and significance of the custom, but in no case has received even a mythical explanation.
>
> In Gifford's excellent paper on Miwok Moieties is the clue

> to a possible solution. A Miwok man is permitted to marry his wife's brother's daughter; but his son also has the same right. If the son marry her, she becomes the daughter-in-law of a man who might have been her husband. Conversation and association between them might then be an embarrassing reminder of that former possibility; and, what is more to the point, *it might give others occasion for suggestive gossip as to the possibility of present clandestine relations.*
>
> The tabu between a man and his mother-in-law may be explained as the logical extension of that between a woman and her father-in-law. If my wife dare not talk to my father, employing me rather as intermediary, what is more natural than that I bear myself similarly toward her mother? The mind strives for symmetry, and in this respect the Indian by no means falls behind the rest of the human race.
>
> It may be objected that this explanation subordinates the mother-in-law tabu to the father-in-law tabu, when in reality the former is the more prominent and the latter apparently secondary. But is it not certain that the mother-in-law tabu is always and everywhere the primary one, from which the other is derived, though in many cases it appears to be so.
>
> Assuming the validity of the hypothesis, we have, as the original tabu, relations between a woman and her father-in-law in a tribe organized on the patrilineal basis, and in a tribe where either a man or his son may marry the same woman. But the converse is not permitted; that is, neither a woman nor her daughter may marry the son of the woman's husband's sister, which would result sometimes in her becoming mother-in-law to a man whom she might possibly have married.
>
> If it should be found that in a matrilineal social organization where the mother-in-law tabu exists, a woman has the right to marry her husband's sister's son, the suggested origin of the tabu would seem to be sustained.[44]

The text of *The North American Indian,* especially early volumes on Plains peoples and Volumes 13 to 15, which were devoted to California peoples, contains numerous instances of the operation of the mother-in-law taboo. There, however, Myers was almost purely descriptive and refrained from theoretical explanations of the sort contained in this unpublished note. The one exception occurred in his chapter on the Miwok, where – in much shorter compass – he put more or less the position outlined in this note. This was probably because of the prominence given to E. W. Gifford's work on the Miwok – so definitive that Claude Levi-Strauss in *The Elementary Structure of Kinship* (1949) later referred to it as having established the lineaments of what he called "the Miwok system" of relationships – and Myers presumably wished to develop it. Kroeber, for his part, in taking up Myers's comment that he would "appreciate an opinion from [Kroeber] and Mr. Gifford as to the . . . plausibility" of his views, was chary of giving approval:

> Your explanation of the mother-in-law tabu is certainly original and penetrating. I am somewhat suspicious of it however because the form of marriage involved is of very limited distribution whereas parent-in-law tabu in some form or other extends over at least half the continent. The general probability therefore would indicate that it was the earlier institution. I am not maintaining that this is proved but that it is the more likely alternative.

While it may initially seem that Kroeber's position was slightly stronger logically, the thrust of subsequent theoretical work on questions of kinship has been to deny the very idea of "earlier" and "later" institutions in favor, generally speaking, of explanations which account for *both* diachronic and synchronic factors as exemplified in any *particular* case – including clan structures, as mentioned by Myers. For structuralist anthropologists, at least, a people's linguistic terms for familial relationships have served as the most reliable key – as in, for example, Levi-Strauss's rereading of Gifford's original Miwok data – and these, while lightening the stress on the sexual relations aspect of the taboo, tend to support Myers's contention of a clear link between the form of property lineage in any given tribe and the taboo.[45]

Document 5B. Letter, William E. Myers to Frederick Webb Hodge, 1924.

> Herewith the Introduction to Vol. XIV, and express receipt for MS of XV. I had a hunch I was wrong in writing 153d st. on the package, but no doubt you will receive it.
>
> For a long time I have been unpleasantly aware that I have not thanked you for the Pueblo bibliography. Please consider

yourself now doubly thanked. Since leaving home [San Francisco] May 5 I have had what the newspaper writers call a hectic time, getting new material, incorporating it in the text, giving the MS a general overhauling, and getting the pictures ready for the engraver and the copyright office. The past week I have been working here [Los Angeles] with a Cochiti delegate to some convention or other.

Thanks for sending me Lowe's [sic] paper on Shoshonean culture. I believe my Paviotso dope in XV checks with it very well.

Happily, my back is much better, though not by any means normal. A few days of driving, and I am likely to spend a day in bed. We are starting for Zuni Sunday morning, and will remain in the Pueblo country all summer unless they run us out. I understand that they think less of white folks than ever.

After reading the MS, please turn it over to Holmes [at the printer's]. I have no carbon copy, and if it were lost in transit I don't believe I would have the heart to tackle it again. The carbon was sent to the Seattle studio some years ago and can't be found.

Myers sent this letter after dispatching the manuscript of Volume 15 to an incorrect address. As he hinted at the end of the letter, his fieldwork and most of his writing of this volume, on certain California and Great Basin peoples, had been completed during the long hiatus between the publication of Volume 11 in 1916 and that of 12 in 1922. Hence his justifiable pride in preceding but also concurring with the findings of another eminent and prolific colleague of Kroeber's at Berkeley, Robert H. Lowie. His work on the Pueblos, as even the tone of this letter suggests, was to prove, as we shall see, much more contentious.[46]

Document 5C. Letter, Stewart Eastwood to Frederick Webb Hodge, 1927.

Now that we're storm bound here [Golovin Bay, Alaska], I have an opportunity to catch up with my correspondence.

Much water has passed under the bridge since we first landed at Nome. There we found that the chief obstacle to work was lack of transportation, not only to out of the way places, but anywhere. After much haggling over price, we solved that foremost difficulty by purchasing a boat . . . The 29th of June we put out to sea for Nunivak Island, and arrived there on the 10th July, after drifting around in the ice block and being hung up on a sand bar. Navigation is uncertain since there is no reliable information on tides, currents, or even charts. We go mostly by guess and God helps us get there eventually.

On Nunivak we had the best of luck since the natives are primitive and unspoiled. They were willing to help us in every way so that we have a fine mass of material and a goodly number of pictures – real pictures illustrative of this mode of living, not merely the portraits we had to fall back on [in Oklahoma] last summer.

Our interpreter [Paul Ivanoff] I cannot praise too highly. He is the local representative of the reindeer company, part Russian, mostly Eskimo, speaking not only the Nunivak dialect but several of the mainland tongues. He worked with [Knud] Rasmussen [the Danish colonial administrator and authority on the Inuit]. I note that Rasmussen and other writers speak of Nunivak as a bare land, almost devoid of means of living. That information must have been hearsay, for we found it quite to the contrary. Berries, plants, grasses and edible seaweeds in abundance – many of which we are bringing out to be identified. Birds in profusion – sea animals and fish in any quantity. While there we came across two "Bone-hunters" from the Smithsonian, [Henry B.] Collins and [T. Dale] Stewart, who are supplementing [Ales] Hrdlicka's [physical anthropology] collection.

From Nunivak we went to Hooper Bay for pictures. The natives there are the filthiest in Alaska – we were only too glad to leave. They have much bird life there but little else. They were kept from starvation by the teacher and the missionary who helped them catch white whales by driving them aground by means of the power boat. Living as they do in mud and dampness, it is estimated that 75% have tuberculosis. Their kyaks and weapons are poor; they have the crudest basketry; no carving in ivory since they don't get it; no wood carving since wood is extremely scarce. And so on. This culture at first glance seems to be a lack of culture.

To be brief. From there we headed North but a stiff blow drove us in here. We intend to re-outfit at Nome for the Diomides, Kotzebue and King Island.

> We're looking forward to getting our first mail at Nome. I succeeded in picking up a copy of Nelson [i.e., Edward W. Nelson, *The Eskimo About Bering Strait,* 1897].[47]

Eastwood did not manage to maintain his correspondence with Hodge during the rest of the trip, and this is unfortunate because the experience affected him deeply. In November 1929, when he was putting the finishing touches to the supplementary details to Volumes 19 and 20 – as well as worrying about the effects of the stock market crash on his mortgage and job prospects – he told Hodge: "Off and on I am digging out an article on Alaska but the progress is slow – about 11,000 words to date." "It may see the light of day if some editor will take pity on me," he continued, "If not it will be a mighty good log of the expedition." It appears that he found no editor to pity him, but his Alaska experience did not go entirely unregarded. On July 24th, 1942, after the United States entered World War II, Hodge wrote a glowing reference for Eastwood to secure him a naval commission, and he cited the younger man's experience as a navigator in the treacherous northern waters of Alaska.[48]

PART THREE

INDIANS INCORPORATED

Good words do not last long until they amount to something.

Chief Joseph, Nez Perce (1879)

Figure 12. Custer's Crow scouts, Curtis, and A. B. Upshaw at Custer Outlook, 1907. This image, by an unnamed member of the project team, depicts (from left to right) Goes Ahead, Hairy Moccasin, White Man Runs Him, Curtis, and Upshaw, probably during their retracing of the Battle of the Little Bighorn; the significance of the papers held by the scouts is not known. (Library of Congress.)

6

ADVENTURE IN THE FIELD

In 1926 Myers, as we have seen, was concerned about the relative status of the photographs and the written text for *The North American Indian,* wishing to avoid a situation that would result in "a miscellaneous collection of photographs around which a text is to be written." Given that Curtis himself had earlier spoken of the "word text" – for example in his 1911 report to subscribers – as necessary only "to round out and intensify the interest of that told in . . . a strictly graphic manner," there was clearly something of a struggle for authority between the two media. On one occasion George Hunt told Boas: "I was with Mr. Curtis taking old fashioned Indian dressed photographs, and he took very few stories. He did not care as long as he got the pictures taken."[1] And we have witnessed that Eastwood tacitly accepted the constraints placed upon the project's work in Oklahoma by the need to acquire pictures uncontaminated by the modern.

This struggle for authority was doubtless intermittent and varied in significance and effect, but it did reflect larger differences among the project's primary personnel. One such difference was that in the world of anthropology Myers was fairly close to such Boasians as Kroeber – in personal relations as much as in approach – whereas Curtis was obviously closer to the old school of Osborn and others. By extension, a major difference was the contrast between Myers's characteristically diffident ethnology and the stress on excitement, danger, and discovery apparent in the writings of Curtis and others. Even Haddon, a seemingly rigorous advocate of neutral observation, focused on the trials and delights of his own participation in Piegan ceremonies. Similarly, a Curtis form letter of 1909 – which seems at first a straight summary of a year's ethnological activity (it begins "Believing that you will be interested in knowing how work on 'The

North American Indian' is progressing") — characteristically contains traces of another discourse.

Addressed to Gifford Pinchot but with the same text as ones to other subscribers, this letter does enumerate the peoples visited (a large number, from ones in the Canadian Pacific Northwest and on the plains to the Pueblos of the Southwest), the sites at which various fieldworkers (Myers, Dalby, Upshaw, Allen, Strong, and Crump) were deployed, and the languages and culture areas encountered. But it also refers to the weather, especially its rigors ("Our first Yakima camp had been pitched amid the snow and frost of spring . . . and our Blackfoot camp found us in search of more blankets, for again the nights had become crisp and frosty"), and at several points dwells upon scenic beauties with a view to their pictorial possibilities ("among the Kutenai, on beautiful Flathead Lake, a field that afforded the opportunity for making some exceptionally fine pictures"). Also, perhaps most tellingly, it revels in the Crow war-party assembled for the entertainment of Ambassador Jusserand that we have already encountered and hints at secrets uncovered by its author. Among the Cheyenne, Curtis recalled, there was "the old-time Sun Dance, called by them the 'Willow Dance' [and] I was most fortunate in having a chance to witness it and to obtain pictures of all its interesting features."[2] These are the kind of representational features to be explored in greater detail for the remainder of this chapter.

Travelers' Tales

Curtis, as we have observed, deliberately cultivated the romance of the fieldtrip and of himself as the archetypal westerner. In this promotion, whether visually in the photographic portrayal of himself in the dashing 1899 "standard picture" wearing a typical field outfit, or verbally in numerous newspaper stories, the emphasis often fell on his "adventures" in the wild west. It ran through the vivid early *Century* account of the trials and triumphs of "the mad rush to the gold fields" of Alaska, for instance, reverberated in the tales of Hunt's alleged rages or the studied attempt to give Jusserand a western adventure by orchestrating a party of mounted "wild" Indians to sweep towards him across the plains, and often issued in dramatic reenactments (see fig. 13). It was perhaps most vividly in evidence in his 1907 speech to Meany's students in Seattle where, together with stories of more purely photographic problems, he spoke of "the elements":

> The rain pours down. What was an arid desert when you made your evening camp is soon a lake. Perhaps in the darkness of the night you have been compelled to gather your camp equipage and carry it to higher ground; or, perhaps it is a fierce wind striking your camp, and if strong enough it will either blow the tents to the ground or whip them into shreds. And then comes the sand storm. No horse can travel against it. If en route you can but turn your wagon to one side to furnish as much of a wind break as possible, throw a blanket over your head and wait for its passing. It may be two hours or it may be ten, and when it is passed your equipment is in a sorry shape. Nothing can keep it out. Cameras, plate box, plate holders, motion machines, food – everything is sifted full of this fine, powdery sand.

"Hail storms will beat down on you and whip your camp into tatters," he continued, before retailing encounters with hunger, with heat, and with snow storms in which the "horses floundered and fell, regained their feet and struggled on, only to give out completely and lay down in the harness." And he told of a time when "a stubborn driver rushed his four-horse team down a bank and into a freshet torrent":

> [In] the fragment of a minute all you could see of that wagon was its canvas top, and a muddy stream for a quarter of a mile was strewn with the wreckage. From a half dozen cameras scarcely one could be patched up out of that wreck; and plates – well, the shortest time to get a new supply was ten days and a trip to cost hundreds of dollars. Another day the pack mule with my only camera fastened to his back slipped and rolled down the canyon a mile. The camera was spread out on the mountain side seeming nothing but fragments. Twelve hours steady, patient work and it was patched up so it could be used. But such a sight! No camera worker ever before saw anything quite its equal. On the outside it was a bunch of ropes bound and twisted in every direction to hold it together.[3]

One news item on Curtis with the catchy title "Lives 22 Years with Indians to Get their Secrets" highlighted the link between tale-telling, adventure, and ethnological information: "If by coaxing you lead him on to a good tale, . . . the chances are 10 to 1 that before he has finished with it he has switched [over] to the discussion of some racial peculiarity of a disappearing tribe." Adventure sometimes took precedence over the ostensible purpose of the expedition. An obvious example of this may be found in a memoir of a field trip to Apache country in about 1906 by Harold Phillips Curtis, who was born in 1894 and was a schoolboy at the time the events described took place: "I had had many delightful but tantalizingly short weeks with Father [and] the Indians, and now I was to be really one of the party and live in camp month after month, winter and summer." He added, "That would be real life." Many years later, in 1927, Beth Curtis Magnuson, Curtis's oldest daughter, when a grown married woman of 33, accompanied her father on his final field trip, to Alaska. In her "log" of the expedition she concentrated on the mishaps to the boat, the character of its captain, "Harry the Fish," the night life of Nunivak and such, and, except for commenting repeatedly on the "filth" of the Inuit of Hooper Bay, barely mentioned the subjects of her father's work. Even Curtis's second daughter, Florence Curtis Graybill, although probably always more interested in Indians than her sister, in some of her reminiscences of similar "adventures" also scarcely touched on the cultures of the Indians they were studying; uppermost for her was the pull of the outdoors, danger (for example, in shooting the rapids on a turbulent California river), camp food, and a tree-bough bed under the stars.[4]

And, when told, these adventures were more like "travelers' tales" than ethnography. Witness Florence's pig story:

> After one of our trips to the coast we returned with a Karok Indian called Obie. His only apparent luggage was a large gunny sack of dried seaweed which he planned to share with his friends in the mountains, considered a great delicacy by the Indians. . . . One day while Dad and Obie were away from camp making Indian contacts and photographs, I remained to write some letters. In that area near Witchepec were many pigs that were wild. Not javelinas, but pigs . . . originally of the domestic variety. They lived largely on acorns as well as anything else they could scrounge. They were a terrible nuisance around the camp, getting into our supplies if possible. This particular morning they did not seem to be around, for which I was thankful. I did recall hearing some characteristic "snuffling" but it did not sound near enough to be of concern. When Obie returned later in the day he let out a shriek and a flow of blasphemy. He

> had put his precious seaweed in back of the tent, unprotected, and the pigs had eaten it all. I felt so badly. . . . The seaweed could not be replaced . . . so many miles from the coast.

With memories of white water struggles particularly in mind, she wrote, "I wondered, as I had before and many times since, if future generations reading *The North American Indian* would have any conception of the work it involved, and the dangers encountered."[5] We might think that such a spirit was special to impressionable young people, or to people who were not themselves primarily engaged on the project, but it was also very apparent in W. W. Phillips's account of his time in Apache country.

In Phillips's case the high point occurred when, according to him, the Indians went on a drinking spree to celebrate July 4th. The day began peacefully enough: "When the morning of the fourth dawned I found myself alone in the cabin. Gray [the Apache interpreter] had heard the call of the *tulapai* in the night. Up and down stream in the various huts all was as quiet as death. Not a soul in sight – not a sound. Everyone was inside drinking *tulapai.*" But the climax was not long in coming:

> Along toward noon, though, there was a noticeable stir of life, and by midafternoon a small edition of bedlam had turned loose. Groups would gather outside of a cluster of huts to gamble with Mexican cards and become engaged shortly in a general brawl. Women fought not only vociferously but viciously; two in one instance finding hair pulling and screaming insufficient, caught up some long dried cows horns lying about and jabbed at each other wickedly until parted by less intoxicated men.

"A lone white man within a radius of sixty miles, I grew decidedly nervous as the day wore on," Phillips claimed. "The little corral provided a first class screen wherein I could sit unseen, yet see out between its close set posts in all directions to watch the revelers. The passersby went on horseback – racing and yelling like mad – on bareback ponies guided only by ropes tied to the under jaw. It was not, however, until along toward dusk that anyone stopped to see me. I had entered the cabin to prepare some supper when from away up stream I heard the clatterty-clatter of a horse's hoofs." Then, Phillips continued:

> I saw a young lad coming . . . straight for my cabin, and he pulled up at the door. He had a deep gash on his left cheek bone from which blood had dripped from his chin all over his shirt and the withers of his pony. That once white wind-spent beast was gray with dripping sweat, having obviously come no mean distance. The boy could speak a little English and gasped: "He come – he come – he killing me sure; – you help."
>
> It required a bit of fast thinking. If others were . . . actually after him, and found him harbored by me, I was doomed at last for a nasty part in their drunken brawl. The boy in his fright could understand no English. My Apache was limited. Down stream some thirty miles away was another Apache camp. I pointed down stream saying, "Apache *kowa*" (houses). "Chuganaai" (sun, one day) holding up one finger, and motioned for him to go. He understood and went off as fast as his sturdy mount had brought him.
>
> No one followed. Several days later he returned. Gray elicited from him that one man in the party at his home had been drinking too much *tulapai*, and when others tried to restrain him he became enraged, caught up a club and threatened to kill them all, the boy being the first to receive an ugly blow. He had made his trip and been cared for carefully. His wound was healing; he could smile over his fright, and had no fears for the lives of those he had left at home.[6]

In travelers' tales, as several commentators have pointed out, the emphasis often falls on quaint and fearful differences, oddities, dangers surmounted, and, above all, not on the life observed but on the *presence* of the traveler. We may remember Curtis's assurance to *Century* magazine about his Klondike report: "I have *myself* passed over the trails, climbed the mountains . . . waded through the mud and snow, and endured the cold and hunger." Here in Phillips's account the mention of "the lone white man" is similarly telling. The adventure story format inevitably dictates that the traveler returns safely. The anthropological context means that the main threat to his or her safety is the people who constitute the subject of the study. Fascination with the Other is figured as dangerous, and these writers habitually return with a story as well as with ethnological information. A good example emerges from Curtis's attempts to secure the Apache chart, as described in Chapter 3: In his reminiscence he said, "the medicine man who was the keeper of the sacred chart was dead. His wife had used the household axe to good purpose and he had gone to the Great Beyond," whereas *The North American Indian* itself was much more genteel and contained no mention of the murder.[7]

Not surprisingly in such tales, an element of sexual adventure sometimes cropped up. If we stay with the project's records of its encounters in Apache territory for a moment, a muted sexual element may be heard in Curtis's account. He told how he devoted his attention to a succession of medicine men in an effort to extract information on Apache religion: "I . . . went to the Cibacu [sic] in an effort to see the reputed bad medicine man. He refused to see me and repeated his warnings, sending word that I must not camp another night on the Cibacu. That I remained for more than two weeks seemingly surprised him. He sent some one to my camp each day to look me over. The spy would invariably ask when I was going to leave. I, as invariably, answered, 'Pretty soon, maybe tomorrow.'" Then, Curtis added: "The old chap was clever and constantly sent women to my camp, thinking that I might take a fancy to some one of them, and thus give him a chance to complain to the Government and shift the responsibility of having me put off the reservation. This obvious trick amused my interpreter greatly." Curtis even claimed that some of the Apache mothers offered him their daughters by drawing "alluring pictures of the advantages of having a camp mate."

Sometimes the element of sexual adventure was indirect, perhaps even unconscious, but no less sexual for that. Phillips recorded an experience with an Apache woman:

> She was dressed in buckskin of the old style, sort of long loose shirt belted at the waist and fringed at the bottom. Her buckskin boots had legging tops capable of reaching to the hips, but the high tops were folded from knee to ankle and back to knee again. Those long folds thus formed deep pockets of real capacity. Her jovial manner was such that I felt no hesitancy at exploring them as we sat side by side on an old pine log. It amused her much when I pulled a butcher knife out of one boot top, and as I kept on and brought out yarn and twine and bone needles and buckskin for patches she laughed until she shook. A solemn old spectator suggested that I played with danger, for he knew that the woman had been on trial once at Agency headquarters for beating her husband. I had Gray ask the old fellow what he knew about old times, and old customs and wars and dances, but before he could reply the woman answered that she knew

> that he knew nothing; at least not more than one thing – to look for pretty women. I found in time that she was approximately one hundred per cent right.

It is obvious that Phillips, groping among the Apache woman's clothes in his restless search for knowledge, felt able to take liberties with her (as the idiomatic expression of the period had it) that would not have been permissible for him in the white world of the early 1900s. There was also – and the linkage in the anecdote itself is telling – an inbuilt assumption that the sexual relations of the Indians were available for discussion in a way that those of the ethnographers themselves were not. Sometimes, as we will see, this tendency could shade over into the published ethnography itself.

If Phillips sometimes felt endangered by events beyond his control in the field, there were also occasions where the sense of adventure was actually produced by the project's effort to acquire information and pictures. "I have grown used to having people yell at me to keep out, and then punctuate their remarks with mud, rocks and clubs, that I pay but little attention," Curtis declared, and he complained of being told to limit his output at traditionalist centers, such as Acoma in New Mexico, and of being "taxed," or charged a fee, by other peoples, such as the Hopi. Indeed, the project's records contain numerous instances of *conquering* Indian resistance, sometimes to ethnological questioning, but mostly to being photographed, and what probably constitutes the earliest newspaper report on Curtis's Indian activities to appear outside the Seattle area was devoted to this topic. Titled "Did You Ever Try to Photograph an Indian?," it appeared in 1900 in the San Francisco *Sunday Call* and, in a display of the nonchalant racism so frequently characteristic of the turn of the century, declared, "There is just one feat more difficult than introducing an Indian to the bathtub, and that is, to make him face a camera." In particular, it reproduced Curtis's own stories of his efforts to portray the sundance of the Blackfeet or Piegan of Montana:

> The average Indian will neither be cajoled nor bullied into posing. Mr. Curtis does very little urging. His rule is an old one – "money talks. . . . " The Blackfoot people have a sun dance once a year commencing in the first week in July and lasting five days. They are five days crammed with weird customs that few white men have been permitted to witness. Mr. Curtis is one of these fortunate few. "Even more interesting than the

> snake dance of the Moquis," says Mr. Curtis, "is the sun dance of the Blackfoot people. . . . It was only through the friendship of White Calf, chief of the Blackfoot tribe, that I was allowed to be present during the ceremonies. As I had, by various means, endeared myself to his people there was little protest against my presence. [Yet] . . . I had some trouble and once almost lost my scalp. It is the custom of the men to collect the logs for the lodges constructed for the sun dance. I wished to get a picture of them riding back from one of these wood sorties and stationed myself accordingly. Three horsemen dashed into sight, at the head an Indian called 'Small Leggins,' who had a particular disgust for the camera. I got the picture, but the quick eyes of 'Small Leggins' saw what I was about and with an angry cry he headed his horse for me, intending to ride over me. By a miracle of good luck Chief White Calf, riding from the other direction, saved my life. Afterward I won the friendship of Small Leggins, but he never lost his distrust for the camera.

Also, according to another newspaper item, at the Nespelem reburial ceremonies for Chief Joseph of the Nez Perce in 1905 Curtis even went so far as to pull out a six-shooter and threaten to kill Chief Albert Waters when he opposed the presence of Curtis's camera.[8]

These supposed victories over Native American recalcitrance also testify to the degree to which the project stressed the esoteric nature of Indian life, especially its ceremonialism. This is most obvious in the case of the Pueblo peoples, as we shall learn, perhaps especially from W. W. Phillips's account of his secret investigation of a mountaintop shrine (Doc. 6A), but we have also already seen it in connection with Apache religion. It could be argued that for Curtis one of the main points of ethnology was to make *public* that which was private or esoteric. This is intimated in some of the picture titles: "Out of the Darkness" (1904), for instance, refers both to the line of Navajo riders emerging from the shadow of the canyon and to a sense that their lifeways are being brought into the light, made available to the viewer's understanding. Other images whose contents and titles play suggestively with the notion of darkness and the esoteric are the doubly ambiguous "In Black Canyon – Apsaroke" (1905), "Into the Shadow – Clayoquot" (1915), and "In the Shadow – Yurok" (1923). For many, of course, there *is* a profound fascination in learning about the lives of others, especially the lives of those who inhabit radically different cultural worlds, and one way of reading the accounts of the project's fieldwork is to see them as testimony to the heroism of the anthropological encounter, perhaps the heroism of the anthropologist.

Insofar as the records disclose the very mechanisms of private probes, their emphasis is on *transcending* racial barriers, not on tearing them down. Curtis's readers and viewers would imaginatively enter an Indian world which, though disappearing, was irretrievably different, Other. One of the openings to the musicale, for example, issued an invitation: "Let us close our eyes for an instant, and in that flash of time span the gulf between today's turmoil and the far-away enchanted realm of primitive man. We have entered what is to us a strange land." In fact, the project repeatedly stressed the exotic. In a newspaper interview with the British Columbia newspaper *Province* about his Northwest work in 1910, Curtis claimed that "*all* . . . [these] Indians . . . exhibit one striking characteristic in their religious ceremonialism, namely, the prevalence of hypnotism. They were under the influence of the priest class to an extraordinary degree. 'I am convinced,' said Mr. Curtis, 'that the participants . . . were all in various stages of hypnosis, [even if] the priests did not know how they obtained these results.'" Apparently, he then went on to claim that the famous Ghost Dance of the 1890s had been an example of hypnosis at work.[9]

Again, the project was not unique in these ways. Indeed, as commentators on other anthropologists have shown, there was sometimes even a stress on competitiveness in securing and salvaging information. David Murray has described, for example, how Frank Hamilton Cushing, in relating his success in absorbing material from the Zuni, even went so far as to say, "my method must succeed. I live among the Indians, I eat their food. . . . Because I will . . . look with unfeigned reverence on their beautiful . . . ceremonies, never laughing at any absurd observance, they love me and I learn."[10] Frequently newspaper accounts of Curtis's activities suggest that he had been able to learn more than others because he, too, had "lived" with the Indians. He himself often boasted thus ("I had, by various means, endeared myself to his people"). And even Myers was not immune to such notions, as when he asserted his determination "to get at the bottom" of the alleged cannibalism of the Kwakiutl or referred disparagingly to the amateurishness of various "green" helpers.

The Adventure of Conquest

Two further important threads to this web of representation need to be traced and disentangled: tourism, with its accompanying commodification of everything within its purview, and, of course, conquest itself. The notion of "the wild west," the arena for these adventures has, of course, always been a construct; Earl Pomeroy pointed out that the West became whatever potential Eastern tourists were thought to want it to be, so for many years they were "reassured . . . that [it] was no longer wild and woolly – until fashions changed and it was time to convince them that it was as wild as it ever had been." There is, indeed, a growing body of scholarship stressing the relationship from the turn of the century onwards between the commodification embodied in the promotion of tourism – especially to the Southwest (by such entities as the Fred Harvey chain or the railroads) – and Indians as part of that commodification; in promotional photographs and the like, Indians were featured as an endorsement of "an exciting past and a picturesque present."[11]

There was a pervasive appropriation of Indian artifacts, architecture, arts, and even personnel, especially native craftspersons or, in Marta Weigle's expression, "subject-producers-of-objects" – all made over as "staged authenticity" to suit a tourist aesthetic, and all to be seen against the backdrop of a natural and built landscape of such antiquity that it matched, even in visual specifics, the sites of the Middle East, even the Holy Land itself. This is most apparent, perhaps, in the visual similarities between some of Curtis's photographs of the Pueblos and actual popular Orientalist imagery. I am thinking of such views as "Street Scene at San Juan" (1925), which, were it not for the presence of the cross atop the church, could easily be read as Middle Eastern, or the general view of Zuni taken in 1903 (see fig. 18). Several of the women depicted in the middleground of exterior Pueblo shots are half concealed by their robes, as if in Purdah, and many of the close-up portraits, especially of males from Taos, are swathed in white cloth, granting them an air of "exotic," "Eastern" mystery. Not surprisingly in this context, Curtis's own articles for *Scribner's* in 1906 and 1909 were almost as much part of the discourse of tourism as they were ethnographic; the one on the Pueblos concluded with the following injunction to the reader: "You, who say there is nothing old in our country, turn your eyes for one year from Europe and go to the land of an ancient primitive civilization. The trails are rarely travelled, and you will go again." Also, as we have seen, he turned some of his Indian images into postcards and others were used specifically as tourist publicity by the Santa Fe Railroad.[12]

Of course, underlying such touristic endeavors to uncover the "authentic" was a desire to get back to the time before whites arrived, or at least the moment of arrival, to look with pristine eyes upon a primordial world. In the case of the North American Indian project there were numerous instances of attempts to replicate the vision of the earliest white entrants upon the land, those first to look with what Mary Louise Pratt has called "imperial eyes." We have already remarked upon such photographic images as "Before the White Man Came" (frontispiece), and in a later chapter we will see that Curtis's most important film was set "In the Days of Vancouver." In the context of the ethnological fieldwork, the most obvious example was the effort to replicate part of the imperial adventure of Lewis and Clark. This is how Curtis remembered the project's motivation:

> In the autumn of 1805 the Lewis and Clark party, travel-worn, hungry, their clothes in rags, reached the Columbia River and in canoes followed its course to the Ocean. It was the last leg of their incomparable march of exploration through unknown and trackless wilds . . . from the Mandan villages on the Missouri River to the Pacific Ocean. . . .
>
> On the banks of the River, from the Dalles to the ocean, they had found populous villages of flatten-headed, fish eating Indians. Many were treacherous and hostile. Their houses of great size were built of cedar planks. These villages of a primitive people living largely on salmon and other fish reeked with a nauseating stench.
>
> Through the Lewis and Clark Journals I had followed in my mind that great exploration on the Columbia River. I had long envisioned such a trip. I wanted to see and study the region from the water, as had the Lewis and Clark party more than a hundred years before; also to make a final check of ancient and present Indian village sites. I wanted to camp where they camped and approach the Pacific through the eyes of those intrepid explorers. . . . [13]

In such motivation there was a persistence of what Patricia Nelson Limerick has characterized as a curious "innocence" about both the actual historical purposes of Lewis and Clark's endeavors and their ultimate results, the conquest and dispossession of Native Americans. In Limerick's formulation, which may remind us of the connection made by the Indian Welfare League's report on the Indian Citizenship Act (see Chapter 1), the history of the West entered "the national memory" in a very different way to that of the South:

> The subject of slavery was the domain of sober national reflection; the subject of conquest was the domain of mass entertainment and the occasion for lighthearted national escapism. An element of regret for "what we did to the Indians" had entered the picture, but the dominant feature of conquest remained "adventure." Children happily played "cowboys and Indians" but stopped short of "masters and slaves."[14]

It is interesting that the only nationally acknowledged setback for whites in the conquest of the West, George Armstrong Custer's defeat at the Battle of the Little Bighorn on July 4, 1876, caused Curtis to swerve away for a time from ethnology as such. On the same day, October 22, 1907, Curtis sent two letters to Edmond S. Meany, who was writing the Sioux historical sketch for *The North American Indian*:

> While speaking of the Sioux history, would you mind having your students make a special search for matter on the Custer fight. One point I am anxious to get information on – Has there been anything published on the fact that Custer, from the highest viewpoint in the region watched Reno's charge, battle and defeat?

"This viewpoint," he elaborated, was "within easy relieving distance from Reno, in fact so close that he could have been to Reno's assistance in less than ten minutes, or have attacked the Sioux camp at its most distant point within 15 minutes." Curtis, who was photographed at Custer's outlook (fig. 12), thought that this information threw "an entirely new light on the entire Custer fight." It was not, he concluded the first letter, "a pipe dream": "I have ridden the battlefield from end to end, back and forth from every important point on it, noting carefully the time of such rides. . . ." In the other letter he said:

> I forgot to mention that in my work on the Custer fight, I have had with me three scouts who led Custer through the valley of the Little Big Horn, and who were with him until he was actively in the fight, they being the last people to see Custer or any of his men alive . . . and no one has heretofore made a careful study of the region assisted by these men.[15]

During his next visit to New York City Curtis gave an interview to the *New York Herald*, published on November 10, 1907, in which he apparently stated that Custer essentially wagered for glory, gambled his men's lives, and that he, Curtis, had concluded this as a result of an investigation lasting some months in the company of a number of Indians. Several correspondents protested this view and, as was mentioned earlier here, Mrs. Elizabeth Custer wrote to the Head of the U.S. Forest Service, Gifford Pinchot, complaining about his encouragement of Curtis's work. Since Pinchot had recently named a National Forest after Custer, he had a double reason for seeking an explanation from Curtis. Curtis's response to Pinchot, composed on May 9, 1908, was conciliatory, urging that the matter be dropped, but also included an offer to send Pinchot "typewritten material" on the issue for his own "personal reading."[16]

Interestingly, as the relevant volume of *The North American Indian* neared publication, Curtis became ever more circumspect. Having informed Meany in January 1908 that he might be going to do so, on August 28 of the same year he told him, "I cut out your matter relative to the Custer fight and brought in my material from the time [Custer] started up the Rose Bud until the end." "Don't have a cold chill when I say I brought in my material," Curtis admonished. "I have been very guarded and while giving a great deal of new and interesting information, I have said nothing that can be considered a criticism of Custer." Curtis also claimed to have the endorsement of General Charles A. Woodruff, "who spent so much time in the field with him [Custer]." He also gave similar reassurances to Pinchot: "I have said nothing that in any way deserves objection by Mrs. Custer. . . ." These reassurances were subsequently largely borne out by the detailed account in *The North American Indian* itself. There, Curtis stressed again his own involvement with and reliance upon White Man Runs Him and other Crow and Arikara scouts, as well as the corroboration of Woodruff. Basically, while he fought shy of imparting blame to Custer, the blow-by-blow account would have enabled a discerning reader to see what Custer could have witnessed from each vantage point on the battlefield – and to judge accordingly.[17]

The crucial point about this diversion from the usually more ethnologically-oriented concerns of the project was that the effort was *not* to assess the impact of the battle and its aftermath on the Sioux, Cheyenne, and other Plains peoples involved, but to seek an "explanation" of the *white* defeat. In turn, that explanation did not lie in any feature of Native American culture, but, it is hinted, in Custer's specific "mistakes." In other words, the Battle of the Little Bighorn was represented wholly as an episode in (white) American expansion.

The North American Indian project as a whole, even when its leading figures went to and fro over battlefields, certainly did not go so far as to fuel, in Limerick's phrase, "lighthearted . . . escapism," but, as we have seen, it did share in this penchant for "adventure." The project, in fact, like so many other western enterprises, was an amalgam of a range of practices, including business speculation, image production, trade, various forms of welfare, "entertainment" in Limerick's sense, and the relatively dispassionate ethnology of Myers. *The North American Indian* produced by the project was, of course, a work of some scholarship in anthropology and history, less obviously and directly determined by this array of practices than the magazine articles and the like, but it too, as I will continue to show in the chapters which follow, was also inscribed with notions of "adventure," not merely transcribed from the notes of a diffident ethnologist.

DOCUMENTS

Document 6A. Excerpts from "Among the Tewas [in c. 1906]," by W. W. Phillips, c. 1911.

This is a further extract from the memoir William Phillips probably wrote in 1911 as a contribution to the publicity campaign for the series of special lectures Curtis gave that year and describes field activities which took place in 1905 or, more likely, 1906. Phillips was born on March 4, 1880, in Little Falls, Minnesota, and, like Curtis, came with his family to the Bremerton area of Puget Sound, where his aunt, Clara Phillips, met and married Curtis. He lived in Seattle with Edward and Clara Curtis as one of the family from the age of sixteen. He supported himself through college by a succession of jobs in the Curtis studio and graduated from the University of Washington in 1904. As the tone of his writing in the memoir suggests, Phillips was at an open and impressionable stage in life during the period it describes. For several years he was the mainstay of the North American Indian project, employed both in the field and seeing volumes through the press in Cambridge, Massachusetts. It was while in the East, in Boston, that he met his future wife, Harriet Caroline Sias, and it was probably his marriage in December 1912, his consequent need for a more stable income, that led him to leave the project. For some years thereafter he farmed at Greenacres, near Spokane, before returning to Seattle in 1916 to engage himself in a variety of business enterprises, including the secretary-treasurership of Fraser, Goodwin, and Colver, a brokerage firm that collapsed in 1931 as a result of the ongoing Depression. He died, suddenly, in 1936.[18]

For endless distances along both sides of the Rio Grande in New Mexico, stretch chains of mountains, ten to twenty miles back, between each of which and the river lie rolling wastes of a most desolate, god-forsaken order, too sandy to grow sagebrush of decent size. These hills, – round-topped, hog-backed, often but gravel – rise abruptly from the water's edge, though here and there the river valley widens – at the confluence of some tiny stream tributary to the main stream. It is at such points, where water may be conducted from up stream for irrigation purposes, that the Tewa Indians have located their homes – compact villages, wherein all buildings are made of adobe, built one adjoining another, sometimes several stories in height, about a hollow square. From the outside, alleyways lead into the central plaza onto which all doors open. The outer walls, which alone are visible from a distance, often present the appearance of barricades, such suggestion being accentuated by small window openings, high up, and projecting roof timbers. All roofs are flat, – of thick, well tamped adobe supported by brush-thatched horizontal timbers.

Under these roofs are found quiet, peace-loving, soil-cultivating Indians who display cleanliness, courtesy and hospitality of an order which betokens a civilization highly advanced when first they were met by Spanish pioneers nearly four hundred years ago. Pueblo, or Village, Indians the Spanish called them. . . . [Their towns vary] from a hundred to a thousand or two in population, but only in those known as the Upper Rio Grande Pueblos are we now concerned, for it was among them that observations were made in the autumn of 1905.

These began with the village of San Ildefonso, where, on September 6th, was held the Tablita ceremony – a dance given for the purpose of tendering thanks to the allseeing benevolent Poseyamo – for the harvests, and the rain that produced them.

Churches, crosses, pictures and images of Christ and the Virgin Mary, and hieratic paraphernalia, whether priests now reside at the villages or not, are found on all sides, to evidence the long years of Spanish, and therefore Catholic, contact the various Pueblos have suffered and enjoyed. In outward semblance the Indians are Catholic in religious faith, stoutly contending that they are converts, but in the wings and behind the curtain, they are as pagan to-day as they were the day Queen Isabella listened with favor to the pleadings of Columbus.

September sixth, as it happens, is the day set aside by the Catholic priests among them on which to pay special tribute to San Ildefonso, the patron saint for whom the village now bearing his name was renamed; Po-hwo-gies they call themselves in their native tongue. On that day annually the San Ildefonso villagers dance. The early morning is devoted to mass – peace made with a foreign god – after which, in an underground chamber, the *estufa,* male dancers robe in cinctures, spruce boughs, moccasins and paint. Women come out bare-footed, garbed in homespun dresses.

Down the center of the plaza these form two long lines, facing each other a few feet apart. The individuals, perhaps thirty in all, ranging in age from thirty to three, are alternately male and female, the latter carrying painted, shingle-like, serrate-edged tablets straight up on their heads. Throughout the day, to the music of drumming and singing furnished by a chorus of middleaged men, the two lines and chorus members dance, at intervals resting and retiring to the estufa, stopping when the sun goes down.

The songs are all supplications to Poseyamo for clouds and rain and snow and bountiful crops – each ending unfailingly with "Thanks to Poseyamo," for he is the one supreme god of gods, whose name in translation means Falling Water.

Water! water! is the cry among all Pueblo Indians of the thirsty, sun-baked region we know as the Great Southwest.

The entering wedge to Tewa customs and beliefs we secured in San Ildefonso, meeting kindly, courteous, but conservative treatment. Government lies in the hands of one man – ruler for life – succeeded at death by the man who is next oldest in membership in a certain secret order. Cacique – chief – the Spanish termed him; to his tribesmen he is the Poantoyu – priest and president. He appoints a delegate yearly to act as governor – to face the daily problems in the open – while he sits back, obscure, but powerful and most observant: for responsibility develops any man.

A week spent in diligent effort at the village of San Ildefonso, probing, through a good interpreter, into secret realms, – mythology, religion, ancient customs and modern ceremony – gave me a good foundation on which to work among other villages of like beliefs farther up the Rio Grande. . . .

We had visited three pueblos, acquiring notes of some value, before decamping from our desert schooner at the village of Santa Clara. A good Indian interpreter was not to be found there, so pictures became the chief objective of that visit, but not until some show of fight for folklore and hints of internal organization had been made. With the aid of our Mexican teamster, I tried the village governor, appointee of the Cacique, through the medium of Spanish. He fought like the proverbial "sixty" to escape divulging anything, . . . but he made a bee line for the village school mistress when leaving us late in the night, and with fiery eyes and guarded voice revealed to her that the Two Americans knew too much, for mention of a little knowledge gave him the impression that we knew much more. Further work became difficult, and when I returned to Santa Clara by horseback one evening to call on the school mistress, a silent sentry stood beside my horse while I was visiting, and silently guided me out of the village on to the desert road when I remounted to return to our camp farther up on the Rio Grande.

This camp was situated just outside the village of San Juan. Good sized stores, a modern church and other improvements gave this place a civilized appearance. Dogs, innumerable, of unnameable extraction, playing a more dramatic part in our research work than we then knew, collected nightly about our tents, for no better reason, apparently, than to fight and turn the stillness into pandemonium. This is noteworthy from the fact that though Indians, generally, keep dogs galore, they are usually the most harmless, least combative canine mongrels that ever gnaw at bones.

[At San Juan] a little silver went further . . . than anywhere that I recall; usually it takes a lot. Products of their fields, – corn, beans, other vegetables and hay, were had at a reasonable figure, and portraits, kitchen scenes and harvest views were obtained without establishing a bank. Some good pottery and excellent pieces of ceremonial paraphernalia were bought there, too, at other than high prices.

But in spite of the very hospitable attitude . . . considerable balkiness was met with when we quizzed for knowledge of what takes place in their secret, underground chambers of worship.

Devotion to things Indianesque an Indian never gives up, no matter where he is, though oftentimes he may refrain from outward show. Even the returned students – the educated youths on whom we had often to depend for interpreters – are rigid in that devotion. The matter of securing good interpreters is most important, and they have always to be selected with great care. The average well-educated Indian is the poorest to be had. The better he knows his English, the longer he has been away at school, and the less he knows his Indian tongue, in its suggestive, idiomatic forms; he is less trusted by his elders too. . . . [At San Juan, without obtaining good results, I went through two interpreters.]

"How goes it with your new man?" Curtis asked one day when I was trying the third one. It was no go as I replied.

"You remember that 'bad-eyed' fellow who sat around here this morning?" he asked again.

"Yes," I answered.

"The store-keeper says he talks fair English that he has picked up by himself, and has a reputation as a renegade; would knife a man for ten dollars when he is hungry."

"I hope he is hungry," I replied, "for we can supply the ten without being knifed, and perhaps he will go in and earn it." He did, too. Sojero was enlisted as right hand man the following day.[19]

He told me all he knew about his people, and all he hoped to know, reveling in the disclosure because he was being a bit tricky and was earning needed money with his wits. He racked his brain to give me clues to things of which I had no knowledge. These were followed out to advantage through other, possibly more reliable, sources. . . . Among other things, [Sojero] mentioned a sacred rain-making shrine which he averred was to be found on the top of one of the highest points in the southern Rockies, some forty miles from the Rio Grande, though he had never been at the spot in person. However, if I would tell no one, and join him on a trip that might mean a gun fight with his brother tribesmen if discovered, he would furnish ponies and take me to the shrine.

Just what we might find, he wasn't certain, but he did know that during dry seasons when crops began to suffer, it was customary for each of six secret societies among his people to send two delegates each to that shrine, together with a personal representative of the village cacique, to dance for rain. They would leave at nightfall after a purifying fast, travel by moonlight across the sand hills, and rest near dawn in the timber beyond. Then in broad daylight the journey would be resumed and the mountain crest reached in the afternoon. There, about a stone altar, on which they placed jewels and feather offerings to the gods, after disrobing, in stark nakedness, the delegates would dance from mid-afternoon till sunset, offering prayers for rain.

Mexican sheep herders long since learned not to follow, and the "unwashed" of the San Juan Tewas never viewed what transpired there. Sojero had heard these trips discussed, having had to bribe his friends to assist him in gaining a surreptitious entrance to the council. If I would pay him a little more per day for the use of his horses, he would take me to the shrine. The bargain was struck.

When Justo, our Mexican camp cook, learned of the plan, he asked me not to go, evincing the gravest fears for the safety of Sojero and myself. I asked him what there was to fear; if any one knew where we were going, but got for a reply, only, "I don't know. You better watch out."

Of course we expected to "watch out," but Justo's attitude convinced me that he had something definite in mind, and he had though I didn't learn what it was until long afterward.

At midnight Sojero came with two good-sized horses. We saddled quietly and hurriedly, setting out toward a Mexican town down stream, when destination lay across the river and up. Once out of the Indian village, however, we turned toward the bald mountain that was to be our goal, crossing the Rio Grande at a ford and taking to the rolling hills beyond, well and securely launched on a trip that promised adventure.

My guide proved to be a wonder. Over hills, through canons and brush thickets, up rocky slopes into forest belts, . . . regardless of trail or track, he pushed his way, by what magic I have not yet divined. With a long, loose end of a halter rope he larruped his rakish sorrel unsparingly, and to keep in sight of him, I had to heap abuses on the black I rode.

We had climbed above the last stream by nine in the morning, but would find a spring, so Sojero said, not far from the mountain's base. He was right, but yet wrong, for when we reached the spot at one o'clock that afternoon, parched with thirst, after clambering alternately up rock-strewn slopes and through thickets, we found barely more than black mud at the base of a huge boulder, covering a patch on the edge of a brushy stretch no larger than a room. The mud was trampled full of holes by stray, wandering ponies, some of the tracks being freshly made. Into one of these, close by the rock, had oozed a cupful of water. Sojero and I dipped a few swallows each with a rubber cup, but ugh! It smelt like a stable and tasted vilely, turning my stomach so that I couldn't eat. Sojero ate but a few morsels of luncheon too; then we moved on, one having to prod our poor beasts, while the other tugged on their neck-ropes, to get them away, for they had not had water enough to dampen their tongues.

Some distance beyond we passed above timber-line into dry ripened grass, and as the mountain then rose abruptly, we unsaddled the horses, tethered them, and climbed on afoot.

That last ascent I thought would never end; the twenty pound camera I carried on my back had grown to twenty hundred, and the altitude was sufficient seemingly to displace air completely. Breathing was like drawing cider through a straw from an empty keg. In time we reached the mountain crest, and oh the relief!

Sojero's tomb-like silence all day had made me skeptical, but fears of disappointment were dispelled when a crescent-shaped line of rocks piled around a slight excavation burst into view. The shrine was a positive entity; and it did not take long to expose plates enough to carry home evidence of its existence.

Out from the chord between the points of the crescent ran three hollowed-out pathways directed toward as many Indian villages on the distant Rio Grande – these to direct the course the rain must take from the mountain-top when it falls in response to the Tewas' sacred rites and most potent prayers offered at the shrine.[20]

Without undue loss of time, the guide and I turned homeward. At dusk that night we reached water – taking a different backward route – where the four of us, horses and men, drank, ate and rested for a time. The descent . . . proved more severe than the ascent. So worn out that she wobbled, the patient black that I rode more than once pitched forward on her knees with a groan when I mounted. But Sojero brooked no delays. Safety lay in getting home in as short a time that even if suspicion should fall upon us, and point to the object of our absence, reason would say nay.

The guide's caution was not unnecessary, for our surreptitious disappearance and return by night aroused no end of suspicion . . . among Indians and Mexicans for miles around, but no one ever suspected that we had visited the mountain-top.

One night a year afterward . . . three hundred miles from the Tewas on the Rio Grande, I called upon Justo, the cook, to assist in translating some old Spanish reports on Indian customs wherein the narrator spoke of Indian gods as witches and wizards who took on the forms of man or beast at pleasure. Justo's eyes lighted: "You remember – San Juan? All those dogs that fight so much? I tell you to 'watch out'. They are not dogs at all. Those Indians can change themselves and see everything that goes on at night – running round like dogs. One old Mexican man who live with them when he was little, say lots of time he wake up at night and find only clothes left inside – the Indians gone off like dogs."

His own superstitious belief in lycanthropy had menaced Justo much while we sojourned in San Juan, and believing that our movements were watched by the numerous dogs, he lived in terror all the time we were there, in the one instance waiting in nervous anxiety for the return of Sojero and myself from the sacred mountain. . . .[21]

Document 6B. Extracts from "Travelling the Route of Lewis and Clark – One Hundred Years Later [in 1910]," by Edward S. Curtis, n.d.[22]

In the autumn of 1805 the Lewis and Clark party, travel-worn, hungry, their clothes in rags, reached the Columbia River and in canoes followed its course to the Ocean. . . .

The boat in which I set forth in the spring of 1910 [to replicate their voyage] was a nondescript, flat-bottomed one, square at the stern and pointed at the bow. In it was installed a small gas engine with sufficient power to give us steerage way. . . . A large Indian canoe served as a supplementary cargo carrier.

Our party consisted of Myers, my field helper of many years; Schwinke, a stenographer; Noggie, the Japanese cook; and an old Columbia River pilot. The previous year I had consulted him as to the feasibility of such a trip and he expressed a great desire to accompany us, stating: "I would like to make one more trip on the old River before I fold up." Well, he made most of the trip. . . .

As we moved downstream Myers and I made notes, watched for places to land and checked on old village sites. Schwinke set his typewriter on a packing case and hammered away typing yesterday's notes. Some days swift water and rapids kept us busy just staying right side up. At night we camped on the shore. Sometimes we picked up an old Indian who could give us pertinent information and took him along for a few days. . . .

We approached Celilo Falls in our small craft in some trepidation. Here the great Columbia pours through basalt cliffs dropping some eighty feet into a tumultuous cauldron. Here the Indians fished for the great Chinook salmon. Hanging precariously to the precipices they used dip nets and spears to capture fish. But Celilo was more than a place to fish. Indians from many tribes and from great distances travelled to this trading center. They came from the seacoast and by river; they came over mountains and valleys by horseback laden with goods to barter. I doubt any other location in the country had seen such assemblages of Indians through the years.

It was here we had the problem of portaging our outfit. How much simpler for us than it was for Lewis and Clark. We loaded our boat on a flatcar and a dinky teakettle of a locomotive would pull it to the unloading point below the Falls. Even with such modern facilities it proved quite a task to put our flat-bottomed barge on the car. We had not appreciated its size and weight. The track extended down an incline into the river and the car was let down until partially under water. Freshet season complicated the loading. Since I was the leader of the party and considered the best swimmer, I fell heir to the job. I handled the boat while the men hauled on the lines from shore. The roar of the Falls was so great they could not hear my instructions which forced me to swim ashore to give directions.

Noggie was sitting on the ground crying. On my inquiry: "What in the hell is the matter with you?" he sobbed, "I know you will be drowned!" Undoubtedly I should have appreciated his concern for my welfare, but on the contrary I was annoyed. I suggested quite forcefully to lay off the sobs and give his attention to his line. At least Myers was able to enjoy a laugh over Noggie's tears and my exasperation. One of my vivid recollections was Myers's comment while sitting in the barge and rolling over the steel rails: "Chief, you should take a picture of our outfit and send it to the Explorer's Club, entitled: 'Hardships of exploring in the wild west'."

In portaging the Falls and rapids of Celilo we passed old friends, the Wishrams, living on the north shore of the river. The Wishram village was one of the oldest and strongest on the Columbia River, and it would have been a great pleasure to visit our old friends, but time did not permit. . . .

Contrary winds, rough water, rains and many villages later, made our progress slow. Arriving near the mouth of the Willamette River Noggie decided that he had lost his taste for cooking in the blowing sand and rain. In fact he was fed up with the great outdoors so he folded his bedroll and departed. The fine old captain decided that while we working near the Willamette he would have a visit with his old cronies in Portland. City life proved too much for him and he embarked on that last journey to Unknown Ports. At least we had a last thrilling trip together down the "Old River." Our party of five was reduced to three and I became both captain and cook. As we neared our goal, the Pacific, and summed up the existing native life from the Dalles to the Ocean, we were greatly impressed [that] scores of populous villages and many sub tribes had passed from existence. The Chinook tribes on the river, which were often spoken of by Lewis and Clark, were practically extinct with the exception of the Wishrams of the Dalles. . . . In that hundred year period there was a ninety-five percent decrease in population and no doubt that is a conservative estimate. . . .

Introduced diseases, uncared for and unchecked, are the foremost cause of their destruction. Small pox, measles and cholera had ravaged them. Whiskey, too, had done its part. . . . At the time of the Lewis and Clark expedition the Indians had not acquired a taste for liquor. This fact was mentioned by the explorers several times. . . .

Nearing the ocean we turned our worthy but nondescript craft adrift that it might float out to meet the ocean breakers and be battered to fragments. . . .

Various aspects of Curtis's reminiscence of this voyage were borne out by an *aide memoire* kept by the stenographer, Edmund Schwinke. Schwinke, who joined the North American Indian project earlier in 1910, was born in 1888 in Warren, Minnesota, of German immigrant parents, originally went to Seattle in 1909 to clerk for a shipping company, and may have been introduced to Curtis through Ella McBride (see Chapter 2). He worked for Curtis for a number of years before settling in Oak Hill, Ohio. From the *memoire*, written on two large index cards, it seems that the party started down the Columbia River from Pasco, that the "old Columbia River pilot" was Captain [Michelle?] Martineau, a steamboat master who had been born in 1848 to an Indian mother and a pioneer father. Martineau had travelled to the Yukon in 1898, had "retired" in the early 1900s to farm, but continued to sail the Columbia from time to time. The cook, dubbed Noggie by Curtis, was named Nakamoto by Schwinke. Schwinke's notes were presumably intended to form the basis of a continuous narrative of his Northwest experiences, for they took the story onwards to Quinault, Seattle, and points north, including Alert Bay in Kwakiutl territory, all locations thereafter of Schwinke's work for the project.[23]

Data collected on this voyage was deployed in *The North American Indian*, Volume 8, most notably a catalogue of village sites along the Columbia which included what Schwinke has as "Nihlwidich," a form of the Chinook name for the principal Wishham village near the Dalles, transliterated in *The North American Indian* as "Nihhluidih." The thrust of *The North American Indian* account was that these people had been virtually extinguished. All round, as the volume's preface put it, "considerable labor was involved in this research, as it required detailed study of the entire stretch of river and the interviewing of every aged Indian to be found on its shores." Much of *The North American Indian* account – minus, for the most part, the adventure element – foreshadowed material in the personal records of Curtis and Schwinke.[24]

Document 6C. Letter, Edward S. Curtis to Edmond S. Meany, 1922.

On August 30, 1922, Curtis wrote from Ukiah, California to his old friend Meany, saying, "I am certain you will be glad to know I am in the field working with the Indians." "I am out on a three or four months trip with the Indians of northern California." "Florence is with me," he continued, "other than that I am alone. Had expected Myers to be with me but he was otherwise tied up and could not manage it. I will make a map with check marks showing where some of the seasons [sic] work is."[25] As the rest of the letter went on to assert, Curtis was confident that the season's work would lead to publication of a further volume of *The North American Indian* (the publishing schedule of which had experienced something of a hiatus) and he outlined plans up to and including Volume 17. As it happened, he was unable, as his postscript explained, to include a map, and the letter that follows was by way of a report on the promised work.

> I believe you will be interested in a few details of my summers [sic] work among the California tribes.
>
> As you know the principal work of this season's trip is the making of the pictures for Volumes XIII and XIV. As a popular title for the trip it might be called "Gathering Up The Fragments." The two volumes in question will cover the many small groups in California north of San Francisco and the Klamath Lake region of Southern Oregon.
>
> This . . . covers a tremendous area and a great diversity of life. The Coast line from Golden Gate to the Oregon line is a precipitous one with a jungle like forest of spruce, redwood and fir coming to the water's edge. In the old days many small groups lived along the coast principally at the mouth of the rivers. These tribes lived much as did the Puget Sound natives in the old days.
>
> The great majority of the California tribes can well be termed a mountain people. Their home grounds were along the countless mountain slopes where fish could be had from the streams and game and acorns from the mountain sides. So steep are the mountain sides that the natives could only find village sites at rare intervals and in many cases to locate a house they had to dig a niche in the mountain side itself.
>
> This limited ground space has in some places brought about a unique and interesting grave yard location. The graves can truly be said to be a part of the domestic establishment, and here the people certainly always have the dead with them. In many cases the graves are within ten feet of the house. To one not accustomed to living in a cemetery one of these old villages does not seem over attractive as here for generations they have buried their dead, and those buried during the last fifty years

Figure 13. Ogalala War Party, 1907, by E. S. Curtis. These Sioux reenact a scene from pre-reservation days.

are enclosed in a whitewashed picket fence. Over the graves and on the fence are placed all sorts of domestic junk. One village visited seemed fully half covered with graves and naturally the graves of the present generation were dug among the bones of the former generations.

One of the difficulties of this California work is the great number of groups to be visited, and the further fact of their being so scattered and last but not least the isolation. The season's work will cover over fifty working places and to reach some of these is no small task. The majority of the places we reached or almost reached with our car, and in the early part of the trip we christened it "Nanny," as nothing but a goat could get over the mountain trails our work has taken us. Northern California has mountains enough to supply the world and still have plenty for home consumption, and motoring into the out of the way niches among these mountains can be termed a sport. So far we have met with no serious mishap but plenty of close shaves. On one occasion while creeping around a mountain side the ground gave way and the car started to roll over. Once in a lifetime one uses good judgment in what seems to be the last moment of existence. This was one of the times. When the car started over I lacked three feet of [distance from] a life saving oak on the mountain side. I gave the car all the gas at once, and it shot ahead far enough to reach the tree, and then toppled over against it. Sitting in the seat I could have tossed my still burning cigarette two hundred feet down to the first ledge of the gorge. . . .

So far the summers [sic] work has given us six crossings of the coast range and there will be six to eight weeks more work before I am through. . . .

Speaking of highways that from Requa to Crescent City surpasses anything I have ever seen. . . . Anyone motoring from Seattle to California should go by the Coast route passing through nearly two hundred miles of redwood forest. To-day we are camped near the mouth of the Smith River. Our tent is under a spruce and so near the ocean that we are almost in its spray. It is a day of constant rain, and no work can be done. Otherwise I would have no time for this letter.

A week from now we should be at Crater Lake. Then down to Klamath Lake where Florence will leave for home and the balance of the trip I will be alone. Some of the main points to be touches [sic] on the southward leg of the trip will be Alturas, Shasta, Redding, Lassen, Susanville, Pyramid Lake, Nevada, Lake Tahoe, Oroville, Yosemite, and Tulare Lake. These, however, are but highway points and the real work will be on the bypaths.

In a technical way the seasons [sic] work covers some most interesting material. I am working with a different linguistic group at every move. At one point where I worked with a large number of Indians gathered for work in the bean fields, there were six languages in the one camp.

At this point we have the Tolowa, a branch of the Athapascan stock. On the Klamath River, . . . we had the Karok, and the Yurok, the latter belonging to the Algonquin linguistic stock [and so, through the Hupa, the Wailaki and Yuki, the Kato, the Pomo, and the Shasta]. Many other stocks and groups will be touched but I think I have given you enough of the linguistic groups to indicate some of the . . . problems involved in these two volumes now at hand.

While the majority of the groups have changed materially

through contact with the white race and mixed bloods predominate, there is still fine picture material and I am confident that the volumes will be rich in illustrations.

I cannot refrain from touching upon the treatment of the California Indians by the early settlers of the state. While practically all Indians suffered seriously at the hands of the settlers and the government, the Indians of this state suffered beyond comparison. The principal outdoor sport of the settlers during the 50's and 60's seemingly was the killing of Indians. There is nothing else in the history of the United States which approaches the inhuman and brutal treatment of the California tribes. Men desiring women, merely went to the village or camp, killed the men and took such women as they desired. Seemingly feeling that the Indians might later be given some protection and rights they killed them off as fast as they could. Camps were raided for men to serve as laborers. Such Indian workers were worse than slaves. The food furnished them being so poor and scanty that they died of hunger. One would think that self interest would have caused them to feed the enslaved men, but apparently there was a feeling that others could be caught when those at hand were dead.

In 1851 a treaty was made with the California tribes but the settlers fearing that some of the land might contain gold, prevented the ratification of the treaty. Thus the Indians became a people without even camping places which they could call their own. No story can ever be written which can overstate the inhuman treatment accorded the California tribes.

It is only fair to say that all early settlers did not join in the brutal treatment of the native as in some cases individual settlers treated the Indians about them with every consideration.

Enough of all this. I will let you know how the trip ends.[26]

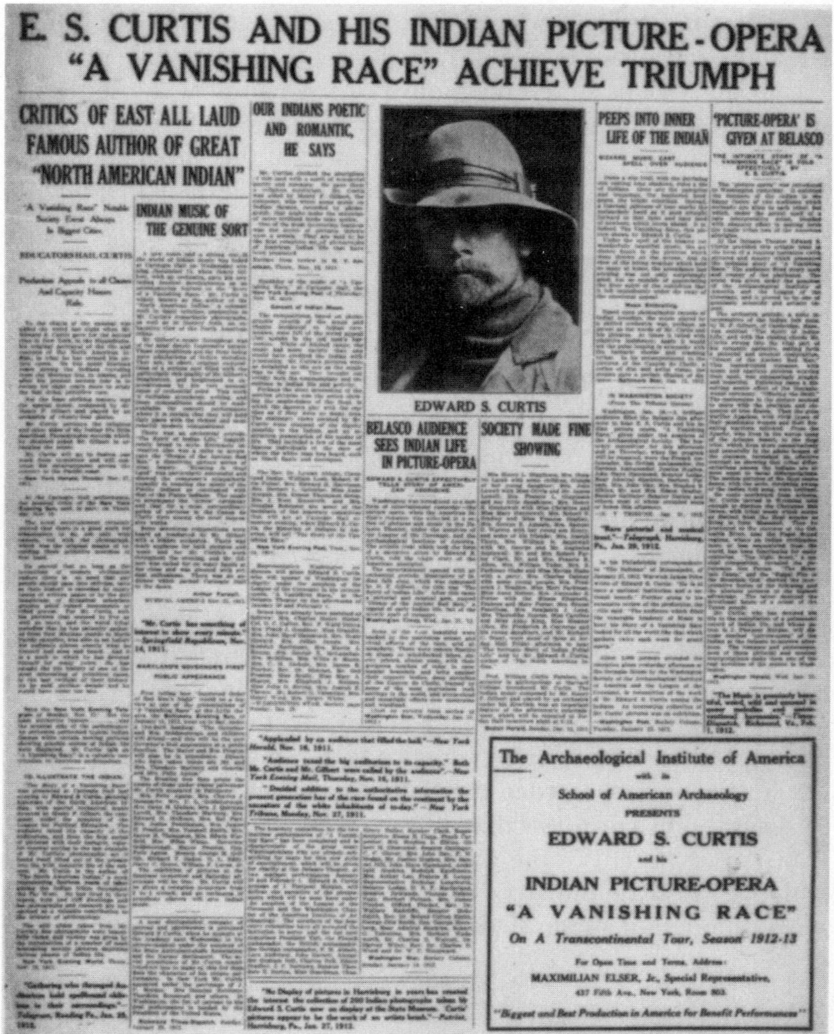

E. S. CURTIS AND HIS INDIAN PICTURE-OPERA "A VANISHING RACE" ACHIEVE TRIUMPH

CRITICS OF EAST ALL LAUD FAMOUS AUTHOR OF GREAT "NORTH AMERICAN INDIAN"

OUR INDIANS POETIC AND ROMANTIC, HE SAYS

INDIAN MUSIC OF THE GENUINE SORT

EDWARD S. CURTIS

PEEPS INTO INNER LIFE OF THE INDIAN

'PICTURE-OPERA' IS GIVEN AT BELASCO

BELASCO AUDIENCE SEES INDIAN LIFE IN PICTURE-OPERA

SOCIETY MADE FINE SHOWING

The Archaeological Institute of America

School of American Archaeology

PRESENTS

EDWARD S. CURTIS

INDIAN PICTURE-OPERA

"A VANISHING RACE"

On A Transcontinental Tour, Season 1912-13

MAXIMILIAN ELSER, Jr., Special Representative,

Figure 14. Simulated newspaper publicity brochure for the musicale, 1911. The inset self-portrait of Curtis in field outfit was made in 1899.

7

"THE VANISHING RACE" IN SIGHT AND SOUND

On November 19, 1911, Curtis wrote to his friend Edmond S. Meany, about his latest triumphs. "Dear Brother Meany," he began, "I think we can say that my lecture entertainment 'arrived'. I wish you could have been present at the Carnegie Hall affair. The tremendous auditorium was filled to overflowing, a sea of people from the stage to the very 'sky' itself." Curtis had been introduced by Henry Fairfield Osborn of the American Museum of Natural History; just before they stepped into view Osborn had looked through the foliage and, according to Curtis, remarked, "'Do you realize that that is almost an appalling audience, and one that few men in their life-time have the privilege of facing?'" "I think," Curtis added, "he was a little nervous on his own account and slightly so on mine, [but] rather than causing nervousness . . . it gave me courage and I was absolutely certain of myself after my first two words." "Osborn's voice," Curtis explained, "lacks the carrying power and his slight nervousness meant a rather halting introduction. This was evidently greatly to my advantage, as the minute I spoke I reached the farthermost corners and my voice caught and held the people."[1]

It certainly was no run-of-the-mill lecture. "The enthusiasm," claimed Curtis, "was quite out of the ordinary. During the impressive musical numbers you could sense the wave of feeling which passed over the audience. They would not cheer as they wanted to hear to the best possible advantage," though "in a few instances they did break into applause during the rendering of the music." Even allowing for the obvious note of self-congratulation and for a measure of hyperbole here, it must have been a memorable occasion. Curtis could barely contain his high spirits and dashed off exuberant accounts to other friends and patrons, including Roosevelt and Pinchot. And the appearance at Carnegie Hall was but one among many: In fact, in the same letter to Meany, Curtis spoke of performances at the Brooklyn Institute and the New York Hippodrome and of the continuation of the national tour through the winter of 1911–12. This did indeed come about, and a further transcontinental tour was scheduled for 1912–13. Roosevelt, on hearing of the Carnegie Hall success, told Curtis, "It is a good thing for the whole American people."[2] It was definitely a good thing for Curtis. He received his first entry in *Who's Who in America* and, in general, 1912 probably marked the acme of his fame.

Moreover, what we are considering here – if we exclude such would-be "popular" ventures as George Catlin's Indian Gallery, with its tipis erected in such venues as the Louvre, and, of course, Buffalo Bill Cody's manifestly circus-like Wild West Show – was the most highly wrought and elaborate of "entertainments" about American Indians ever devised.[3] Curtis called it his "musicale" or "picture-opera." The present chapter constitutes an effort to uncover the musicale's origins, development, content, and contemporary reception, in the belief that such cultural archaeology may lead us towards an understanding of its significance.

Constituting the Musicale

From quite early on in his career Curtis appreciated the benefits that might derive from investment in public lectures. In 1900 he spoke at a major photographic convention in San Francisco. In Seattle, his home town and studio headquarters, he gave talks fairly often, including an appearance at Christensen's Hall in 1904. In 1905 he lectured to the Century Club in New York and the Cosmos Club in Washington, D.C. The talks brought in a useful income. They also enhanced Curtis's self esteem and his reputation as an authority; this was most overtly displayed in a 1906 letter to one of his earliest patrons, Judge Thomas Burke:

> Last night I gave a stereopticon picture talk at the Century Club. The room was crowded; I did my part well, perhaps better than I have ever before. I put the pictures on the screen and talked like a whirlwind for an hour and fifteen minutes, showing them about one hundred and thirty pictures. The audience . . . [was] breathlessly quiet, occasionally cheering a picture. When the last picture went on the screen, and I thanked them feelingly for

> their interest in the pictures . . . the whole roomful of men rose to their feet with a cheer of thanks. Nothing [has] caused quite the feeling of pleasure that this demonstration did. . . . As you know, it is a Club having in its membership the best artists in America, and last night they were out in force, and when a gathering like that will show such enthusiasm one cannot help but feel he is right in the work.[4]

But the primary merit of such engagements was that they constituted *events* and, as such, were newsworthy in a way that photographing and writing in themselves – even publications, even exhibitions – were not. Gilbert H. Grosvenor of the National Geographic Society, in commending Curtis to Richard Watson Gilder of *Century* magazine, described the impact of one such event in 1905: "He gave our Geographic Society the most wonderful exhibition last night I have seen. We had about 1000 people and they just sat and clapped and clapped. He showed 130 pictures and they applauded nearly every one, though our audiences are usually very staid." In one early interview, in speaking about the success of his talks, Curtis admitted, "My stereopticon exhibits attracted a good deal of attention, and while that had not been my former plan, I have . . . arranged for considerable so-called lecture work for the coming season . . . " As we saw earlier, a consequence of the financial arrangement with Morgan was Curtis's enforced assumption of responsibility for keeping the North American Indian work in the public eye and for selling subscriptions, so it is not surprising that from the spring of 1906, when the agreement with Morgan was reached, speaking engagements became a pretty regular thing.[5]

By the summer of 1911 the finances of the project were not in a healthy state. On June 7, Curtis wrote to Hodge, outlining some of his plans:

> I have got to confess that I am face to face with a complete change of plans for the year, and want to go over them with you. Outside of some absolute miracle there is no chance whatever for my getting funds for field work this year. Within forty eight hours I will probably have started on my plans for a new order of things, which will be a big and active selling campaign personally conducted, covering all parts of the United States, beginning in October, and ending next spring. I have been face to face with this thing for some weeks, so that I can write now with

> some degree of sanity. In other words, the worst of the misery is over. The time between now and autumn will be used in preparation for the winter campaign. . . .

Curtis went on to outline other aspects of the plan, including the insistence that it should not be known that the change was "forced" upon them "through the lack of funds" and stressing the last ditch nature of the campaign. Curtis put the matter in a more general manner to Charles Walcott, Hodge's superior at the Smithsonian: "The work of preparation for this whirlwind lecture campaign has been very heavy, and I hope that the results will justify the work involved. . . . The purpose of the tour is to attract attention to the book, and to close up sales enough to put [it] on its feet." But he also had to confess, "at the same time I must, if possible, make the lecture part self-supporting."[6]

And it did become a campaign; for example, to the University of Pennsylvania Museum Curtis offered both the musicale and the promotion services of a Mr. Conrado or Conradi, describing him as "a quiet, matter-of-fact, dignified type of a man . . . who does a good deal of work through the schools, etc. to promote a serious interest in the entertainment." Also, the North American Indian office followed up the Museum's acceptance with a series of publicity initiatives, and to coincide with the Philadelphia performance Curtis arranged exhibitions of his photographs both in the Museum itself and in Wanamaker's department store window. Curtis urged Mrs. E. W. Scherr, one of his New York patrons who knew show business herself as a performer, to scatter the publicity leaflets "like autumn leaves" and to "tell the friends of the cause that this is the time they need to be counted on the right side." Bright red programs were printed ("They are so attractive," Curtis claimed, "that the ushers steal them"), and the other material available included posters, a supply of "Indian stories" prepared for the press, multiple copies of the Hawthorne review of *The North American Indian*, window displays, and newsclippings.[7]

Curtis lectures were either illustrated by magic lantern slides or delivered in the context of an exhibition of photographs or photogravures. Also from early on, Curtis began to incorporate movie footage into his presentations. Quite when or how the notion arose of including music in the 1911–12 tour is not known. Native American music, though, had been a concern of the ethnological work for *The North American Indian* from the beginning. As early as 1905

Roosevelt had written to Curtis: "When you come to publish that book, the very best person you could get to write up the songs and music of the Indians, and especially the southwestern Indians, is Miss Natalie Curtis." "I wish you would get into touch with her," he added. It has not been ascertained whether anything came of this particular initiative, but phonographic equipment was regularly taken into the field, ceremonies and songs were recorded, and the contents of the phonographic cylinders were transcribed by competent musicians so that scores could be published in *The North American Indian.*[8]

One of the musicians engaged in this task was Henry Franklin Belknap Gilbert of Cambridge, Massachusetts. Gilbert, a composer and conductor in his own right, also contributed an interesting "Note on the Indian Music" to Volume 6 of *The North American Indian*, which was published in 1911. Perhaps conscious of the great popularity of Gilbert's *Pirate Song* (1902), it was to Gilbert that Curtis turned for compositions to accompany his "material" for the big campaign. Moreover, according to Curtis's letter of contract with the musician, written on July 26, 1911, Gilbert was not only to supply some "twenty-six numbers" by the end of September (all to be copyrighted by Curtis), but also to arrange them for an orchestra *and* hire, direct, and conduct the orchestra during the coming tour. On the same day, Curtis sent Gilbert a parcel of eight phonographic records of musical items he intended to depict visually in the course of the performance. Gilbert, it seems, was expected to build his own compositions from this data.[9]

The performance – whether the standard general treatment sometimes titled "The Intimate Story of Indian Tribal Life" or a variation of it covering a more restricted geographical area, such as "Indians of the Southwest" (which highlighted the Hopi Snake Dance; see fig. 15) – was divided into segments, some plainly expository and some more sensory, even emotional, in their appeal. The music was written to bring out the mood and atmosphere of the picture sequence or motion picture. Occasionally, as might be expected, this was done by musical quotation from or allusion to the aboriginal music that had originally accompanied the action or which was produced by the particular tribe concerned. Sometimes, though, it was simply done by a rhythmic musical echo of a visual action (such as running or, indeed, dancing), as was the fashion with most music intended to accompany silent films at that time. Hence, in the case of a Flathead dance that was to be presented in still pictures, Curtis had this advice for

Gilbert: "The dancing here is not motion picture dancing, and if you wanted to get the thought of dancing in your music it would be only to suggest it. . . ." "It is simply like a painting," he added, "and any dance idea would be satisfactory."[10] For the most part, Gilbert made a delicate compromise between giving a musical "idea" of something – whether maidens gathering water in Hopi country or a Plains war party descending a slope – and actual orchestral renditions of songs he had heard on his phonograph, such as the prayers of the Sioux Hunkalowampi ceremony. Clearly, it was Gilbert's contribution that turned a lecture into a "musicale."

Gilbert and the 1911 Tour

Gilbert's association with the ethnological work of the North American Indian project was basically a happy one. For a start, as he himself later admitted, the assignment produced a reasonably steady, if relatively small, income. This income was really useful to him as a composer, serving to underwrite his dedicated vocation. One of the fieldworkers, usually Myers, would send him wax cylinders and he would transcribe from them, then return both cylinders and scores. He would also read proofs of the transcriptions at the appropriate time. In 1910 alone he transcribed at least sixty cylinders. Not surprisingly, perhaps, the material itself – hearing in his own living room, as he put it, "the Indian singing his barbaric song out in the wilds of Idaho or some place out there" – gradually came to be an inspiration to him in its own right, and this is a matter to which we will return.[11]

Gilbert's involvement with the lecture tour, on the other hand, was shot through with difficulties and disappointments. Upon engagement he was given only about two months in which to produce over twenty "numbers." He expected the tour to start at the beginning of October (though, as it happened, it did not start until half way through the month), and much of the material he was to work from and with, both movie footage and slide sequences, did not reach him until well into August. And Curtis changed his mind quite drastically about the program at least once, saying, "All things in this world are a compromise, and we will simply have to do the very best we can."[12]

Gilbert found the negotiations with musicians and with Curtis's tour manager, Charles Rice, both awkward and distasteful. Rice, who was conscious of Curtis's true financial situation to a degree that

Figure 15. Hopi Snake Dancer in Costume, 1904, by E. S. Curtis. This man, a member of the Antelope clan, holds a feather used for hypnotising the snakes used in the ceremony.

Gilbert was not, laid down parameters that were hard to meet. "We want good men," he wrote, "the best we can get, but in the manner of expense I've got to go slow." Speaking of Curtis, he added, "He's carrying an expense now no other lecturer has ever carried before." Gilbert seems ultimately to have carried the day in getting a higher rate for the musicians – probably thinking that only better pay would attract musicians of the right caliber, capable of playing his music. Even so, it is doubtful whether he succeeded in full; certainly, Curtis seems to have worried as to whether the musicians would be sufficiently sober![13]

The tour itself – which began in Boston, travelled to several centers in New England before arriving in New York, moved on to Newark, Baltimore, and points south, and then concluded in Washington, D.C. – was not always the unparalleled triumph that Curtis experienced at Carnegie Hall. In several towns audiences were small; in others the company seems to have been over dependent on the patronage of wealthy citizens prepared to lend their names to the enterprise, rather than the attendance of ordinary folk. Sometimes the orchestra was ragged. At a later point Gilbert described how at least once the synchronization failed to work:

> Each series of pictures was accompanied by a piece of music composed especially to fit it. The picture series were arranged similarly to the old dissolving views, one fading into the other. In composing the music I had planned exactly where these changes should occur, marking them plainly in my score. In my left hand I held an electric signal bulb – a rubber bulb connected by a wire to the booth of the lantern operator. Therefore I was [able] to . . . signal to the operator to change the picture, with one hand, while I conducted the orchestra with the other. The pictures were all arranged in proper order so that if the operator got the right series started everything was bound to happen as it should. [In] one performance . . . the operator got the series mixed. The lecturer had given an account of a wild and wonderfully beautiful gorge . . . which was to be followed by a series of somber and impressive pictures. I started my rather rugged and grandiose music and gave the signal for the first picture whereat there flashed upon the screen a splendid picture of an Indian papoose in a perfect whirlwind of rage and tears. . . . [14]

Most important of all, the tour was not a financial success. There were ten to fifteen-thousand printed programs left over which had to be junked and many debts had been incurred. The principal effect of this for Gilbert was that he was not paid in full for his work. In December 1911 Curtis wrote, "we will keep your memorandum on the hook, and trust that we will be able to reach it before we have all made our appearance before Saint Peter," and the following spring, his assistant, Schwinke, concluded a letter with the words, "We still have your bill in mind, but our treasure ship has not yet reached port."[15]

Despite all this, Curtis himself was not unduly discouraged. He seems to have believed that most of their losses had come about through a combination of too many performances in small towns and insufficient advance publicity. He hired a new tour manager, entered into a sponsorship agreement with the Archaeological Institute of

America, engaged a Mr. Ryan to replace Gilbert as conductor and organizer of the musicians, and envisaged a bigger and better tour for the winter of 1912–13, again using Gilbert's music.[16]

Musicale Defined

The word "musicale" was a late nineteenth century Americanism derived from the French "*soirée musicale.*" While the French term referred to a musical evening, American usage emphasized the social or party aspect of the occasion. Though exposition, pictures, words, and music were all featured in Curtis's entertainment, some of this inheritance – of prestige, of social cachet – stayed with the word as Curtis adopted and adapted it; his musicale was meant to be an event in the social calendar whenever it was performed. It was often sponsored by charitable or socially exclusive groups: the Nurses Settlement of Richmond, Virginia, the League for Political Education in New York, and the League of the Covenant in Washington, D.C.[17]

The upper echelons were called upon to act as official patrons. In New York City alone, the chief patrons were Morgan, Roosevelt, and Roosevelt's sister, Corinne Robinson. In Baltimore, the musicale marked the first public appearance of Maryland's Governor Goldsborough, and Boston brought out its Brahmins, including members of the Lowell, Agassiz, Parkman, and Fenollosa families. Perhaps most glittering of all, the patrons of the performance at the Belasco Theater in the Federal capital included President Taft himself, the ambassadors of Britain, France, and Germany, inventor of the telephone Alexander Graham Bell, novelist Thomas Nelson Page, the Speaker of the House, and numerous judges, senators, congressmen, secretaries, commissioners, and other officials. Warwick James Price, one of the reporters of the Philadelphia performance, described the Academy of Music audience there as looking "for all the world like that which gathers twice each week for grand opera."[18] Perhaps hoping to build financial success on the base of such social acclaim, Curtis began more frequently to refer to the musicale as his "picture-opera."

But his increased use of the term also had its musical dimension. On February 5, 1912, he urged Gilbert to compose new material "of the greatest possible picture and musical importance":

> It will be a series lasting at least fifteen minutes – more or less . . . a synopsis . . . of the whole field. As I see it now, it will

> open with the music, the house in darkness. Quickly following the beginning of the music a sunrise scene will be thrown on the screen (slowly), possibly with a human figure. . . . Then the Vanishing Race, leaving it on the screen fully a half minute, possibly a minute. Then we start with the South, using an entirely new picture, perhaps of the palms, then the Indians of the Colorado, again those of the southern desert, now the Pueblo life, then on to a point somewhere between that and the plains, with their tipis, the earth lodges of the upper Missouri, the woods Indian of the mountain, the Kutenai of the lakes, the Columbia, the Coast of Washington, of British Columbia, and of Alaska. The closing scene will be of the Arctic – a sunset over icebergs. In the music we want to carry the mood of the whole, well knit together, yet suggesting the local material in every case where we can.

Encouraging Gilbert to think seriously about it, Curtis also offered to send the pictures and information as an aid to the musical "part" of the work, and suggested that "fragments of music already in hand" might well "lend themselves" to the scheme. Essentially, what Curtis had in mind was, in operatic terms, an overture.[19]

Unfortunately, it seems that no such composition came into being. In fact, Gilbert did continue to develop his Indian material, but for his own purposes and, as we shall see, not always with Curtis's full approval. It may well be that Gilbert became somewhat disaffected with Curtis. He was certainly hurt and angry that Columbia Records issued a recording of the Indian music without giving him any credit as composer. While he was incensed enough to initiate legal proceedings, it must have been intensely galling to receive the following reaction from Curtis:

> Why don't you hire a bill poster to spread your name over a mile or two of billboards and then get a nice seat somewhere where you can spend a few weeks gazing at it. . . . Personally I have given so small thought to anybody's name on the phonograph record . . . that I didn't even know of the absence of my own name on it until receiving this letter from your attorney. I have not seen the [Columbia Record] catalog in question and do not know anything about it. I simply gave instructions to the people in the office to turn over dope to go on the record and that sort of thing, and as to what came from it I must confess

> ignorance and indifference. . . . If our everlasting reputations depend on this Columbia disc, God help our reputations! It has just about as much bearing on our affairs as a single fly-speck on the moon. . . .

Curtis was somewhat disingenuous here in that, at least in the May 1913 Columbia catalogue, his own photograph appeared by record A5457, which contained two items "from Edward S. Curtis's Indian Picture Opera," and a reader would have had to read the small print to find that they had been "arranged" (not composed) by Gilbert. Finally, Curtis softened the tone of his letter by adding, "You are too big a man and your time is worth too much to waste it in any such nonsense as is taken up in the [attorney's] letter. . . . Let us both forget it." Although Gilbert did ultimately receive credit for the music on the recording, it appears that he never did get any financial recompense from Columbia – or, insofar as he might have been culpable, from Curtis.[20]

For his part, as the letter above underlines, Curtis was not normally one to cry over spilt milk. In the aftermath of the financial failure of the 1911–12 tour, he compiled for the 1912–13 tour a simulated newspaper publicity brochure of ecstatic press comments; he titled it *E. S. Curtis and His Indian Picture-Opera "A Vanishing Race" Achieve Triumph* (fig. 14). He had a remarkable capacity for eliminating failure from his mind. Even at a low point in the first tour, just after a small audience in Philadelphia, he was able to write to the local sponsor of the event, George Byron Gordon, director of the University Museum, in an upbeat way. After bemoaning the audience's size and offering to reimburse the museum for its losses, he added:

> Here is a little incident which you may appreciate. As my son, Harold, and I were walking towards the hotel, one of the house policemen . . . came up and put his arm around my shoulder, and with considerable feeling wished that they might have that sort of thing four times a week, and as he was leaving us he called out, "Come again, and we will give you a house so full that we will have to turn them away." It is a great deal of satisfaction to be able to please even a policeman.

But most of all he concentrated only on the New York successes. This, for example, is how he concluded a brief note to Clark Wissler, the leading anthropologist at the American Museum of Natural History, in thanking him for the loan of some of the museum's massive Plains tipis for the performance at the Hippodrome: "They added much to our very striking stage picture. . . . We used first [the theater's] big forest drop, and then a foreground of real trees. The screen was placed easel-like well forward of the forest background, which gave us a splendid effect, particularly as . . . it was possible to keep the forest lit with a twilight effect rather than leaving it a somber, heavy background." "In other words," he concluded, "all through the entertainment we had a picture within a picture."[21]

The Musicale and the Significance of Gilbert's Indian Music

As it happened, the 1912–13 tour, like the previous one, despite an auspicious opening before a packed Metropolitan Theater in Seattle, was a financial failure, and Curtis's association with the Archaeological Institute could not be sustained. The basic problem, as Curtis himself intuited, was that the costs of the venture – transport and wages for himself and nine to twenty-five members of the orchestra, plus publicity and management expenses, hall hire, and numerous other smaller items – simply could not be covered unless each venue was packed out by an audience paying admission prices at least equivalent to those actually paid for grand opera at that time. In the arrangement used, a 50/50 split of profits (or losses) with local sponsors, it was difficult for anyone to break even.[22] In effect, he was discovering the situation that managers of most opera and ballet companies experience today: Without a considerable subsidy, a working profit is virtually impossible to achieve. Moreover, there is little evidence to suggest that the musicale tours were successful in their original aim of increasing subscriptions to *The North American Indian*.

Nevertheless, on both tours the musicale was regularly introduced by eminent figures – Osborn in New York, Professor William Curtis Farabee of Harvard in Boston, Meany in Seattle; it played to some very large, enthusiastic audiences; and it received much laudatory press comment. The reporter for the *New York Evening World* said that the audience at Carnegie Hall "taxed the capacity of the auditorium" and "found itself lifted out of the prosaic into the wild romantic life of the redman" by the musical and pictorial effects. In Seattle the performance received a prolonged ovation from a huge crowd and was highly praised by critic Charles Eugene Banks, himself something of a collector of Indian lore. The *Washington Star* pointed particularly to "the marvelous sunset and cloud effects of the rare, arid atmosphere," and of "canoes floating on glassy or wind-flecked lakes, sinewy priests, almost nude, with their gorgeous touches of color in ceremonial bracelets and belts against coppery bodies . . . and storm-cloud and moonlight effects over mountains and woodland." The *New York Evening Post*, on the other hand, singled out the musical features – "full of the weird appeal that speaks in the red man's harmonies" – features that the *Baltimore Star* claimed sometimes "lulled with a plaintive insistence," while at others they "set the pulse leaping in sympathy with . . . barbaric chords and crashing rhythm." The *Times-Dispatch* of Richmond, Virginia, also heard the music as "genuinely beautiful, weird, wild and unusual in queer melodies and unconventional harmonies."[23]

The *Washington Herald* did not, from the start, separate out the various constituents. The performance, it said, "unfolded the romance of the Indian in the happy fusion of two mediums which normally are alien to each other, but which, under the . . . spell of a rare interpretative artist, blended with eloquent effect. . . ." Agreeing with its rival, the *Washington Times* reserved most praise for what it dubbed "a pictorial and musical gem," the sequence titled "Dream of the Ancient Red Man": "a legend of early Indian life, full of the mystic spell of romance." All told, the musicale was hailed as both an innovation in itself and as testimony to the enduring value of the total Curtis enterprise. The *New York Evening Telegram* called it "a valuable contribution to American anthropology" and, in what perhaps constituted the supreme commendation, Warwick James Price, after seeing the performance for *The Minneapolis Bellman*, declared of Curtis himself: "He is at once a national institution and a national benefit."[24]

For Gilbert, the composition work for the musicale was, to some extent, an uneasy interlude. After his direct involvement with it ceased, he continued, as before, to transcribe phonographic records from the field. He received a batch of six for Volume 9 from Myers in mid-May 1912 and, at the same time, Myers hinted that there would be a very much larger selection for Volume 10, devoted to the Kwakiutl.[25] As the Kwakiutl volume was both projected as and proved to be a particularly rich resource, it is not surprising that it did, indeed, involve Gilbert in more than the usual amount of musical work.

Myers hoped that Gilbert would also write a note for the Kwakiutl volume on the various "baton rhythms" of the tribe. "The Kwakiutl Indians," he explained, "keep time by means of sticks with which they strike a long board, hence the phrase 'baton rhythms.'" In the same letter, though, Myers had to point out that such a note was "a matter that will have to wait, inasmuch as there are a great many more records to be transcribed for this volume and Curtis is not able to see his way to giving it immediate or early publication." Two years later, when they were actually ready to go ahead with the volume, Curtis himself urged Gilbert to undertake more transcriptions, but to no avail.[26]

Gilbert's decision, without doubt, was due to discontent with Curtis and his business arrangements, especially over the musicale, rather than to any loss of interest in Indian music. In a program note for a Boston Symphony Orchestra concert of his music in 1921, Gilbert recorded the profundity of his involvement: "I . . . eventually pursued my studies . . . far beyond the material which the phonographic cylinders afforded me, examining in detail the collections of North American Indian music which have been made by Alice Fletcher, Franz Boas, Benjamin Ives Gilman, Natalie Curtis, Frances Densmore, and others." "The suggestions," he added, "of barbaric wildness in certain of these fragments of melody – their frequent waywardness of rhythm – and above all the savage and insistent drum beat with which most of the songs were accompanied – stirred my blood and aroused my romantic enthusiasm."[27]

One of Gilbert's chief claims to significance is that he was credited as the very first "serious" American composer to use black music – Negro spirituals and ragtime – in concert orchestral works. His *Negro Episode* was first performed in 1896, and he went on to produce such works as the *Comedy Overture on Negro Themes* (c. 1906), *Negro Rhapsody* (c. 1912, performed 1915), *Negro Dances* (1914), and, perhaps most important of all, *The Dance in Place Congo* (c. 1908), a symphonic poem with dance music, which was first presented as a ballet, in revised form, by the New York Metropolitan Opera Company in 1918. In a sense, his work with Indian rhythms for the musicale represented a parallel effort.

Using the twenty-one short orchestral pieces produced for the musicale as a source, Gilbert actually published five of them, as arranged for the piano, in his *Indian Scenes* (1912). This publication – despite Curtis's initial worries over his copyright in the material – had his blessing, used some of his photographs for illustrative purposes, and kept very close to the music that had been used to accompany various of his picture sequences. Gilbert's titles for the pieces – namely "By the Arrow," "The Night Scout," "In the Kutenai

Country," "Signal Fire to the Mountain God," and "On the Jocko" – exactly correspond both to the titles of specific Curtis photographs and to selected segments of the musicale program.[28]

Gilbert wished to go a stage further, and ultimately did so, in his "Indian Sketches." These were reworkings, revisions, of musicale material as purely orchestral works. Here Curtis was more than simply worried. "You say you want to revamp certain of these numbers for orchestra use," he wrote in October 1912, "but you do not say who is to receive the returns from this. Do I get in on it or does the music in this way virtually pass out of my hands?" "As revamped," he added, "I take it that it would scarcely fit the pictures to be given in connection with them. Let me know. . . ." And later in the month Curtis put his point even more emphatically:

> I fear that the publication of the elaborated music will spoil the value of the material as it now stands. This music, published and available for concert use, would remove all novelty of the music in connection with the pictures. I do not know whether I will ever make any great use of the music in this way, but my investment in it is still rather heavy.
>
> Frankly, my natural inclination is to tell you to go ahead. I certainly do not like to think of myself as a dog in the manger. Frankly, what effect do you think this elaboration will have on my music and its future use in connection with the pictures, and would I in any way be associated, as far as publicity is concerned, with the elaborated music if published.

Eventually, though, Curtis relented. "Now as to your music, further compositions, and that sort of thing. Don't grow peevish," he admonished. "I think I am a pretty reasonable sort of a chap, and my letters were more or less of an inquiry. . . . Most assuredly, make use of the number you have revamped, and as to drawing upon material in The North American Indian, I assure you that you are more than welcome," he declared. "That is what the stuff is for, and the more use you can make of it the better I will like it." Then, in a characteristically impish touch, he added, "I trust that I will have the pleasure of seeing you some time later in the winter, and then if you are still cross you can have all the fun you like abusing me."[29]

Ultimately, at least six "Indian Sketches" emerged and were performed by the Boston Symphony Orchestra on March 4, 1921. As will be recognized immediately from the titles of each of the movements except the last, the relationship between this suite and the musicale numbers was tangential: "Prelude," "Invocation," "Song of the Wolf" ("a short development of one of the somber and poignant cries of the Kutenai"), "Camp Dance," "Nocturne" (a "larghetto of somewhat romantic feeling, such as one might have if [one] were alone at night paddling a solitary canoe on one of our Western rivers. . . ."), and "Snake Dance." The suite was scored primarily for conventional western instruments – wind, percussion and strings – with the addition of an Indian drum and an Indian rattle. Also, as Gilbert's friend and fellow composer of "Indian music," Arthur Farwell, noted in his review of the original musicale for *Musical America*, Gilbert's music *was* his own: "These compositions are far from being mere adaptations of Indian melodies. They are . . . original compositions . . . filled with the particularly rich quality of Mr. Gilbert's imagination. . . ." And, it must be admitted, by comparison with their Indian "sources," they are rather genteel.[30]

Farwell was the founder of the Wa-Wan Press, which published much of Gilbert's first work. Named after an Omaha Indian ceremony, the Press called itself "a movement for American music." Farwell would have been aware, then, that Gilbert's Indian work, like his better-known compositions based on African-American materials, was a significant departure from classical European models towards appropriate musical expression of the New World. One of the publicity leaflets for the musicale stressed this aspect: "Mr. Curtis felt that he was securing the collaboration of the American composer best qualified to render in music the primitive thought – a man with the courage to strike out for himself regardless of European influence or beaten paths." Gilbert was not alone in so striking out. One literary parallel of the time was Mary Austin's *The American Rhythm* (1923), a book of poems which she called "re-expressions" of Indian chants, prayers, love songs, invocations, and so forth, together with a long essay. It is notable that on February 28, 1911 – earlier in the same year as the opening productions of the musicale – Austin's verse play based on Indian materials, *The Arrowmaker*, was first performed on the New York stage. Curtis saw it at least twice. "It draws me as all Indian things do," he declared to Austin, "and I know it will be a short time till I am again there watching and listening."[31]

The chief significance of the musical aspect of the picture-opera was that – like the (admittedly uncharacteristic) work of Gilbert's own major mentor, Edward MacDowell, in his *Indian Suite* (1891–5) – it marked an early serious return to, an investment in, indeed a "re-expression" of, aboriginal America as a positive constituent of modern American expression. Interestingly, in the same period as the musicale, in the course of an "interview" with Edward Marshall in which he was much more pluralist in his attitudes towards race than usual, Curtis himself declared that "the Indians" could have "helped us in our music; their music was a real part of their lives, a genuine expression of emotion," and would have been a welcome constituent in forging American music. From this perspective, it is unfortunate that plans made in 1913 by Curtis and Gilbert to present the picture-opera as a "musical pageant" at the MacDowell Colony came to naught.[32] The MacDowell Colony, in which Gilbert was a regular and active annual participant, acted as a kind of hothouse for new musical plants. This was one that may have been stunted by not receiving such nurture.

The Musicale as Representation

The precise import of the visual aspects of the musicale is also difficult to determine. The main visuals, the lantern slides – despite the colorful and vivid tinting remarked upon by contemporary reviewers and apparent in the relatively few surviving examples – were essentially another form of the photographic images reproduced as photogravures in *The North American Indian* itself, and their significance cannot be assessed separately.[33] It might be more productive, at this juncture, to give some brief consideration to the musicale as a total entity – slides, motion pictures, music, and, of course, words, both scripted and anecdotal – an entity which, in turn, most publicly expressed the aspirations of the Curtis Indian enterprise as a whole.

Whatever its financial failings, it *was* a popular show. Precisely because of the musicale's broadly based appeal, Curtis expected – and had to withstand – some opposition from professionally trained anthropologists. This was why, in his exuberant letter quoted at the opening of this chapter, Curtis was so pleased to tell his friend Meany of his success not only at Carnegie Hall, but at one of the bastions of intellectual endeavor, the Brooklyn Institute:

> Last night we were at the Brooklyn Institute and I was face to face with a hostile element. Opposition had attempted to poison the atmosphere and Prof. [Franklin W.] Hooper himself was somewhat inclined to be indifferent, critical and a bit sarcastic,

> but in spite of that feeling . . . they had a record house and the enthusiasm was quite out of the ordinary. At the close Prof. Hooper came to me and said that he considered it one of the most important affairs given by them; that they had heard many phases of Indian life and seen fragments . . . , but I was the first to . . . give them what he considered the real Indian; . . . that he thought the entertainment a message of more than national importance; that it should be heard in every town in the United States . . . by the adults . . . [and] school children . . . and [he would] state [this] in [his] address before the Academy of Science at its annual meeting. . . .

Some of the press commentary, too, would seem to indicate that such a point was taken. Curtis "proved," declared the *New York Evening Sun*, "that as long as the inventions of modern civilization endure there is no need that any people should pass into oblivion, save as their history is recorded by musty tomes of written pages or by the dull imaginings of dryasdust scientists groping amid ruined monuments or rifled graves." The musicale, in other words, was a successful piece of popularization, which, ironically, moved audiences that the heavy "tomes" of *The North American Indian* itself could not hope to reach. The *New York Evening Sun* even went so far as to claim that the musicale enabled Curtis "to set before his audience almost exactly what he himself had seen and heard."[34]

Clearly, if Gilbert's music constituted cultural appropriation of at least a potentially positive sort, the musicale as a whole stood for appropriation of a more double-edged kind. On one side, there was some recognition at the time – registered in remarks like Hooper's and in Roosevelt's "It is a good thing for the whole American people" – that aboriginal imagery and history were integral parts of American imagery and history. On the other side, the press commentary reveals that it was the exotic otherness of Indians that most impressed the musicale's audiences: "the wild romantic life of the redman," "the weird appeal," "the beautiful, weird, wild," "the romance of the Indian," "the mystic spell of romance," and so on. As I remarked at the outset of this book, what these audiences experienced in sight and sound was not "the real Indian," to use Curtis's impossible formulation, or, even, what he himself had witnessed in the field, but a representation shot through with all the intricacies, assumptions, and tensions of an attachment to the current ideology of Indians as "the vanishing race." The musicale's Indians were envisioned as *both* beautiful and curiously static, as if immune to the passage of time, perhaps already disappeared from the earth, ethereal, and – as befits their lantern-slide presentation – caught forever, as it were, in a kind of slow dissolve.

DOCUMENTS

Document 7A. Program Notes for "The Intimate Story of Indian Tribal Life," 1911.[35]

ORCHESTRA PRELUDE, "The Spirit of the Indian Life."

Foreword by Mr. Curtis.

I. PICTURE AND MUSICAL COMPOSITION, "Dream of the Ancient Red Man." This dissolving series with impressive music depicts the life of the plains Indian from youth to the afterworld. The scene opens with an old man beside a stream, musing of the past. He is seen as a proud young warrior, and in the days of his courtship. Then with a mounted war-party – statuesque horsemen under the starlit sky. Following that we see the camp of the enemy, the wild ride of battle, and the return of the victorious warriors.

II. DISSOLVING SCENIC EFFECT of the Hunkalowanpi ceremony, "Offering the Skull." In picture pantomime with music is enacted a most inspiring prayer to the Great Mystery.

III. THE INDIANS of the Palm Canyons and the Cactus Plains.

IV. THE APACHE. – A remarkable series of pictures of these desert and mountain people, and a glimpse into their most interesting religious development. Their sacred paintings. Their priests. An analysis of their theology throws remarkable light on religious thought among the various tribes of Indians.

V. THE HOPI AND THEIR SNAKE DANCE. – The story of the Snake Dance. Many separate pictures of the most sacred incidents of the Snake rite. Motion pictures of the dance, accompanied by the orchestra.

VI. "EVENING IN HOPI LAND," a changing series of nine scenes, with orchestra accompaniment. The scene opens with a picturesque house-top group at the end of day. As the men look across the desert they see the returning shepherd and his flock, and in the sunset glow the maidens appear at the well. Next is an inspiring Hopi sunset, and as darkness gathers groups of women appear on the high-perched houses against the starry sky. We now see the wonderful moonlit trail passing the gap, and the scene closes with a glorious sunrise across the desert sands.

INTERMISSION AND INTERLUDE.

VII. PICTURESQUE and characteristic scenes from the northwest plains life.

VIII. NORTH PACIFIC COAST TRIBES. – The whaling Indians. Their grewsome mummy ceremony.

IX. DISSOLVING MUSICAL SET, "On the Shores of the North Pacific," depicting life by the moonlit ocean.

X. "INVOCATION TO THE BUFFALO," a dissolving musical composition of powerful and impressive appeal to the Infinite.

XI. "THE MOUNTAIN CAMP," a dissolving series of five pictures with accompanying music. The sunlit camp in the forest is the first scene, then a nearer view is had showing the Indians in their dance, and in the third we see the participants more distinctly, the full enthusiasm of their ceremony upon them. This changes to a wonderful evening picture of the camp, gradually subdued by the darkness and quiet of night and slumber.

XII. "THE KUTENAI OF THE LAKES," a musical series of unusual beauty. It opens with a firelit camp upon the shore, changing to a closer view of the women entering the lodges. Then we see canoes and canoe life at dawn; the rush gatherer, the hunter upon the still waters, a sunny shore scene, and the farewell of the lovers. Across the waters, appears a canoe laden with happy, care-free youths, and again, farther away, a woman, with steady stroke of paddle, homeward bound. The series closes with a far distant glimpse of a canoe against the setting sun.

XIII. THE PUEBLO OR STONE-HOUSE PEOPLE. – General pictures, illustrative of their life.

XIV. "BY THE ARROW," a musical series of declaration and devotion.

XV. "SIGNAL FIRE TO THE MOUNTAIN GOD," a dissolving scene with musical accompaniment, depicting the devotional hours of a priest of the Tañon people. First he is seen at sunset before one of the wonderful rock shrines or altars of the high mountains. The sacred fire is scarcely visible. The sunset blends into starlight and night, and the glowing flame carries its message of faith and supplication. All through the night he stands on watch, lest the Divine Ones find him unfaithful, and as the Gods of Day drive away the Mysteries of the night, our priest poises in the gray dawn, watching the dying flame.

XVI. THE NAVAHO and their interesting desert life.

XVII. "A JOURNEY THROUGH CANYON DE CHELLY." – This is a changing series of eleven dramatic pictures with accompanying music.

XVIII. THE RELIGION OF THE NAVAHO. – Their Yebichai dance. Yebichai motion picture.

XIX. "SUNSET IN NAVAHO LAND," and "The Vanishing Race," an evening scene suggesting the thought of the race, already robbed of its tribal strength, its primitive faith, stripped of its pagan dress, going into the darkness of the unknown future.

Document 7B. Excerpts from a Typescript of a Script for the Musicale, 1911–12.[36]

My greatest desire tonight is that each and every person here enter into the spirit of our evening with the Indians. We cannot weigh, measure, or judge their culture with our philosophy. From our analytical and materialistic view-point, theirs is a strange world. Deity is not alone in a supreme being after their own image, but rather is everywhere present – world or universal voice, universal spirit. I want you to see this beautiful, poetic, mysterious, yet simple life, as I have grown to see it through the long years with the many tribes.

Toward that end let us close our eyes for an instant, and in that flash of time span the gulf between today's turmoil and the far-away enchanted realm of primitive man. We have entered what is to us a strange land. Man and nature are one, and atune. All about us are the mysteries of the Infinite. We wander through the forest, and the murmur of the pines is the voice of the tree people, who speak to us. The waving of the grasses in the mountain meadow brings its response, and when we look into the limpid pool we see mirrored there the high-flying birds and drifting clouds. They also possess a soul, and touch our hearts. Far away on the mountain-side we see the elk, the deer, and the bear, and from the somber forest depths comes the call of the wolf, and our related hearts are touched. Let us turn our eyes from the sky and the mountains, and look to the lowly things. The earth and the pollen upon the breezes are the parents of all that springs from the soil. The smallest of the animate and inanimate, even the pebbles at the brookside and the insect beneath our moccasined feet, are scarcely less important than the King of Birds, the eagle. The winds of the east, the west, the north, and the south, are personified and deified. When we feel the breath of the South upon our faces we say, "You of the spring and summer, give us a good day." And when we hear the thunder of the west roll up the valleys and across the mountains, we cry out, "O, ye Nation of Thunderers, withhold your anger!" And when the cold breezes of winter sweep down upon us, we shrink and say, "You Mysteries of the North, you have defeated the South, and soon the chilly snows will be upon us." Truly it is a strange land to which we have for a minute journeyed, and now we must return to more material things.

When we start to unknown lands we naturally study, even if but hurriedly, the country and the people which we propose to visit. Tonight we go to the land of the Indian, and as in other travels, let us glance at the scope of the subject.

First, what is the Indian? The American Indian is one of the five races of man, and of this race there are [more than] fifty linguistic stocks in North America. When I say stocks I mean just that – languages fundamentally differing. Of dialects there were at the time of the discovery fully one thousand in North America.

We must not lose sight of the ethnological importance of the American Indian, and we must keep in mind that they represent fully seventy-five per cent. of the world's languages. . . .

Passing linguistic groups, let us glance at the life and manners. We have natives of the sub-tropics dwelling beneath the waving palms in the land of perpetual warmth, and, to the contrary, natives of the Arctic directing their frail skin craft among the dangerous ice-bergs. And between these extremes are countless tribes, all, according to habitat, differing in culture.

The first and greatest problem before all human beings is that of food, and naturally the culture of any group is largely determined by this. Students of primitive religion will tell you that the question of food is the first thought in the majority of religious systems. This admitted, let us take a broad glimpse at it in relation to the Indian. . . .

We pass from the proud, buffalo-hunting Indian to the less

favored. We had the strictly sedentary Indian, dwelling in stone or less substantial, but permanent homes, living largely from cultivated crops. We had tribes, like the Yuma, living largely from cultivated crops . . . on streams filled with fish easy of taking; we had tribes living in the inhospitable desert, who depended largely on plant seeds, roots, insects, and small game; we had natives like those of southern California, who took wild fowl in countless numbers; and also those depending on salt water fish. This was particularly so of the north Pacific coast natives, who had such vast quantities of salmon. Some of the tribes of this region secured much food by the capture of whale, and still others by the capture of seal. And the last important item I will mention was without question of the greatest value to the largest number of natives, it being the many varieties of shellfish. Originally all Indians were without doubt coast dwellers, and shellfish was naturally the principal food. It was taken without implement or skill, and cooking was not absolutely necessary.

I have asked you to take this broad glimpse at the Indian subject, that you may have firmly in mind that we cannot refer to the Indian as a unit, as is often done, but rather we must in a measure consider each group as a subject unto itself.

Now I will return to the thought passed a minute ago – that of Indian religion. We have caught a glimpse of the many sources from which food was had, and now we must fix in our minds that while the fundamentals of their religious thought are broadly alike, the details are determined by the surroundings. The agricultural Indians have their God Father and God Mother of the Growing Things, but the game hunters would know nothing of such divine ones, but would supplicate those who control the game of the forest and plains. The whaling tribes would invoke those of the Infinite who controlled the storm of the ocean and the life of its waters; and so we might go on for the whole evening. There seems a broadly prevalent idea that the Indian lacked a religion. This erroneous impression was perhaps fathered by our own presumption in considering our reaching out to the Infinite to be religion, and the Indian's like act to be heathenism. Rather than being without a religion, every act of his life was according to divine prompting. True, the gods bore strange names, but the need was as great, the appeal as devout.

The pictures which I am to show you tonight deal largely with the devotional and ceremonial life, and were selected with the dual purpose of being instructive and giving pleasure as pictures.

As to the music, each number has been composed by Mr. Gilbert to accompany a definite series of pictures. As basic material he has used largely phonographic records made of the Indian songs and chants, the effort being to produce music which would be truly primitive, harmonizing with the pictures and expressing the composer's interpretation of them.

BLANK – (Talk on Dream of Ancient Red Man)

The scene opens with an aged man sitting on the banks of a mountain stream. We presume him to be watching the ribbon-like, endless flow of water, dreaming of the days of the past. He thinks of himself as a proud young man, and the second picture shows him as a magnificent youth with two companions on a high cliff overlooking the home camp. . . . Next we see in motion picture a war-party riding away. Then a small group of the warriors on a high hill-top, they have travelled far, and are looking down upon the camp of the enemy. It is a magnificent, statuesque, starlight picture. Now our group is seen riding rapidly to the attack, followed by a night picture of the enemy's camp, as the invaders see it from the distance. The wild ride and rush at the close of the attack, a picture of vigor and atmosphere. Then we have a scene of action, but free from strife. It is the tribesmen riding out to greet the returning victorious warriors. Our old man's mind travels as through the many incidents of life, and he sees before him the burial scaffold on the hilltop, and he knows that there rest many of his old companions, and that soon he too will have journeyed on to the after world.

DISSOLVING VIEW. DREAM OF THE ANCIENT RED MAN.

BLANK – (Talk on Hunka Ceremony)

The Hunkalowanpi ceremony is an important one with the Sioux, and in slightly varying forms and under different names exists with many of the buffalo hunting tribes. . . .

DISSOLVING SET – HUNKA CEREMONY

BLANK – (Palm Canyon and Cactus Pictures)

The Indians of the Palm Canyons belong to the Yuman stock, and live in the region of the wonderful palm groves of southern California. They depend largely on the fruit of the palm for food, and this tree, which is of such great value to them, they invest with personality, believing it to possess a soul. I first saw these wonderful palm canyons at the end of a long, hot August day. . . .

PICTURES * PALM CANYON AND CACTUS.

BLANK – (Apache Talk)

The Apache, our next group to treat, is in many respects noteworthy. His birthright was a craving for the warpath, and his cunning beyond reckoning. His character is a strange mixture of savagery, courage, and ferocity, with a remarkable gentleness and affection for his family, particularly his children. They have made so much of a fighting record, that to the majority the name stands for savagery alone. Yet they have a mythology and theology rich to imagery and strong in its concepts. Their Genesis is particularly poetic, and their pantheon includes the gods of the sky, of the earth, of the elements, gods of intellect and oratory, and the Goddess of Fecundity and the Goddess of Purity, in whose honor young girls at certain ceremonial occasions wear a white shell fastened in the hair, as an emblem of virtue. . . .

PICTURES * APACHE

BLANK – (Hopi Talk)

Now we come to the Stone House or Hopi people. Their homes are high perched on the mesas of the desert. One feels that it is a land of mystery. Everywhere about is heard the droning chant of the priest and priestess. . . .

GENERAL HOPI PICTURES AND BUFFALO DANCE PICTURES

BLANK – (Talk on Snake Dance)

The Hopi's greatest religious rite is the so-called Snake Dance. Strictly speaking it is not a dance, but rather a dramatic . . . rite, in fact, a dramatized prayer. Time is lacking to fully describe the ceremony, consequently I will try to show you its thoughts, and then outline both the esoteric and public rites. . . .

Let me remark that the Hopi Snake rite is but one of the countless forms of snake worship existing among primitive people. Practically all the Pueblo tribes of the United States know it in some form. In the Rio Grande region it became a part of their phallic ceremonies. The Hopi in their highly dramatized form of snake veneration, have developed a beautiful rite passing beyond the mere worship of the reptile, in that the snakes are but messengers to the divine ones. It is a ceremony lasting nine days and nights, participated in only by the priests of the Snake cults, assisted by their brothers of the Antelope order. The priests of the Snake order live quite apart from the tribe during the ceremony, sleeping in the kiva or on its top. Food is brought near and placed on the ground. Then, when its bearer has disappeared, the men come out and carry in it.

(Personal Note)

GENERAL PICTURES OF SNAKE DANCE and SNAKE DANCE MOTION PICTURE

BLANK – (Talk on "Evening in Hopi Land"). . . .

DISSOLVING VIEW. EVENING IN HOPI LAND.

INTERMISSION – (five minutes with house lights – then two minutes interlude with house lights off.)

BLANK – General words on plains pictures.

We now journey from the delights of Hopi Land and the desert, to the far northern plains, where we see glimpses of the vigorous and picturesque hunting tribes.

PLAINS PICTURES

BLANK (Words on coast Indians.)

From the proud natives of the plains we will go to the coast tribes of the Pacific.

COAST PICTURES.

BLANK – (Talk "On the Shores of the North Pacific.")

DISSOLVING SERIES * ON THE SHORES OF THE NORTH PACIFIC

BLANK – Talk on Jocko Set.

The coming dissolving series opens with a quiet camp in the mountain forest. . . .

DISSOLVING SET * JOCKO CAMP

BLANK – (Talk on Kutenai Pictures)

Now we have a characteristic glimpse of the Kutenai, the canoe Indians of the Mountain Lakes. Their very picturesque canoe was different from any used by the other American natives, being a framework of wood with a covering of elkhide. The opening picture is a night scene on the forested shores of a mountain lake. . . .

KUTENAI PICTURES

BLANK – (General reference to Pueblo people and their life.)

GENERAL PUEBLO PICTURES.

BLANK – (Talk on "By the Arrow")

"By the arrow I make my vow" is the thought in the coming dissolving view. In the first scene we have the striking figure of the priest against the sunlit sky, holding the arrow to the dying day. The theme of picture and music is the rigor of declaration and devotion. This sunset changes to one of our blanket-wrapped priest with arrow high held to the starlit sky, a powerful figure of invocation. Then creeps on gray dawn. As the sun appears our priest has again thrown off his robe, and stands imploring the spirits of the east and the newborn day.

BY THE ARROW DISSOLVING SERIES.

BLANK – (Signal Fire Talk)

We now have the dissolving musical effect "The Signal Fire to the Mountain God," bringing to us the impressive devotional hours of a priest of the Tanon people. . . .

SIGNAL FIRE DISSOLVING SERIES.

BLANK – (Navaho Talk.)

The last group of the evening will be the Navaho. This very interesting tribe is the second largest in the United States. They, like the Apache, belong to the Athapascan stock. There is a vast difference in their characteristics. The Apache were warriors to a degree unparalleled, while the Navaho were noticeably lacking in the war spirit. . . . The Navaho were when first observed a semi-nomadic people depending partially on agriculture for food, and partially on game. For some reason they seemed to possess the shepherd instinct as no other tribe of North American Indians. They are strikingly independent, and ask little but to be left alone. Of course, as we take it upon ourselves to be our brother's keeper, we cannot permit that, but from the fact that they are so broadly scattered, our paternal influence is not deeply penetrating, and these desert people are yet delightfully themselves.

GENERAL NAVAHO PICTURES

BLANK – (Canyon de Chelly Talk)

Our coming dissolving series is a journey through a remarkable canyon in the Navaho country – Canyon de Chelly, pronounced by the Navaho, Tisay – the Canyon of the Divine Ones. To the Navaho it is the rift in the earth from which the gods emerged to direct and teach men. The echoing walls send back voices from those who no longer walk the earth, as it is not alone the home of the gods, but of the prehistoric people. . . .

I have made many journeys through this miles-stretching

amphitheater, have travelled and camped there during every one of nature's moods, have ridden its long miles through the hot summer sun; and during the bitter snow of winter, have seen it lashed with the fury of the sand storm, and its floor a rushing, devouring freshet torrent. In the coming dissolving series I desire to give a slight impression of its mysterious depth. . . .

CANYON DE CHELLY DISSOLVING SET.

BLANK – (Talk on "Sunset in Navaho Land" and "The Vanishing Race.")

DISSOLVING SERIES ("Sunset in Navaho Land" etc.)

Document 7C. Excerpts from Program Notes for "Lecture on the Indians of the Southwest," c. 1911[37]

ORCHESTRAL PRELUDE, "The Spirit of the Indian Life."
Foreword by Mr. Curtis.

Opening picture, characteristic of the American Indian at the height of his existence, followed by "The Vanishing Race." This is the favorite picture of the whole series, wonderfully full of sentiment, and conveying the thought of the race . . . going into the darkness of the unknown future.

I. THE INDIANS OF THE EARTH HOUSES. – The Coahuilla, and their homes among the beautiful palms. The Pima, Papago, Mohave, Yuma, Havasupai.

II. THE APACHE. – . . . Jicarilla Apache of northern New Mexico.

III. THE HOPI AND THEIR SNAKE DANCE. – "Hopi Land," a changing series of nine scenes. . . . Individual pictures of Hopi life. The story of the Snake Dance. . . . The Buffalo Dance in separate and in motion pictures.

INTERLUDE BY THE ORCHESTRA
(Knabe Piano used)

IV. THE STONE-HOUSE OR PUEBLO PEOPLE. – Descriptive pictures. Dissolving scene with musical accompaniment, "Prayer to the Mountain God". . . . Acoma, the most beautiful of all the pueblos. Taos, nestling in the foothills of the forested mountains. Dramatic musical composition, "By the Arrow". . . .

V. THE NAVAHO, and their wonderfully picturesque homeland. . . . "A Journey Through Canyon de Chelly". . . . The

Yebichai ceremony, a dance in motion picture, with music. "Sunset in Navaho Land". . . .

The lecture will present the general culture and manners, with special attention to the ceremonial and religious life. Mr. Curtis has participated in the Snake ceremony as one of the priests, and has pictures even of the ceremonial capturing of snakes. He took part also in the Yebichai ceremony of the Navaho, and shows some most remarkable views even of this rite and of its participants.

Document 7D. Excerpts from a Typescript of a Script for the Musicale Titled "S.W. Lecture," 1911.

Now we take up the consideration of the gentle, smiling, liquid-voiced Hopi [whose] greatest religious rite is the so-called Snake Dance. . . .

In the instance in mind I was the new member, and the priests felt that it augured well that the gods were pleased at their having taken me as one of them, when they found within a minute a large snake. Now came my first surprise. I had agreed to do without question what my brothers asked or directed, and as the first snake was taken, one of the men, who clumsily spoke a few words of English, explained that when they took with them a new brother, on capturing the first snake they wound it around his neck four times. Then my good prompter continued to explain: "Soon we will get another snake. That will be a blue racer. We will put that around your neck. Then we will get a rattle-snake, and that we will put around your neck, and that will be all." I yet have in mind a very vivid picture of that rattle-snake wound about my neck, its head extending far enough forward that I could clearly see its apparently angry expression. . . .

YEBICHAI

. . . I was fortunate enough to be initiated . . . [in this] rite . . . , certain parts [of which] are held in secret. . . . [It] is a very exacting ritual of about twelve hours each day for nine days, without a written word or prompter. The ritual is learned by the young men desiring to become priests through constant attendance at different ceremonies.

A person thinking himself afflicted will send word to some

priest that he desires him to give this ceremony. Then the patient calls on the members of his clan for assistance, as the expense of the ceremony is considerable. The priests and all their helpers must have certain presents, and all spectators and visitors must be fed. Goods and chattels to at least a value of $500.00 would be necessary. An important part of this ceremony is the sand paintings. . . . These are prepared on the floor of the hogan in which the ceremony is held. The ground is first covered with a fine brown earth, and after carefully smoothing the central part, the priests begin to lay in the design. The colors are secured by grinding to a powder the different colored stones. In applying the colored powder the sand is sifted through the fingers in a fine stream, making a line, if desired, as fine as could be done with a broad pencil. On an elaborate sand picture six or eight men work from early in the forenoon until late in the afternoon.

The great event of the Yebichai ceremony is the ninth and closing night. By this time all the spectators are present, perhaps a few hundred or perhaps a thousand or more. The masked characters impersonating the different deities participate in a night-long dance. From different parts of the Navaho country groups of dancers have arrived. Each group will have their own masks and paraphernalia, and each is composed of the same number of men impersonating the same myth characters. There is great rivalry to see which of these separate teams are the best actors and dancers.

The dance is in the open between two long lines of fire. It is fall or winter, and the many spectators group themselves about these for warmth. All through the night team after team of dancers appears, and just as the dawn begins to break, one of these groups starts to give the mystic blue-bird song. This is a signal for all to disappear, as no one must remain to hear the last fragment of this song. And what a sight it is! About the fires in the cold dawn are grouped we will say two thousand people, the majority on horseback, and as the air of the bluebird song starts, one feels the movement of this great throng, and as it nears the close, they ride away into the half lights, melting, as it were, into the desert. There are no roads – no trails. They go in a thousand directions. In less than ten minutes from the beginning of the song the scene of the days of activity is but a few smoldering fires and a cloud of dust, raised by thousands of beating hoofs. They came silently from the desert and pinon and pine-clad plains, and as silently they have melted away. . . .

Figure 16. Curtis and George Hunt filming in Kwakiutl country, 1914, by E. A. Schwinke. Hunt, with megaphone, helps orchestrate a ceremonial dance sequence for *In the Land of the Head-Hunters.*

8

"BRONZE IN ACTION"

The poet Vachel Lindsay, in what probably constitutes the earliest aesthetics of the cinema, *The Art of the Moving Picture*, which was published in 1915, found space to praise Curtis's documentary feature film *In the Land of the Head-Hunters* (1914):

> The photoplay of the American Indian should in most instances be planned as a bronze in action. The tribes should not move so rapidly that the panther-like elasticity is lost in the riding, running, and scalping. On the other hand, the aborigines should be far from the temperateness of marble.
>
> Mr. Edward S. Curtis, the super-photographer, has made an Ethnological collection of photographs of American Indians. This work of a lifetime, a supreme art achievement, shows the native as a figure in bronze. Mr. Curtis's photoplay, The Land of the Head Hunters [sic] (World Film Corporation), a romance of the Indians of the North-West, abounds in noble bronzes.

It may be that the film was drawn to Lindsay's attention through his own temporary residence in Spokane, Washington, and his consequent extra knowledge of artistic activities in the then relatively remote Pacific Northwest, because other sophisticated commentators of the time – and for a sixty-year period thereafter – failed to notice it.[1]

The trade and popular press, on the other hand, did respond. The *New York Times*, for example, was awed by the film's tinting, which, it claimed, represented the invention of a "new color system." *Variety*, for its part, singled out for special commendation the film's photography, its "sunlight effects," and the sea lion and whale sequences; it also expressed wonder over the fact that "every participant" was "a genuine American Indian." This latter point was one of the film's features praised by a local Seattle reviewer, Charles Eugene Banks. "These Indians," he said, "shame all attempts at animal masking by white people. Their bears, foxes, eagles, goats, wasps, wolves and other animals are wonderful figures" and "weirdly convincing." W. Stephen Bush, writing in the *Moving Picture World*, attributed the startling success of such scenes not to the Indians' acting ability – which, rather oddly, he denied – but to Curtis's "extraordinary perception of artistic and dramatic values, in an uncommon skill of selection and in a sort of second sight with the camera." He declared the film "a wonderful study in ethnology" and "an epic" which set "a new mark in artistic handling of films in which educational values mingle with dramatic interest."[2]

In the Land of the Head-Hunters was in fact the very first movie of its kind, antedating the endeavors of Robert Flaherty, creator of what has hitherto been considered the earliest full-length narrative documentary, *Nanook of the North* (1922), by over seven years. That is, the transmission of "authentic" documentary material (ceremonies, religious beliefs, customs, and the like) via a linear "fictitious" narrative, conventionally thought to have been inaugurated by Flaherty's story of his Inuit hero's epic journeys and tense hunting struggles in order to secure his family's survival in the frozen north, were foreshadowed by Curtis's story about Motana, his visions, his courting of the beautiful Naida, and his battles with sea lions, whales, and wicked sorcerers. In fact, Flaherty himself visited Curtis in 1915 and was inspired by his work.[3]

Curtis's fictitious narrative, although based in terms of plot on *Romeo and Juliet*, was most heavily influenced by Henry Wadsworth Longfellow's immensely popular *The Song of Hiawatha* (1855), with its blending of Native American lore collected by Henry Rowe Schoolcraft and the verse form of the Finnish national epic *Kalevala*. Like *Hiawatha*, Curtis's narrative was set in a supposedly primordial time before the arrival of whites and, more importantly, it reached after *epic*. Some of its incidents were reminiscent of episodes in Hiawatha's story; for example, Motana's neck band and a lock of his hair were stolen during his sleep just as Mudjekeewis took "the belt of Wampum/ From the neck of Mishe-Mokwa,/ From the Great Bear of the mountains," and the film's majestic ceremonial wedding paralleled Hiawatha's wedding feast. And in the book version of *In the*

Land of the Head-Hunters (1915), Curtis, although writing in prose, sometimes even used the sort of inversions of regular diction that were so characteristic of Longfellow's verse: Where the poet had a construction like "Homeward then he sailed exulting,/ Homeward through the black pitch-water,/ . . . With the trophies of the battle," Curtis had: "Short and sharp was the battle. Bruised and limping were those who met its brunt. Thus did the youth prove himself worthy of a wife."[4]

The long winters experienced by the Kwakiutl were devoted to a cycle of rituals involving the whole community in performances, which both provided a kind of entertainment and established or confirmed people in their social relationships. The documentary element of Curtis's film was largely devoted to this complex ceremonialism, which included the use of extraordinary theatrical effects, and to the depiction of some of the material goods of this hierarchical society: massive canoes and wooden houses, furs, game, and food from the sea. The Kwakiutl had the Hamatsa ceremony, involving a figure who came in from the wild who *apparently* indulged in cannibal practices and had to be humanized. They made and used beautifully painted, large wooden masks. (It is noticeable in the film that there is a contrast not just in style, but also in quality, between the two main acting conventions: "Kwakiutl" ceremonial "acting" and the "acting out" by Indians of what we might call the white story line; as Charles Eugene Banks and the otherwise blinkered commentator in Document 8C realized, the Kwakiutl were clearly more comfortable with the ceremonial acting.)

Curtis's film was conceived during the period in which the musicale was failing, and it may be that it emerged partly as a consequence of that failure. In the inception of *In the Land of the Head-Hunters,* Curtis looked to the motion picture as *the* mass medium of the age. Movies, moreover, not only attracted huge audiences, but were coming to be seen as the most appropriate vehicle for historical reconstruction on an epic scale. This was manifestly evidenced by the appeal of the most famous example of its kind and time, D. W. Griffith's *The Birth of a Nation* (1914). After seeing *The Birth of a Nation,* President Wilson, in an oft-quoted remark, declared that it was "like writing history with lightning." Curtis may have hoped that his movie would generate at least some quotient of the public acknowledgment that Griffith's film received for its rendition of the supposed renewal of the South after the traumas of the Civil War.

His movie treated a large and dramatic historical subject, Indian life when first encountered by whites "in the days of Vancouver" (that is, 1792), or even earlier, and Stephen Bush did recognize it *as* an "epic," saying "it fully deserves the name." "It seemed to me," he elaborated, "that there was a most striking resemblance all through the film between the musical epics of Richard Wagner and the theme and treatment of this Indian epic." Whatever the purely formal innovations of *The Birth of a Nation*, so often saluted by film historians, we should now recognize that it was not so much "writing history with lightning" as celebrating with thunder the ideology of white supremacy.[5] Needless to say, in such things as its sensationalizing of alleged Indian "head-hunting," Curtis's film, if less obviously contentious to its original audiences, also represented prevailing ideological assumptions about the nature of aboriginal culture. At the same time, since Vancouver does not actually arrive in the finished version of Curtis's film, his movie Indians, *unlike* Indians in the then-emerging Western genre, were not opposed to whites. They occupied a space outside white history – which is a point to be considered later.

To achieve even the level of recognition registered in the contemporary notices quoted here, Curtis's cinematic expertise when he made his Kwakiutl film must have been based on a long apprenticeship to the medium. The present chapter, in sequence, outlines that early work, fills out the known record of *In the Land of the Head-Hunters* somewhat, offers some clues as to Curtis's later activities in the film world (including Hollywood), and then discusses related aspects of the project's representation of Indians.

Curtis's Earlier Movie Work

Earle R. Forrest, the writer and photographer, recorded in his book *The Snake Dance of the Hopi Indians* (1961) that Curtis had made movie footage of the Oraibi Snake Dance contemporaneously with his still images (such as fig. 15), that is, as early as 1906: "I heard at the time that he had paid the Snake Society two hundred dollars for the privilege of filming motion pictures in the Snake *Kiva*, but I cannot vouch for this statement." "In a recent letter, Robert E. Callahan, of Los Angeles," he continued, "declared that making pictures in the Indian country in 1906 could hardly have been possible; that the process had not been adequately developed at that time. He should have told that to Mr. Curtis, who took those movies and the next winter toured eastern states showing them in theaters, once in Pittsburgh, Pennsylvania." Forrest was a very reliable source on photographic matters, and in this instance evidence survives which supports his supposition. Curtis's original outline for *The North American Indian,* submitted to J. Pierpont Morgan in 1906, for instance, mentions motion-picture equipment and the "considerable value" of film of "the Indian's ceremonial life." When he spoke at the University of Washington during the winter of 1906–7 he referred to his "photographic and other equipment" as if it normally included "a motion picture machine." Moreover, the 1906 summer fieldwork was largely devoted to various tribes of the Southwest.[6]

However, it is more likely that the movie work began even earlier. The *Portland Oregonian* of January 15, 1905, carried an item devoted to one of Curtis's illustrated talks which had the following subheading: "New and Remarkable 'Motion Pictures' of Snake Dance and Other Mystic Ceremonies." This implies that the films were made during the summer of 1904. The *Seattle Times* for May 22, 1904, told, it seems, the story of the first such motion picture:

> When Mr. Curtis was in Washington, D.C. recently, government scientists who have devoted a lifetime to the study of Indians, chanced to mention the great Yabachi dance. It seems this dance is hidden among the most sacred rites of the Navajos. It is a ceremony that lasts nine days, all told. Smithsonian Institution men told Mr. Curtis that pictures of the dance . . . would be priceless from the standpoint of the Indian historian. But they also told him that the government had been working to get the views for twenty years without result, and . . . had reached the conclusion that it was beyond the pale of the possible. . . . [When] Curtis started for the land of the Navajo . . . he took with him a moving picture machine, something he had never carried before. To all questions he answered: "I am going to Arizona. I don't know how long I will be gone." And he went to Arizona, and he stayed just long enough to accomplish that which Uncle Sam, with all his power and authority, had tried . . . and failed. . . . In addition to individual pictures of the masked dancers and the "fool," Curtis brought back a "moving picture" of the dance itself . . . something that . . . will convey to the onlooker the exact and lifelike picture of a dance that, in its reality, had never been seen by light of day, or . . . looked upon by the eyes of a white man. . . .

In November 1904 the same newspaper recorded a similar Curtis coup in the case of the Hopi snake dance. Curtis had apparently hired an Oraibi roof top; "it was from this roof," he said, "[that] I proposed to work the motion picture machine or kinetoscope. My other work I planned to do from the ground and get in as close and often as I could." When Curtis told the stories of such events during the course of lectures, he described his own participation with tremendous verve and vividness, while at the same time presenting his photographs and movies. It is quite possible that in this way a conflation of years occurred in Forrest's mind: He witnessed Curtis at work in the summer of 1906 and later assumed that the movies he saw in the winter of 1906–7 were made then.[7]

The most elaborate lecture performances of Curtis's career were, of course, his musicale appearances in 1911 and 1912. These, as we know, included motion pictures; part of one performance script, for example, reads: "MOTION PICTURE SNAKE DANCE." A program note for another lecture contains a section which heralds *In the Land of the Head-Hunters*:

> III. The Tribes of British Columbia, and their remarkable ceremonial life. Pictures show the general life and manners. "The Kominaka Dance," or dance of the skulls. The Whaler. The Whale Ceremony. Motion Picture, "Dance of the Mummy." "On the Shores of the North Pacific," a dissolving composition depicting life by the moonlit ocean. This series of pictures . . . contains some of the most remarkable ever taken of the secret rites of Indians.

Since this same note has references to the music composed especially for the 1911 tour, it is likely that Curtis had by then already conceived much of what was to become *In the Land of the Head-Hunters.* The film certainly contains sequences which could be described by the phrases used here: Motana dances with skulls, there is a ceremony followed by a remarkable whale hunt, and, as we have seen from the laudatory review comments, the movie offered some stunning light effects. Curtis had certainly made still photographs of Hamatsa ceremonies – what is called here the "Dance of the Mummy" – as early as 1910, and it seems very likely that film footage of such scenes was made at the same time. On the other hand, the British Columbia movie sequences made as early as 1910 and shown during the 1911 musicale may not have been the same as the sequences of the actual feature-length film, which seems to have been shot mostly during 1914. Rather, it appears that the early movie footage constituted a first run for segments of the more narratively unified feature film.[8]

Representing Kwakiutl Life in Film and Writing

Curtis was in fact moving from the musicale to the movie. On March 28, 1912, he wrote from his New York office to Frederick Webb Hodge; in the midst of general discussion, he began to impart ideas for movies: "I am still doing some figuring on the possibility of a series of motion pictures, and am very much in hopes that it will materialize, as such an arrangement would materially strengthen the real cause [the fieldwork and publication of *The North America Indian*], as well as giving us some most valuable material in the motion pictures themselves." By May 2 of 1912 Curtis had turned this vague notion into the grandiose scheme that he outlined to Secretary Walcott of the Smithsonian Institution: "It has been suggested," he wrote, "that I make . . . a complete series of motion pictures of the most important tribes, such pictures illustrating . . . the activities of their lives, particularly domestic and ceremonial, not carelessly caught fragments . . . but rather carefully studied . . . subjects, in order that every picture be an unquestioned document." He went on to stress "the utmost care" that would need to be taken over costuming and other props and he illustrated the kind of film he had in mind by giving a précis of subjects to be covered if a film of "British Columbia coast tribes" were being produced. "Pictures should be made," he said, "to illustrate the period before the white man came, keeping in mind all their activities." Several of the many activities he then listed did eventually appear as segments of *In the Land of the Head-Hunters*, including whaling and its attendant ceremonies, the return of a war party, "many beautiful masked dancers," a wedding, and so on.[9]

Curtis hoped that Walcott would endorse the educational value of such a venture as part of his efforts to raise extra funds for the thorough kind of job such preparation required. A partial context and spur to Curtis's approach was that in 1911, during the commercial American cinema's first cycle of Westerns with Indian characters and themes, there was a lively debate on the need to represent Indian culture "correctly." An editorial in the *Moving Picture World*, for example, called for a new kind of film: "While we still have the real Indians with us, why cannot thoroughly representative films be produced, making them at once illustrative and historic recorders of this noble race of people, with their splendid physique and physical powers?"

"It is to be hoped," the piece continued, "that some of our Western manufacturers will yet produce a series of films of REAL Indian life, doing so with the distinct object in view that they are to be of educational value, both for present and future use." Several of the contributors to the debate were particularly concerned about costume. Edward W. Buck, editor of the *Nevadan,* was incensed about inappropriate headdresses and wrote to the *Moving Picture World*: "Let's have this thing done right. Let the show people post up a little on the dress of the noble aborigine."[10]

In Curtis's efforts to get things "right," he sought additional help from George Byron Gordon of the University Museum, Philadelphia, telling Gordon that he was "submitting this subject to but three friends, Dr. Walcott, Prof. Osborn, and yourself," adding, "with letters from such a trio I feel I can easily carry my point." Both Walcott and Gordon complied. "Your plan to make a permanent motion-picture record of the existing primitive life of our Indians while the opportunity still lasts, and to restore scientifically, as far as may be practicable, that part of their life that has passed, is so important to education," wrote Walcott, "that I am very much pleased to know that there is a prospect of [it] being done." Gordon, for his part, though writing in haste before departing for a visit to London, went on at length about the need for correct costumes – "both that which was appropriate to them as a people and also to the occasion which is illustrated." "There is only one right thing to do . . . and I have given the matter a good deal of attention," he said. "The Indians should be dressed throughout in correct tribal costume wherever it is possible to provide them, either by originals or by reproductions made for the purpose." Whether there was any connection to such endorsements as these or not, in the making of the British Columbia film costumes were, indeed, reproduced – and house fronts were erected, totems were carved, canoes were repainted, and masks were made in elaborate profusion.[11]

When Curtis approached Edgar L. Hewett in 1913, saying that for "a couple of years" he had "been working towards the making of a great motion picture dealing with the tribes of British Columbia" and using Gilbert's music, it was with a more developed proposal. Hewett, an anthropologist who went on to hold such influential positions as the director of the School of American Research in Santa Fe, was serving as director of exhibits for the world's fair held in San Diego in 1915, the Panama Exposition. Curtis suggested that the Exposition sponsor the completion of the film to the tune of "about $20,000.00" to finish the picture in return for publicity showings of it and a share in its profits. He stressed the beauty of the animal dances and the secret nature of the ceremonies, as in this example:

> A particularly fine group of . . . characters is a series of forty birds. The masks . . . are particularly beautiful and I question whether they have been seen, as it is one of their very sacred rites and the masks are destroyed as a part of the ceremony. All of this material will be available for our picture the coming year.

Hewett may well have entertained Curtis's proposal seriously because at the San Diego Exposition there was a marked emphasis on evolution and racial types, movies provided a significant amount of the entertainment and education on offer, and they were greatly used to publicize the show. However, for whatever reason, the funding Curtis requested did not materialize.[12]

Nevertheless, soon after securing the backing of the eminent anthropologists he had approached, Curtis managed to raise the necessary funds elsewhere in the commercial world. In replication of the financial base achieved for the production of *The North American Indian* itself, his Continental Film Company, soon transformed into the Seattle Film Company, came into being, and the film itself, "produced" by the World Film Corporation, followed two years later.[13] In certain crucial respects it differed from the kind of product commended by Walcott and Gordon, primarily in that, as we have seen, it was structured as the story of Motana, his triumph over forces of evil, and his successful wooing of and marriage to a young bride. That is, the depiction of aspects of what Curtis, in his outline for Walcott, called "the primal life," were subsumed into an unfolding story – just as they were in the later *Nanook.*

The positive print was finally made from the negative in the middle of October 1914. On December 1 Curtis sent complimentary tickets to the curator of ethnology at the American Museum of Natural History, Clark Wissler, and also included some for Herbert J. Spinden, another leading ethnologist of the time:

> You will no doubt recall our discussion on Indian motion pictures. Following the plan I had in mind at that time, I have produced one dealing with the tribes of the British Columbia coast and it is to have its initial showing on December 7th. I am enclosing seats and hope you can join us.

> I think you will find much in it of interest. The picture is a compromise between what I would like to make, if I was in a position to say – "the public be damned" – and what I think the public will support.
>
> I am enclosing a couple of additional tickets which I would like to have you pass on to Mr. Spindon [sic] if he is in town.

A little later, the film was put on at Carnegie Hall as, Curtis said, "a benefit affair for one of the Social Center efforts," and he invited Theodore Roosevelt to share a box with him. Roosevelt, however, was obliged to decline.[14]

In view of the fact that the movie slipped into virtual obscurity for so long, it seems that "the public" did not support it. But the initial reviews, as we have seen, were favorable. W. Stephen Bush went so far as to call it "a gem of the motion picture art" which had "never been surpassed." The anonymous critic of the *Independent* invoked ideas similar to the sculpture-in-motion notions expressed by Lindsay (themselves reminiscent of A. C. Haddon's use of "living bronze," as quoted in Chapter 5):

> It was thought to be a great educational advance when [museums] set up groups of Indians modeled in wax and clothed in their everyday or gala costumes. But now a further step of equal importance has been taken. . . . The masks and costumes of the eagle and the bear which seemed merely grotesque when we saw them hung up in rows in the showcase at the museum become effective, even awe-inspiring, when seen on giant forms on the prow of a canoe filled with victorious warriors. . . . Mr. Curtis appreciates the effectiveness of the silhouette and the shadow and he is not afraid to point his camera in the face of the sun, contrary to the instructions of the Kodak primer. The scenes that elicited most applause from the audience were after all not those of Indian combats, but those of waves and clouds at sunset, the herd of sea lions leaping from the rocks and the fleet of canoes being driven swiftly forward. . . .[15]

And – for modern viewers too – the film contains other stunning visual effects: the use of a canoe-borne camera actually *among* other moving boats, for instance, or the mythical figures of Grizzly Bear, Thunderbird, and Wasp dancing in the prows of the advancing carved canoes, or the theatrical display of the dance privileges.

Figure 17. The Fire Drill – Koskimo, 1914, by E. S. Curtis. This Kwakiutl man (actually, it seems, George Hunt) will make fire by creating a spark through friction between the two pieces of wood.

There is the same power even when reconstruction of the sort mentioned above was involved. Curtis's Kwakiutl still pictures often exhibit an element of reconstruction, most emphatically "The Fire Drill" (fig. 17; 1914), in which – though the Kwakiutl had used Hudson's Bay Company matches for more than a generation – an old man sits at the root of a tree about to ignite tinder with two pieces of wood. Interestingly, while this and other still images – the masked figures "Kotsuis and Hohhuq" (1914), for example, or "Coming for the Bride" (1914) – paralleled sequences in the motion picture, there is no doubt at all that *The North American Indian* was a much lower-key product than the film. While it included such relatively mundane images as "A 'Begged from' Cedar" (1914), showing a living tree from which a plank has been hewn, and many other aspects of workaday Kwakiutl life, the film tended to move through a series of climactic events. This is most obvious, of course, in its emphasis on headhunting, but also in such sequences as Motana dancing in the graveyard bedecked with skulls. The anthropological account of the

Kwakiutl in *The North American Indian* was by no means unbiased; witness this quotation from its preface:

> It is an inhospitable country, with its forbidding, rock-bound coasts, its dark, tangled, mysterious forests, its beetling mountains, its long, gloomy season of rains and fogs. No less inhospitable, mysterious and gloomy, to the casual observer, is the character of the inhabitants. They seem constantly lost in dark broodings, and it is only after long acquaintance and rather tedious process of gaining their confidence that one discovers an uncertain thread of cheerfulness woven in the somber fabric of their nature. Even then one is impelled to question their knowledge of any such thing as spiritual exaltation or mental pleasure, except as may be aroused by the gratification of savage passions or purely physical instincts. Chastity, genuine, self-sacrificing friendship, even the inviolability of a guest, – a cardinal principle among most Indian tribes, – are unknown. It is scarcely an exaggeration to say that no single noble trait redeems the Kwakiutl character.[16]

And it also included much gory data on warfare. But the primary stress of *The North American Indian* fell on the explication of Kwakiutl social organization (especially the potlatch system) and Kwakiutl mythology (including several photographs of extraordinary transformer masks).

By contrast, in *its* representation of Native Americans, Curtis's film – though it undoubtedly contains a considerable amount of "record" material of the kind promised to Walcott and others – tried to meet the discernible requirements of its medium, and went after greater sensation. In one exchange with Gordon, Curtis managed *both* to stress the sensational aspect of his earlier Kwakiutl movie footage *and* to imply that it had no place in an educational endeavor like his musicale. "I will omit, as you suggest, all the motion pictures except the snake dance. . . . I will gladly omit the mummies, as I am not particularly fond of 'sweet food' at the best," he said.[17] Indeed, *In the Land of the Head-Hunters* itself manages – along with scenes offering a vision of some material splendor – to touch several points on the gamut of well-known negative white preconceptions of Indians: Its Kwakiutl are savage, cunning, superstitious, cruel, etc. As a telling scene-setting sentence in one of its scenarios put it: "They were head-hunters, and cannibalistic" (see Doc. 8A).

It is likely that the element of sensationalism and the stirring quality of the film's photography stayed in the minds of staff members of the American Museum of Natural History just as much as the educational impact of what Lindsay called its "noble bronzes." In the early twenties – when, as we shall see, Curtis was engaged in another part of the film world – Pliny Earle Goddard, then curator of ethnology there, approached Curtis in the hope of buying a print of *In the Land of the Head-Hunters.* Goddard wrote on January 25, 1923, and then again on March 9:

> I have a strong feeling that your film ought to be preserved in some institution like our museum and besides we can make excellent use of it for our lecture work. You know how public institutions are. They are often out of money. This is the beginning of a year, however, and I am hopeful that some money might be found for such a purchase. If you will give your price I will do what I can toward securing it.

Curtis replied affirmatively from his Los Angeles studio at 668 South Rampart on March 1, 1923, adding, "The picture as now arranged is approximately 6,000 feet in length. As originally put out, while I had it on in New York, it was 10,000 feet. I question however the loss of much that was really vital in its trimming down. Few important incidents were left out; the trimming was largely in the form of shortening scenes."

This exchange marked the opening of protracted negotiations by correspondence between the two parties, and its elements are implicit here. The museum procrastinated, primarily because of lack of funds, and Curtis's print of the film was physically in less than a fully satisfactory state. In a letter of January 17, 1924, a year after his initial inquiry, Goddard summarized the Museum view:

> You will think I have been very slow in regard to the Head-Hunter films. The Curator of the Department of Education last fall informed me that he could not purchase the film for his department. I decided, however, to keep it with the hope that some other arrangements could be made. Recently I ran it for Professor Franz Boas to see. He thought several sections of it should most certainly be preserved as a record. This had been my opinion, but since I had seen very little of Northwest Coast life I could not speak with authority. Our budget for 1924 is not

> complete but I am informed that it is not likely that there will be funds for the purchase of the film. When I consider a thing so essential as this, I never give it up for the lack of money.
>
> What I really want is a negative of about 1,000 or 1,500 feet of the film covering in particular the dances and boat scenes. This negative, of course, could be made from a fresh positive, hardly from the positive that I have here.

Goddard went on to suggest a joint purchase with the collector George G. Heye, originator of the Museum of the American Indian (of which Hodge had become director).

Clearly, what Boas and Goddard wanted was the film's set pieces; they were not interested in the narrative aspect of it, which, from the viewpoint of film history, made it unique in its own time, however absurd the story was in some respects. Moreover, it was precisely "dances," games and the like that Boas himself had the Kwakiutl perform "as a record" for *his* movie camera a few years later. Boas and Goddard, unlike Flaherty, did not understand the credibility that, paradoxically, fictional narrative – even "romance," in Lindsay's term – can achieve. But then, as a number of commentators have pointed out, figures like Curtis and Boas represent completely different approaches to anthropology. On this matter, if not on others, Gordon of the University of Pennsylvania Museum would have agreed with Boas. He, too, was interested in set pieces and in 1921 asked Curtis for his "fine film of the snake dance" for use in his museum's "educational work with children," but when Curtis offered instead the Kwakiutl film, he declined.[18]

In 1924 the American Museum of Natural History was not the only party running out of money. On October 8 Curtis wired that because he was short of funds he would sell the "master print and negative" for $1,500. A week later, on October 16, he sent the following letter:

> I shipped the film yesterday and included in the case first the negative which I think is complete. However, fearing that it might not be, I have sent the positive to you; also, I have included about a thousand feet of extra negative as it may contain some bits which may be of value to you, and I also included a few pieces of positive print which may not be included in the assembled print. I am enclosing a bill covering the matter; also, it is understood by this letter that I relinquish any claim to the copyright upon the film.

In a postscript to his letter, Curtis asked for the return of any unwanted positive film, but there is no record of any such transaction. More important, it is not known what happened to all this footage thereafter.[19]

Curtis's Later Movie Work

Gifford Pinchot, as we have seen, was acquainted with Curtis from at least 1899. He encouraged Curtis, subscribed to *The North American Indian*, and even lent him money. In August 1914, Curtis, in a letter typical of his efforts to keep his project alive in the mind of a subscriber, told Pinchot of his movie activities, including the filming of seal and whale hunting:

> You will be interested to know that during my summer's field work I had a splendid sea lion picture hunting expedition, and further than that, a corking whale hunting trip, and I now almost consider myself a professional whaler. I was in at the exciting killing of several big ones. In a few days I will go out on another short trip, and expect to have a couple of weeks of active whaling, and during the winter I will perhaps have a chance to show you with movies how we do it.

A little later in 1914, on October 6, Curtis wrote to Roosevelt with similar enthusiasm:

> Incidentally, I had a great trip this summer, photographing sea lions and a corking whaling trip. Two or three times during the heighth [sic] of the whaling excitement, I wished you were there, and the captain of the whaler remarked "Tell Teddy that he should go whaling and have the fun of shooting a sulphur bottom."[20]

The following year Curtis was both involved in other aspects of the film world and tried to get into more regular movie making. C. B. Barkley of the Universal Culture Lyceum of 56 West 45th Street, New York, wrote to Curtis's old friend Meany that Curtis "had charge" of the Lyceum's "department of Ethnology," and that the Lyceum had "for its object wide spread culture, Moral Uplift and Visual Education through the agency of Motion Pictures." It seems that the Lyceum was one of a burgeoning group of organizations founded at that time to tame and harness the new medium; Barkley went on to outline the "positively harmful" effect of many movies – which were seen by "twenty million Americans every day" – through their treatment of "SEX PROBLEMS, MURDERS," etc.[21] It is not known what came of Curtis's role in the short-lived Lyceum; but, with or without a concern for moral uplift, his own next movie project was beginning to take shape.

In February 1915 he wrote to his assistant Edmund Schwinke, who had often acted as a cameraman during the shooting of *In the Land of the Head-Hunters*, about the possibility of "a month's motion picture work and scenic stuff." By May this had hardened into a plan for "a picture tour of the beauty spots of America," with "fifty-two weeks of a scenic picture a week." "The stills are going to Leslie's," he continued, "and the motion pictures going through motion picture channels." They were to start at the Grand Canyon, and then proceed to Yosemite and Yellowstone. As it happened, Schwinke chose not to participate in the venture, but the absence of a key person did not prevent at least some of these projections, including work in Indian country, coming into being.[22]

But one aspect did fail: President Wilson, who had so lauded the efficacy of motion pictures, refused to be filmed. "Aside from my pictorial Indian work, which has been under way for so many years, I am this year beginning a picture tour of the United States. This is primarily a tour in the interests of Leslie's Weekly, and I am to furnish travel pictures for one page of their magazine for each week for a year," Curtis told him, after being introduced to his private secretary by the sculptor Gutzon Borglum. He then outlined what was clearly meant to be taken as the less commercial aspect of the plan for the year, emphasizing the "greatest educational good" of the work and its concentration on government land, and enclosed letters of endorsement from Franklin Lane and others. "The first series is to be Washington, the Capital of the United States. For this number," Curtis went on, coming to the pivot of his request, "I am most anxious to secure a short piece of picture of you, perhaps as you are walking to your car at the entrance of the White House, or in any way satisfactory to you." He added that he dared to be so "presumptuous" only because of "the unusual educational value" of his undertaking, which was, he said, "to teach America to Americans," and insisted that "the picture making need occasion no serious loss of time" because it could be done when the president was "naturally going or coming." Wilson's private response to this and an accompanying request to make "a few pictures of the White House grounds" was curt: "Please decline this for me."[23]

The actual landscape work was doubtless more welcomed, if by figures less powerful. On April 22, 1915, Curtis asked his old friend Meany for permission to join the Mountaineers on the club's ascent of Mount Rainier that summer, saying that he would be on an "active tour of the United States," working both in "regular photographs and motion photography." It seems that Curtis was expected to visit the Mount Rainier National Park during August in the company of the assistant secretary of the Interior, Stephen T. Mather. The following February, on the 22nd, Curtis wrote to Pinchot, partly to explain a delay in his loan repayment and partly to boast that the secretary of the Interior had asked him "to go out to the Yellowstone and make a series of motion pictures of the animals." "They tell me," he added, "that there is an unusually large number down in the valley where they are being fed to some extent, and I should be able to get some splendid things." By the spring of 1916 the work was probably complete, for Curtis invited Pinchot to a private view of what he termed, in his letter of April 12, "my park and Indian motion pictures."[24]

Many years later Curtis provided the University of Washington Library with a copy of a letter from Herbert A. Smith, a former editor of *The Forester*, the journal of the U.S. Forest Service, in which – perhaps having heard about the photographer from his chief, Pinchot – he had asked Curtis to combine his work for *Leslie's* with securing pictures suitable for Forest Service use as "lantern slide illustrations, and for transparencies, bromides, etc." In an accompanying note to the University Librarian, Curtis added a gloss to the effect that he had selected Yosemite as the best location (and here he was probably conflating two different commissions, since Yosemite was not administered by the Forest Service), that he was "furnished an army mule for [his] camera equipment," that "the trip through the high mountains" took "several weeks," but that he "and his helper" had "made enough motion picture footage for a [sic] evening program and enough still pictures to fill several magazines."[25]

It has not proved possible to locate any publication of the still photographs for certain; some may have appeared in materials issued by the National Park Service and the Morgan Library does possess a series of Curtis transparencies which includes views of the Grand Canyon and other beauty spots, mule trains, and what might well be a party of VIPs. The film footage was shown during 1916 by William Randolph Hearst's International Film Service as a series of "Curtis Scenics." Each scenic was approximately five minutes long and comprised half of a split reel, the other half being occupied by cartoons, such as the Katzenjammer Kids and Krazy Kat. These "motion picture cocktails," as they were advertised, were circulated on a weekly basis to cinemas throughout the nation. Whether any survive is not known.[26]

In the years after 1916 it is unlikely that Curtis made any films of his own. For a start, Bureau of Indian Affairs policy was opposed to the kind of ethnographic films Curtis was interested in. The *Annual Report of the Commissioner for Indian Affairs* for 1917 carried a note to the effect that the increasing number of requests for Indians to appear in motion pictures were habitually refused unless Indians were to feature in present-day scenes, not "'made-up' exhibitions of their old time customs and dances." In any case, *In the Land of the Head-Hunters* had proved a financial disaster, and Curtis simply did not have the money for further film ventures of its kind. In fact, in the same letter in which he first told Pliny Earle Goddard that he would be willing to part with his Kwakiutl movie, he added that he had enjoyed a very satisfactory summer of fieldwork in California and southern Oregon the previous year. "I found far more interesting material for pictures than I had expected," he said, "and my only regret is that I could not [give] more time to the trip. Unfortunately I did not have a motion picture camera with me as funds were not available for any work along that line." In the ethnological field – if we except the 16mm footage of Curtis's 1927 Alaska trip with his daughter Beth Curtis Magnuson – there were never again funds for work "along that line."[27]

It is, therefore, especially ironic that Curtis was simultaneously deeply involved in other people's productions for Hollywood. "I am now working," he informed Goddard on May 15, 1923, "on the picturization of the 'Ten Commandments' and aside from breaking the one which mentions the fact that we should keep the Sabbath holy, I am working about eighteen hours a day, both on said Sabbath and on the days between." *The Ten Commandments* (1923), directed by Cecil B. de Mille, was one of the epics of the silent cinema. The first book on the North American Indian project, Ralph Andrews's *Curtis' Western Indians* (1962), included mention of Curtis's work as a "stills photographer" on the film, and this is very likely, since such images survive. Interestingly, de Mille himself, in his 1959 *Autobiography*, listed Curtis as "the second cameraman," and slightly more recently film historians have also begun to record his definite employment as a movie camera operator.

In fact, Curtis's Hollywood connections, despite the apparent absence of any screen credits at all, would repay further investigation. For instance, after his daughter Beth moved the Curtis Studio from Seattle to Los Angeles on the breakdown of her parents' marriage just after the First World War, many of the studio's clients for portraits were movie people, such as character actor Hobart Bosworth and screenwriter John Monk Saunders. Curtis knew de Mille and D. W. Griffith personally and was very friendly, apparently, with William S. Hart, the cowboy star, and Gene Stratton-Porter, the popular novelist, nature writer, photographer and writer-producer for the movies.[28]

Stratton-Porter, who was almost incredibly popular at the time – and not above using her popularity to press her racist and eugenicist views in some of her monthly editorials in *McCall's* – wrote to her daughter Jeannette Porter Meeham in 1922: "Mr. Curtis, the Indian photographer, made a new boots-and-breeches picture of me in one of the cañons the other day," and in another letter admitted that her Indian love story *The Fire Bird* (1922) was heavily indebted to his aura of the "Indianesque," even though he was ensconced in Hollywood. In the 1924 and 1926 editions of *Who's Who in America*, Curtis listed the Screen Writers' Club among the societies to which he belonged, and at least once, in 1922, he gave a friend knowing advice about writing for the cinema. He was associated with de Mille's *Adam's Rib* (1923) and, probably, the Tarzan films, most likely the serial begun in 1921 with Elmo Lincoln in the title role.[29]

The last film with which Curtis seems to have had a connection was a Western, *The Plainsman*, made in 1936 with Gary Cooper as the male lead. With an undated letter to his friend Olive Daniels, Curtis sent a photograph, now lost: "This picture I did while working on De Milles [sic] The Plainsman. . . ." Along with Cooper, a fictionalized Buffalo Bill and an invented General Custer, the film also featured several hundred Sioux Indians who were drafted in from the Rosebud Reservation to participate in this version of the events of 1876. This is an intriguing episode in a number of respects. It would be interesting, for example, to know what both Curtis and the Sioux thought about Anthony Quinn playing an Indian. It is almost certain that some of the Sioux present would have recognized Curtis as the man who, almost thirty years before, in 1907, had urged numbers of their people to undertake a very different type of reconstruction of war and raiding parties, to follow the course of the same Little Big Horn battle, and to sit for portraits of themselves for *The North American Indian*.[30]

In Curtis's *In the Land of the Head-Hunters* movie, as we have seen, George Vancouver has not (yet) arrived: Native Americans remain outside white history. Yet, paradoxically, it was white history – in this case the development of an even more sophisticated machine than the still camera – that had made possible the fiction of ahistoricity. Curtis's feature film, in other words, purported to offer the same kind of transparent and unproblematic representation of Native Americans that he had striven for in the still photograph titled "Before the White Man Came" (frontispiece) discussed at the close of Chapter 1. Thus, despite the essential narrativity of film in comparison to photography, the project's subject, "the North American Indian," was placed in the same position as in that photograph. Whatever the status of Gutzon Borglum's other comments (in Doc. 8D), his observations on the continuities and connections between the media seem both just and directly applicable to Curtis: "The Kodak awakened the possibility of freezing this strange, evanescent gold [the mystery of life] . . . and the instantaneous camera set for the movements of animals in action carried it further – but the moving picture, wrongly and poorly named, has made or is making a fine art." But, then again, "art" – like "history" itself (as in such projections as "Writing History with the Camera") – is also an ambiguous concept in this regard, one that maintains the tension between fact and fiction, document and (re)construction, that we have observed throughout this study.

DOCUMENTS

Document 8A. Introduction to Scenario, "In the Days of Vancouver," c. 1913.

In keeping with Curtis's desire to film the Kwakiutl "before the white man came," the earliest surviving script materials either name Vancouver in the title or mention 1792, the date of his voyage to the Northwest Coast.

IN THE DAYS OF VANCOUVER

Geography of picture: The shores of Vancouver Island. Rocky, abrupt shoreline, in places open beach. Narrow waterways, many small islands, in places heavy surf. Shoreline practically a virgin forest. Trees of great size, undergrowth so dense that it makes a veritable jungle.

Tribes live in many small villages scattered here and there at the edge of the water on the bays and inlets. Natives large, vigorous, good-looking, temperament vicious and sensual, proud to a degree, saturated with superstition, wrapped in ritualistic forms. Constant intertribal and intervillage warfare. They were head-hunters, and cannibalistic. Travel wholly by canoe, large and small. Depend largely upon the sea for food; fish, shellfish, seal, porpoise, whale. Skilled in working wood with primal tools.

Clothing: Men wore a single blanket of fur or woven from the bark of cedar trees. Women used same type of blankets, and also went about wearing simply a cedar-bark skirt. A rain cape – poncho-like – made from cedar-bark, was used by both sexes. Great wealth of most extraordinary ceremonial costumes. These are largely the masked characters participating in the ceremonies. Warriors dressed in striking and distinct ways. War implements were short spears which could be used in canoes, war-clubs, bows and arrows, and war slings. The last were used for throwing heavy stones a great distance.[31]

Document 8B. Handbill for Moore Theater, Seattle, 1914.[32]

MOORE THEATER
December 7 to 15 Matinees Daily
The World Film Corporation presents
In the Land of the Head Hunters
A Drama of Primitive Life on the Shores of the North Pacific
From Story Written and Picture Made by
EDWARD S. CURTIS
Every Participant an Indian and Every Incident True to Native Life. . . .

SYNOPSIS

To gain power from the spirit forces, Motana, the son of a great chief, goes on a vigil journey. Through the fasting and hardships of the vigil he hopes to gain supernatural strength which will make him a chief not less powerful than his father, Kenada.

First upon a mountain's peak he builds a prayer-fire to the Gods. After long dancing about the sacred flames he drops from exhaustion, and in vision sleep the face of a maid appears in the coiling smoke, thus breaking the divine law which forbids the thought of women during the fasting.

Now he must pass another stronger ordeal. Leaving his desecrated fire to go to the Island of the Dead, he meets Naida, the maid of his dream, and wooes [sic] her. She tells him she is promised to the hideous Sorcerer. Motana bids the maid return to her father and say that when this vigil is over he will come with a wealth of presents and beg her hand in marriage. Now he renews his quest of spirit power and tests his courage by spending the night in the fearful "house of skulls." And to prove his prowess he goes in quest of sea lions and then achieves the greatest feat of all – the capture of a whale.

Then, for his final invocation to the Gods, Motana again builds his sacred fire upon the heights. While he fasts and dances there about his prayer fire the Sorcerer in a dark glade of the forest has gathered about him fellow workers in evil magic and they sing "short time songs" to destroy him. The Sorcerer sends his daughter to find Motana and in some way get a lock of his hair, that they may destroy his life by incantation. This ever-treacherous plotting woman on seeing Motana asleep by his fire becomes infatuated with him and decides to risk even the wrath of her Sorcerer father and win the love of Motana. When she awakens him with caressing words, he bids her begone, as he is not thinking of women, but of the spirits. With angry threats she departs, but in stealth watches the faster until he drops asleep; then creeping up steals his necklace and a lock of hair, and disappears.

Motana returning ask [sic] his father to send messengers demanding the hand of Naida. Her father, Waket, replies to the messengers: "My daughter is promised to the fearful Sorcerer. We fear his magic. If your great chief, Kenada, would have my daughter for his son's wife, bring the Sorcerer's head as a marriage gift." With song and shout they start upon the journey and attack the Sorcerer's village. With song triumphant they return with the Sorcerer's head; and in great pomp of primitive pageantry Naida and Motana are married.

Even while the wedding dancers make merry a cloud of tragedy hangs above them, for Yaklus, the fearful war-chief, returning from a fishing expedition, learns of the attack and is preparing to avenge the death of his brother, the Sorcerer.

In his magnificent high-prowed canoes he starts upon his war of vengeance. It is a tribal law that the war party destroy all who are met, whether friend or foe. While on their foray fishing parties and travelers are encountered.

Then they make their night attack upon the village of Motana. Kenada and his tribesmen give way before the infuriated Yaklus, and amid the smoke and flames of the burning village Motana is wounded and Naida is carried away to captivity.

Yaklus returning to his village gives a great dance of victory. The frenzied warriors demand the life of Naida. Yaklus bids her come and dance for them. If she dances well enough to please him he will spare her life. If not, they will throw her to the "hungry wolves." So well does she dance that Yaklus spares her.

In the sleeping hours Naida sends her fellow captive-slave with a token and message to Motana, who has been revived by the surviving medicine men of his village. When he receives the message from this bride-wife Motana calls for volunteers.

By stealth he rescues her. Yaklus in rage starts in pursuit. Motana, hard pressed, dares the waters of the surging gorge of Hyal, through which he passes in safety. Great was his "water magic." Yaklus attempts to follow, but the raging waters of the gorge sweep upon him and he and his grizzly followers become the prey of the evil ones of the sea.

Document 8C. Newspaper item, 1914.[33]

HOW TO GET AN INDIAN TO "DIE" BEFORE CAMERA

The many realistic scenes of tribal warfare reproduced by Edward S. Curtis, with great vigor and dramatic flavor, are among the most distinctive features of his stirring Indian photodrama, "In the Land of the Head Hunters," to which many have been drawn to the Moore this last week, and which will be seen here but three days more. Mr. Curtis appears to have had the most ready response from his North Pacific Indians in the action of these conflicts.

When the whole truth is told, however, a full share of credit must be given the producer, because, in preparing for the many mimic battles in "The Head Hunters," he encountered the strongest kind of opposition from the natives. To see them in the picture one would imagine that they needed no coaxing to swing their whalebone bludgeons about and mow down the enemy or perish in an unequal combat. On the contrary, all the powers of persuasion of which Mr. Curtis is possessed were needed to draw them into it. He found that these very scenes touched upon a very firmly embedded superstition of the Kwakiutls – they would not play "dead," for they believe that to do so brings real death within a year.

To play the victorious warrior was a part easily filled, but to play the unfortunate warrior, who goes down in defeat and is slaughtered, found no applicants. The older men were absolutely fixed in this belief, and for a time Mr. Curtis had an army of victors only, and none willing to play an heroic death scene before the camera.

With the promise of a little extra reward, the younger Indians were finally cajoled to fill the ranks of the defeated, and, once committed to it, their squeamishness disappeared and they found much sport in grieving their parents by dropping dead with a little extra realism whenever possible.

Document 8D. Letter, Gutzon Borglum to Edward S. Curtis, 1914.

Borglum was the extraordinarily energetic sculptor of such massive works as the presidential faces on Mount Rushmore. This letter was not the spontaneous outburst that it might at first appear. Curtis used it for publicity purposes immediately: He enclosed it with a letter to Roosevelt inviting the former president to a showing of the film. Borglum, in fact, was one of the directors of The North American Indian, Inc.[34]

I have to-night seen your pictures of the Head Hunters for the third time . . . and I cannot let the occasion pass without thanking you for entering this field of educational entertainment and lifting this form of expression into the realm of the fine arts.

The moving picture has been to the dramatic roust-about what the tin horn has been to the boy with an insufficient vocal organ. It has been diverting, and in its rapidity of action alone it has caught the tired eye of the world. In its rapid reappearance with an occasional promise, it has held the attention of humanity.

I think I am not making a new observation though I have not seen this expressed, that the best in life, much of its wonderment, of its mystery, much of its psychology that is "felt" however vaguely seen – rarely presented or described, yet, like a golden thread this mystery runs through every scene of life. The Kodak awakened the possibility of freezing this strange, evanescent gold, which I call the soul of any subject, be it good or bad; and the instantaneous camera set for the movements of animals in action carried it further – but the moving picture, wrongly and poorly named, has made or is making a fine art.

You have, as one of the poets of our day, a natural consciousness of this thread of gold – of truth – of beauty – of beautiful reality and you found it in your subject The Wooing of the Head Hunters, and revealed it.

I am not surprised at your photography. It compares favorably with your other masterpieces of the people of the plains. . . . The great thing that we all must congratulate ourselves upon is that you have entered the field of film production and will lift its standard to the realm of the fine arts. God Bless You!

Figure 18. Postcards of Curtis photographs (Zuni, Zuni Girl, Mohave Girl), c. 1904. Such postcards yielded both income and visibility for the project.

9

REPRESENTING THE INDIAN

I wish to open this final chapter by looking at the North American Indian project's representations of religion, so often throughout history *the* category of difference. It was certainly the topic most frequently declared to be of special interest to the project – and others beyond the project, such as A. C. Haddon, appreciated this. There were, for example, numerous newspaper stories about Curtis's views on the origins of Indian shakerism in the Pacific Northwest, the prevalence of hypnotism in native communities, and on a host of other such matters, as if it was known that this religious and ceremonial emphasis was the project's bread and butter.[1] In particular, we will focus on the religious rites of the Pueblos, a group of peoples who were of major concern to Curtis and his associates. While, as we know, the project was not a seamless whole, our findings may seem initially to indicate a more marked deviation than others from the overall pattern of the project's representation of Indians. My ultimate point, however, is that this seeming deviation actually underlines the strength and persistence of that pattern. Indeed, the principal threads of the pattern itself are what I want to unravel. The remainder of the chapter will be devoted to that task.

Representing Religious Rites

When Curtis delivered one of his musicale performances in 1911 he said, as we have seen, "There seems a broadly prevalent idea that the Indian lacked a religion. This erroneous impression was perhaps fathered by our own presumption in considering our reaching out to the Infinite to be religion, and the Indian's like act to be heathenism." "Rather than being without a religion," Curtis continued, "every act of his life was according to divine prompting" (Doc. 7B). In 1927, when he wrote to Hodge on behalf of Eastwood and himself about the applicability of the word "theology" in "Wichita Theology," a subtitle they proposed to use in Volume 19, he took a similarly relativistic position – "You seemingly object to the use of the word other than associated with Christian religion. I see nothing in Webster to indicate that Christianity has the exclusive use of the word" – before offering to "compromise" on "Religious Beliefs." (This questioning of the presumption of Christianity was also apparent when Curtis recalled George Hunt's glee over a Christian misreading of a totem pole and, more baldly, in his 1927 Alaska logbook entries on the corruptive role of missionaries among the Inuit.) Again, in "Indian Religion," the script of a lecture probably produced in 1912, Curtis bemoaned the tendency among whites to ignore the "variety" of Native American life, for "individuals acquainted with but one small group" to "say that the Indian beliefs are so and so." "If they stated 'the Zuni' for instance 'believes so and so', all well and good," he continued, "but when they say 'the Indian', it is quite another matter . . . the beliefs of one locality cannot in any sense be applied to all." Yet, in the same 1927 letter to Hodge that I quoted from above, Curtis purported *not* to see the force of Hodge's criticism of Eastwood on precisely this point: "On the paragraph which begins – 'Indian religion, that is instinctive worship of the divine ones', you make the comment 'It is too late to make such a statement in print'. You do not indicate what part of the statement cannot be made. . . . "[2]

The tensions here, although already extreme, are taken to breaking point when seen in conjunction with religion among the Pueblo peoples. It will be remembered that Myers felt the Pueblos were inhospitable to whites, especially ethnologists, and that venturing among them was highly fraught and could even prove dangerous. It is also clear that he assumed that some aspects of Pueblo culture, mainly their religious practices, were not only hard to find out about, but positively evil: Writing to Hodge in 1924 he described Santo Domingo as "one of the very worst nests of the lot."[3] Moreover, he seems to have taken it for granted that Hodge would naturally share his views.

During the early twenties – which, as we saw in Chapter 1, witnessed a highly transitional phase in Indian–white relations generally – there was in fact much ferment among and concerning the Pueblos. The time's most contentious issue was the Bursum Bill, a piece of proposed legislation which, had it been enacted, would have expropriated land traditionally within Pueblo control in favor of recent white settlers. The various Pueblos, acting both as individual tribes and in concert with one another, received an unprecedented amount of support from reformist whites, especially under the auspices of the Indian Defense Association and the General Federation of Women's Clubs, and this enabled the defeat of the most threatening aspects of the Bursum Bill and of its most devious successor, the Lenroot Bill.[4] The other hot issue concerned Native American ceremonial dances and, indirectly, sexual practices. Basically, in furthering the overall thrust of then-current Bureau of Indian Affairs policy to assimilate Indians as individuals into mainstream (white) ways, there was renewed pressure to eradicate tribal religious rituals.

The most blatant expression of this pressure was a circular "To All Indians" from the commissioner for Indian Affairs, Charles H. Burke, dated February 24, 1923. Burke was "against Indian dances, as they are usually given" and "against the display of their old customs at public gatherings held by whites," saying "something must be done to stop the neglect of stock, crops, gardens, and home interests caused by these . . . ceremonies. . . . " Burke emphasized individual endeavor, warned against "evil or foolish things," inveighed particularly against "'give-away' customs at dances" and, with specific reference to the Hopi and Pueblo peoples, he condemned the handling of "poisonous snakes in . . . ceremonies." He claimed that he had the right to issue an order "against these useless and harmful performances" but that he would rather they stopped of the Indians' own accord, and, therefore, he urged each group to reach agreement with its superintendent to hold no gatherings at certain times of the year and always to meet only for a short time "and to have no drugs, intoxicants, or gambling, and no dancing that the superintendent does not approve."[5]

While in this particular circular the emphasis fell primarily on economic matters, at the back of it was also much agitation on the part of such "friends of the Indian" as the Indian Rights Association about the sheer paganism, as it was seen, of such ceremonies and, especially, what Matthew K. Swiffen, editor of *Indian Truth*, the Association's magazine, called "immoral ceremonies, such as the Koshare Dance at Santo Domingo" and, as Kenneth Philp has reported, the "indecency" of other Pueblo dances. These opponents of the ceremonies, like the very influential Board of Indian Commissioners, were also profoundly worried that Indian ceremonial life tended to draw into it even "educated" Indians, thus inhibiting what they saw as efforts towards progress. On the other side, in support of the dances, were those like John Collier who believed that the ceremonies were socially cohesive and worthy of respect as profoundly religious expressive forms. As well as engaging in such means of protest as meetings, legal proceedings, and representations to other branches of government, Collier also wrote a prodigious number of letters to the press and a pamphlet for the Indian Defense Association titled *The Indian and His Religious Freedom*, completed in July 1924. In such writings, Collier refuted many of the aspersions that were routinely promulgated by opponents of the dances: that the caciques of the Pueblos used dictatorial methods and enacted cruel punishments on nonadherents, that many ceremonies involved the impregnation of women participants, including educated young girls, and the like.[6]

Among the intellectual supporters of the dances was the Southwestern writer Mary Austin. She composed a questionnaire on the alleged indecency of Indian ceremonies and sent it to some of the leading ethnologists of the day, including Jesse Walter Fewkes, who had written extensively on Hopi and Pueblo cultures; John R. Swanton and J. N. B. Hewitt of the Smithsonian; Francis La Flesche, who was himself Omaha; and Hodge, then working for the Museum of the American Indian as well as for Curtis. None of them reported seeing anything "indecent," in that any sexual references had always appeared to them to form part of a larger, holistic conception of the rhythms of nature, of life itself. On May 31, 1924, Austin sent a very angry note to Commissioner Burke, claiming that he was embarked on "an errand of suppression of native religious faith." In view of Curtis's position in the controversy – basically pro-Bureau, as I will elaborate (and as we might expect, given the evidence of Chapter 1) – it is ironic that in his editor's reply to Austin one of the works on Indian ceremonial life that Hodge recommended that she consult was *The North American Indian* itself! A further irony was that Hodge seems to have kept quiet to Myers and Curtis on these matters, whereas he was incensed enough to write to newspapers denouncing Bureau policy; more intimately, to Austin, he said, "My observations convince me that the Indians most devout in their native religious beliefs and practices are far more trustworthy than those who have been 'converted' to the beliefs of white people."[7]

Curtis attempted to enter the fray with an essay that deliberately echoed the title of Collier's polemical article: "The Indian and His Religious Freedom."[8] It opened with a ringing declaration in favor of religious tolerance, as "granted by our Constitution," but immediately proceeded to the heart of its argument:

> No moral or constitutional law grants the right of the individual or associated individuals to compel others to worship in conformity with their beliefs. When a religious order whips, maims, brands, fines, or ostracizes individuals . . . because they do not see fit to follow the religious practices of the order, then it ceases to be religious freedom and can be nothing but religious persecution. Further a crime, a misdemeanor, a wrong, committed in the name of "religion" is no less wrong even if it is done in the name of an Indian religion.

Curtis admitted that "the present storm of protest against government interference" had come about because of "an unfortunate, ill-advised, and ambiguously worded letter emanating from the Indian Department," but when he began to characterize "the storm center of this controversy," "particularly the Pueblo Indians," he was downright hostile: "In this controversy, the white friends – the agitators – and the orthodox Indians are not asking for religious freedom, but for religious tyranny. . . ."

He outlined the Pueblo system of government, averring that "each tribe is a state within itself," having its own "Governor, surrounded by a council," with "back of this visible government" what he termed "the real power, – the cacique" who "names or selects the governor and the council." Because, as he put it, "Aside from their own religion these Indians are practically all Catholics," he accused them of being "religiously polygamous." He gave an example from his own experience, in which a service that began "at the church" turned into a ceremony featuring "the Koshare dancers, nude with the exception of a gee string and with bodies grotesquely painted. . . ." The Koshares were responsible, he said, "for the greater part of the lewd and obscene phases of these dances. In other words, they are the last word in paganism in North America." He claimed that "education is the only factor which will cause the giving up of the old practices."

Curtis then expanded upon the struggle for the allegiance of the younger generation between the "Indian priesthood" and the "educated Indians" and particularly bemoaned the intrusive role of what he called "white agitators, backed by great numbers of our most intelligent people," who were doing their utmost "to encourage the old cacique organization to force the younger generation to participate in the ceremonies." And they did so, he claimed, "under the cry of 'religious freedom.'" "Yet," he said, what they were "actually doing" was "encouraging religious tyranny of the rankest sort . . . which . . . destroys all good done by our own educational work." Acknowledging "that those who are primarily interested in the picturesque side of the Indian [would] make a cry of protest," he went out of his way to stress his long experience "in the field," especially of "ceremonies and religion." The following constituted his considered judgment:

> Many of the ceremonies are colorful . . . [but they do] contain features which from the point of civilization are decidedly objectionable. All humanity in coming up from paganism has passed through the same phases of religious debauchery. In many cases the objectionable features are the secret parts of the "public" dances. The casual observer of these dances sees nothing but the spectacular and beautiful public performance; he does not see the secret rites which precede or follow the public ceremony. Students term many of these features "Phallic rites." It is a nice, polite term used in covering no end of sex liberty. In the beginning these "Phallic rites" may have been beautiful ceremonies intended to symbolically . . . encourage perpetuation of the race; but . . . they have [degenerated] and . . . are but sex debaucheries and the means by which the Indian priests gain possession of the maturing girls. The nature of these religious sex features . . . cannot be described in an article going before the general public. It is safe to say that the situation is no worse than we are led to believe it was at Sodom and Gemorrah [sic].

Curtis thought it would be obvious to the reader why educated Indian girls would object to taking part in the ceremonies and why many parents would not wish them to do so, and expressed anger that "white agitators" were "encouraging the caciques in forcing the school girls into the ceremonies." He then proceeded for the bulk of the essay to "cite a few cases," claiming that "every instance" could be backed up by "sworn statements and affidavits." It is not possible to summarize all the incidents recounted, but they included: the fining of a man who would not let his fourteen-year-old schoolgirl daughter participate in the dances; the stoning "to death" of a woman who had defied the council; the confiscation by the priesthood of property owned by individuals who had refused to observe ceremonial customs; the punishment of an absent man's wife "for the refusal of her husband to dance" (she was allegedly stripped and "left for a half day or more in a cold room" before being called naked "before the assembled council," where she became "the object of their lewd wit");

the selection of young girls for the sexual use of the priests, and the subsequent group "debauch"; the whipping of a young man, naked, for "the offense of wearing American clothes"; and the mass flogging of "about twenty returned students" who had quietly withdrawn from the ceremonies.

Curtis swore that the "purpose" of his article was not to stop the ceremonies, but "to inform . . . well meaning people" so as to "discourage" their support for "propagandists" who, he said, "go about among the Indians encouraging them in opposition to the government and in maintaining all existing ceremonies and further the revival of those they have on their own part discontinued." He insisted that the efforts of such "propagandists" during the previous three years had "set the Pueblo Indians back a generation." "Let public sentiment and the Indian Department stand back of the . . . progressive Indian and we will quickly have ten where we have one now," he affirmed. "Were I Indian Commissioner," he concluded, "I would write a proclamation to the Indians," stating emphatically that coercion would not be permitted. Then, "without any wavering," he said, "I would enforce that proclamation if it required a troop of soldiers in every Pueblo."[9]

The vehemence of Curtis's engagement also showed in a public talk he gave at the new anthropology museum in Santa Fe the same year (quoted in Chapter 1) and in a letter to his editor of November 28, 1924. In the letter he specifically vilified Collier – "in his complete ignorance of the subject and desiring some popular angle . . . to which he can draw support . . . [he] has done much to encourage the revival of the most objectionable ceremonies" – and told Hodge of his own and Myers's fieldwork that summer:

> . . . we have, I think, secured a great deal of new material bearing upon [Pueblo] ceremonies – particularly at Santa [sic] Domingo; and, as you know, Santa [sic] Domingo is the hot-bed of all of the old ceremonies . . . and . . . furnishes the killing committee to care for any offenders regardless of the village in question. It was a group of men from Santa [sic] Domingo which disposed of the man who told too much to Mrs. Stevenson. . . . [10]

Whether Curtis's polemical article was ever published is not known, but in any case his views were sufficiently circulated for Collier to remember them – and resent them – a decade later. In September 1934, four years after the publication of the final volume of *The North American Indian*, Curtis received a three-page letter initiated by Collier in his new role as the first Indian Affairs commissioner dedicated to the pursuit of a policy based on cultural pluralism, a policy more or less embodied in the Indian Reorganization Act of that very year. The letter was from Secretary of the Interior Harold L. Ickes. Collier – who may well have been in Curtis's mind when he referred in the article to "one of the foremost agitators" – had urged Ickes to take such action after consulting the Solicitor's Office and a prominent Albuquerque legal partnership about its likely success. He was seeking, he told Ickes, a "knockout for Mr. Curtis and his book." "This grandiose publication, financed by J. Pierpont Morgan, sells for $2,000," he declared. "In my days of ignorance, in 1912, I helped Curtis get the money. His pictures represent the top mark of photography of Indians. These books will be quoted for the next two hundred years."[11]

Ickes reserved the right to initiate legal action against Curtis at some subsequent point and, in general, the tone of the letter was far from friendly:

> My attention has been called by the officials of the Pueblo of Santo Domingo, through the Indian Superintendent at Santa Fe, to false and highly damaging statements contained in Volume XVI of the publication entitled "The North American Indian." It appears from the title page of this volume that you are the author of these statements and that the book was published by you.

Ickes drew attention to certain passages, identified by quotation and page number, each one of which he considered brought "the Indians into a position of contempt" in the eyes of the reader. The offending passages concerned such alleged acts on the part of the priesthood as the encouragement of "cohabitation" between children at puberty, the stripping and whipping of a Santa Clara woman married to a Santo Domingo man for refusing to take part in dances, and the enforced display of nakedness as a punishment for arriving late for ceremonies. The extract potentially most difficult for Curtis to uphold, perhaps, given the accompanying commentary, was one of the most bizarre and certainly the most specific, perhaps even containing a veiled reference to Collier himself in its use of the expression "an American enthusiast":

> Page 164:
>
> "In 1923 an American enthusiast took various Pueblo Indian 'delegates' to Washington, ostensibly to plead for religious freedom. Three men were taken from Santo Domingo. A principal feature of the program was exhibition dancing. Soon after their return two of the Santo Domingo men, Agustin Aguilar and Santiago Pena, were executed, because they had participated in the dancing, 'showing their secret feathers'. The body of one was placed at the base of a wall, a portion of which was thrown down, to demonstrate that he had met death by accident. The method of execution is explained as an application of supernatural power. The actual means employed is not known, but probably is either garrotting or poisoning."
>
> Agustin Aguilar and Santiago Pena, stated by you to have been murdered by their own Pueblo, are probably the two most distinguished Santo Domingo Indians. Each has repeatedly held high office in the government of the Pueblo; each has been sent by the Pueblo on important missions to Washington, and each is today alive. Both of them are well known to the Indians and also to the white people of Albuquerque and Santa Fe.

"I consider your offense to be of practical importance," Ickes concluded. "The demand of large numbers of people that the Government . . . destroy the cultural, tribal and religious life of the Indians leans for its support on such apparently authoritative, and yet irresponsible and malicious, publications as your own," he said, and suggested that such "defamatory statements" did more damage to Indians than "all of the hostile special interests" opposed to them. He demanded that Curtis circulate "printed apologies," that he "expunge" the offending passages "from any undistributed copies" of the volume, and that he "notify" the previous purchasers about the "incorrectness" of some of the book's statements.

Curtis, reeling somewhat from the shock, could not then suddenly admit that it was Myers who had been the principal author of the offending volume, and he forbore to remind Ickes that his preface to it had indicated that both the Pueblo volumes (16 and 17) had been compiled from "admittedly incomplete data." Instead, he sent Ickes a holding letter, promising to "exercise all possible diligence in forwarding . . . a detailed statement," but pointing out that it would be necessary to contact his "field assistants." In mitigation, he also mentioned that "all material" had been "collected directly from members of the tribe" and "prepared with all possible care and edited by Dr. F. W. Hodge." "To date," he added, "this is the first protest to reach our organization concerning material contained therein."

As we saw in Chapter 5, Myers had been greatly interested in Pueblo "sex stuff," so there must have been some relevant data in the project files. Also, Santo Domingo, like other Pueblos at the time, did have some individuals and factions who favored cooperation with the bureau, so it is conceivable that there were at least some "affidavits" testifying to what the witnesses believed were "wrongs." In any case, Curtis devoted much time for several months to amassing evidence in defense of the book, and though his response to Ickes of January 29, 1935, received an extremely waspish reply, he must have said enough to convince government officials that further action, legal or otherwise, would have been fruitless, especially in that Ickes's final communication was not dispatched until August 29, 1935. "I am persuaded," Ickes wrote, "that no correction or redress can be expected of you as a matter of fairness or honor or as a concession to the scientific spirit." "In my opinion," he continued, "you have done a wrong to tribes of Indians who have never wronged the white man, in violating the tenets of anthropological science and in giving lodgement in the most expensive of books to the most disreputable of pornographic gossip." "You have shown yourself," he jibed, "to be lacking in a decent regard for the rights of others. In particular, you have no sense of sportsmanship."[12]

Representing the Pueblos – and Others

There could hardly be a more graphic instance of the ideological dimension to the representation of other cultures than this episode. Each of the protagonists explicitly demonstrated his awareness of it, most forcefully Ickes when he referred to the "practical importance" of the project's ethnographies. Also, there was a definite sense of interconnectedness between the pages of Volume 16 of *The North American Indian,* devoted to Santo Domingo and related Pueblos, and the overt polemics of Curtis's article. Here there was a consistency and a continuity between *The North American Indian* and other forms of representation to which the project gave rise. This contrasts with other tribal groups; in the case of the Kwakiutl, for example, we discerned correspondences between the "Head-Hunter" movie and Volume 10, but we were more conscious of the film's sensationalizing differences. Volume 16 included in its Introduction much the same charges about indecency and so forth that appeared in the article, though less directly about Santo Domingo, and the body of the text contained several accounts of executions for various kinds of heresy.[13] Indeed, if this continuity between the political statement and the published ethnography had not been apparent, there would have been less of a basis for Ickes's intervention.

In a deeper sense, though, the Pueblo peoples were not represented differently to other Native Americans treated in *The North American Indian*; rather, they were represented more extremely. There was often a tendency for the project to stereotype Indians in general – as a group lower down than whites on a racial hierarchy – and individual tribes in particular, in a hierarchy of tribes. We have seen how Indians (as exemplified by the Sioux) were compared to their "Caucasian" competitors, for example (Doc. 1C), and how the Kwakiutl were characterized as notably gloomy, with scarcely "a single noble trait." And away from the pages of *The North American Indian* itself, Curtis frequently admitted this sort of typological thinking, as when he glossed his picture "An Apache Group" (1904) for the benefit of Pinchot:

> The thought in mind in making [it] was following the Apache's name . . . meaning "enemy." That is, enemy in its broadest sense – every man's enemy. This group of old Apaches in their plotting and scheming seemed to me to best illustrate their name.[14]

To the project – and the dominant culture as a whole – all Indians were mysterious. In 1904, in her discussion of Curtis's images, Gertrude Metcalfe went so far as to characterize "the Red Man" as the "most disconcerting mystery that ever confronted us as a nation." She claimed that "after four centuries' embarrassing acquaintance with him," when "we look into his solid, unrevealing face" we "know that his inner life is still a sealed book to us. We have no intelligent comprehension of the ideas that underlie the secret rites of his tribal life."[15] If all Indians were mysterious, the Pueblos were seen as deliberately secretive. As we witnessed in the field accounts of Phillips and Myers, the received wisdom was that they were excessively reticent about their beliefs and religious practices.

Yet, at the same time, as we saw in Chapter 6, the Pueblos – more than any other group – were regularly treated as a resource for tourism; they, their artifacts and, most significantly in this instance, their ceremonies, were commodified for white consumption. In "The Indian and His Religious Freedom" Curtis spoke of "the picturesque side" of their dances and admitted that many of the ceremonies were "colorful" to any onlooker's eyes. In *The North American Indian* itself there is a graphic description of the intrusions of tourism – the railroad, automobiles – on the otherwise quiet life of Isleta Pueblo.[16] Several of its images, such as "Zuni Girl" (see fig. 18; 1904) and "Girl and Jar – San Ildefonso" (1905), depict women face-on, carrying or with prominent painted pots; this has the effect of both displaying the artifact and, in visual parallelism, exhibiting the woman. Both woman and pottery are commodified.

The paradox here is that while tourism commodified Pueblo culture and made it accessible to whites to a greater degree than it did those of other Native American groups, the fact that Pueblo culture also maintained a dynamism of its own and that the people resisted thorough appropriation meant that they were seen as duplicitous. It was thought that they lived virtually a double life. We can discern such a thrust in, for example, the distrust expressed by both Phillips and Curtis about the Pueblos' allegiance to *both* Catholicism and "paganism" and in Curtis's polemical differentiation between the public and private parts of their ceremonies. "Unquestionably he lives a dual existence, and the surface characteristics that we see give no true clue to the real man within," thought Metcalfe. "This has been kept hidden from us with a pertinacity and cunning that probably has no parallel in the history of mankind."[17]

Note the obvious element of projection here: "Our" ignorance is not our responsibility, but is attributed to *their* cunning. It could be argued that, given the well-documented thesis that for mainstream (white) Americans the twenties, with its flappers and so on, was a period of marked change in gender relations and sexual mores, the concern for Pueblo sexual morality was *also* a projection. Before the white man came, to appropriate Curtis's picture title, nakedness was "innocent" and unbridled sexuality was part of the "natural" order – "All humanity in coming up from paganism has passed through the same phases of religious debauchery," Curtis asserted – but once "the white man" had come, well, "he" brought to the Indians all the anxieties of "his" own deracinated culture. But that is too large a topic for discussion here. What I do wish to emphasize is that this episode, in a parallel fashion, points up the possibility that while a Collier could be active in preserving – even, as Curtis himself saw, reviving – traditional *practices*, the project's attempts to extinguish them in life may well have reflected its resolve to preserve them in word and image, in representation.[18] Moreover, what seemed appropriate for preservation was a people whose development had been arrested at a definitively "pagan" stage – or who had elected, as it were, to arrest their own development.

Interestingly, the corresponding photographs of Pueblo religious practices seem particularly still, even static. While there are a very few images of group performances – of the San Ildefonso Tablita Dances, for example, or "Picuris Harvest Dance" (1925) – with all their inherent intimations of a potentially unfolding drama, the majority of the religious views depict single individuals engaged in acts of personal devotion. In "An Offering at the Waterfall – Nambé" (1925), which shows a man kneeling to place a feather in the water, the "flow" of the waterfall is, of course, arrested by the action of the camera and presented as a frozen white glow around the man's features.

Most telling, perhaps, are three images made at San Ildefonso. "The Offering" (1925) depicts a loin-clothed man in middle distance atop a ridge of rock, his arm extended to make a morning offering of corn to the sun. Similarly, almost like a companion piece, "Offering to the Sun" (fig. 19; 1925) has a male figure standing between walls of stone, both hands holding feathers and raised skywards, facing a sun almost eclipsed behind rock. These figures, which in life must have been in motion, when shown surrounded by stone, are made to seem just as still as "The Sentinel" (1925), a man posed pressed against, and looking out from, a wall of rock. Indeed, in that even parts of the mens' bodies, especially in "Offering to the Sun," visually echo or tessellate with the rock forms around them, there is a suggestion that these figures – particularly as originally reproduced, in sepia, which shades their bodies the same as the stone – are actually sculpted from rock. This is reminiscent of one of Francis Parkman's pronouncements: "The Indian is hewn out of rock. . . . He will not learn the arts of civilization, and he and his [habitat] must perish together. The stern, unchanging features of his mind excite our admiration for their very immutability; and we look with deep interest on the fate of this irreclaimable son of the wilderness."[19]

Representing Indians in The North American Indian

After the publication of the final volume of *The North American Indian* in 1930, Curtis, despite his advancing years, involved himself in a variety of activities, including some demanding ones, such as camera

Figure 19. Offering to the Sun – San Ildefonso, 1925, by E. S. Curtis. Note the studied composition of this image.

work for the movies, and some strenuous ones, such as the identification of remote, seemingly exhausted western mines that might yet be exploited at a profit. But he seems to have lost contact with Myers and other North American Indian project workers and, despite the unwelcome spur applied by the Secretary of the Interior, to have maintained only an erratic anthropological interest in Native Americans. In the early to mid-thirties, although on one occasion he admitted to Meany that he was "a bit lost" in the aftermath of the ending of the all-consuming project, Curtis worked at several mainly autobiographical books on Indian life, and in 1934 he told Julian Hawthorne that he had completed one on the Northwest Coast.[20] Despite the fact that such works went unpublished, in the forties, when aging and various ailments restricted his movements to the environs of his home in Southern California, family members encouraged him to write his memoirs, and – like some of them – he did so.

In the late forties and very early fifties, up to his death on October 21, 1952, in the course of what was becoming a lively correspondence with Harriet Leitch, history librarian at the Seattle Public Library, Curtis wrote up further memories of his earlier years. In much of this writing there was not only a nostalgic element – he often reused the phrase "in the long ago" – but also an elegiac note, as if the Indian project had already passed from public memory. While the University of Washington Library mounted a Curtis exhibition in 1948, his sense of neglect was then, as was hinted at the outset of this book, largely justified. Robert Lowie and other prominent anthropologists continued to cite *The North American Indian* in their own, mainly specialist publications, but the project's life as an ongoing and influential enterprise looked as if it was over. Such a status is akin to that of death for individuals, and we might well ask, in Eduard Goldstücker's piercing formulation, "Is the process of living not a continuous *becoming* upon which only death paradoxically confers the immutability of *being*?"[21] Looked at from beyond its endpoint, perhaps we need attend less to the project's diachronic elements, its ever-changing vicissitudes; if we remain aware of the simplifying aspect of what we are doing, we can view it more synchronically, as a text. Here *the* text is *The North American Indian* itself.

We have had occasion to note disparities between events and cultural lore collected or written about "in the field" and their rendering in *The North American Indian*, and many more such could be enumerated. W. W. Phillips, for example, in writing about experiences that took place among the Northern Cheyenne in 1905, recounted several "superstitions" of these people that do not appear in the seemingly comprehensive account of their culture in Volume 6 of *The North American Indian.* Sometimes interpreters and informants who seemed crucial in the field go unrecorded in the text itself, sometimes tense encounters are ignored as if they had never happened, and some things are greatly deemphasized in the final publication. One of these is the supposed "filthiness" of the Inuit of Hooper Bay. This was remarked upon almost obsessively by each member of the project present, and Mary Louise Pratt has pointed out that such observations are a frequent trope of travel writing by whites and constitute part of the cultural work of that genre to reinvent such places as Hooper Bay as "backward and neglected," as "manifestly in need of the rationalized exploitation that Europeans bring" as part of the "white civilizing mission" – a sense particularly clear in Eastwood's formulation, in which he noted the beneficial technological interventions of "the teacher and the missionary." (This points to a further paradox in the project's approaches: In almost the same breath, as we observed above, Curtis himself was *celebrating* Inuit lack of contact with missionaries because it allowed the perpetuation of the people's innocence!)[22]

A particularly sharp example of disparity between participants' travel accounts and *The North American Indian* itself concerned the Western Apaches. In Curtis's tale of extracting religious information from Goshonne and other shamans, one of his ostensible purposes was to enhance his own heroic role as an ethnologist, able to salvage valuable material from the most recalcitrant of informants, but he also revealed, in passing, that the Apaches themselves were highly factionalized along religious-political lines. Phillips too, in his Apache account, rendered a similar impression. In the light of this, it is interesting that *The North American Indian* itself gave no sign that the Apaches were so riven. Indeed, with very few exceptions, such as the Hopi (where treatment of factionalism could not be avoided, since a whole village was forced to decamp elsewhere as a result of political divisiveness), the volumes of the big work represented Native American tribes as devoid of politics. Sometimes, it seems, this was because they were seen as so "primitive" as not to have developed politics, and sometimes – in a more benign variation of the same predilection – it was because they were seen as seamless, organic communities. Needless to add, whether Native Americans were envisaged as easily duped, as in Curtis's religious freedom article here, or as prepolitical, as in *The North American Indian,* it would be clear to most readers from the dominant culture that there was ample justification for U.S. government political intervention in and control of their affairs.[23]

In general, the subjectivity of the fieldwork accounts is (relatively) overt, whereas in the published volumes there is a veneer of objectivity that tends to disguise it. In that – as we have often observed in this study – the North American Indian project shared many features with anthropology as a whole, this is not surprising, for similar disparities have been enumerated in the case of other studies. In fact, in recent years critical attention has often switched from the examination of anthropological fieldwork – what was collected, where, when, whether informants were likely to have known much about what they were saying, etc. – to scrutiny of the actual composition, especially the writing, of ethnographic texts. It was in the production, after all, in the particular representation itself, that the subjects, "others" and their cultures, were not so much even reconstructed as *constructed.*

Looked at this way, it is clear that anthropologists tended to compose their accounts from a narrative point of view that largely excluded signs of their own presence, which in turn made their ethnographies appear wholly coherent (even when incomplete), objective (if sympathetic), and, above all, authoritative. The indigenous people and their cultures were fixed, so to speak, as if unchanging (and possibly unchangeable), in what Johannes Fabian has analyzed as "the ethnographic present tense," which further accentuated their essentialization.[24] In the case of the North American Indian project, I hope I have demonstrated that Curtis's public appearances, the eye-witness testimony of project workers, the various newspaper accounts of the project's life "among the Indians," and other such phenomena, were all important aspects of the totality of the project's representations of Indians. Let me now recall some of the ways in which the representations embodied in *The North American Indian* itself fall within analytical categories such as those identified by Fabian and others.

If we turn first to the point of view, invocations of a tableau – or, as an extract we are about to examine has it, a "panorama" – are readily apparent. In the Introduction to the first volume of *The North American Indian,* Curtis spoke openly of "the fact that the Indian and his surroundings lend themselves to artistic treatment." "Indeed," he continued, "to overlook those marvelous touches that Nature has given to the Indian country, and for the origin of which the native ever has a wonder-tale to relate, would be to neglect a most important chapter." *The North American Indian* would offer, he said, "a record of the Indian's relations with . . . the phenomena of the universe . . . as a broad and luminous picture." The following is a passage from near the opening of the Crow volume, and it appears after a description of the Crows' homeland as "the veritable Eden of the Northwest":

> The larger camps were always the scene of great activity. Horses were tethered everywhere close at hand; on the slopes far and near thousands were grazing, while on the nearby hilltops groups of people were statuesquely outlined against the sky. Here are chiefs and councillors in quiet discussion of tribal affairs. As they pass the pipe . . . and look down upon the village with its hundreds of lodges their eyes are glad, for the picture is one of plenty, . . . On another hill proud youths are seen, decked in the savage trappings that make glad their

> hearts. . . . Not far distant is a group of maidens gaily dressed in garments of soft skins . . . on other outlooks are old women who live only in the past. . . . Farther from the village mourners cry out in anguish . . . and on distant peaks are lonely men fasting . . . for spiritual strength. In the camp itself there is an endless panorama of activities. . . .

The move into the present tense, the emphasis on the visual – "look down," "picture," etc. – and the syntax make the Indians passive, the object of our gaze, and grant "us" the active vantage point. Even the Indians' emotions are not so much expressed as visualized ("their eyes are glad"). The use of the phrase "statuesquely outlined against the sky" is particularly telling; these Indians are stilled and sculpted, aestheticized, for our delectation.[25]

Another feature of the viewpoint that is immediately obvious is that, whereas the tellers of what I have presented as "adventure in the field" frequently stressed their own presence, the viewpoint adopted in *The North American Indian* itself – while resting on the reader's sense that the study being absorbed is the product of direct experience (usually established by first-person references to the fieldwork in each volume's preface) – was more distant, third person, and systematic. Travelers' tales are necessarily partial in every sense – in that they consist of the teller's story – whereas each volume of *The North American Indian* was arranged in a relatively fixed sequence treating such recurring topics as: homelands and habitations; historical sketches (of Indian–white contact); religious beliefs and practices; tribal organization; social customs; ceremonies; arts and crafts; food, hunting, and fishing; war and the chase; mythology; songs and tales. That is, like other anthropological treatises, *The North American Indian* was ordered according to the schematics of the discipline as then understood, and, as A. C. Haddon testified, was offered as a "body of knowledge."[26]

Furthermore, this sense of systematic coverage was augmented by the use in each volume of appendices offering "Tribal Summaries" and, often in tabular format, linguistic data, such as comparative vocabularies. And the presentation of the images in the published volumes of *The North American Indian* also tended to obscure the presence of the observer. Whereas several of the documents reproduced here speak of the dangers and difficulties of photographing Indians, the images themselves disguise any such problems and proffer the illusion of representational transparency. For example, the viewer frequently has the sense of looking in on something that was being enacted regardless of the camera, whether it was a (in actual fact reconstructed) war party ready for the charge, or "The Potter Mixing Clay" (1921), in which the Hopi woman, her arms visibly lined with age, is given sufficient surrounding space to appear wholly absorbed in the circle of her work.

The degree to which *The North American Indian* generally imparted a sense of almost unquestioned coherence, comprehensiveness, and objectivity to its ethnography may best be seen at another point at which it threatened to break down. As we saw in Chapter 5, in 1927 Eastwood and Curtis found that most of the peoples displaced to Oklahoma had become so acculturated to white ways that it proved difficult to collect the "traditional" data they required. In one letter to Hodge, Curtis went so far as to confess that in the case of the Comanche the material they had gathered did not make "a strong showing," adding "but one can not make something from nothing." He continued:

> We covered the ground with the most intelligent of the present day educated men as interpreter and helper. With his help, we talked with all of the old men of the Tribe. Day by day we struggled to get [material]. Finally, our interpreter, Mr. Tebo, turned to me in some exasperation and stated: "You are trying to get what does not exist." The only material we could find was countless, meaningless, fragmentary obscene stories of the camp-fire type; no point to them beyond that of obscenity. Aside from this . . . there [were] fragmentary experiences of the old men in hunting and warfare but even in these . . . it was not possible to find comprehensive stories . . . worthy of publication.

The treatment of the Comanche as published in Volume 19 is certainly short, but there is no hint of such difficulties or, even, of radical discontinuity, something that might have been attributed to the Comanche people's "vanishing" status.[27]

Indeed, except in the case of the Introductions to certain volumes – those where, as we have seen, Curtis openly admitted approval or disapproval of particular peoples – *The North American Indian* generally presented each Native American culture, however briefly, as coherent (if strange), with an internal logic of its own. Interestingly, even the contrast between most of the images in Volumes 1 to 18, some of which were undisclosed reconstructions, and the Oklahoma pictures, in which a noticeable number of people who sat for portraits were too "civilized" to fit in easily, is both muted and unremarked. This means that the Oklahoma experience was not allowed to disrupt the longstanding premises of salvage ethnology upon which *The North American Indian* was built. In reality, since in principle all cultures are dynamic – and we know empirically from the evidence of countless observers, including members of the Curtis project, that early-twentieth-century Native-American cultures were no exception – the project definitely encountered varying degrees of transcultural change in the case of *every* tribe. However, apart from each volume's Historical Sketch (which, perhaps paradoxically, exclusively treated the period after contact with whites: trading, wars, introduced disease, and so on), the texts of the volumes concentrated on "traditional," precontact lifeways to a very similar degree. Thus, for example, in the Eskimo volume of *The North American Indian* there is no mention of the anti-missionary sentiment we noted above or, even, of missionaries; indeed, the text on the Kotzebue actually states that "the medicine men, who rule the village, supervise ceremonies, advise hunters, treat the sick . . . ," and generally gives the impression that precontact life continued.[28]

The same may be said of the accompanying photographs. Just as signs of the presence of the camera-wielding observer were excluded, so to a large extent, as Christopher Lyman has shown, were tokens and traces of "white" culture and "the modern" generally. Automobiles, alarm clocks, and trade marks were retouched away. This is not wholly the case: There are deliberately titled images of, for example, "Modern Hupa House" (1923), "A Mixed Blood Coast Pomo" (1924), and "Modern Blackfoot Burial" (1926), as well as the occasional portrait of men with shorn hair and neckties (such as "Wilbur Peebo – Comanche" [1927]), but it is as if these were included almost as exceptions to prove the rule. Needless to say, Curtis was not alone in these practices; as was stated in the Introduction, other photographers did similar things.

Indeed, the representation of Native Americans in the visual arts at that time – including painting, which was just as likely as photography to have served as an actual influence on Curtis – was remarkably consistent. The West was always both a decreasing physical space and, as so many critics have observed, a dimension – an Eden or Garden or some such equivalent formulation – open to corruption and, therefore, almost invariably a site of nostalgia for artists. In the vision conjured up by Curtis there was a strong element of a kind of hushed awe before a more "primitive" existence. William Cronon has provided us with a trenchant summary of artistic efforts "to erase evidence that Indians and Europeans had already mingled quite profoundly by the time an image was made." Although his characterization of Curtis himself is oversimplified, he sets Curtis's specific efforts at such "erasure" in context, saying "Euro-American outsiders and their influence almost always manage to evade the artist's frame, so that we are forced to infer their presence on the margins of the composition without actually seeing them."[29] Several of Curtis's images of such ceremonies as the Hopi Snake Dance – which, as I have pointed out, constituted almost a regular meeting-point for photographers – present the audience of tourists as an indistinct blur. In "Assiniboin Hunter" (fig. 20), taken as late as 1926, Curtis even used his own shadow – recognizable only upon close examination, of course – to "push" the standing hunter back into the middleground; there, symmetrically framed by birch trunks and his pack dogs, the man seems almost a fixture of the landscape. One image, of a group of stationary Crows looking down from a rocky outcrop was actually titled "Rigid and Statuesque" (1911).

All this speaks of essentialization and, as we saw at the close of Chapter 1, the timeless. Rhetorically and especially visually, Indians were framed according to the canons of European taste in the broadest sense (with, for example, the blankets of Plains chiefs depicted more as classical-style togas), but such devices served only to underline their difference. Indians were seen, predominantly if not exclusively, as unalterably Other, and their otherness was that of the primitive savage. As Grinnell, Curtis's mentor, put it in *The Story of the Indian* (1896): "Long association with the Indians enables a white man ultimately to share their thoughts and feelings; and he who has reached this point understands the Indian. He understands that the red man is a savage and has savage qualities." It was this kind of "long association," via the project, that supposedly enabled Gilbert, in his music for the musicale, to "reach the primitive," as Curtis told Charles Lummis, and "in a most delightful way." Metcalfe, too, spoke of Indians' "untamed savagery" and of the "intelligence of high order" that gleamed from their eyes – but it was "not the intelligence of civilized man"; it was, rather, the attribute of some special breed apart. Needless to say, this view of the immutability of Indianness was both buttressed by and in tension with the notion of Indians as "vanishing" as formulated, for example, by Sidney Allan (Sadakichi Hartmann) in an article for *Wilson's Photographic Magazine*: "Walt

Figure 20. Assiniboin Hunter, 1926, by E. S. Curtis.
The photographer's own shadow in the foreground is a critical aesthetic factor in this reconstruction of Northern Plains hunting practices.

Whitman . . . expressed . . . his regret at . . . the extinction of this wild and beautiful race. And, although some authorities claim that the Indian race is not dying out . . . , one can hardly be sanguine. . . . Mr. Curtis's undertaking can not easily be repeated. The red savage Indian is fast changing into a mere ordinary uninteresting copy of the white race."[30]

Hence the emphasis on reconstruction, most blatantly, as we have seen, in such images as "Ogalala War Party" (fig. 13; 1907), with its band of Sioux, war lances at the ready, or "On the War-Path – Atsina" (1908), or "A Mountain Fastness" (1908), with its party of mounted Crow warriors in Pryor Canyon, Montana. While these images represent Indians as a fierce force to be reckoned with – and of the Crows the caption adds "nowhere do they seem more at home" – at the time they were taken the Plains Wars had been ended absolutely by the Wounded Knee Massacre and the actual figures depicted in them were hemmed onto reservations. Interestingly, when Curtis came to defend such images in a letter to Hodge, he opposed the position of such anthropologists as James Mooney by arguing for the accuracy of his images precisely *as reconstructions*:

> Let us return to the title of the picture in question ["A Cheyenne Warrior"]. It does not necessarily imply that the man is engaged in battle, or at the instant of going into the fight. An Indian *of the old days* was a warrior 365 days of the year, a very small part of which would be spent in actual fight. . . . If a war party were starting out they would . . . don all their fine clothing and ride around the camp. A picture made of them then could be titled "Warriors," and the title be beyond just criticism.[31]

Moreover, there is a curious sense in which a reconstruction *cannot* leave its objects as mere "children of nature." It was, precisely, the *culture* of Indians which was changing under the pressure of events and which had to be reconstituted, composed into, in these cases, pictorial conventions appropriate to a warrior culture.

In other words, "the warrior" (and, of course, its larger, embracing typological category "the Indian") was an allegorical figure and, as Wai-chee Dimock observed in a different context, "To be personified at all . . . is already to submit to the dictates of the timeless, the dictates of destiny." To be nostalgically personified in this sense – as the warrior, or the sentinel, when policies and (however enforced) patterns of life were moving on – was to be inert, to be, as we saw earlier, as unchanging as rock. It is in this connection that the relative dearth of smiling faces among the portraits in *The North American Indian* may be significant. While we should note that there are some radiant exceptions – "Innocence – Umatilla" (1910), for example, or "Clayoquot Girl" (1915), or "Boys in Kaiak – Nunivak" (fig. 21; 1927) – most of the faces encountered in the collection are unsmiling, even grave, and wear expressions usually taken to betoken thoughtfulness, concern, and, above all, resignation. This is not just a matter of the preponderance of expressions commonly associated with stillness as against the smile as the key expression thought to indicate change and animation. The majority of these portraits also participate in the perpetuation of visual aspects of the enduring trope of "Indian melancholy" so brilliantly analyzed by Werner Sollors, who has drawn out the deep structural link in American thought between dying/van-

Figure 21. Boys in Kaiak – Nunivak, 1927, by E. S. Curtis. These smiling Inuit boys were photographed during the project's final season of fieldwork.

ishing Indians, the passage of time, and the triumph of the republican American empire.[32]

Here a formulation offered by Walter Benjamin may prove helpful. "If the object becomes allegorical under the gaze of melancholy, if melancholy causes life to flow out of it and it remains dead, but eternally secure, then it is exposed to the allegorist, it is unconditionally in his power," he observed. "That is to say it is now quite incapable of emanating any meaning . . . of its own: such significance it has, it acquires from the allegorist. He places it within it, and stands behind it; not in a psychological but in an ontological sense." The *very being* of "the Indian," that is, and the nature of that being's essence, was granted by the allegorist. In a letter to Judge Burke about his keynote image "The Vanishing Race" (fig. 3), Curtis expressed his gratitude that the judge saw "the thought of the picture" as he did: "a touching, melancholy poem."[33] An essential component of the ontology of "the Indian" was, precisely, his tendency to vanish.

Representing Vanishment

> So mutely, uncomplainingly, they go!
> How shall it be with us when they are gone,
> When they are but a mem'ry and a name?
> May not those mournful eyes to phantoms grow –
> When, wronged and lonely, they have drifted on
> Into the voiceless shadow whence they came?
> – Ella Higginson, "The Vanishing Race"

Wai-chee Dimock, among others, has reminded us that notions of Indian vanishment have had a long history. Revolutionary General Benjamin Lincoln said: "If the savages cannot be civilized and quit their present pursuits, they will, in consequence of their stubbornness, dwindle and moulder away, from causes perhaps imperceptible to us, until the whole race shall become extinct." As Dimock says, "'Extinction' is what happens in an autotelic universe: it naturalizes the category of the 'doomed', not only by recuperating it as an evolutionary category but, most crucially, by locating the cause of the extinction within the extinct organism itself. . . . Indians die out [as] a function of their 'stubbornness,' their benighted refusal to quit their savage ways. This is the logic of blaming the victim. . . ."[34]

We discerned a very similar view in Chapter 1 when Curtis is quoted as speaking in 1912 of the "strange chance" by which "the precursors of this branch of the human race" had been "held for ages in the grip of darkness," of "the inevitable transformation of the Indian's life," and of Indian demise as an effect of "Nature's laws." Moreover, referring to nineteenth-century justifications, Dimock perceived that "Barbarians are doomed . . . because they have outlived their allotted time span, because their very nobility marks them as anachronistic. The Indian . . . perished not in spite of but *because* of his 'stateliness', his 'heroic virtues', his 'fine figure', commanding voice, noble beauty." This is remarkably similar to Curtis's 1912 belief that "American Indians possess many noble traits which were no doubt not common to the average primitive man of the same state of development."[35] These noble traits – repeatedly captured in photographs and evoked in prose – were traits that precisely *unfitted* Indians for survival. And they did so just as effectively as the ignoble and repressive traits said to have characterized the unreconstructed "paganism" of the Pueblos.

There was always something loose, baggy, and problematic about the notion of "vanishing" – and not only in the project's usage. Sometimes it referred to the exemplary death of an Indian hero – as, for example, in Cooper and Longfellow. Sometimes it was applied to the loss of indigenous languages or the acquisition of English, as in Curtis's 1911 exchange with Pinchot (see Chapter 1). Often it indicated the abandonment of traditional lifeways. Sometimes, as in Hartmann or D. H. Lawrence, it evoked a vague sense of dissolution or racial merging. Sometimes, as in the otherwise banal second verse of Higginson's "The Vanishing Race" quoted above, there was a hedged acknowledgment of "our" role: "They" were important, but that importance was measured solely in "our" terms ("How shall it be with *us* when they are gone"). And always there was a whiff of the euphemistic about "vanishing"; it is a peculiarly intransitive word, as though Indians were here one minute and gone the next almost without good reason, as if they did, as we say, *just* vanish.

The most hostile formulation of the schematics of this relationship as it applied to the Curtis project has been pressed by Minnesota Chippewa author Gerald Vizenor: "He [Curtis] traveled with his camera to capture the neonoble tribes, to preserve metasavages in the ethnographic present as consumable objects of the past." In the same essay, "Socioacupuncture: Mythic Reversals and the Striptease," Vizenor seems to anticipate – or indeed call forth – the visual playfulness of the Native American artist Richard Ray (sometimes known as Whitman). Speaking through a collective persona, Vizenor continues, "we were caught dead in camera time, extinct in photographs, and now in search of our past and common memories we walk right back into these photographs." Both Vizenor and Ray acknowledge the power of the North American Indian project's representations, implicitly if not explicitly admitting that they cannot and should not be categorized as in some straightforward sense "untrue," and consigned to oblivion. Rather, they treat the project as a given, a resource so pervasive that it must be dealt with. One effective way of doing so is to subvert it, and Ray has certainly visually subverted the vanishment trope in his "Edward S. Curtis Rip-off (Vanishing Americans) . . . Hardly. . . ." (1972). By presenting a copy of an early Curtis Navajo portrait with, "behind" it, as it were, and half obscured by it, a lighter-shaded replica of the same image, Ray, as Jean Fisher has commented, "steals back a studio appropriation and doubles it to expose Curtis's imaginary Indian surrogate as a pale shadow revealing nothing of the 'real' behind the white image of the 'red'. . . ."[36]

Themes of time – change and stasis – have ruffled the pages of this chapter, indeed of this book, and I have been unable to smooth them out. Indeed, this intractability is an important facet of what I am attempting to say. In his "Theses on the Philosophy of History," Walter Benjamin warned us against trying to recognize the past "the way it really was" or reliving it by an effort to "blot out everything [we] know about the later course of history." Rather, he intuited that such erasure was actually a sign of empathy for "the victor" and the victors' successors. "Whoever has emerged victorious participates to this day in the triumphal procession in which the present rulers step over those who are lying prostrate," he said. Then, in an image evoking actual victory marches, he equated "the spoils . . . carried along in the procession" with "cultural treasures," and put it that we should view such trophies "with cautious detachment" because they owe their origin not only "to the efforts of the great minds and talents who created them, but also to the anonymous toil of their contemporaries."[37]

Despite the fact that the North American Indian project – with its aspiration to become a "monument" to a vanishing race – was literally funded by the "rulers" of Curtis's own day, it would be an oversimplification to assimilate its erasing endeavors to the kind of history Benjamin abjured. At the same time, it is worth noting that – using peculiarly appropriate terms in the present context – Benjamin went on to offer the aphorism that serves as the epigraph for this study: "There is no document of civilization which is not at the same time a document of barbarism." The project threatened to still, to fix, even to freeze, Indian culture(s) into a rocklike unbreakable form – and not only in its representation in text, but in life, in history too. As Benjamin also saw, our task should be "to brush history against the grain."[38] Looked at "against the grain," as it were, the project does also constitute a resource for Native Americans and others, a set of texts to be appreciated, studied, exploited, played with, and, perhaps in the manner of Richard Ray, played against. Yes, *The North American Indian* is, ultimately, a "monument" – but not to a vanishing or vanished people in the original sense in which Curtis and others used the term. Rather, it is a monument to the enterprise, at a particular moment, of the dominant culture that produced it and, more importantly, to the beauty and capacity for change of the subjugated, damaged, yet resilient cultures that actually sustained it.

NOTES

Abbreviations

AMNH = Department of Anthropology Archives File 110, American Museum of Natural History, New York, N.Y.

Austin = Mary Hunter Austin Papers, Huntington Library, San Marino, Calif.

Bancroft = The Bancroft Library, U of California, Berkeley, Calif.

Commissioner = Letters to the Commissioner, Bureau of Indian Affairs, Record Group 75, National Archives, Washington, D.C.

Flagstaff = Museum of Northern Arizona, Flagstaff, Ariz.

Gilbert = Henry F. Gilbert Papers, Yale Music Library, Yale U, New Haven, Conn. (All letters to and from Gilbert are from this collection.)

Haddon = A. C. Haddon Papers, Cambridge U Library, Cambridge, England.

Hodge = Frederick Webb Hodge Collection (MS.7.NAI.1), Braun Research Library, Southwest Museum, Los Angeles, Calif. (Unless indicated, all letters to and from Hodge are from this collection.)

Huntington = E. S. Curtis File, Huntington Institutional Archives, Huntington Library, San Marino, Calif.

Kernberger = Karl Kernberger's (private) Collection, Santa Fe, N.Mex.

LACMNH = North American Indian Materials, Los Angeles County Museum of Natural History, Los Angeles, Calif.

LC = Manuscripts Division, Library of Congress, Washington, D.C.

Meany = Edmond S. Meany Papers, Manuscripts and University Archives, U of Washington Libraries, Seattle, Wash. (Unless indicated, all letters to and from Meany are from this collection.)

NAA = National Anthropological Archives, Smithsonian Institution, Washington, D.C.

NAI = Edward S. Curtis, *The North American Indian*, ed. Frederick Webb Hodge, 20 vols., 20 portfolios (Cambridge, Mass.: University P, then Norwood, Mass.: The Plimpton P, 1907–30).

Newcombe = Newcombe Collection, Provincial Archives, Victoria, British Columbia, Canada.

NW = Northwest Collection, U of Washington Libraries, Seattle, Wash.

PCUW = Photography Collection, Special Collections, U of Washington Libraries, Seattle, Wash.

Philadelphia = Letters to the Director, Museum Archives, U of Pennsylvania Museum, Philadelphia, Pa.

Pinchot = Gifford Pinchot Papers, Manuscripts, Library of Congress, Washington, D.C. (All letters to and from Pinchot are from this collection.)

PML = E. S. Curtis Materials, Pierpont Morgan Library, New York, N.Y.

Roosevelt = Theodore Roosevelt Papers, Manuscripts, Library of Congress, Washington, D.C. (Unless indicated, all letters to and from Roosevelt are from this collection.)

SB = E. S. Curtis File, Library, Santa Barbara Museum of Natural History, Santa Barbara, Calif.

Smithsonian = Secretary's File, Record Group 45, Smithsonian Institution Archives, Smithsonian Institution, Washington, D.C.

SPL = E. S. Curtis File, History Department, Seattle Public Library, Seattle, Wash.

UW = Manuscripts and University Archives, U of Washington Libraries, Seattle, Wash.

Introduction

1. Signs of the "revival" included: the publication of T. C. McLuhan's anthology (with Curtis photographs), *Touch the Earth: A Self-Portrait of Indian Existence* (New York: Scribners, 1971), A. D. Coleman and T. C. McLuhan, eds., *Portraits from North American Indian Life by Edward S. Curtis* (New York: Dutton, 1972), the Aperture volume of photographs *The North American Indians* (New York, 1972), and such selections as Mick Gidley, ed., *The Vanishing Race: Selections from Edward S. Curtis' "The North American Indian"* (Newton Abbot: David and Charles, 1976, and New York: Taplinger, 1977; reprint ed. Seattle: U of Washington P, 1987); exhibitions at the Pierpont Morgan Library, New York (1972) and the U of California, Irvine (1976); and the reissue of the film *In the Land of the Head-Hunters* (1914) as *In the Land of the War Canoes* by the U of Washington P in 1973. The original major publication was *NAI.*

2. Curtis to Meany, November 19, 1911; quoted more fully in Ch. 7. Ross, "Edward Curtis," *Death Valley and Other Poems in America* (London: London Magazine Editions, 1980), 75–6, my emphasis.

3. See Hanna Fenichel Pitkin, *The Concept of Representation* (Berkeley, Los Angeles, London: U of California P, 1967), especially 63–115; Howard S. Becker, "Telling about Society," in his *Doing Things Together* (Evanston, Il.: Northwestern UP, 1986), 121–35; and W. J. T. Mitchell, "Representation," in Frank Lentricchia and Thomas McLaughlin, eds., *Critical Terms for Literary Study* (Chicago and London: U of Chicago P, 1990), 11–22. The most celebrated instances of the ascription of greater realism to photography are Roland Barthes's "The Photographic Message" (1961), in his *Image-Music-Text,* trans. Stephen Heath (London: Fontana, 1977), 15–31 and *Camera Lucida,* trans. Richard Howard (London: Cape, 1982). A general study true to its title is David Freedberg, *The Power of Images: Studies in the History and Theory of Response* (Chicago and London: U of Chicago P, 1989). The distinction drawn here between an entity called reality and a domain called representation should not be maintained with absolute rigidity; see Paul A. Bové, "Discourse," in Lentricchia and McLaughlin, 50–65, which treats related theoretical issues.

4. Mitchell, "Representation," 15; also, Pitkin deals primarily with political representation.

5. See Berkhofer, *The White Man's Indian: Images of the American Indian from Columbus to the Present* (New York: Vintage, 1979); Dippie, *The Vanishing American: White Attitudes and U.S. Indian Policy* (Middletown, Conn.: Wesleyan UP, 1982); and Ch. 4 of Werner Sollors, *Beyond Ethnicity: Consent and Descent in American Culture* (New York and Oxford: Oxford UP, 1986), 102–30. For specific visual and written examples comparable to the project, see William Truettner, "Science and Sentiment: Indian Images at the Turn of the Century," in Charles C. Eldredge, Julie Schimmel, and Truettner, *Art in New Mexico, 1900–1945: Paths to Taos and Santa Fe* (Washington, D.C.: Smithsonian Institution and Abbeville P, 1986), 17–41; he argues that "the Indian" was generally romanticized, nationalized, and incorporated at this time.

6. Said, *Orientalism* (New York: Pantheon, 1978). For the effects of Said's work, see Francis Barker *et al, Europe and its Others,* Papers from a Conference at the U of Essex, 2 vols. (Colchester: U of Essex, 1985). See also Mick Gidley, ed., *Representing Others: White Views of Indigenous Peoples* (Exeter: U of Exeter P, 1992). Clifford, "On *Orientalism,*" in his *The Predicament of Culture: Twentieth Century Ethnography, Literature and Art* (Cambridge, Mass., and London: Harvard UP, 1988), 258. "How the Indian Composes Songs," an obvious publicity item, appeared in the Tacoma *Tribune* on December 17, 1914; clipping in NW. For some of Curtis's "inaccuracies," see Christopher M. Lyman, *The Vanishing*

Race and Other Illusions: Photographs of Indians by Edward S. Curtis (Washington, D.C.: Smithsonian Institution P, 1982); also, in an interview with the author in July 1977, Erna Guenther, the Puget Sound scholar, pointed out that the image "Puget Sound Baskets" (1912) also includes Yakima and Fraser River area baskets, and that the braids shown in "Quilcene Boy" (1912) were an aberration. A 1986 British Museum conference of predominantly western world anthropological museum curators took as its very honest title "Exhibiting Ourselves."

7. See, for example, Talal Asad, ed., *Anthropology and the Colonial Encounter* (London: Ithaca P, 1973); several others are cited in Clifford, "On *Orientalism*," 256. While the U.S.A. has rarely been seen as a colonial site in the same sense, that view is partially corrected by such works as David Murray, *Forked Tongues: Speech, Writing and Representation in North American Indian Texts* (London: Pinter, 1991). See also Edward W. Said, "Representing the Colonized: Anthropology's Interlocutors," *Critical Inquiry*, 15 (Winter 1989), 205–25.

8. Becker, 126 and *passim*. Becker believes in the retention of some element of the real in the representation, as if by adhesion, while at the same time stressing that it "leaves out much, in fact, *most*, of reality."

9. Armstrong, "Play and Cultural Differences," *Kenyon Review*, NS 13 (Winter 1991), 157. A good statement of the problematics of representation in connection with Indians is Michael E. Staub, "(Re)Collecting the Past: Writing Native American Speech," *American Quarterly*, 43 (September 1991), 425–56, who rightly favors texts which "question their own (always problematic) authority, foreground their own partiality, and acknowledge their own limits as 'factual' sources while at the same time insisting on the validity of their subjects' perspectives" (451). Achebe, "The Song of Ourselves," *New Statesman & Society*, February 9, 1990, 30–2. Achebe, like a number of Native American figures, has discerned not just a desire, but a *need* for indigenous writers to celebrate the continued presence of their peoples in their respective continents. Cultural historians like Ana Maria Alonso have shown that a people's own representations of the past are central to the very constitution of social and individual identities; see "The Effects of Truth: Re-Presentations of the Past and the Imagining of Community," *Journal of Historical Sociology*, 1 (March 1988), 33–57. This is the formidable task undertaken by Achebe, Silko, and other indigenous artists. Ngugi wa Thiong'o advocates the further step of "writing" in indigenous languages as sensitively as possible to the oral properties of both language and culture, an approach also adopted by, for example, the Cheyenne poet Lance Henson; see Ngugi, *Decolonising the Mind: The Politics of Language in African Literature* (London: Heinemann, 1986), especially 63–86. This does not completely answer Armstrong's rightly anguished question; the means of transmission, for example, even for Henson and Ngugi, cannot be a wholly indigenous form, and Armstrong and others have stressed the necessity – indeed, the desirability – of a "play" between and across forms of cultural expression. It is such play or intertextuality that produces that "hybridity" of structure and meaning which Bill Ashcroft, Gareth Griffiths, and Helen Tiffin, authors of *The Empire Writes Back* (1989), call "the primary characteristic of all post-colonial texts, whatever their source" (excerpted in Dennis Walder, ed., *Literature in the Modern World: Critical Essays and Documents* [Oxford and New York: Oxford UP, 1990], 298–303).

10. See the essays by many of the Native American contributors to Lucy R. Lippard, ed., *Partial Recall* (New York: The New P, 1992); Smith's is 59–63. Silko, *Storyteller* (New York: Arcade, 1981), 1. Also, as James Clifford has pointed up, there is a sharp difference between the image as experienced by strangers and as experienced by locals: In the likeness of a figure offered as the very type of the Nootka, captioned in *NAI* as "A Hesquiat Woman" (1915), a

local person recognized her own mother and, of course, knew her name; see Clifford, "Four Northwest Coast Museums: Travel Reflections," in Ivan Karp and Steven D. Lavine, eds., *Exhibiting Cultures: The Poetics and Politics of Museum Display* (Washington, D.C.: Smithsonian Institution P, 1991), 212–54, especially 232.

11. Gidley, "Into Apache Lands: Reminiscences of Edward S. Curtis's North American Indian Project," *European Review of Native American Studies*, 8, no. 1 (Spring 1994), 15–22; the figures were Curtis's young son Harold, W. W. Phillips, and Curtis himself. For another field account, see Gidley, "A. C. Haddon Joins Edward S. Curtis: An English Anthropologist Among the Blackfeet, 1909," *Montana*, 32 (Autumn 1982), 20–33.

12. Trachtenberg, *The Incorporation of America: Culture and Society in the Gilded Age* (New York: Hill and Wang, 1982), 4.

13. Takaki, *Iron Cages: Race and Culture in 19th-Century America* (New York and Oxford: Oxford UP, 1990 [1979]), 173; H. Craig Miner, *The Corporation and the Indian: Tribal Sovereignty and Industrial Civilization in Indian Territory, 1865–1907* (Columbia, Mo.: U of Missouri P, 1976) treats the *direct* impact of corporate enterprises (railroads, cattle companies, etc.) on indigenous peoples settled in Oklahoma.

14. Myers to Hodge, n.d. but received March 27, 1926.

15. *Touch the Earth*, cited above. Typical of the eulogistic accounts is Florence Curtis Graybill and Victor Boesen, *Edward Sheriff Curtis: Visions of a Vanishing Race* (New York: Thomas Crowell, 1976), and Barbara A. Davis, *Edward S. Curtis: The Life and Times of a Shadow Catcher* (San Francisco: Chronicle Books, 1985). Lyman's *The Vanishing Race and Other Illusions* has not been succeeded by book-length studies, but numerous works accept his account as an orthodoxy, including, for example, Peter Jackson, "Constructions of Culture, Representations of Race: Edward Curtis's 'Way of Seeing'," in Kay Anderson and Fay Gale, eds., *Inventing Places: Studies in Cultural Geography* (Melbourne: Longman Cheshire, 1992), 89–106, and Alison Griffiths, in "Science and Spectacle: Native American Representation in Early Cinema," in S. Elizabeth Bird, ed., *Dressing in Feathers: The Construction of the Indian in Popular American Culture* (Boulder, Colo.: Westview, 1996), 86–91. For the best critique of Lyman, which stresses Curtis's "accuracy," see Bill Holm's review in *American Indian Art*, 8 (Summer 1983), 68–73.

16. Wissler, *Indian Cavalcade or Life on the Old-Time Indian Reservations*, republished as *Red Man Reservations* (New York: Collier, 1971), 197–207. See Akin, "Frederick Monsen of the Desert," followed by Monsen's own "The Destruction of Our Indians: What Civilization is Doing to Extinguish an Ancient and Highly Intelligent Race . . . ," *The Craftsman*, 11 (March 1907), 678–82 and 683–91, respectively; see also, Lee Clark Mitchell, *Witnesses to a Vanishing America: The Nineteenth Century Response* (Princeton: Princeton UP, 1981), 140–5. For Dixon, see: his own *The Vanishing Race* (1913; reprint New York: Popular Library, 1972); Dippie, 211–15; Peter Gold, "Returning Photographs to the Indians," *Studies in Visual Communication*, 9 (Summer 1983), 2–14; and Paula Richardson Fleming and Judith Lynn Luskey, *Grand Endeavors of American Indian Photography* (Washington, D.C.: Smithsonian Institution P, 1993), 103–7. Curtis–Dixon connections are broadly contextualized in Gidley, "The Repeated Return of the Vanishing Indian," in Brian Holden Reid and John White, eds., *American Studies: Essays in Honour of Marcus Cunliffe* (London: Macmillan, 1991), 189–209, and in a review of *Grand Endeavors* in *American Indian Culture and Research Journal*, 17, no. 2 (1994), 235–9; the *Photographic Times* pieces appeared in volume 44, the issues of April and June 1912, 124–8 and 206–12, respectively.

17. For Hartmann, see Doc. 2B. Dimock, *Empire for Liberty: Melville and the Poetics of Individualism* (Princeton: Prince-

ton UP, 1989), 7, my emphasis. Dimock's argument about Melville appeals as a paradigm for Curtis: "Melville's authorial enterprise can be seen . . . as a miniature version of the national enterprise" (10).

Chapter 1

1. Roosevelt to Curtis, February 6, 1906.

2. Details of Curtis family history were taken from books on Curtis, corrected and supplemented by unpublished materials and family interviews, including one with Ray Curtis's daughter, Mrs. H. A. Schall of Colton, Calif., in August 1977. Mrs. Betty McCullough, Asahel Curtis's daughter, kindly supplied a copy of a Curtis family genealogy taken from the front page of the family bible.

3. Phillips, "Curtis," typescript, 9 , private collection. Though undated, internal evidence suggests that this was written in 1911 to publicize the musicale, described in Ch. 7. Subsequent extracts are from the same source. For more on Phillips, see extracts from his writing in later chapters and, especially, commentary in Ch. 6.

4. For information on the brickyard see Bill Holm and George I. Quimby, *Edward S. Curtis in the Land of the War Canoes: A Pioneer Cinematographer in the Pacific Northwest* (Seattle and London: U of Washington P, 1980), 20.

5. See William H. Goetzmann and Kay Sloan, *Looking Far North: The Harriman Expedition to Alaska, 1899* (Princeton: Princeton UP, 1982).

6. Curtis to Hodge, September 15, 1903.

7. Curtis to Pinchot, October 12, 1904.

8. Curtis to Hodge, October 28, 1904. Holmes to Curtis, March 9, 1905, E. S. Curtis File, Thomas Burke Papers, UW.

9. Roosevelt to Curtis, December 16, 1905. See the accounts too numerous to cite which claim erroneously that Roosevelt introduced Curtis to Morgan. Unfortunately, none of the studies of Morgan's patronage mention his sponsorship of the Curtis project, surely the most unusual of his ventures in this area. Neil Harris's "Collective Possession: J. Pierpont Morgan and the American Imagination," in his *Cultural Excursions: Appetites and Cultural Tastes in Modern America* (Chicago: U of Chicago P, 1990), 250–75 and 408–15, provides a lively summation of Morgan's cultural significance as a collector and patron.

10. Information on Morris from his unpublished "The Autobiography of a Son of New England" (1938), typescript, Yale Law Library, New Haven, supplemented by entries in *Who's Who in America*. Unfortunately, due to his admitted reluctance to discuss any matter involving his first wife, it contains no direct references to Curtis. Financial and administrative information from data on The North American Indian, Inc., sent to Henry E. Huntington with Curtis to Huntington, June 3, 1911, Huntington. Also, interview with Harold Curtis (who after the separation of his natural parents was raised by the Morrises), February 1977.

11. See the outline reproduced as Doc. 1A; also Curtis to Pinchot, January 27, 1906; further details of the arrangements appear here in Ch. 4. Family information supplied by Harold Curtis.

12. See William Dinwiddie to Walcott, April 12, 1907, and Walcott to Dinwiddie, April 16, 1907, Smithsonian. Dinwiddie was the first sales representative and manager of the New York office of the project.

13. Information on Hodge from: his own publications, an interview with his widow, Grace Meany Hodge, on August 10, 1977, and a transcript, provided by Mrs. Hodge, of Corinne Gilb, "Frederick Webb Hodge, Ethnologist: A Tape Recorded Interview, April 1956," Regional Cultural History Project, Berkeley, Calif. For more on Myers, see Ch. 5.

14. Curtis to Roosevelt, August 17, 1906. The Foreword appears here as Doc. 1B.

15. A photocopy of the typescript speech, headed "New Museum – Santa Fe, July 27, 1924," was kindly provided by Manford E. Magnuson, Curtis's son-in-law, after an interview in April 1977. Subsequent quotations are from the same source.

16. The notes that follow are necessarily an abbreviated view of a complex phase of Native American history. Fuller accounts may be found in vol. 2 of Francis Paul Prucha, *The Great Father: The United States Government and the American Indians* (Lincoln and London: U of Nebraska P, 1984), and Frederick E. Hoxie, *A Final Promise: The Campaign to Assimilate the Indians, 1880–1920* (Cambridge and New York: Cambridge UP, 1989). A succinct account is provided in Wilcomb E. Washburn, ed., *History of Indian–White Relations* (Washington, D.C.: Smithsonian Institution, 1988), 51–81, vol. 4 of the *Handbook of North American Indians.*

17. Curtis to Jones, June 2, 1904 (and to Acting Commissioner Tonner, July 2, 1904), Commissioner.

18. Curtis to Leupp, October 17, 1905, Commissioner. *NAI*, vol. 2 (1908), 95; also reprinted in Gidley, ed., *The Vanishing Race*, 30.

19. Gidley, ed., *The Vanishing Race*, 99 and 31. Curtis was one of many Leupp supporters who urged President Taft to retain him as commissioner when the new president came into office; see Curtis to Pinchot, March 1, 1909.

20. Curtis to Leupp, August 14, 1905, with note by Leupp and response, Commissioner.

21. Leupp's *Annual Reports* for 1905 and 1906 were reprinted in extract form in Wilcomb E. Washburn, ed., *The American Indian and the United States: A Documentary History* (Westport, Conn.: Greenwood, 1973), vol. 2, 735–46 and 751–3, respectively. For a concise account of Leupp's policies, see Donald Parman's essay on him in Robert M. Kvasnicka and Herman J. Viola, eds., *The Commissioners of Indian Affairs, 1824–1977* (Lincoln and London: U of Nebraska P, 1979), 221–32. Leupp's "The Red Man's Burden" appeared in *Hearst's Magazine*, May 1913, 741–52. *NAI*, vol. 3 (1908), xii. Information on the physical condition of the Pine Ridge people from the interview, cited above, with Harold Curtis, for whom it was a vivid memory. It may be, however, that Harold witnessed this starvation in 1905, rather than 1907, and, if so, this could have been the reason the Pine Ridge Sioux had so forcefully "got into" Curtis's brain when he first wrote to Leupp.

22. Pinchot to Curtis, May 25, and Curtis to Pinchot, May 27, 1911.

23. Curtis to Bagley, September 23 and October 12, 1911, Bagley Papers, UW. Eells, "The Decrease of the Indians," *The American Antiquarian*, 25 (May–June 1903), 145–9.

24. Curtis to Hodge, October 13, 1911. See Thornton, *American Indian Holocaust and Survival: A Population History since 1492* (Norman: U of Oklahoma P, 1987), especially 91–133 and 159–85. Sherburne F. Cook, in *The Population of California Indians* (Berkeley and Los Angeles: U of California P, 1976), has pointed up the difficulties of arriving at precise figures for all California peoples, but especially for those actually in hiding (see 59–71).

25. On Marshall, see Curtis to Roosevelt, November 3, 1911, Roosevelt. Quotations from "The Vanishing Red Man . . . Discussed by Edward S. Curtis," foreword and interview by Edward Marshall, *The Hampton Magazine*, 28, no. 4 (May 1912), 245–53, 308.

26. Anon., "Writing History with the Camera," *Photographic Times*, 44 (April 1912), 124. It is conceivable that the newspaper clipping Pinchot sent Curtis had some connection to the later Ishi story, in that there were several newspaper reports on the Berkeley Anthropology Department's "expeditions" to make contact with a tribe that subsequently turned out to have been Ishi's; see those reproduced in Robert F. Heizer and Theodora Kroeber, eds., *Ishi the Last Yahi:*

A Documentary History (Berkeley and London: U of California P, 1979), 76–87. For Ishi himself, see also Theodora Kroeber, *Ishi in Two Worlds: A Biography of the Last Wild Indian in America,* reprint ed. (Berkeley, Los Angeles and London: U of California P, 1976) and Gerald Vizenor's reflective "Ishi Bares His Chest: Tribal Simulations and Survivance," in Lucy R. Lippard, *op. cit.*, 64–71.

27. "Indians Increasing," unpaginated clipping from the *Post-Intelligencer*, October 18, 1916, Curtis Biography file, NW.

28. Information on Curtis's relationship with Leupp was taken from Curtis to J. Pierpont Morgan, June 21, 1906, PML; he wrote on the Chemehuevi in Curtis to Leupp, November 17, 1906, Commissioner. Intro., *NAI*, vol. 13 (1924), xi–xii; reprinted in Gidley, ed., *The Vanishing Race*, 59.

29. Curtis, "Plea for Haste in Making Documentary Records of the American Indian," *American Museum Journal*, 14, no. 4 (1914), 163–5.

30. Brief commentary on Lane may be found in Prucha, *The Great Father*, vol. 2, 770 and 879. Curtis to Lane, April 12, 1915, Major James McLaughlin Papers, State Historical Society of North Dakota, Bismarck, N.D.; Father Louis Pfaller kindly searched the papers for Curtis letters when they were at Assumption College, Richardton, N.D. For Curtis's relations with the Crow, see especially Ch. 3. For medical advice, see Acting Commissioner F. H. Abbott to Curtis, November 6, 1909, Crow File 96051–1909, Commissioner.

31. See Curtis to Lane, May 15, 1915, McLaughlin. For Last-Arrow ceremonies see Hoxie, 180–1.

32. In general, there was much dispute over Indian Office abuses on the Crow Reservation; see, for example, Prucha, *The Great Father*, vol. 2, 774. In hearings of the Congressional and Senate Committee on Indian Affairs, April 1–13, 1908, Mrs. Grey made several charges of maladministration on the Crow Reservation; see the report of the hearings, "A Company for breeding horses on the Crow Reservation . . . and on bill S2963, for surveying and allotment of Indian lands," issued by the Government Printing Office, 1908. Lane to Curtis, April 13, 1915, McLaughlin.

33. McLaughlin to Curtis, June 23, 1915, and Albert to McLaughlin, June 24, 1915, McLaughlin. The "declaration" was reprinted in Sells's *Annual Report* of 1917; extracted in Washburn, ed., *The American Indian and the United States*, vol. 2, 867–9.

34. For more detailed contextualization than can be provided here, see Randolph C. Downes, "A Crusade for Indian Reform, 1922–1934," *Mississippi Valley Historical Review*, 32 (1945), 331–45; Kenneth Philp, *John Collier's Crusade for Indian Reform, 1920–1954* (Tucson: U of Arizona P, 1977), especially Chs. 2– 5; and William G. Robbins, "Herbert Hoover Indian Reformers under Attack: The Failures of Administrative Reform," in Carl E. Krog and William R. Tanner, eds., *Herbert Hoover and the Republican Era: A Reconsideration* (Lanham, Md.: UP of America, 1984), 95–119. See also Ch. 9 here.

35. Little information seems to have survived on the League, but some was found through scattered, mainly L.A., newspaper references, interviews with Curtis family members, and Harry C. James, *Pages from Hopi History* (Tucson: U of Arizona P, 1974), 180–1, 190. Most important was a pamphlet kindly supplied by Stephany Eger of the Museum of New Mexico, Santa Fe, titled "Activities of the Indian Welfare League" (c. 1924). Information on Ryan from "Author of 'Told in the Hills' Back in Los Angeles," *Los Angeles Examiner*, January 22, 1906, 6; her own books and other publications, including "Fragments of Amber," *Los Angeles Times*, Sunday Magazine, September 18, 1921, 7; a gossip column, "Lee Side o' LA," *Los Angeles Times*, August 17, 1930, pt. 2, 4; her obituary in the *Los Angeles Times*, July 12, 1934, pt. 2, 1; and interviews with Curtis family members. Information on other figures from such directories as *Who's Who in America*.

36. Most information on the League's role in the Citizenship Act was taken from "Activities of the Indian Welfare League." The League goes unmentioned even in the detailed account provided by Gary C. Stein: "The Indian Citizenship Act of 1924," *New Mexico Historical Review,* 47 (1972), 257–74. For sensitive discussion of citizenship issues, see Hoxie, especially 211–38; see also Dippie, 309–17.

37. Unfortunately, it has not proved possible to unravel the intricacies of any of these cases, but some light on the Southern California situation was shed by Sells in one of his reports; see Washburn, *The American Indian and the United States,* vol. 2, 899–902.

38. See works cited by Prucha, Hoxie, and Philp; see also Berkhofer, *op. cit.,* especially 166–97, and Dippie, *op. cit.*

39. Roosevelt to Curtis, February 27, 1910, and February 3, 1909.

40. "In Memory of J. Pierpont Morgan"; quotation taken from version bound in with *NAI,* vol. 9 (1913). Curtis to Prager, November 22, 1911, Oregon Province Archives of the Society of Jesus, Crosby Library, Gonzaga U, Spokane, Wash.

41. See Willard B. Gatewood, "Theodore Roosevelt and the Coinage Controversy," *American Quarterly,* 18 (Spring 1966), 37. Truettner, *The West as America: Reinterpreting Images of the Frontier, 1820–1920* (Washington, D.C., and London: Smithsonian Institution P, 1990), especially 38–53.

42. For coverage of relevant racist ideology in the period, see David Spitz, *Patterns of Anti-Democratic Thought* (New York: Macmillan, 1949), 137–62; Thomas F. Gossett, *Race: The History of an Idea in America* (New York: Schocken, 1965), 353–63, 390–8, 426–7; and Allan Chase, *The Legacy of Malthus: The Social Costs of the New Scientific Racism* (New York: Knopf, 1977), especially 163–75, 256–301.

43. Curtis to Morgan, enclosing untitled typescript outline, January 23, 1906, PML.

44. Foreword, *NAI,* vol. 1 (1907), n.p.

45. Intro., *NAI,* vol. 3 (1908), xii–xiii.

Chapter 2

1. Phillips, "Curtis," cited Ch. 1, n. 3; subsequent Phillips quotations are from the same source.

2. As mentioned in the Intro., the insistence on Curtis's desire to produce outstanding pictures, at whatever cost, is the significant contribution of Lyman, *The Vanishing Race and Other Illusions.* Curtis to Merriam, May 29, 1900; also letters of May–July 1900, C. Hart Merriam Papers, BANC FILM 1958, Bancroft.

3. Quoted in Robert Doty, *Photo-Secession: Photography as a Fine Art* (Rochester, N.Y: George Eastman House, 1960), 24.

4. *Scenic Washington* (Seattle: Edward S. Curtis, n.d. [1898]). The only copy examined is in Bancroft. The massive catalogue of Curtis negatives held (in photocopy form) by the Manuscript Division, Clark Library of the U of California, L.A., contains long series runs of Washington views, mountaineering pictures, and other non-Indian sequences. O. M. Moore, ed., *Washington Illustrated, Including Views of the Puget Sound Country, [etc.]* (Seattle: Puget Sound Bureau of Information, 1900) and Edmond S. Meany, ed., *Art Work of the State of Washington* (Oshkosh, Wis.: Art Photogravure Co., 1900). Meany, a good friend to Curtis, himself co-founded a Seattle-based climbing organization, the Mountaineers, in 1906. Another co-founder was Edward's brother Asahel, and Edward joined later. Meany's *Mountain Camp Fires* (Seattle: Lowman and Hanford, 1911) contains a frontispiece of Rainier by Edward Curtis. The "hobby" claim was made by Goetzmann and Sloan in their otherwise fine *Looking Far North* (Ch. 1, n. 5), 181.

5. Curtis, "The Amateur Photographer," *The Western Trail,* 1, no. 4 (February 1900), 273; the only copy of this seen is in the NW. "Curtis's Photographic Studio," *Argus,* 5, no. 45 (December 17, 1898), 28, col. 4.

6. Edward T. Parsons, "Rainier" [an account of the Mazamas' ascent in

1897], *Mazama*, 2, no. 1 (October 1900), 25–34; other quotations about the 1897 climb are taken from this article.

7. "Mazamas on Mt. Rainier," *Harper's Weekly*, 41 (August 28, 1897), 848–50. Arthur Inkersley, "To the Top of Mt. Rainier with the Mazamas," *Good Words*, 42 (February 1901), 101–7.

8. Curtis to Publishers, *Century*, October 14, 1897, Century Company Records, Rare Books and Manuscripts Division, New York Public Library, Astor, Lenox and Tilden Foundations; this is the earliest known Curtis letter.

9. Curtis to *Century*, n.d., and Curtis to *Century*, telegram, December 6, 1897, Century. Curtis, "The Rush to the Klondike Over the Mountain Passes," *Century*, 55 (March 1898), 692–7.

10. Information on Edward and Asahel pictures, in the form of photocopies of photographs known to be from the same sequence as those in Curtis's *Century* article, kindly supplied by the late Robert D. Monroe, former Head of Special Collections, U of Washington Libraries. On credits, it is worth noting, for example, that although D. G. Inverarity took some of the Harriman Alaska pictures, all were credited to Curtis and all were initially copyrighted in Harriman's name. Other data are from the following: "Will Go to the Klondike," *Argus*, 4, no. 45, (December 18, 1897), 4; Grosvenor, "Harriman Alaska Expedition in Cooperation with the Washington Academy of Sciences," *National Geographic Magazine*, 10 (June 1899), 225–7, my emphasis. Also, the *National Geographic* of April 1898 contains an article on Alaskan resources with two photographs by Edward S. Curtis taken, it says, in the "Fall of 1897" and "February, 1898."

11. Katherine Gile, "Mount St. Helens," *Mazama*, 2, no. 3 (July 1903), 125–9; all information on the Mazamas' 1898 outing comes from this source. Harry Fielding Reid, "Glaciers," *Mazama*, 2, no. 3 (July 1903), 119–22; this includes a page of photographs of the 1901 expedition credited to Edward S. Curtis.

12. Curtis to Harriet Leitch, n.d., SPL. See virtually any account based on Curtis family history, for example, Graybill and Boesen, 10–12.

13. Curtis to Merriam, April 20, 1899, Merriam, Bancroft. Curtis's money worries were occasioned by his partial refurbishment of the studio in the Downs Block, Second Avenue, that he had recently acquired from Frank La Roche. It was probably for such services as acquiring packers that Curtis was made a member of the "Executive Committee" for the Expedition.

14. Some of Edward's mountain pictures formed a public exhibition at the Mazama Portland headquarters; see "The Curtis Collection," *Mazama*, 2, no. 1 (October 1900), 50–1. It would be interesting to know what happened to these photographs. Curtis to Leitch, November 17, 1950, SPL. For information on Ella McBride, who died aged 102 in September 1965, the clippings in the Washington-Biography and Meany Pioneer Files in NW were consulted. She was also mentioned in the 1897 *Mazama* account cited and described as "a photographic artist" in C. H. Hanford, *Seattle and Environs, 1852–1924* (Chicago and Seattle: Pioneer History Publishing Co., 1924), vol. 1, 643–6.

15. See, for example, Graybill and Boesen, 7 and 10–14. The quotation is from Genthe's "A Critical Review of the Salon Pictures with a Few Words upon the Tendency of the Photographers," *Camera Craft*, 2, no. 4 (February 1901), 310. At this point Genthe was yet to shoot to popular prominence for his views of the 1906 earthquake. For information on Genthe, see his own autobiography, *As I Remember* (Chicago: Reynal & Hitchcock, 1936) and Gidley, "Genthe, Arnold," in *Contemporary Photographers*, ed. George Walsh, Colin Naylor, Michael Held (London: Macmillan, 1982), 272–3.

16. Curtis to *Century*, March 4, 1899, Century. See David Sucher, ed., *The Asahel Curtis Sampler: Photographs and Puget Sound Past* (Seattle: Puget Sound Access,

1973) and Richard Frederick and Jeanne Engerman, *Asahel Curtis: Photographs of the Great Northwest* (Tacoma: Washington State Historical Society, 1983). Much wariness is required in distinguishing between the early scenic work of the two brothers.

17. Frontispiece, *Lewis and Clark Journal,* 1, no. 6 (June 1904). Several of Edward's mountain views, together with many of Asahel's, were printed in John H. Williams, *The Mountain That Was God: Being a Little Book about the Great Peak which the Indians Named "Tacoma" But Which is Officially Called "Rainier,"* 2nd ed. (Tacoma: John Williams, 1910; New York and London: Putnam's, 1911). Grosvenor to R. W. Gilder, February 18, 1905, Library, National Geographic Society, Washington, D.C. For later scenic tour, see Holm and Quimby, 108, and Ch. 8 here. Robert Sterling Yard, ed., *The National Parks Portfolio*; there were several editions from 1916 onwards – each with views credited to Edward S. Curtis, along with many of Rainier by Asahel and his company – and I saw the third (Washington, D.C.: Government Printing Office, 1921).

18. Phillips, "Curtis," 4. Copies of these named studies have so far not been traced, but similar views of a slightly later date, c. 1901, are reproduced from the journal *Camera Craft* in Lyman, 42, 43, 46, and 47. A bluetone of "Aphrodite" was displayed at A Gallery of Fine Photography, New Orleans, in the fall of 1990. The *Argus* items were cited in Davis, 19 and 251.

19. Information on Burke from various reference works and the Thomas Burke Papers, UW, especially letters by Curtis to Burke of July 29, 1902, requesting Burke's presence for a new portrait, and January 21, 1906. Curtis Studio likenesses of all these other figures appear in the portraits file of PCUW. The Samuel Hill Papers, Maryhill Museum, Goldendale, Washington, contain receipts for pictures made at the Curtis Studio. Higginson's poem is quoted in Ch. 9; when she later came to publish her *The Vanishing Race and Other Poems* (Bellingham, Wash.: C. M. Sherman, 1911), the whole volume was dedicated to Curtis, "with homage for his art." There are several references to Kincaid in *Looking Far North* (Ch. 1, n. 5). Information on Cheasty was in the story of his dramatic death, "Cheasty is Killed by Fall," *Post-Intelligencer,* June 13, 1914, 1.

20. PCUW portrait file contains a mass of Curtis Studio Arctic Club portraits, including those mentioned here. For brief commentary on Brainerd and Curtis, see Graybill and Boesen, 17, and for same on de Mille, see Ch. 8 here. A similar file of Curtis Studio portraits is to be found in the Seattle Historical Society. For Joseph, see Gidley, *Kopet: A Documentary Narrative of Chief Joseph's Last Years* (Seattle and London: U of Washington P, 1981), 58–60. Curtis spoke of the Riis lecture in a letter to Pinchot, December 16, 1904.

21. See "E. S. Curtis Here to Handle Exhibit," clipping from the *Seattle Times* of May 28, 1909, in *Seattle AYPE Scrapbook,* no. 8, 27, and "Many Exhibits of Aboriginal Work and Picture History of Photographer Curtis Give Redman Conspicuous Place," *Seattle Times,* August 29, 1909, clipping in Curtis Biography File, both NW. Nadeau's portrait is in the portrait file at the PCUW, while Duncan's is in the Federal Archives, Seattle. Brief notes on the Harriman party's views of Metlakahtla may be found in *Looking Far North* (Ch. 1, n. 5), 38–43. Pavlova's portrait was in the collection of Manford Magnuson in August 1978, as was that of Tagore, reproduced in Davis, 68, where it is credited to Edwin Johanson. (If it was not by Curtis it is more likely that it was taken by Edward Johanson, Edwin's father, who worked at the Seattle studio during World War I.) In an interview in December 1976, Florence Graybill mentioned several Hollywood portraits she remembered her father taking in the early twenties. A Curtis Studio portrait of Meeker made in the L.A. Curtis Studio after 1920 is to be found in PCUW.

22. Curtis, "The Amateur Photographer," *The Western Trail*, 1, no. 6 (May 1900), 469. Child competition details on 1 of *The Ladies' Home Journal*, 20 (October 1903). Subsequent reports, none of which named Curtis, appeared in issues for the following February, May, and September. Unfortunately, though Russell did not die until the age of 90 in 1962, no further information on his relationship with Curtis could be found; basic data in many editions of *Who's Who in America*, especially vol. 32 (1962–63), 2701.

23. See "Curtis Goes to Oyster Bay," clipping dated June 3, 1904 in Curtis Biography File, NW, and *McClure's*, 25 (July 1905), 284–92. Lot 0512 of The Prints and Photographs Division of the Library of Congress contains thirty two 6 × 8 sepia prints of Sagamore and its occupants dated 1904. Curtis to Pinchot, August 2, 1904, December 16, 1904, and April 14, 1905. Roosevelt, *An Autobiography* (London and New York: Macmillan, 1913).

24. Curtis to Pinchot, April 14, 1905. Curtis to Alice Roosevelt, April 12, 1905, author's collection, gift of Alice R. Longworth in letter dated June 19, 1974. The Alice Roosevelt Longworth portrait file in the Prints and Photographs Division of the Library of Congress contains several Curtis portraits, wedding pictures, and a study apparently made for *Frank Leslie's Magazine* in 1902, though this last has not been traced in published form.

25. There is a file of La Roche prints in PCUW. For Frank Nowell and Darius Kinsey, see Ralph W. Andrews, *Photographers of the Frontier West: Their Lives and Works, 1875–1915* (New York: Bonanza, 1965), 38–59 and 72–83, respectively. For A. C. Warner, see Robert D. Monroe, "First at the Summit: Arthur Churchill Warner on Mt. Rainier," *The Record* (Friends of the Library, Washington State U), 39 (1978), 6–27. For Hegg, see Murray Morgan, *One Man's Gold Rush: A Klondike Album* (Seattle and London: U of Washington P, 1967).

26. See *Argus* item cited (Ch. 2, n. 5). For Muhr, see Omaha city directories, Robert Bigart and Clarence Woodcock, "The Rinehart Photographs: A Portfolio," *Montana*, 29 (Autumn 1979), 24–37, and Holm and Quimby, 23–5. For Cunningham at the Curtis Studio, see the report of her talk to the Chemical Society of the U of Washington in *Pacific Wave*, 15, no. 38 (February 18, 1908), 4, col. 1, UW, and her reminiscence in "Camera Dean Back in Seattle," *Seattle Times* (May 20, 1965), Art Department Scrapbook, Seattle Public Library. For Kunishige (and further information on McBride), see Robert D. Monroe, "Light and Shade: Pictorial Photography in Seattle, 1920–1940, and the Seattle Camera Club," in *Turning Shadows into Light: Art and Culture of the Northwest's Early Asian/Pacific Community*, ed. Mayumi Tsutakwa and Allan Chong Lau (Seattle: Young Pine P, 1982), 8–32. Information on Throssel from Peggy Albright to author, October 19, 1994; see also Albright's forthcoming study of Throssel.

27. Information on Inverarity from interviews with his son, Robert Bruce Inverarity, from Autumn 1976 onwards, entries in the *Seattle City Directory*, and C. Bagley, *History of Seattle* (Chicago: S. J. Clarke, 1916), vol. 3, 1115–6; one of Inverarity's architectural photographs appeared in the *Argus*, 5, no. 45 (December 17, 1898), 26. It may be the case that Inverarity encouraged Curtis to take his very first Indian pictures; see Holm and Quimby, 22.

28. PCUW holds the short run of *Anderson's*. Caffin, *Photography as a Fine Art*, reprint ed. (New York: Amphoto, 1972). Beck, *Art Principles in Portrait Photography* reprint ed. (New York: Arno, 1973).

29. Quotations from *The Western Trail*, 1, no. 3 (January 1900), 186; no. 4 (February 1900), 273; no. 5 (March/April 1900), 379; and no. 6 (May 1900), 468–9.

30. For indications of the Snake Dance as photographers' meeting place, see: Gidley, "R. B. Townshend's Hopi Snake Dance Photographs in Focus,"

European Review of Native American Studies, 1, no. 2 (Autumn 1987), 9–14; Luke Lyon, "History of Prohibition of Photography of Southwestern Indian Ceremonies," in Anne van Arsdall Poore, ed., *Reflections: Papers on Southwestern Culture History in Honor of Charles H. Lange,* Papers of the Archaeological Society of New Mexico, no. 14 (Santa Fe: Ancient City P, 1988), 238–72; and Sharyn R. Udall, "The Irresistible Other: Hopi Ritual Drama and Euro-American Audiences," *The Drama Review,* 36 (Summer 1992), 23–43. Other information from *Catalogue of the Fine Arts Exhibit of the Lewis and Clark Centennial Exposition: Portland, Oregon, June 1 – October 15, 1905* (Portland: Albert Hess, [1905]), 77–9; "Exhibition Notes," *Camera Work,* no. 11 (July 1905), 57; David Calvin Strong, "Sidney Carter and Alfred Stieglitz: The Canadian Pictorialist Exhibition (1907)," *History of Photography,* 20 (Summer 1996), 160-2. Steichen's Morgan portrait is reproduced in Doty, 55. "The Curtis Portraits," NW; given the reference to the St. Louis Exposition, this must have been produced in 1904 or, at the latest, 1905. Once Curtis began to be listed in *Who's Who in America,* in 1912, his entry regularly noted his membership of the National Arts Club, the prestigious New York institution that mounted early pictorialist exhibitions and to which such figures as Caffin, Remington, and Stieglitz also belonged; unfortunately, the Club has no records of his activities.

31. Caffin, as quoted in Estelle Jussim and Elizabeth Lindquist-Cock, *Landscape as Photograph* (New Haven and London: Yale UP, 1985), 65. The Eugene portrait of Stieglitz is reproduced in Doty, 8, and the profile by Käsebier in Caffin, 71.

32. "Edward S. Curtis: Photo-Historian of the North American Indian," Seattle *Sunday Times,* Magazine Section, November 15, 1903, clipping in Curtis Biography File, NW; emphasis added. See Goetzmann, *The First Americans: Photographs from the Library of Congress* (Washington, D.C.: Starwood, 1991), 99. Curtis to Hodge, June 26, 1907. An orotone of "Maid of Dreams," dated 1925 (but definitely taken earlier), was displayed at A Gallery of Fine Photography, New Orleans, in the fall of 1990.

33. Anon., "Writing History with the Camera," *Photographic Times,* 44 (April 1912), 124–8.

34. Text of Kurtz's comments taken from a *North American Indian* publicity prospectus [c. 1909], photocopy, author's collection.

35. The Curtis Studio published a 16-page *Catalogue of The Curtis Indian Prints On Exhibition in the Forestry Building . . .* (Seattle: Curtis Studio, n.d. [1905]) containing details of 304 prints; copy examined was in the New York Public Library. For Curtis's affinities with pictorialism, see: Beth B. DeWall, "The Artistic Achievement of Edward Sheriff Curtis," U of Cincinnati (Master's Thesis, 1980), especially Ch. 3; Christopher Varley, Introduction to *Edward S. Curtis in the Collection of the Edmonton Art Gallery* (Edmonton Art Gallery, c. 1980); Lyman; A. D. Coleman, "Edward S. Curtis: The Photographer as Ethnologist," *Katalog* (Odense, Denmark), 5, no. 4 (June 1993), 25–34; and Fleming and Luskey, *Grand Endeavors,* 99–117; looser discussion of the influence of the studio on the field, but with reference to specific images, may be found in Goetzmann, *The First Americans,* 41, 78, 109, and 117. For Curtis's Portland talk, see "Notes and Comment," *Mazama,* 2, no. 4 (December 1905), 264–5.

36. Caffin, quoted in Doty, 51. For the development of the Photo-Secession, see also Weston Naef, *The Collection of Alfred Stieglitz* (New York: Viking, 1978), and for "straight" photography, see such standard accounts as Beaumont Newhall, *The History of Photography* (New York: Museum of Modern Art, 1939; 1982).

37. The literature on the picturesque – though it rarely takes cognizance of photography – is vast and sophisticated; among the works that treat ideological aspects, and whose insights

could be applied to the more recent past, is Ann Bermingham, *Landscape and Ideology: The English Rustic Tradition, 1740–1860* (Berkeley: U of California P, 1986). Lyman, 71, points out that modern wagons were retouched out of the Little Bighorn image.

38. Berger, *Ways of Seeing* (Harmondsworth: Penguin with the BBC, 1972), 104. On Emerson, who wrote influentially about photography as an art, see Nancy Newhall, *P. H. Emerson: The Fight for Photography as a Fine Art* (New York: Aperture, 1978), in which the images mentioned above are reproduced.

39. Grinnell, "Portraits of Indian Types," *Scribner's*, 37 (March 1905), 259–73, an article illustrated by Curtis photographs; quotation from 70–3.

40. An earlier analogy for this process of nationalization is the work of Bingham; see Angela Miller, "The Mechanisms of the Market and the Invention of Western Regionalism: The Example of George Caleb Bingham," *Oxford Art Journal*, 15 (Spring 1992), 3–20.

41. "Telling History by Photographs. Records of Our North American Indians Being Preserved by Pictures," *The Craftsman*, 9 (March 1906), 846–9. This article, illustrated by three Curtis photographs, may have been composed by Gustav Stickley, the publisher of *The Craftsman* who, as well as championing the Arts and Crafts movement in the U.S.A., gave early recognition to photography as an art.

42. Allan, "E. S. Curtis, Photo Historian," *Wilson's Photographic Magazine*, 44 (August, 1907), 361–3. For information on Hartmann and a selection of his photographic writings, see *The Valiant Knights of Daguerre*, ed. Harry W. Lawton and George Knox (Berkeley and Los Angeles: U of California P, 1978).

43. The speech was in Box 58, "Miscellaneous Manuscript Articles," Meany. For further information on Meany, see the biographical sketch in Gidley, *Kopet*, 8–10 and, especially, references to him in subsequent chapters here. See "Curtis Tells of Indian Pictures," *Pacific Wave* (November 10, 1905), 1, col. 4, and 2, cols.1 and 2, an account of the 1905 field season. For contemporary pictures of Curtis in the field, see, for example, illustrations to Graybill and Boesen. "E. S. Curtis Back in Seattle," *Seattle Times* (January 19, 1907), 8, cols. 1–3. The text of the speech used here is that of the typescript; it also appeared, with a brief additional note on *NAI* publication plans, as "My Work in Indian Photography," *Photographic Times*, 39 (May 1907), 195–8 and was reprinted in the *British Journal of Photography*, 54 (August 23, 1907), 636–7, as "A Triumph of Record Photography," with a head note expressing the hope of a Curtis exhibition in Britain. Curtis wrote to Meany on October 22, 1907. Most of the details of timing, etc., were corroborated by dates on relevant correspondence. The ethnologists were Myers and Phillips, who also acted as secretary.

Chapter 3

1. Curtis to Candelario, October 31, 1905, Candelario Collection, Museum of New Mexico; see also Curtis letters of October 7 and 19, 1905. A laudatory piece by Adolf Muhr in *Photo-Era* spoke of the studio as "the home of Mr. Curtis and of the Curtis Indian" ("E. S. Curtis and His Work," *Photo-Era*, July 1907, 9–13). Curtis photos were often sold with a notice on the verso of the frame calling his studio "the home of the American Indian." At the same time, it would be a mistake to overemphasize this point; other photographers of Indians – Adam Clark Vroman and Roland Reed among them – decorated their studios with Indian artifacts, and even some practitioners who were not primarily interested in Indians, such as Henry Peabody and Frances B. Johnston, had studios at least partly cluttered with such objects. They were obviously considered appropriate exotica for travelling photographers.

2. Grinnell, "Diary of the Harriman Alaska Expedition," Grinnell Papers, Southwest Museum, Los Angeles; Merri-

am, "Journal of Harriman Alaska," vol. 1, 233, C. Hart Merriam Papers, LC. Curtis to Merriam, December 27, 1905, with annotation in Merriam's hand, C. Hart Merriam Papers, Bancroft. Bok to Curtis, November 18, 1903, Edward S. Curtis Vertical File, UW.

3. Curtis to Bowditch, May 19, 1908, January 24, 1910, and July 27, 1915, SB. Curtis to Bowditch, November 5, 1910, January 10 and January 21, 1913, E. S. Curtis File, Manuscript Collection, Flagstaff.

4. Curtis to Gordon, August 24 and September 6, 1911, Philadelphia. Southwest Museum information from various accession notes, etc., in Hodge, and Frances E. Watkins, "The Stewart C. Eastwood Collection," *The Masterkey*, 16, no. 6 (November 1942), 199–202. Some of the other museums with items first collected by Curtis are the British Museum, the Burke Museum, Seattle, the Denver Art Museum, and the Los Angeles County Museum of Natural History.

5. Curtis to Hodge, December 4, 1908. Information on Wilson from Carolyn Gilman and Mary J. Schneider, *The Way to Independence: Memories of a Hidatsa Indian Family, 1840–1920* (St. Paul: Minnesota Historical Society P, 1987), which constitutes both a history of Wilson's ethnological activities and a partial catalogue of items he collected; it is clear that his activities did sometimes arouse disquiet among the Hidatsa (see, for example, 286–7), and Wolf Chief's disposal of the skull shrine was particularly contentious (see 294–301). *NAI*, vol. 4 (1909), 163–5 and 138. It is unlikely that Curtis himself harbored any ill-will towards Wilson, whose brother, the artist F. N. Wilson, contributed drawings to Curtis's *Indian Days of the Long Ago* (Yonkers-on-Hudson: World Book Co., 1914).

6. See Clifford, "Histories of the Tribal and the Modern" and other essays in *The Predicament of Culture* (Intro, n. 6), and Jeanette Greenfield, *The Return of Cultural Treasures* (Cambridge and New York: Cambridge UP, 1989), which, though it does not deal with expropriation "internal" to a nation, contains much pertinent commentary. See the many letters from Samuel A. Barrett to C. F. Newcombe, Newcombe. *Looking Far North* (Ch. 1, n. 5), 161–8.

7. Curtis to Hubbell, August 20 and December 7, 1906, and February 1, 1907; Curtis to Hubbell, April 1 and 5, May 27, July 14, and October 4, 1907; and April 19 and June 2, 1909, all Hubbell Papers, Special Collections, U of Arizona, Tucson. Information on subscription from Curtis to Hubbell, May 10 and 20, October 18, November 4, 1912, and May 5, 1913, also Hubbell Papers.

8. Information on the Days may best be found in Clifford E. Trafzer, "Sam Day and His Boys: Good Neighbors to the Navajos," *Journal of Arizona History*, 18 (Spring 1977), 1–22. The Samuel Edward Day Collection of manuscript material is in the Cline Library, Special Collections and Archives, Northern Arizona U, Flagstaff, and Charlie's photographs are at the Museum of Northern Arizona, Flagstaff. See also Curtis to Charlie Day, November 19, 1908, Day Collection.

9. See Trafzer, 16–8, and, for the full context, the same author's edition of one of the protest letters: "An Indian Trader's Plea for Justice, 1906," *New Mexico Historical Review*, 47 (July 1972), 239–56. Day to Curtis, February 10, 1905, enclosed with Curtis to Leupp, March 15, 1905, Commissioner.

10. Curtis family lore about Day appears in, for example, Ralph W. Andrews, *Curtis' Western Indians* (Seattle: Superior, 1962), 26–7, and Graybill and Boesen, 25–6. Curtis to Day, December 20, 1904, Day Collection. Also, "A Seattle Man's Triumph," *Seattle Times*, May 4, 1904, clipping in the NW fully reproduced in Lyman, 65–9. James C. Faris, basing his case on a comparison of published Curtis images with ones in Day family hands, has argued convincingly that Day himself was the subject of cer-

tain masked portraits; see his "The Navajo Photography of Edward S. Curtis," *History of Photography*, 17 (Winter 1993), 377–87. Faris has also contended that some of the Yebichai images were actually *taken* by Day rather than by Curtis, and such would have been consistent with what we know of the relationship between the two men (if not of Curtis's photographic practice, at least from the onset of the Indian project); but here his grounds – an *assumption* that Curtis was not there at the right time of the year – are less firm, in that he *was* in Navajoland and the Southwest at times other than the summer (see, for example, Doc. 2C).

11. Stevenson to Walcott, November 17, 1908, Matilda Coxe Stevenson Papers, NAA. Wissler, *Red Man Reservations* [1938] (New York: Collier, 1971), 200. The question of what actually constitutes the "selling" of religion, if it is indeed possible, is more complex than these polemical positions can indicate. There were Stevenson letters to Curtis indicating full support on February 21 and May 5, 1907, and April 9, 1908, E. S. Curtis Vertical File, UW. For Stevenson's bossiness, see Nancy Oestereich Lurie, "Women in Early American Anthropology," in June Helm, ed., *Pioneers of American Anthropology: The Uses of Biography* (Seattle: U of Washington P, 1966), especially 53–4, 60–2, 233 n. 41, 234 n.53.

12. Curtis to Leitch, March 3, 1951, SPL. Ronald P. Rohner, "Franz Boas: Ethnographer on the Northwest Coast," in Helm, *op. cit.*, 149–222, and letter to the present writer, December 7, 1976.

13. For material on Hunt, see Rohner, *op. cit.*; Helen Codere, "Introduction" in her edition of *Kwakiutl Ethnography* by Boas (Chicago: U of Chicago P, 1966); Ira Jacknis, "Franz Boas and Photography," *Studies in Visual Communication*, 10, no. 1 (Winter 1984), 2–60; and Irving Goldman, *The Mouth of Heaven: An Introduction to Kwakiutl Religious Thought* (New York and London: John Wiley, 1975), especially 9–12. Brief theoretical commentary on the Hunt–Boas relationship – including some on the way Boas frequently did not grant Hunt appropriate human consideration – in the constitution of a representation of Northwest Coast culture may be found in Murray, 100–4, as cited in Intro, n. 7. A more hostile view of Hunt may be found in J. Cannizzo, "George Hunt and the Invention of Kwakiutl Culture," *Canadian Review of Sociology and Anthropology*, 20, no. 1 (1983), 44–66.

14. See Holm and Quimby, especially 66–9; for still Curtis images of Hunt, see Leland Rice, *Edward S. Curtis: The Kwakiutl 1910–1914* (Irvine: Fine Arts Gallery, U of California, 1976), and Goetzmann, *The First Americans*, 136. For Hunt's changeableness and other relevant aspects of his character I consulted Graybill and Boesen, 61–5, a typescript of an undated and more elaborate Curtis memoir in the possession of Victor Boesen, vol. 10 of *NAI*, and an undated one-page typescript Curtis reminiscence of Hunt in the LACMNH; since the latter was found with other short pieces on Northwest Coast history, it may have formed part of a book Curtis compiled in the thirties on aspects of the region.

15. See Holm and Quimby, *passim* but especially 127–8, where Hunt's accounts are reproduced. "Grotesque Indian Mask in Curtis Collection," *Seattle Times*, November 10, 1912, clipping in the Curtis Biography File, NW.

16. For further discussion of Hunt's role in the transfer of arts, see Douglas Cole, *Captured Heritage: The Scramble for Northwest Coast Artifacts* (Seattle: U of Washington P, 1985). The Curtis memoir is fully reproduced in Graybill and Boesen, 64–7.

17. Ibid.

18. Harold Curtis, interview with the author, January 1977; for further details of Harold's experiences with the Sioux, see Homer H. Boelter, with Lonnie Hull, *Edward Sheriff Curtis: Photographer-Historian* (Los Angeles: Westerners Brandbook, Los Angeles Corral, 1966), n.p. The

Meany financial account was found in the uncatalogued portion of his papers. Apache story told in an untitled typescript by Curtis in LACMNH; this extract, and variations upon it, was probably composed for the 1911 musicale tour.

19. See Rohner, "Franz Boas: Ethnographer of the Northwest Coast," *passim*, but especially 172, and Marie Mauzé, "The Destiny of a Shrine: The Yukwot Whaler's Washing Shrine at the American Museum of Natural History," a paper on the reconstruction of a Nootka whaling shrine, delivered at the Tenth European American Indian Workshop, Vienna, April 1989.

20. Gifford to Myers, September 12, 1915, Museum Archives, University Archives, Bancroft.

21. Phillips, "Beside an Old Chief's Resting Plot," typescript, 9 , private collection. Phillips's field notes of the visit to Nespelem survive in the LACMNH. The North American Indian was often at pains to use appropriate Indians as brokers; for example, on April 8, 1912, Curtis wrote to Gordon of the U of Pennsylvania Museum, Philadelphia, about his forthcoming visit to the Museum, expressing his hopes of interviewing, presumably as preparation for Northwest Coast fieldwork, "the Alaska Indian" working there, namely Louis V. Shotridge of Haines, Alaska, who later wrote such essays as "Tlingit Woman's Root Basket" for his institution's *Museum Journal*, 12 (September 1921), 162–78.

22. Phillips, "Through the Country of the Crows," typescript, 10, private collection; subsequent quotations are from this piece. In a passage not quoted here Phillips made detrimental remarks about Carlisle, but despite these adverse comments, Curtis seems to have recruited other workers from, and perhaps through, Carlisle, and only some were disaffected.

23. Some of Upshaw's father's deeds are recorded in *NAI*, vol. 4 (1909), 18–20. Information on Upshaw himself came from: Daniel F. Littlefield and James W. Parins, *A Bio-bibliography of Native American Authors, 1772–1924* (Metuchen, N.J. and London: Scarecrow, 1981), 170 and 303; Upshaw's own "What The Indians Owe to the United States Government," *Red Man and Helper*, 14 (April 1897), 8; Phillips; and interviews with Harold Curtis, January 1977, and Florence Graybill, December 1976, who remembered her father speaking of Upshaw's death. Curtis reported on him to Hodge in December 26, 1907, Hodge, and his contribution to *NAI* was remembered in the preface to vol. 7 (1911), xii.

24. "Six Weeks Among the Indians," 1905 newspaper clipping in Clarence Bagley scrapbook no. 5, 110, NW. The surviving manuscripts of *NAI* include a wealth of handwritten notes, typed materials, vocabularies, etc. There is much evidence of contributions by Upshaw. Most impressively, in a file labeled "Blackfeet" there are two copies of material titled "Upshaw Notes," typescripts of interviews and histories, and, in one carton of typed material on the Apsaroke and Hidatsa peoples, the typed and indexed volumes of field notes cite Upshaw's name, as might be expected, frequently. The brief note on Upshaw's White House visit, which lent him an aura of the exotic as "a full-blooded Crow Indian," appeared in the *Washington Post*, March 26, 1909 (reproduced in a Curtis publicity brochure, *The North American Indian*, n.d. [c. 1911], author's collection).

25. Typescript reminiscence by Curtis, probably written in the mid-thirties, quoted very fully in Andrews, 39–42.

26. Interview with Fritz Dalby, Edwin Dalby's son, August 1978, who misidentified Allen – who also later served as William Elmendorf's principal informant on the Skokomish – as Skykomish.

27. File 389/1911, Crow 311, Commissioner. File 41014–08–321 Crow, also Commissioner; Curtis's letter is dated February 3, 1909.

28. "Edward S. Curtis: Photo-Historian" (Ch. 2, n. 32). Information on pres-

ent-day Navajo responses supplied by William B. Lee in an interview with the author, August 1980; Dr. Lee's evidence is also fully reported in Lyman, 69. Similar experience with Navajos and the film footage was communicated by Clifford Trafzer in discussions during the spring of 1985. (It should be pointed out, however, that Luke Lyon believes that the Yebichai footage shown to present-day Navajos was simply wrongly printed in laterally reversed form; see his "History of Prohibition of Photography," cited in Ch. 2, n. 30). Pratt, *Imperial Eyes: Travel Writing and Transculturation* (London and New York: Routledge, 1992).

29. "Edward S. Curtis: Photo-Historian," *op. cit.*.

30. The Curtis file in the New York Public Library Manuscript Division includes this gravure of "The Oath." Dorris, "Indians on the Shelf," in Calvin Martin, ed., *The American Indian and the Problem of History* (New York: Oxford UP, 1987), 102.

31. "Edward S. Curtis: Photo-Historian," *op. cit.*.

32. There follows a yarn about Curtis in the company of Seattle newspaper man E. L. Rebner – or, possibly, Reber, as the story itself says – being ordered off an Arizona reservation by its (unnamed) agent. The project's relations with the Bureau of Indian Affairs seem to have varied partly according to the level of the official concerned, as will be evident from Ch. 1; usually thereafter project members went into the field armed with permission letters for which Curtis applied directly to the commissioner.

33. Whatever the veracity of this story of Indian trade practices, its stereotypical rendering suggests that this "Charley" was a generic construct and had no connection with Charlie Day, who in any case was closer to the Navajos than the Hopis.

34. The report, which originally appeared in the *Seattle Sunday Times* of August 11, 1907, was taken from an advertising brochure for *The North American Indian*, c. 1910, author's collection. At Curtis's urging, Meany produced a more elaborate account for national consumption: "Hunting Indians with a Camera," *World's Work*, 15 (March 1908), 10004–11. Many of the pictures and much of the data obtained among Red Hawk's folk did duly appear in vol. 3 of *NAI* later in 1908.

Chapter 4

1. Printed invitation to Curtis Exhibit at Christensen's Hall, and typescript memorandum of January 28, 1904, "To the Honorable Board of Regents, University of Washington [signed by Alden J. Blethen and one other]," E. S. Curtis Vertical File, UW. Photocopy of printed invitation to the Waldorf-Astoria exhibition attached to a facsimile of a letter from Theodore Roosevelt to E. H. Harriman of March 2, 1905, author's collection.

2. Information from subscription lists in PML. For further insights into Curtis's financial dealings, see Curtis to Morgan, June 21, 1906, Curtis to King, July 10, 1907, and, for King's commentary on the request for early payment that this represented, King to Morgan, July 18, 1907, all PML.

3. Information primarily from holograph copy by Edmond S. Meany of an agreement to aid Curtis in the name of J. W. Clise, Meany.

4. Curtis to Meany, August 20, 1907.

5. Curtis to Meany, September 4, 1907.

6. Curtis to Meany, October 22 and 24, 1907; Curtis to Meany, January 27, 1908 (and Curtis sent similar letters on February 24 and July 31, 1908); typescript, amended in Meany's hand, of a statement dated June 24, 1908, presumably to be placed in a presentation copy of volumes of *NAI*. Some of the figures named had served as patrons to Curtis before, namely Alden Blethen, J. E. Chilberg, J. W. Clise, C. H. Cobb, Samuel Hill, and F. S. Stimson.

7. Curtis to Hodge, September 18, 1908.

8. Curtis to Morgan, November 5, 1907, as quoted in Davis, 54. A knowledgeable account of Morgan's crucial role in the 1907 panic may be found in Vincent P. Carosso, *The Morgans: Private International Bankers, 1854–1913* (Cambridge, Mass. and London: Harvard UP, 1987), especially 534–47. Curtis to Pinchot, January 24, 1910.

9. Myers to Hodge, May 28 and June 19, 1925. Information from the Curtis materials in PML, especially the book labeled "The North American Indian, Inc.: Corporate Records."

10. Curtis to Greene, April 6 and July 2, 1914, PML. The "attached balance sheet" did not remain with the letter in PML. The "annual report of January 1913" was reprinted quite fully in Douglas C. Ewing, "*The North American Indian* in Forty Volumes," *Art in America*, 60 (July–August, 1972), 84–8, and Beth Barclay DeWall, "Edward Sheriff Curtis: A New Perspective on *The North American Indian*," *History of Photography*, 6 (July 1982), 223–39, with further data. The PML also holds six copyright "Assignments."

11. The comment on Dinwiddie appeared in Curtis to Hodge, January 27, 1908. Curtis to Grosvenor, December 20, 1910, Archives, National Geographic Society, Washington, D.C.

12. For Cosmos Club, see Curtis to Pinchot, October 28, 1904, and Pinchot's reply, and Curtis to Pinchot, December 30, 1904. Correspondence referring to letters of introduction include Pinchot to Curtis, January 5, 1906 (La Farge), Curtis to Pinchot, January 21, 1906 (John Hays Hammond), Pinchot to Curtis, March 30, 1907 (Stokes, Vanderbilt, and others), Curtis to Pinchot, April 5, 1907 (Melvil Dewey, New York State Librarian), and Pinchot to Curtis, February 28, 1912 (three influential Chicago people). Mrs. Custer's comment is in her letter to Pinchot, April 19, 1908. All Pinchot.

13. Curtis to Pinchot, January 21, 1906. Butler to Curtis, January 15, 1906, Nicholas Murray Butler Papers, Butler Library, Columbia U, New York. Curtis to Mrs. Robinson, December 31, 1909, Houghton Library, Harvard U, Cambridge, Mass.

14. Curtis to Riggs, January 23, 1909, Manuscripts, Denver Public Library, and to Boothe, March 15, 1910, Library, Washington State Historical Society, Tacoma. Curtis to Huntington, May 24, 1911, Huntington.

15. Curtis to Mrs. J. B. Montgomery, November 5, 1906, and April 23, 1907, MAP Montgomery Collection, Manuscripts and Archives, Yale U Library, New Haven.

16. Curtis to Pinchot, March 27, 1906; Pinchot to Curtis, March 29, 1906. For sales, see, for example, Curtis to Bowditch, June 10, 1911, SB; and Curtis to Roosevelt, April 28, 1911, and Roosevelt to Curtis, May 2 and 5, 1911. For appearance patronage, see Curtis to Roosevelt, November 3, 1911, and Roosevelt's secretary to Curtis, November 10, 1911, Roosevelt. For The Modern Historic Records Association, see Curtis to Doane Robinson, Secretary of South Dakota Historical Society, May 21, 1912, South Dakota Historical Society, Pierre; there is also a brief comment in Ch. 3 here.

17. Curtis to Huntington, March 4, 1909, Huntington. From an agreement in the same file dated March 3, 1910, it seems that Huntington was persuaded to exchange his subscription to the Japanese tissue edition but not to convert to paid-up status.

18. Curtis to Pinchot, April 4, 1908. See *The North American Indian: Extracts from Reviews of the Book, and Comments on the Work of its Author, Edward S. Curtis* n.d. [c. 1910], author's collection. Nomination forms included with, for example, Curtis to Bowditch, January 3, 1916, Flagstaff. For commendations, etc. see Curtis to Pinchot, May 12, 1915; for picture gifts, Curtis to Pinchot, December 16, 1904, March 27, 1906, and Pinchot to Curtis, January 23, 1911, December 27, 1912, January 9, 1914, etc.; for "sup-

plementary readers," see, for example, Curtis to Hubbell, October 12, 1914, Hubbell Papers, U of Arizona, Tucson.

19. Curtis's description of the portrait appeared in a letter to Leitch, December 29, 1950, SPL. Curtis to C. Hart Merriam, April 29, 1908, Merriam, Bancroft.

20. Jusserand, who wrote the famous *English Wayfaring Life in the Middle Ages* (1889), was patron of the Curtis Picture-Opera in Washington as described in Ch. 7 here. Accounts of the episode in Curtis to Pinchot, November 15, 1909, Pinchot, *and,* for example, Curtis to Bowditch, November 18, 1909, SB.

21. Curtis to Vallentine, June 25, 1909, and Abbott to Curtis, July 13, 1909, File 51246–1910, Crow Dept., Commissioner.

22. Undated entry in File 356 (dealing with advertising), Northern Pacific Index, Minnesota Historical Society, St. Paul. Curtis to Pinchot, April 14, 1905, and Pinchot to Curtis, April 25, 1905. By June 17 Curtis was able to report that twenty Seattle business men had lent him $5,000 for a year in what was, in effect, a forerunner of the larger deal Meany negotiated for him in 1907. Information on Pinchot loan from Curtis to Pinchot, June 27, 1915, February 22, April 19, May 17 and 24, July[?], 1916, and May 19, 1917; Pinchot to Curtis, February 12, 1917, and Woodruff to Curtis, January 9, 1920.

23. Curtis to Huntington, with enclosures, June 3, 1911, Huntington.

24. Curtis to Penrose, April 11, 1907, and Penrose to Whom it May Concern, enclosed with Penrose to Curtis, April 17, 1907, Library, Whitman College, Walla Walla.

25. Curtis to Merriam, November 28, 1908; Curtis to Merriam, April 10, 1906, both Merriam, Bancroft. Putnam to Curtis, January 22, 1908, and Curtis to Putnam, February 11, 1908, University Archives, Pusey Library, Harvard U, Cambridge, Mass.

26. Curtis to Stevenson, February 21, 1907, M. C. Stevenson Papers, NAA. See Dinwiddie to Walcott, April 12 and November 22, 1907; Curtis to Walcott, April 20, 1907, December 7, 1908; Hodge to Walcott, December 15, 1908; Walcott to Dinwiddie, October 6, 1908; Walcott to Curtis, December 12, 1908, Smithsonian.

27. See, for example, Curtis to Walcott, January 25 and December 16, 1910; Walcott to Curtis, January 3, 1911, and February 14, 1912. See Curtis to Walcott, April 4, 1911, and Walcott's response; also group of letters expressing appreciation to Mrs. Harriman. All Smithsonian.

28. Curtis to Gordon, September 5, 1906, Philadelphia. Curtis to A. F. Larrabee, December 7, 1906, Commissioner; File no. 86532–1907 contains the rest of the correspondence concerning Jamestown, except the diploma letter, which appears in File no. 76171–1908; information on Turin from Curtis to C. F. Hanke, February 7 and 17, 1911, and Hanke to Curtis, November 4, 1911, all in File no. 4463–1911, Record Group 75, National Archives, Washington, D.C. Wisconsin information from *Catalogue of Collection of Photographs of North American Indians by Edward S. Curtis Exhibited in the Museum of the State Historical Society of Wisconsin at Madison July–August 1908*, an illustrated brochure in the Milwaukee Public Museum Reference Library, supplied in photocopy form by courtesy of the U of Washington Libraries; Francis W. Grant (for Curtis) to Thwaites, February 22 and Thwaites to Grant, February 28, 1907, Archives and Manuscripts, State Historical Society of Wisconsin, Madison. American Museum information in Curtis to Osborn, February 24, 1912, AMNH, and in an invitation to an exhibition there, February 1–16, 1916, with Curtis to Hodge, January 11, 1916. San Diego information in Curtis to Hewett, July 9, 1913, Edgar L. Hewett Papers, Fray Angelico Chavez History Library, Museum of New Mexico. New Mexico information from Ledger of Minutes of the New Mexico State Historical Society for August 1914, Museum of New Mexico.

29. Grinnell's *Scribner's* article, "Portraits of Indian Types," is cited in Ch. 2, n. 39. Grinnell to Hodge, April 24, 1908; "Wonderful Indian Pictures," *Forest and Stream,* 70 (April 1908), 652; Curtis to Hodge, April 20, 1908. Curtis to Gordon, April 20 and May 13, 1908, Philadelphia; G.B. Gordon, Review of *NAI,* Vols.1 and 2, *American Anthropologist,* 10 (July–September 1908), 435–41; Curtis to Pinchot, November 28, 1908; Curtis to Walcott, December 7, 1908, Smithsonian; Curtis to Huntington, December 4, 1908, Huntington.

30. Curtis to Hodge, April 3, 1909. McGee to Curtis, May 1, 1906, Letter book, Miscellaneous no. 2, March 31, 1906– , 90, McGee Papers, LC. Curtis to Hodge, October 9, 1909 and July 21, 1910 (in which he mentions also prodding McGee); W. J. McGee, Review of *NAI,* vol. 5, *American Anthropologist,* 12 (July–September 1910), 448–50.

31. Information on Hodge and ten Kate from correspondence in Hodge; Curtis to Hodge, April 3, 1909. Other aspects covered in Curtis to Hodge, with ten Kate's letter (dated November 1, 1909), November 13, 1909; ten Kate to Hodge, November 7, 1909; Curtis to Hodge, January 23, 1910; ten Kate, "A Translation of Report of the Royal Netherlands Geological Society," Second Series, vol. 27, 1910, Pt. I, in *NAI: Extracts,* cited in n. 18 above and, under the same title, as a brochure, n.d. [1910], n. [12], Hodge.

32. Curtis to Hodge (with enclosure), June 7, 1911. Curtis to Hawthorne, May 22, 1911, Hawthorne Family Papers, BANC MSS 72/236z, Bancroft. A copy of the Hawthorne publicity brochure is in SB.

33. For Roosevelt, see Roosevelt to Curtis, February 3, 1909, and Curtis to Roosevelt, November 16, 1911. For *World's Work,* see Curtis to Meany (enclosing Walter Hines Page to Curtis of October 28), November 5, 1907, and January 11, 1908, and *World's Work* to Meany, March 8, 1908; Meany, "Hunting Indians with a Camera" appeared in the magazine in vol. 15 (March 1908), 10004–11. For Ankeny, see Ankeny to Meany, March 23, 1908, and Curtis to Meany, April 6, 1908. For Hubbell, see Curtis to Hubbell, May 10, 20, and 30, October 18, and November 4, 1912, May 5, 1913, and October 12, 1914, Hubbell Papers, U of Arizona, Tucson.

34. Curtis to Stevenson, May 5, 1907, Stevenson Papers, NAA. Curtis to Wissler, March 3, 1909, AMNH; Curtis to Osborn, May 11, 1913, Osborn File, Library, American Museum of Natural History.

35. Curtis to Hodge, December 1, 1907. Curtis to Hodge, December 17, 1907; Ayer to Hodge, January 17, 1918, and other letters between 1918 and 1920, especially November 20, 1920.

36. Curtis to Osborn, February 4, and carbon of Osborn to Curtis, February 6, 1911, Osborn File, Library, American Museum of Natural History.

37. For accounts of anthropological dispute, see Joan Mark, *Four Anthropologists: An American Science in Its Early Years* (New York: Science History Publications, 1980); Neil M. Judd, *The Bureau of American Ethnology: A Partial History* (Norman: U of Oklahoma P, 1967); George W. Stocking, *Race, Culture and Evolution: Essays in the History of Anthropology* (New York: Free P, 1968), especially 270–307; and Stocking, ed., *The Shaping of American Anthropology, 1883–1911: A Franz Boas Reader* (New York: Basic Books, 1974), especially Pt. 9, "The Propagation of Anthropology." In several places it has been reported that Curtis claimed that in 1907 Roosevelt received a complaint from Boas about Curtis's lack of training and the inadequacy of the project's fieldwork. In response, Roosevelt set up a commission consisting of Henry Fairfield Osborn, Charles D. Walcott, and William H. Holmes to investigate. After examining the evidence, including a trunk of reference books and the field notebooks kept by Myers, the tribunal, to Roosevelt's obvious delight, exonerated Cur-

tis (see, for example, Graybill and Boesen, 28–30 and Goetzmann, *The First Americans*, 22). However, after exhaustive searches, there is no record of any correspondence relating to such an issue, in 1907 or any other time, in the surviving papers of *any* of the alleged participants, Roosevelt, Boas, Osborn, Walcott, or Holmes. For two particular complaints about Boas, see Curtis to Hodge, December 27, 1909, and Curtis to Meany, April 12, 1911. For an elaboration of the allegations involved, see Gidley, "Footnotes to an Anthropological Quarrel" (forthcoming).

38. Curtis to Hodge, December 26, 1907, February 3, 1914, and, also, February 6, 1914.

39. Typescript of report in PML. For quotations from Carnegie and further commentary on the nature and discourse of Carnegie and other relevant robber barons, see Trachtenberg (Intro., n. 12), 78–86.

40. Parts of this report, with slightly different wording, appeared as the "General Introduction" to the first volume of *NAI*. Its sentiments had entered into general circulation; for example, Hartmann quoted several sentences verbatim in the piece cited in Ch. 2, n. 42.

Chapter 5

1. Curtis to Hodge, December 17, 1907. For the 1911 draft, see Doc. 4A.

2. Curtis, handwritten and typescript reminiscences included with letters to Harriet Leitch, SPL; also quoted fully by Andrews, 44, and Graybill and Boesen, 29–30. On the complaint, see Ch. 4, n. 37 here.

3. *NAI*, vol. 18 (1928), xii.

4. Extract from President's Report to the North American Indian, January 1913, enclosed with Curtis to Belle de Costa Greene, April 6, 1914, PML; also reproduced in Ewing, cited in Ch. 4, n. 10.

5. Corinne Gilb, Transcript of "Frederick Webb Hodge, Ethnologist," cited in Ch. 1, n. 13, 104.

6. Family and Springfield information kindly supplied by Janet McCrosky of the Springfield Library Friends Genealogical Research Group in a series of documented letters to the author during May–July 1977.

7. Information from copies of Myers's educational records kindly supplied by Patrick M. Quinn, University Archivist, Northwestern.

8. A typical request for general access is Curtis to Leupp, June 17, 1905, and similar correspondence seeking access on behalf of Myers to Arizona and New Mexico appears in Curtis to the Commissioner, August 16 and September 13, 1911, Commissioner. Myers to Newcombe, April 15, 1913, Newcombe.

9. Handwritten letter in Schwinke Collection, now located at the Burke Museum, U of Washington. On Kwakiutl theatricals, see Holm and Quimby, especially 102.

10. Myers to Gifford, September 6, 1915, U of California, Berkeley, Department of Anthropology Records, CU–23, Bancroft.

11. Myers to Hodge, January 25, 1910; Myers to Hodge, August 13, 1915, enclosed with Hodge to Pliny Earl Goddard, Hodge File, AMNH; Graybill and Boesen, 30.

12. Myers to Hodge, March 10, 1910. Myers to Newcombe, November 10, 1913, Newcombe. Myers's conclusions about the "cannibal feast" are indeed outlined in *NAI*, vol. 10 (1915), 221–42, including the finding that it was most likely achieved theatrically rather than actually practiced.

13. Curtis to Hodge, January 27, 1914. Myers to Kroeber, March 6, 1919, Department of Anthropology Records, CU–23, Bancroft.

14. Myers to Kroeber, March 8, 1919. In *NAI*, vol. 13 (1924), Myers gave due credit to each of these authorities (see 38 and 68).

15. Two letters, Kroeber to Myers, March 13, 1919.

16. Kroeber to Myers, March 18,

1919. See, for example, *NAI*, vol. 13, 263–72, for Yurok-Wiyot vocabularies. See Myers to Kroeber, July 26, 1919, and Kroeber to Myers, August 16, 1932. One of Kroeber's graduate students remembers him talking respectfully of Myers, especially his work on the Kwakiutl, and speculating upon his whereabouts; personal communication, Bernard G. Hoffman to the author, June 16, 1984.

17. Curtis to Hodge, June 26, 1907. Myers to Hodge, January 14, 1908; an account of Hu ^{n}Kálowa^{n} pi appears in *NAI*, vol. 3 (1908), 71–87. See also Myers to Hodge, October 30, 1908. See, for example, issues raised in letters from Myers to Hodge of November 17, 21, 22, 25, and 28, 1908. All in Hodge.

18. Curtis to Hodge, September 18, 1908. Myers to Hodge, December 7, 1908. Both Hodge. The article Myers read for Hodge was probably G. H. Pepper and G. L. Wilson, "An Hidatsa Shrine and the Beliefs Respecting it," which appeared in the *Memoirs* of the American Anthropological Association for 1908, 273–328.

19. Myers to Hodge, December 2, 1908. There is a large collection of field material for *NAI* in the LACMNH. When I was able to view it, in August 1978 and 1980, it was uncatalogued and somewhat disorderly, but there was no doubting its importance. The "green" hands referred to by Myers were Edwin J. Dalby and, probably, Edmond S. Meany.

20. Myers to Hodge, December 30, 1913. Unfortunately, there are gaps in the Myers–Hodge correspondence, and a particularly long one between 1908 and 1913, so it is difficult to tell precisely when Myers became the principal author, but it seems to have occurred very early on. (As it happened, Hodge also found it impossible to acquire *olivella biplicata* shells.)

21. Intro., *NAI*, vol. 10 (1915), xii. The surviving field and manuscript material for this volume also, of course, bears out Myers's authorial role.

22. Myers to Hodge, July 4, 1914; Myers to Hodge, August 13, 1915, enclosed with Hodge to Pliny Earle Goddard, August 24, 1915, AMNH; and Myers to Hodge, August 5, 1919.

23. Myers to Hodge, June 28 and September 10, 1923, and March 22 and September 7, 1924. Again the surviving field materials, including a folder on the snake cult, attest to Myers's activity in this area. The "show" was the celebrated annual frontier days of Gallup, New Mexico. The relevant volume of *NAI*, vol. 16, while containing many references to historical documents, especially Spanish ones, did not in fact cite much previous ethnological work. The relative proportions of the treatment of Keresan pueblos in vol. 16 did roughly follow this breakdown, though in the 1924 census figures given on page 259, Picuries, with 105 residents, was by no means the smallest pueblo.

24. Myers to Hodge, September 21 and December 12, 1924; and several other letters in Hodge not quoted.

25. Myers to Hodge, August 8, 1925; see also Myers to Hodge, August 18, November 1 and 17, December 6 and 17, 1925. Note on separate publication of "phallic dope" is in a letter to Hodge of December 24, 1925, but publication does not appear to have happened (see also Ch. 9). For new plans, see Myers to Hodge, January 7, 1926.

26. Myers to Hodge, August 9, 1925.

27. Myers to Hodge, November 1, 1925. It has not proved possible to discover the identity of this spectacular wellspring of information; it is conceivable that it was not a person, but the journals of Samuel Hearne, published as *A Journey from Prince of Wales's Fort in Hudson's Bay to the Northern Ocean in the Years 1769, 1770, 1771 and 1772* (1911), a work quoted innumerable times in vol. 18 because its author, according to *NAI*, vol. 17 (1927), "more than any other traveler in the far north . . . was interested in human beings rather than trade" (7).

28. Myers to Hodge, February 9, 1926; Hodge to Myers, February 15, 1926.

29. Hodge to Myers, February 15,

1926. For Myers's withdrawal, see Curtis to Hodge, April 9, 1926, and Myers to Hodge, April 25, 1926. For alternative plans, see Curtis to Hodge, April 9, and Hodge's reply, April 15, 1926. Myers to Hodge, April 15, 1926. Myers to Hodge, April 25, 1926. Finally, see Myers to Hodge, n.d. but received May 28, 1927.

30. Information from issues of Seattle *City Directory* and various files of correspondence. Letter quoted is Myers to Hodge, January 7, 1926.

31. Information from scattered comments in Myers's own letters, personal communication to the author from Bernard G. Hoffman of March 17, 1985, and Myers to Henry F. Gilbert, May 14, 1912. Other information from San Francisco *City Directory*, addresses on Myers's letters, and in a helpful communication to the author from Wallace Wortman, Director of Property, San Francisco Real Estate Department, February 25, 1977.

32. Myers to Hodge, November 1, 1925. Myers to Curtis, n.d. but transcribed in a letter from Curtis to Hodge, April 9, 1926.

33. Information gleaned from the San Francisco *City Directory* and San Francisco telephone directories, the *Sonoma County Directory*, the *Petaluma City Directory*, Myers's death certificate issued by the State of California Bureau of Vital Statistics, Sacramento, and obituaries kindly obtained for me by Dennis Anderson from the Santa Rosa *Press Democrat* of May 1, 1949, 10A, cols. 3 and 6. Unfortunately, I was not able to trace other items which might have yielded further information, such as a marriage or death certificate for Eveline Myers, and Myers's closest surviving relative, a niece, twice refused to see me. It is possible that someone who had himself listed as an "author" in a city directory continued to write, but I have failed to locate any materials published under his own name. Meticulous person that he was, it is almost inconceivable that Myers left *no* record of his writing.

34. Information on Eastwood gleaned from Eastwood's correspondence with Hodge in Hodge (the repository for each Eastwood letter quoted hereafter), and Frances Watkins, as cited in Ch. 3, n. 4.

35. See *NAI*, vol. 19 (1930), 112–28.

36. See *NAI*, vol. 19, 35–104, especially 72–4. See *NAI*, vol. 19, 197–220 for "The Peyote Cult, the 'Stomp' Dance, and the Forty-nine Dance"; this is partially reprinted in Gidley, ed., *The Vanishing Race*, 71–6. For peyotism, see Weston La Barre, *The Peyote Cult* (Norman: U of Oklahoma P, 5th ed., 1989), especially 151–61 on Wilson.

37. See *NAI*, vol. 19, 181–8 (reprinted in Gidley, ed., *The Vanishing Race*, 21–9) and 35 and 36.

38. Eastwood to Hodge, April 16, 1927. Hodge to Eastwood, May 1, 1927, and, for evidence of rewriting, Eastwood to Hodge, December 31, 1927. Also, Curtis to Hodge, December 7, 1927.

39. Information on Haddon (1855–1940) found in Haddon, especially his unpublished "The Morning Star Ceremony of the Pawnee," and A. H. Quiggan, *Haddon the Headhunter* (Cambridge: Cambridge UP, 1942). See Haddon's presidential address to the Royal Anthropological Institute, "What the United States of America is Doing for Anthropology," *Journal of the Anthropological Institute*, 32 (January–June 1902), 8–24. On Haddon at the AYPE, see Robert W. Rydell, *All the World's a Fair: Visions of Empire at American International Expositions, 1876–1916* (Chicago: U of Chicago P, 1984), 199.

40. See Curtis to Hodge, November 16 and 18, 1908. From Osborn to Haddon, April 11, 1893, Haddon, it is clear the two had known each other well for some time. Data on Dalby from: Curtis to Meany, July 31, 1908, and Dalby to Meany, August 5, 1908, both Meany; an interview with Dalby's son, Fritz Dalby, in August 1978; Dalby Family Papers, especially Meany to Dalby, August 13, 1908; Costello's "Scrapbook of the Seattle Press Club," vol. 23, 36, Seattle Public Library; and "Ed Dalby Will Gather

Material for Curtis," *Pacific Wave,* 16, no. 59 (January 8, 1909), 1, col. 3. Curtis later remembered Dalby much less charitably; he told Harriet Leitch that when his assistant had complained of mosquitoes he had said, "If you can't stand the mosquitoes it won't take you but two days to walk out to the railroad" (SPL). Dalby's subsequent fieldwork was among the Coastal Salish peoples of Washington and British Columbia. Thereafter he served as the Seattle *Post-Intelligencer's* waterfront correspondent for almost three decades.

41. Curtis to Haddon, November 2 and December 23, 1909, Haddon. Curtis to Dalby, n.d., Dalby Family Papers. Haddon to Wissler, November 17, and Wissler to Haddon, December 2, 1908, AMNH.

42. See Emilie de Brigard, "The History of Ethnographic Film," a paper prepared for the Ninth International Congress of Anthropological and Ethnological Sciences, Chicago, 1973, 4–5. Haddon's affection for photography was such that for his eightieth birthday in 1935 some 10,000 photographs, many of which he had collected or taken himself, were deposited in the Haddon Library of the Cambridge U Museum. The letter advocating Rivers's system, undated, is in the Dalby Family Papers. Clipping, unidentified, July 17, 1909, Envelope 14, Haddon; Curtis to Hodge, July 13, 1909, indicated that Haddon was to be with him from July 20 to September 5; also, Dalby confirmed part of this arrangement, Dalby to Haddon, July 12, 1909, Haddon. Haddon's Kutenai assistance was acknowledged in the Intro. to *NAI,* vol. 7 (1911). "Indian Ethnological Expert Begins to Study Blackfeet," *Christian Science Monitor,* September 2, 1909; quoted fully in *NAI: Extracts* (Ch. 4, n. 18).

43. For evidence of later contact, see, for example, Curtis to Haddon, October 8, 1914, Haddon. Haddon, reviews of McClintock, *The Old North Trail, Folklore,* 22 (1911), 126–8, and *Nature,* 86 (1911), 83–4; "The Soul of the Red Man," *Rational Press Association Annual* (London: Rationalist P, 1914), 39–43. Haddon's memoir, reproduced from a typescript in Haddon, appears with further contextualization in Gidley, "A. C. Haddon Joins Edward S. Curtis. . . . " (see Intro., n. 11). Much material directly parallel to Haddon's observations appeared in the Piegan section of vol. 6 of *NAI.*

44. This note appears as a typescript with Myers to Kroeber, March 6, 1919.

45. See *NAI,* vol. 14 (1924), 140–1, and Kroeber to Myers, March 13, 1919. The key paper by E. W. Gifford was "Miwok Moieties," *University of California Publications in American Archaeology and Ethnology,* 12 (1916), 139–94. For Levi-Strauss, see *The Elementary Structure of Kinship,* rev. ed., trans. James H. Bell, R. J. von Sturmer, and Rodney Needham (London: Eyre and Spottiswoode, 1969), especially Ch. 22. For another interesting airing of the difficulties of such issues, see Sol Tax, "Some Problems of Social Organization," in Fred Eggan, ed., *Social Anthropology of North American Tribes,* enlarged ed. (Chicago and London: U of Chicago P, 1955), 3–32.

46. Myers to Hodge, June 21, 1924. Lowie's work was "Notes on Shoshonean Ethnography," *American Museum of Natural History Anthropology Papers,* 20 (1924), 185–314. For further material on *NAI* and the Pueblo tribes, see Chs. 6 and 9.

47. Eastwood to Hodge, August 1, 1927. *NAI,* vol. 20 (1930), also mentions Ivanoff, but only as an informer for the book's map of Inuit dialects (3). The "bone-hunters" were Henry B. Collins and T. Dale Stewart, Smithsonian employees on a collecting expedition; for information from Collins's point of view, see the extended review by Joanne Cohan Scherer of Lyman's *The Vanishing Race and Other Illusions* in *Studies in Visual Communication,* 11 (Summer 1985), 78–85. Alleged Inuit filthiness is discussed in Ch. 9 here.

48. Eastwood to Hodge, November 21, 1929; Hodge to U.S. Navy, July 24, 1942.

Chapter 6

1. Quoted in the transcript of the Odyssey television program devoted to Boas (Boston: Public Broadcasting Associates, 1980), 8.

2. The letter is Curtis to Pinchot, November 15, 1910. The identity of Crump is unknown. For Charles M. Strong, see "Instructor Leaves About February 8," *Pacific Wave*, 16, no. 67 (January 22, 1909), 4, col. 2; Strong was also credited for his Southwestern work in the introduction to the relevant volumes of *NAI*. Unfortunately, it was not possible to trace his papers, though some notes by him survive among the manuscripts of *NAI*, LACMNH. The other figures feature elsewhere here.

3. Curtis to Leitch, December 29, 1950, SPL. The other incidents feature in Chs. 2 and 4 here. Other parts of the 1907 speech appear here as Doc. 2C.

4. "Lives 22 Years with Indians to Get their Secrets," a *New York Times* story of April 16, 1911, reprinted in *The North American Indian* publicity brochure, author's collection. H. P. Curtis, in an untitled typescript in Kernberger which is reprinted as part of Gidley, "Into Apache Lands . . . ," cited in Intro., n. 11. Summaries of Beth Magnuson and Florence Graybill writings were made from photocopies of them provided by Florence.

5. F. C. Graybill, in an undated typescript produced for the use of her coauthor Boesen in the production of their writing on Curtis. It was probably written in the later forties as part of the family effort to encourage Curtis in the composition of his autobiography; other brief extracts from the full memoir were published in Andrew's *Curtis' Western Indians* and, of course, in the two Graybill and Boesen books.

6. Quotations from Phillips, "The Gods Forbid," a further "chapter" of his reminiscences, c. 1911, private collection.

7. For the rhetoric of the travelers' tale and related matters, see Pratt, *Imperial Eyes* (Ch. 3, n. 28). Apache story told in an untitled typescript by Curtis in LACMNH; it, and variations upon it, were probably composed for the 1911 musicale tour. Compare *NAI*, vol. 1 (1907), 23–42.

8. "Did You Ever Try to Photograph an Indian?," *Sunday Call*, October 14, 1900, Clipping, Southwest Museum, Los Angeles. For corroboration of early Blackfeet experiences, see Gertrude Metcalfe, "The Indian as Revealed in the Curtis Pictures," *Lewis and Clark Journal* [the journal of the Lewis and Clark Exposition, Portland, Oregon, 1904–5], 1, no. 5, 13–19. For the family view, together with a reminiscence of the sun dance by Curtis many years later, see Andrews, 23–4, 114–15. For the long, illustrated account of the Piegan sun dance, see *NAI*, vol. 6 (1911), 31–58, in which Small Leggins went totally unmentioned. Other information from "Sacred Rites of the Mokis and Navajoes," *Seattle Times*, Magazine Section, November 27, 1904, Curtis Biography file, NW. For Albert Waters incident, see Gidley, *Kopet*, 76.

9. The musicale script referred to here is in Kernberger (see Ch. 7, n. 36). Newspaper item is "Will Study Indians of Pacific Coast," *Province*, April 22, 1910, 1, col. 2.

10. See Murray (Intro., n. 7), both in general and for this quotation (134–5).

11. Pomeroy, *In Search of the Golden West: The Tourist in Western America* (New York: Knopf, 1957), 89. The other quotation is from Peter Bacon Hales, *William Henry Jackson and the Transformation of the American Landscape* (Philadelphia: Temple UP, 1988), 266. The ultimate in commodification is the analogy between the collection of artifacts for the museum and the display of objects in the department store. Indeed, we have noted that Curtis exhibited his pictures in both venues. For a discussion of the cultural work of "objects," see Leah Dilworth's essay-review of two exhibitions, "Object

Lessons," *American Quarterly*, 45 (June 1993), 257–80.

12. See Marta Weigle, "Southwest Lures: Innocents Detoured, Incensed, Determined," *Journal of the Southwest*, 32 (Winter 1990), 499–540, and "Exposition and Mediation: Mary Colter, Erna Fergusson, and the Santa Fe/Harvey Popularization of the Native Southwest, 1902–1940," *Frontiers*, vol. 12, no. 3 (1992), 116–50. The same orientalist point could be made about some of Curtis's Apache and Navajo pictures, for example, "Many Goats' Son" (1904); the trope of pastoral desert Indian peoples as surrogate Arabs had started much earlier, in the nineteenth century. The Curtis quotation is from "Indians of the Stone Houses," *Scribner's*, 45 (February 1909), 161–75.

13. Pratt, *op. cit.* Curtis, "Travelling the Route of Lewis and Clark – One Hundred Years Later," an undated typescript of a Curtis memoir produced by Graybill for the use of Boesen, the co-author of *Visions of a Vanishing Race*, in which a revised version was published (see 57–8).

14. Limerick, *The Legacy of Conquest: The Unbroken Past of the American West* (New York and London: W. W. Norton, 1987), 19. Although Curtis goes unmentioned, the arguments of the book as a whole are relevant to his particular case.

15. Curtis to Meany, both October 22, 1907.

16. Curtis to Pinchot, May 9, 1908; Mrs. Custer to Pinchot, April 19, 1908. Interestingly, Curtis referred to the *Herald* piece as a "so-called interview."

17. Curtis to Meany, January 17 and August 28, 1908. Curtis to Pinchot, November 28, and Pinchot to Curtis, December 2, 1908. See also *NAI*, vol. 3 (1908), 44–50.

18. Information on Phillips from an interview with his son, Wellington S. Phillips in August 1978, corroborated by data in the Seattle *City Directory* and U of Washington records. The extract is taken from a typescript in a private collection.

19. Sojero went unmentioned in vol. 17 (1926), the Tewa volume of *NAI*.

20. This is probably the same shrine as that briefly described in *NAI*, vol. 17, 11–12, though none of the plates Phillips said he made were used.

21. Curtis also told of the belief that dogs were sometimes inhabited by the spirits of humans, and could thus act as "spies," in his short piece "Inherited or Family Names for Dogs," *The Animal News*, 1, no. 3 (May 1912), 2.

22. This Curtis memoir is cited in n. 12 above.

23. Information on Schwinke from a clipping of his obituary in a local Oak Hill newspaper, which was supplied by Mrs. Walter Davis of the Oak Hill Public Library soon after his death in 1977. Information on Martineau taken from *An Illustrated History of Klikitat, Yakima and Kittitas Counties* (1904), 477. Schwinke's *aide memoire* transcribed in 1977 from index cards in the possession of Schwinke's widow, Oak Hill, Ohio.

24. *NAI*, vol. 8 (1911), xii. The Chinookan material, devoted almost entirely to the Wishham, appears as 85–107, followed by a collection of myths, with the register of village sites on 180–3.

25. Curtis to Meany, August 30, 1922.

26. Curtis to Meany, October 8, 1922. On white treatment of California Indians, see the very similar sentiments expressed in the preface to vol. 13 of *NAI*, xi–xii; reprinted in Gidley, ed., *The Vanishing Race*, 59.

Chapter 7

1. Curtis to Meany, November 19, 1911.

2. In his letter to Roosevelt, Curtis said, "It was a success beyond my greatest expectations," November 16, 1911; also Curtis to Pinchot, November 16, 1911. There were similar letters to Hodge, November 19, 1911, and, for example, to Bowditch, November 19, 1911, SB. Roosevelt's response in Roosevelt to Curtis, November 21, 1911.

3. For a detailed account of Catlin's

venture, with which Curtis's enterprise had much in common, see William H. Truettner's *The Natural Man Observed: A Study of Catlin's Indian Gallery* (Washington, D.C.: Smithsonian Institution P, 1979); Don Russell's *The Wild West* (Fort Worth, Tex.: Amon Carter Museum, 1970) treats popular wild-west shows.

4. Contemporary sources of information about Curtis's public appearances include "Convention Aftermath," *Camera Craft*, 1, no. 5 (September 1900), 269; "Will Lecture On His Work," clipping from *Seattle Times*, November 20, 1904, and "Ed Curtis Back from Gotham," undocumented clipping of May 5, 1906, in the Washington-Biography file, NW; Curtis letters to Pinchot of December 30, 1904, and January 21, 1906, spoke of his engagements at the Cosmos and Century Clubs; and an advertisement for talks at the Waldorf-Astoria in 1905, NW. In a letter from Curtis to Gordon of the U of Pennsylvania Museum, September 5, 1906, he gave his fees as $100 for a slide lecture and $125 when motion pictures were included (Philadelphia). Curtis to Burke, January 1, 1906, Thomas Burke Papers, UW.

5. Grosvenor to Gilder, February 18, 1905, Library, National Geographic Society, Washington, D.C. Interview comments from "Ed. Curtis: Explorer, Clubman, Photographer, Historian, and President's Friend," clipping from the *Seattle Sunday Times*, May 21, 1905, in Washington Biography File, NW. Examples of such speeches include Doc. 2C.

6. Curtis to Hodge, June 7, 1911, and Curtis to Walcott, October 9, 1911, Smithsonian.

7. See Curtis to Gordon, November 19, 1911; Charles Rice to Gordon, December 16, 1911, January 6 and 20, 1912; Curtis to Gordon; January 3, 1912, and Gordon to Curtis, two letters, December 23, 1911, Letter Book 8, 52 and 53, all Philadelphia. For slightly more elaborate comments on both the "absolute" necessity of publicity, but the need for it to be "dignified," see Curtis to Hodge, October 1, 1911. Curtis to Mrs. E. W. Scherr, October 31, 1911, Copley Library, La Jolla, Calif. Mrs. Scherr, the wife of a prominent financier and patent attorney, Emilius W. Scherr, was better known by her maiden name, Amy Lay Hull, for her stage recreations of historical figures, such as Dolly Madison; see her obituary, *New York Times*, February 14, 1959, 21, col. 2. The musicale leaflet was enclosed with Curtis to Clarence B. Bagley, September 23, 1911, Bagley Papers, UW. Bagley, who was an avid amateur historian of the Northwest and a Seattle city government official, also acted as a local patron for a tour in the succeeding year, for which he received publicity material from Seattle agent Paul Hedrick (see Hedrick to Bagley, September 26 and October 11, 1912).

8. Roosevelt to Curtis, February 7, 1905. Natalie Curtis became the compiler-author of *The Indians' Book* (1907), an influential rendition of Indian songs, myths, and stories. Some of the field recordings for *NAI* survive in the holdings of the Archives of Traditional Music at the U of Indiana, Bloomington; see Dorothy Sara Lee, *Native North American Music and Oral Data: A Catalogue of Sound Recordings, 1893–1976* (Bloomington and London: Indiana UP, 1979), 55–8.

9. Biographical accounts of Gilbert (1868–1928) appear in Katherine M. E. Longyear's unpublished thesis, "Henry F. Gilbert, His Life and Works," Eastman School of Music, Rochester, 1968, and in her entry on Gilbert in Stanley Sadie, ed., *The New Grove Dictionary of Music and Musicians* (London: Macmillan, 1980), vol. 8, 372–3; *NAI*, vol. 6 (1911), 165–6. Myers was certainly conscious of the popularity and worth of the *Pirate Song*; in a letter to Gilbert he wrote: "Mrs. Myers joins me in best wishes to Mrs. Gilbert and yourself. Last fall in a little New Mexico town we happened into a general store and heard [a record of David] Bispham singing the "Pirate Song," and thereafter we made it a daily practice to have business there so long as we were in

the town. It's a fine thing" (Myers to Gilbert, May 14, 1912). Information on composition from Curtis to Gilbert, July 26, 1911; also further letter of July 26 and ones of August 7 and 12, 1911.

10. Curtis to Gilbert, August 7, 1911.

11. Gilbert, "A Chapter of Reminiscence," Pt. 2, *The New Music Review,* 20 (1921), 91. Myers to Gilbert, September 22 and October 7, 1910, May 14, July 11, August 26, and November 26, 1912; and Curtis to Gilbert, February 17, 1914.

12. Curtis to Gilbert, July 26, 1911; also, Curtis to Gilbert, August 25 and September 7, 1911.

13. Rice to Gilbert, August 24, 1911; also Rice to Gilbert, August 31 and September 14, 1911, and Curtis to Gilbert, August 18 and October 2, 1911, all Gilbert.

14. See the second half of Curtis's exuberant letter to Meany of November 19, 1911, in which he described the "seventeen kinds of hell" through which he had traveled to success at Carnegie Hall; also, Curtis to Hodge, January 6, 1912. Gilbert, "A Chapter of Reminiscence," 91.

15. Curtis to Gilbert, February 5, 1912; and December 30, 1911; Schwinke to Gilbert, March 2, 1912.

16. Curtis to Gilbert, February 5, 1912, and Curtis to Hodge, January 6, 1912. The note "Mr. Edward S. Curtis's 'Picture-Opera'" in the *Bulletin of the Archaeological Institute of America,* 3, no. 3 (June 1912), 188, constituted an endorsement of the musicale.

17. *E. S. Curtis and His Indian Picture-Opera "A Vanishing Race" Achieve Triumph,* a simulated newspaper brochure produced to advertise the 1912–13 tour, author's collection. Unless otherwise indicated, all of the quotations and much of the information on the reception of the musicale is taken from it; subsequent citations, for quotations only, are to the original newspaper source as given in the brochure (though not all of these could be checked).

18. Price, *The Minneapolis Bellman,* January 27, 1912.

19. Curtis to Gilbert, February 5, 1912.

20. Curtis to Gilbert, June 4, 1913; also letters by F. T. Hammond to Gilbert, July 16, August 8, October 15 and 22, November 7 and 13 (with enclosures), 1913, all Gilbert. *May Columbia Records,* 1913; I am grateful to Paul Wells for finding this for me. By 1915, the *U.S. Columbia Record Catalog* did list the same disk as Gilbert's *Dream of the Ancient Red Man*; it was noted as incidental music to Curtis's "The Vanishing Race" illustrated lecture and consisted of "Dream of the Ancient Red Man" together with "Signal Fire to the Mountain God" and "Song of the Wolf" played by [?] Prince's Orchestra.

21. Curtis to Gordon, January 16, 1912, Philadelphia. Curtis to Wissler, December 4, 1911, AMNH.

22. On December 2, 1912, Curtis gave an "ordinary" illustrated lecture to a full house at the Metropolitan Theater, and this served as an appetizer for the more expensive showings of the musicale itself on December 6 and 7; see "Indian Historian Receives Ovation," clipping in the Washington Biography File, NW. The same file includes a full program of the Metropolitan version. Curtis to Hodge, January 6 and 14 (together with enclosure to Francis W. Kelsey), and March 28, 1912. Details of financial provision given in "Memorandum of Agreement" dated December 16, 1911, between Curtis and the U Museum, Philadelphia (Philadelphia).

23. *New York Evening World,* November 16, 1911. Charles E. Banks, "Primitive Glory of Indian Shown," undocumented newspaper clipping in Washington-Biography file, NW. *Washington Star,* Wednesday, January 31, 1912; *New York Evening Post,* Thursday, November 16, 1911; "Peeps Into Inner Life of the Indian," *Baltimore Star,* January 13, 1912; *Times-Dispatch,* February 1, 1912.

24. "Picture-Opera is Given at Belasco," *Washington Herald,* Wednesday, January 31, 1912; "Belasco Audience Sees Indian Life in Picture-Opera," *Washington*

Times, Wednesday, January 31, 1912. *New York Evening Telegram*, Monday, November 17, 1911; Price, as cited in n. 18 above.

25. Curtis to Gilbert, April 25, and Myers to Gilbert, May 14, 1912.

26. Myers to Gilbert, November 26, 1912, and January 4, 1913; Curtis to Gilbert, February 17 and 26, 1914. Unfortunately, no notes on the music by Gilbert appeared in the published volume, though most of the transcriptions were his.

27. Gilbert, "Program Notes [Indian Sketches]," *Boston Symphony Orchestra Programs 1912–21*, ed. P. Hale (Boston, 1921), 1074.

28. Gilbert, *Indian Scenes* (New York: H. W. Gray, 1912). In this publication each piece was preceded by the appropriate Curtis picture – though two, "In the Kutenai Country" and "On the Jocko," were mistakenly substituted for one another, a matter upon which Curtis vented his irritation in a letter to Gilbert of April 25, 1912. For Curtis's blessings on this venture, see also his letters to Gilbert, December 23 and 30, 1911, and February 12, 1912.

29. Curtis to Gilbert, October 3 and 28, and November 22, 1912.

30. See Gilbert, "Program Notes," cited above, 1072–7. Farwell's review was reprinted in the simulated newspaper cited in n. 17. Myers, who certainly knew Indian music, called Gilbert's compositions "Indianesque music" in a letter to Gilbert, January 4, 1913. I am grateful to the late David Cawthra of Exeter U for playing *Indian Scenes* so that I could compare them with the field recordings.

31. An untitled essay of Farwell's which put the case for Indian music most trenchantly was printed as an introduction to a group of compositions published by the Press in September 1903; a reprint may be found in Brice Farwell, ed., *A Guide to the Music of Arthur Farwell and the Microfilm Collection of His Work* (Briarcliff Manor, N.Y.: Brice Farwell, 1972), 78–81. For a sensitive reading of this phase of American musical development, albeit with but few examples of Gilbert's own role in it, see Gilbert Chase, *America's Music* (New York: McGraw-Hill, rev. 2nd ed., 1966), especially the "The Americanists" chapter. An analogous career is that of Charles Wakefield Cadman who, in 1910, brought "Princess" Tsianine Redfeather, an Omaha with a trained soprano voice, to New York to sing "Indian melodies" in the context of his lecture recital advocating the importance of aboriginal sources, and who composed a piece called *To A Vanishing Race* (1925); see *The New Grove*, vol. 3, 593. The publicity leaflet was enclosed with Curtis to Walcott, October 9, 1911, Smithsonian. Austin, *The American Rhythm: Studies and Re-expressions of Amerindian Songs* (New York: Cooper Square, 1970) is a reprint of the enlarged edition of 1930; 41–3 of this book record some instances of the rise of appreciation of Indian cultural expression in early twentieth century America, a subject treated at length in Michael Castro's *Interpreting the Indian: Twentieth Century Poets and the Native American* (Albuquerque: U of New Mexico P, 1983). Curtis to Austin, n.d. [early March 1911], Austin.

32. See "The Vanishing Red Man . . . Discussed by Edward S. Curtis," with Edward Marshall (Ch. 1, n. 25); quotation from 250. If the title of a brief contemporary review that I have been unable to check is significant, it may have pressed this very point: Louise Llewellyn, "Indian Tunes and National Music," *Musical America*, 16 (February 3, 1912), 2. Interestingly, earlier in this period, Anton Dvorak, who had already exploited the folk music of his own native land, used Indian tunes (along with others) in *his* rendition of "America" in the *New World Symphony* (1892). For evidence of the MacDowell proposal, see Curtis to Gilbert, April 11, 1913.

33. Unfortunately, most of the slides that survive appear to be in inaccessible private collections; I am grateful to Thomas V. Lange, formerly of the PML,

for showing me the PML's collection of uncatalogued slides.

34. *New York Evening Sun*, Thursday, November 16, 1911.

35. Reproduced from a brochure in the NW.

36. This script, like the other documents which follow, is in Kernberger.

37. These program notes were undated and may have been produced for either the 1911 or the 1912 tours.

Chapter 8

1. Lindsay, *The Art of the Moving Picture*, rev. ed. 1922 (reissued, New York: Liveright, 1970), 114. Why the film fell into obscurity is unclear. It was rescued largely through the efforts of George Quimby, who came across a print at the Field Museum, Chicago, in the forties, and Bill Holm, the scholar of Northwest Coast art and culture. Prints of the modern version, edited by Holm and Quimby, as *In the Land of the War Canoes* (1973), are available from the U of Washington P. Holm and Quimby continued their work in a book frequently cited above, *Edward S. Curtis in the Land of the War Canoes* (1980). This book makes a number of valuable contributions. It gives a detailed account of how the film was discovered and edited, with annotations on all changes made. Second, by using a series of photographs I traced, it offers a reconstruction of the process by which the original film was made; one of these photographs, by Edmund A. Schwinke, is reproduced here (fig. 16). Third, it provides a profound assessment of the relationship of the Kwakiutl to the film process. Finally, it gives useful information on Curtis and other participants in the project. The present chapter, therefore, concentrates on matters not addressed by Holm and Quimby. Quimby has subsequently advanced the proposition that it was World War I which caused the movie's demise; see "The Mystery of the First Documentary Film," *Pacific Northwest Quarterly*, 81 (April 1990), 50–3. Another reason, and perhaps ultimately a more telling one, is that the film fitted the parameters of none of the emerging cinematic genres.

2. "New Color Photography in Film," *New York Times*, December 2, 1914. *Variety* review of December 25, 1914, reprinted in *Variety: Film Reviews 1907 –* (New York and London: Garland, 1983). Banks, "Curtis Film Tale Epic of Indians," unidentified clipping in Curtis Biography File, NW. Bush, "In the Land of the Head Hunters, Remarkable Motion Picture Produced by Edward S. Curtis, Famous Authority on North American Indians," *Motion Picture World*, 22 (1914), 1685; this review is fully reproduced in Holm and Quimby, 14.

3. Jay Ruby of Temple U transcribed entries from Frances Flaherty's diary to this effect; see Holm and Quimby, 30.

4. Edition of *The Song of Hiawatha* consulted was that edited by Daniel Aaron (London: Everyman, 1992). Curtis's book version, *In the Land of the Head-Hunters*, originally published by the World Book Co. of Yonkers, N.Y, was reissued in 1975 in camera-copy form by the Tamarack P; quotations from 66 and 53, respectively. Curtis knew *Hiawatha* in more than a popular sense; see, for example, his reference to it in Doc. 4A. Interestingly, however, in terms of characterization, his story echoed not so much Longfellow as James Fenimore Cooper's noble and ignoble savages.

5. For an eloquent discussion of the ideology of Griffith's film, see Michael Rogin, "'The Sword Became a Flashing Vision': D. W. Griffith's *The Birth of a Nation*," *Representations*, 9 (Winter 1985), 150–95.

6. Forrest, *The Snake Dance of the Hopi Indians* (Los Angeles: Westernlore P, 1961), 54–5. For the Morgan outline, see Doc. 1A; for the winter speech see Doc. 2C, which also includes data on the 1906 season, as does the 1913 report of the fieldwork reproduced in Ewing (Ch. 4, n. 10).

7. The *Portland Oregonian* item was

reprinted in *NAI: Extracts* (Ch. 4, n. 18). "Seattle Man's Triumph," *Seattle Times*, Magazine Section, May 22, 1904 and "Sacred Rites of the Mokis and Navajoes," *Seattle Times*, Magazine Section, November 27, 1904, both in Curtis Biography file, NW. Teri C. McLuhan's film *The Shadow Catcher: Edward S. Curtis and the North American Indian* (1975), which is available, for example, from Phoenix Films, New York, includes some of this very early footage, including parts of the Yebichai and Snake dance ceremonies. Katherine Bartlett of the Museum of Northern Arizona, Flagstaff, kindly informed me that she also thinks this was how Forrest's mistake arose; Forrest's photo records on deposit there contain no indication of a 1904 visit to Hopi land, but such do exist for 1906, though unfortunately there are no known Forrest pictures of Curtis at work.

8. The script and note from which these quotations were taken are in Kernberger; see also the documents in Ch. 7 here. Leland Rice's contribution to *Edward S. Curtis: The Kwakiutl 1910–1914*, the catalogue cited in Ch. 3, n. 14, dates relevant photographs as of 1910. Compare Holm and Quimby, 33, where the 1914 chronology of the final film version is established largely by reference to the Schwinke photographs.

9. Curtis to Hodge, March 28, 1912. Curtis to Walcott, May 2, 1912, Smithsonian, quoted in full in Holm and Quimby, 32–3.

10. Editorial, *Moving Picture World*, 8 (March 4, 1911), 473, and letter from Buck, 12 (May 25, 1912), 731. I am indebted to Richard Maltby for these references. See also his "John Ford's Indians, or Tom Doniphon's History Lesson," in Gidley, ed., *Representing Others*, 120–44.

11. Curtis to Gordon, May 6, 1912, Philadelphia; Walcott to Curtis, May 4, 1912, Smithsonian; Gordon to Curtis, May 7, 1912, Letterpress Book Number 8, 489, Philadelphia. See Holm and Quimby, 44–57.

12. For the role of film at San Diego, see Robert W. Rydell, *All the World's a Fair*, 214–20. The letter itself is Curtis to Hewett, February 17, 1913, Edgar L. Hewett Papers, Museum of New Mexico. The outline enclosed by Curtis was the same as that mentioned in n. 31 below.

13. Unfortunately, it has not been possible to discover anything about the detailed financial arrangements of these film companies. It is worth adding that the financing of the project must always have been somewhat more risky than Holm and Quimby indicate; see, for example, the letter to Hewett cited in n. 12 above. Holm and Quimby give a full account of the film's elements, including extracts from its scenario, etc.

14. See Curtis to C. F. Newcombe, October 12, 1914, Newcombe. Curtis to Wissler, December 1, 1914, AMNH. Subsequent American Museum letters are from this file. Curtis to Roosevelt, January 26, and Roosevelt to Curtis, February 3, 1915.

15. Bush, *Motion Picture World*, 1685; quoted in Holm and Quimby, 14. "Ethnology in Action," *Independent* (January 11, 1915), 72.

16. *NAI*, vol. 10 (1915), 3–4; reprinted in Gidley, ed., *The Vanishing Race*, 34.

17. Curtis to Gordon, January 16, 1912, Philadelphia.

18. Boas's 1930 Kwakiutl film footage, with printed notes by Bill Holm, is available from the U of Washington P. For commentary on approaches to visual anthropology, see Jay Ruby on page 13 of the transcript of the Odyssey television program devoted to Boas (Boston: Public Broadcasting Associates, 1980) and Jacknis (Ch. 3, n. 13). Information on Gordon transaction from Gordon to Curtis, March 2, 1921, Letterpress book no. 28, 463, and April 11, 1921, Letterpress book no. 29, 96, Philadelphia.

19. In August 1980 Barbara Conklin of the Anthropology Department and Pamela Haas of the Photographic Collection assured me, after searches, that the film was no longer in the holdings of the American Museum. It is conceivable that the print received by Quimby at the Field

Museum in 1947 was this same footage that Curtis parted with in 1924.

20. Curtis to Pinchot, August 5, 1914, Pinchot; subsequent Pinchot letters are from this collection. If one is to believe this letter, and there is no reason not to, Curtis *did* go whale killing and seal hunting in earnest (compare with doubts expressed in Holm and Quimby, 67–9), but it was not in connection with the filming of *Indian* hunting practices, and the letter to Pinchot does not include details of any injuries to Curtis from a whale or of a night spent stranded on a partly submerged island, stories Curtis was to tell later. For further elaboration of this episode, see George I. Quimby, "Curtis and the Whale," *Pacific Northwest Quarterly*, 78 (October 1987), 141–4. Curtis to Roosevelt, October 6, 1914. Incidentally, this letter provides further evidence for the correctness of Quimby's view that Curtis went out with commercial, rather than Indian, whalers.

21. Barkley to Meany, November 4, 1915. For a broader context, see Richard Maltby, *Reforming the Movies* (New York: Oxford UP, forthcoming).

22. See Curtis to Schwinke, February 15 and May 4, 1915, Schwinke Papers, Burke Museum Archives, U of Washington; quoted in the context of further data on Schwinke in Holm and Quimby, 108.

23. Curtis to Wilson, May 12, 1915, Wilson Papers, LC. The letters of introduction Curtis enclosed were from A. F. Potter, Associate Forester; Cato Sells, Commissioner of Indian Affairs (who dubbed him "the famous artist"); W. A. Ryan, Controller, Department of the Interior Reclamation Service; Franklin Lane, Secretary of the Interior; and William G. Redfield, Secretary of Commerce.

24. Evidence from Curtis to Meany, April 22, 1915, J. H. Weer (Chairman of the Mountaineers Outings Committee) to Meany, June 23, 1915, and copy of Weer to Curtis, July 27, 1915, all Meany.

25. Copy of Smith to Curtis, April 13, 1915, with letter by Curtis to Ronald Todd, July 8, [c. 1948], E. S. Curtis Vertical File, UW.

26. For a possible National Park Service outlet, see Ch. 2, n. 17. Information on the Hearst connection was kindly supplied by Lou Pizzitola of New York City in letters of January 25 and February 15, 1990, together with a photocopy of an advertisement in the *Motion Picture Mail*, December 9, 1916, 11. Mr. Pizzitola also discovered that at least one of the scenics was copyrighted.

27. *Annual Report of the Commissioner for Indian Affairs for 1917* (Washington, D.C., 1918), 40. Some of Beth's Alaska footage appears in McLuhan's *The Shadow Catcher*.

28. Andrews, 56. The California Historical Society, San Francisco, has a number of *Ten Commandments* stills. See de Mille, *The Autobiography of Cecil B. de Mille*, ed. Donald Hayne (Englewood Cliffs, N.J.: Prentice Hall, 1959), 252; and Charles Higham, *Cecil B. de Mille* (New York: Scribners, 1973), 115. Other Hollywood information kindly supplied by Curtis's family in interviews with the author: Harold Curtis (January 1977); Florence Graybill (December 1976 and August 1978); Manford E. Magnuson (August 1978).

29. Stratton-Porter's letters are from Jeannette Porter Meeham, *The Lady of the Limberlost: The Life and Letters of Gene Stratton-Porter* (Garden City: Doubleday, Doran, 1928), 220 and 227–9. Fuller contextualization of Stratton-Porter's views may be found in the closing chapters of Judith Reick Long, *Gene Stratton-Porter: Novelist and Naturalist* (Indianapolis: Indiana Historical Society, 1990); passing references to Curtis appear on 225 and 231. Unfortunately, it has not been possible to trace further documents on this Hollywood relationship. Curtis gave screenwriting advice in Curtis to Meany, April 5, 1922. See also Kevin Brownlow, *The War, The West and The Wilderness* (New York: Knopf, 1978), 338–44, a brief survey that relies primarily on *The Shadow Catcher* and interviews with McLuhan. There was an Elmo Lincoln Tarzan still reproduced in a sales catalogue

published by the L.A. photographic dealers, the G. Ray Hawkins Gallery: *Edward S. Curtis Photographs* (1976), illustration to item 20.

30. I am grateful to the late Robert Hitchman for granting me access to the Olive Daniels letter. See the works on de Mille cited above; see Meany, "Hunting Indians with a Camera" (Ch. 3, n. 34).

31. From typescript of a full scenario in Kernberger. With the exception of this additional page, this scenario is the same as that taken from another source and reproduced as Appendix 2 in Holm and Quimby, 115–18.

32. Handbill in NW.

33. Clipping in Curtis Biography File, NW.

34. Borglum to Curtis, December 15, 1914, enclosed with Curtis to Roosevelt, January 26, 1915, Roosevelt. Borglum's name appears as that of a director on a number of the company documents in PML, especially in "The North American Indian, Inc.: Company Records," most often between 1919 and 1929. Further information on Borglum – though not, unfortunately, on his relationship with Curtis – may be found in the clippings file devoted to him in the Library of the Museum of Modern Art, New York, and, at the anecdotal level but with some information on Borglum's half-acknowledged racism, in Howard Schaff and Audrey Karl Schaff, *Six Wars at a Time: The Life and Times of Gutzon Borglum* (Darien, Conn.: Center for Western Studies, Angustura College in cooperation with Permelea Publishing, 1985).

Chapter 9

1. For Haddon, see item cited in Intro., n. 11. For Shakerism, see "Curtis Here to Handle Exhibit," a *Seattle Times* clipping dated May 28, 1909, in the AYPE Scrapbooks, no. 8 (May 23–June 13, 1909), 27, NW; see *NAI*, vol. 8 (1911), 53, and, more important, vol. 9 (1913), 116–7. For hypnotism, see the newspaper item cited in Ch. 6, n. 8.

2. Curtis to Hodge, December 7, 1927. Curtis, "A Rambling Log of the Field Season of the Summer of 1927," typescript kindly provided by Florence Graybill, who reproduced parts of it in her books with Boesen. Curtis reminiscence of Hunt cited in Ch. 3, n. 14. "Indian Religion," an unpublished typescript in the LACMNH, almost fully reproduced in Gidley, "'Indian Religion': [unpublished] Lecture by Edward S. Curtis," *Talking Stick*, no. 2 (Summer 1994), [10–12].

3. For Myers's sentiments, see Doc. 5B and the letter quoted, cited in Ch. 5, n. 24.

4. For a full account of these struggles see Kenneth Philp (cited in Ch. 1, n. 34), 26–54.

5. Charles H. Burke, Official Circular to All Indians, February 24, 1923. The copy examined was enclosed with a letter to Mary Austin from Secretary of the Interior Hubert Work, April 16, 1923, Austin.

6. For a full account of this context see Philp, Ch. 3, "Indian Dances Defended," but especially 55–60.

7. Information from Mary Austin papers, including Austin to Burke, May 31, 1924, and Hodge to Austin, August 28, 1923, with enclosure; also Hodge to the Editor, *New York Times*, December 20, 1923, 6, and October 26, 1924, 12.

8. Typescript, LACMNH. Subsequent quotations are from this script.

9. Many of the specific "cases" outlined by Curtis bear a similarity to ones discussed in Philp, 62–70, and elsewhere, though of course they embody Curtis's own particular interpretation.

10. Curtis to Hodge, November 28, 1924.

11. Ickes to Curtis, September 13, 1934, filed with memorandum from Collier to Ickes, September 8, 1934, and R. H. Hanna to Collier, July 19 and 20, 1934, Indian Office File 47090–1934, Record Group 75, National Archives. On Collier's possible assistance in raising money for Curtis in 1912, see Curtis to

Hodge, January 6, 1912, in which he refers to "the Collier plan," which had been abandoned, and the "Institute," probably the People's Institute in New York, an organization with which Collier was connected for many years, which offered moral uplift to immigrants through lectures and the like.

12. Curtis to Ickes, October 3, 1934, Indian Office File 47090–1934, National Archives; unfortunately Curtis's letter of January 29, 1935, is missing. Ickes to Curtis, August 29, 1935, author's collection, courtesy of Manford Magnuson.

13. *NAI,* vol. 16 (1926), xiii and, for example, 163–5.

14. Curtis, Intro. to vol. 10, quoted in Ch. 8. Curtis to Pinchot, August 2, 1904; similarly, in *NAI* itself (vol. 1) the caption for "The Renegade Type – Apache" indicates that Genitoa is "the type" of Indian who has yielded to peace "not because he prefers it, but because he must." In comments written in green ink on the flyleaves of various volumes of Curtis's own set of *NAI* when he sold it to the U of Oregon in 1932, he made such comments as: "The Sioux were a great people. Collecting the material for this volume was a delightful piece of work" (Special Collections, U of Oregon, Eugene).

15. Metcalfe (Ch. 6, n. 8), 13.

16. *NAI,* vol. 16 (1926), 12.

17. Metcalfe, 13.

18. A comparison might usefully be made with, for example, Frances B. Johnston's pictures of the Hampton Institute, as treated in James Guimond's "The 'Vanishing Red': Photographs of Native Americans at Hampton Institute," *Princeton University Library Chronicle,* 49 (Spring 1988), 235–55. In contrast to Curtis's, they treat Indians according to an ideology of "advancement": at Hampton Indians were to be raised through education to a more "advanced" stage of civilization, so the pictures stress pastoral pursuits and artisanship (but since Hampton was also segregationist, believing still in specific racial traits, their "Indianness" was not elided as it was, say, at more assimilationist Carlisle, where Johnston also photographed).

19. Parkman, as quoted by Dimock (Intro., n. 17), 135.

20. Evidence of Curtis's mining activities runs through a series of his thirties letters to Edward (Ted) C. Shell, especially those of 1933, E. S. Curtis Vertical File, UW. Curtis to Meany, January 12, 1932. Curtis to Hawthorne, June 20, 1934, Hawthorne Family Papers, Bancroft.

21. Numerous letters, Curtis to Leitch, SPL. The small 1948 exhibition was remembered in October 1980 by the late Robert Monroe, head of special collections, U of Washington Libraries, and Lucile McDonald was inspired to produce "Photo Historian of the Indians," *Seattle Times,* Magazine Section, May 8, 1949, 4. Lowie frequently cited the Plains volumes of *NAI* with approval from 1909 onwards (e.g, "Social life of the Crow Indians," *Anthropological Papers of the American Museum of Natural History,* 9, Pt. 2, 185 and 192), most notably in *The Crow Indians* (New York: Rinehart, 1935), 355, and his successors in the field, while wary of the photographs, did too; see, for example, John C. Ewers, *The Horse in Blackfoot Indian Culture,* Bureau of American Ethnology *Bulletin,* 159 (1955), 109 and 234. Goldstücker, Review of Ernst Fischer's autobiography, *An Opposing Man,* in *The Guardian,* February 28, 1974, 9.

22. Information on Phillips and Cheyenne from a further typescript "chapter" of his memoirs, "With the Cheyennes," private collection. Remarks on the dirt of Hooper Bay are to be found in: Curtis, "A Rambling Log," cited in n. 2 above; Beth Magnuson's handwritten log of the trip, as supplied by Florence Graybill, who used parts of it in her two books on Curtis; and Eastwood, as cited in Ch. 5, n. 47. The less subjective account of this alleged filthiness appears in *NAI,* vol. 20 (1930), 97–8. For Pratt, see *Imperial Eyes* (Ch. 3, n. 28), 152.

23. The Curtis and Phillips Apache accounts are cited in Ch. 6, n. 7 and n. 6, respectively. See *NAI*, vol. 1 (1907).

24. See, for example, James Clifford and George E. Marcus, eds., *Writing Culture: The Poetics and Politics of Ethnography* (Berkeley, Los Angeles, London: U of California P, 1986), Clifford Geertz, *Works and Lives: The Anthropologist as Author* (Stanford, Calif.: Stanford UP, 1988), and Murray, *Forked Tongues*. Fabian, *Time and the Other: How Anthropology Makes its Object* (New York: Columbia UP, 1983).

25. *NAI*, vol. 1 (1907), xiii–xv; and 4 (1909), 4–6, which is excerpted in Gidley, ed., *The Vanishing Race*, 39–40.

26. For travel writing, and connections between such work and ethnography, see Pratt, *Imperial Eyes* (Ch. 3, n. 28), and "Fieldwork in Common Places," in Clifford and Marcus, eds., *op. cit.*, 27–50. The list of topics covered by *NAI* is a distillation of the actual practice of the various volumes and repeated descriptions of the project's goals in publicity material for the text. Haddon's memoir is reproduced in the item cited in Intro., n. 11.

27. Curtis to Hodge, December 7, 1927. For the Comanche in *NAI*, see vol. 19 (1930), 181–8, extracted in Gidley, ed., *The Vanishing Race*, 21–9.

28. *NAI*, vol. 30, 165; compare with "Rambling Log", cited in Ch. 9, n. 2.

29. Lyman, cited in Intro., n. 6. Cronon, "Telling Tales on Canvas," in Jules D. Prown, ed., *Discovered Lands, Invented Pasts: Transforming Visions of the American West* (New Haven and London: Yale UP, 1992), 37–87, 197–200; quotation from 56; in the same book Dippie extends the treatment accorded Indians in his *The Vanishing American*, frequently cited here, to make the claim that the image of the West in general was always overwhelmingly nostalgic ("The Moving Finger Writes," 89–115), as does Howard Lamar, to whom viewers of western imagery had "been already so acculturated, [that] their nostalgia was probably almost instantaneous" ("Looking Backward, Looking Forward," 170).

30. Grinnell, *The Story of the Indian* (New York: Chapman and Hall, 1896), ix. Curtis to Lummis, February 5, 1912, Lummis Collection, Southwest Museum. Metcalfe, *op. cit.*, 13; Allan, cited in Ch. 2, n. 42, 361.

31. Curtis to Hodge, January 12, 1908, my emphasis.

32. Dimock, cited in Intro., n. 17, 25. James Faris (Ch. 3, n. 10), while offering insights into Curtis's photographic treatment of the Navajo people, has also put forward the view that the representation would have been more rounded and respectful to the "humanity" of Navajos if the published volume had included "A Navaho Smile" (1903); however, as we saw in Ch. 2 with reference to "The Pima Woman," smiles can just as easily betoken generic conventions. For Sollors, see *Beyond Ethnicity*, cited in Intro., n. 5, 115–19.

33. Benjamin, *The Origin of German Tragic Drama*, trans. John Osborne (London: New Left Books, 1977), 183–4; quoted in Dimock, 24; in that Benjamin revered allegory, I am appropriating him here. Curtis to Burke, January 21, 1906, Thomas Burke Papers, UW.

34. Higginson, as cited in Ch. 2, n. 19, 5. Dimock, 116.

35. Dimock, 118, my emphasis. Curtis quotations from the item cited in Ch. 1, n. 29.

36. Vizenor, "Socioacupuncture: Mythic Reversals and the Striptease," in Calvin Martin, cited in Ch. 3, n. 30, 182 and 186. Fisher, "Unsettled Accounts of Indians and Others," in Susan Hiller, ed., *The Myth of Primitivism: Perspectives on Art* (London and New York: Routledge, 1991), 292–313; quotation on 307, facing reproduction of Ray's image. This is an instance of the possibilities for "play" mentioned in the Intro., n. 9.

37. Benjamin, *Illuminations*, ed. Hannah Arendt, trans. Harry Zohn (London: Fontana, 1992), 247–8.

38. Benjamin, 248.

INDEX

Numbers in italic script refer to an illustration or caption on that page.